Hollywood Cinema and the Real Los Angeles

Hollywood Cinema and the Real Los Angeles

Mark Shiel

REAKTION BOOKS

For Alyce and Anouk

Published by Reaktion Books Ltd
33 Great Sutton Street
London EC1V 0DX, UK
www.reaktionbooks.co.uk

First published 2012

Printed and bound in Great Britain by TJ International, Padstow, Cornwall

British Library Cataloguing in Publication Data
Shiel, Mark.
    Hollywood cinema and the real Los Angeles.
    1. Motion picture industry – California – Los Angeles – History.
    2. Motion pictures – Production and direction – California – Los Angeles – History.
    3. Hollywood (Los Angeles, Calif.) – History.
    4. Los Angeles (Calif.) – History – 20th century.
    5. Los Angeles (Calif.) – In motion pictures.
    I. Title
    791.4'3'0979494-dc23

ISBN 978 1 86189 902 6

Contents

Introduction 7

1 The Trace 18

2 Navigation 69

3 The Simulacrum 128

4 Geopolitical Pressure Point 211

Epilogue 273

Appendix 284

References 289

Select Bibliography 320

Acknowledgements 323

Photo Acknowledgements 325

Index 326

Introduction

> Here the cows give cream, not milk; the bees make honey
> that is pure sugar; the squash and oranges and petunias
> grow bigger; the girls are prettier and the men more virile;
> the days are accounted sunnier and the nights more star-
> spangled. Here all life is better than anywhere else in the
> universe.
>
> Ralph Hancock on Los Angeles, *Fabulous Boulevard*, 1949[1]

Where is the line between reality and representation to be drawn? In Los Angeles, from the end of the nineteenth century to the middle of the twentieth, and especially during the formation and heyday of the Hollywood studio system, the city shaped films and films shaped the city in symbiotic, incestuous and internecine ways. The relationship between cinema and the city was arguably more intense than in any other city then or now, and it made 'Los Angeles' an automatically meaningful landscape for millions in the United States and worldwide.

Whether filming the actual city on location or recreating it in the studio, films variously represented Los Angeles as an escapist utopia or a nightmare that was all too real. From orange groves, beaches, mountains and desert, to boulevards, suburbs, factories and slums, the *mise en scène* of Los Angeles constituted one of the most interesting cinematic locales, and one whose iconic value rivalled the image-making of cities such as Rome, Paris, London and New York, which began their self-mythologizing generations or centuries before. Meanwhile, in cinematography and film editing, the distinctive topography of the Los Angeles basin and the increasingly de-centred planning of its

7

growth facilitated particular kinds of cinematic point-of-view and narrative, thereby influencing cinematic representation in general. This was evident, for example, in the prominence of the long shot of the boulevard filmed from a rapidly moving automobile, the montage of pursuer and pursued in chase sequences filmed on commodious suburban streets, or the sublime vista from an elevated angle of the cityscape sprawling across the frame, an array of twinkling lights by night or in the heat haze of the sun by day.

The vista, in particular, masked the fact that Los Angeles was exceptionally heterogeneous in terms of race, gender and class, and that its social geography and cinematic representation were complex and conflicted. While the studios were often perceived in terms of ethnic difference, as predominantly Jewish enclaves, the majority of films of Los Angeles reinforced its domination by white Anglo-Saxon Protestants. Concentrating their narratives and settings in the increasingly middle-class West Los Angeles, most films aided the dominant culture's suppression and appropriation of the earlier histories of Native American, Spanish and Mexican Southern California. Most marginalized African Americans and Latinos, except when including them for ridicule or romanticization, and most betrayed an increasing privatization of Los Angeles' social space, especially in the proliferation of suburban single-family homes, which created pressurized domestic environments often antithetical to working-class solidarity and progressive political action.

The spatial complexity of the image of the city was matched by the intricate and evolving geography of the film industry on the ground where Hollywood cinema and the place known as 'Hollywood' were never one and the same. Within Los Angeles, film-making was established early on not only in that fabled district but in downtown, Edendale and Westwood, and in nearby municipalities such as Glendale, Burbank and Culver City. In its external relations, Los Angeles used motion pictures to challenge older cities such as New York, Philadelphia and Chicago, with which Los Angeles' film industry competed for creative talent, film production and corporate finance, and whose primacy Los Angeles began to overtake.

In the early twentieth century Los Angeles was remarkable for the great distances between it and other major cities. However, these were increasingly eroded by social, political and economic integration, facilitated by new means of transport and communication, which were prominent in the films, and in whose growth the film industry played

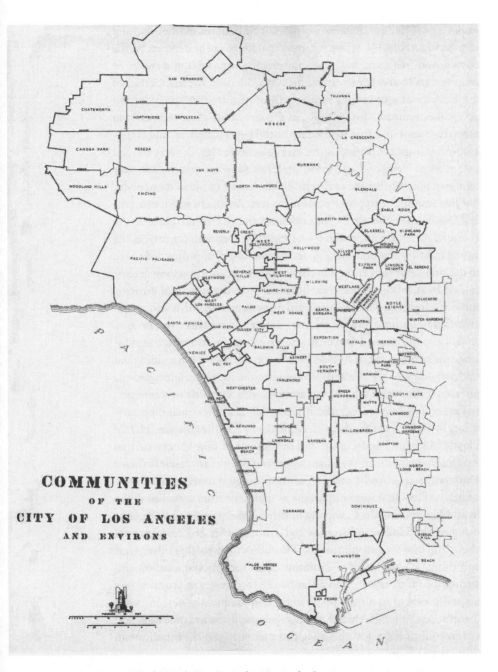

Map of communities of Los Angeles, from Mel Scott, *Metropolitan Los Angeles: One Community* (1949).

important roles. Yet there was often not only harmony but conflict between Los Angeles' cinematic representation and the efforts of the city's government and business interests to promote it as a centre of industry, trade and commerce. This was evident in the association of the industry, at least in conservative minds, with excessive lifestyles and political extremism – for example, in the sex scandals that gripped it in the early 1920s and the 'Red Scare' of the late 1940s and '50s. These and other important ideological struggles were significantly shaped by outsiders' views of 'Hollywood' and 'Los Angeles', and the way they unfolded not only helped to determine the nature of life in those places but had important ripple effects on modern American history in general. Such crises also threw into question the role of the place as the centre of American filmmaking – in the early twentieth century, as the young industry was becoming an institution of global proportions and, in the middle of the century, as the studio system began a long decline caused by shrinking audiences, industrial restructuring and growing financial insolvency. This historical timeframe, and this process of growth and decline, provide the over-arching narrative of this book.

I explore a broad and representative range of films that demonstrate the richness of Los Angeles' history on the screen while aiding our understanding of the relationship between the movie business and the real city and between the real city and its myth. I provide new interpretations of well-known and readily accessible examples, including early shorts by D. W. Griffith, slapstick comedies by Charlie Chaplin, Harold Lloyd, and Laurel and Hardy, and milestones of film history such as *A Star Is Born* (William Wellman, 1937) and *Murder My Sweet* (Edward Dmytryk, 1944). And I make a point of bringing to the surface now-neglected films that were important in their day, from actuality shorts by the Thomas Edison Company to behind-the-scenes publicity films made by the Hollywood studios and numerous lesser-known movies about the movies and film noirs. This allows me to chart the terms and timing of Los Angeles' evolution as an exceptional location and setting for films, taking into account the fact that 'Los Angeles' was often not named in films while 'Hollywood' frequently was, and tracing the ways in which the landscapes, geography, urban planning and architecture of those real and imagined places shaped the films in both content and form.

A surprisingly neglected subject to date, but one that is also crucial here, is the role of the film industry in the explosive growth and urban sprawl of Los Angeles. To facilitate industrial expansion, but also for ideological reasons, the film industry established studios in greenfield sites on the edges of what was a relatively small city in the 1910s and '20s. These sites were often very large, and they generated employment, investment, revenues and synergies with other Los Angeles industries such as automobiles and aviation. With these facts in mind, I explain the causes and effects of the studios' precise locations, their internal structure and appearance, and their evolving relationship to the streets, neighbourhoods and city in which they materialized.

In Los Angeles at this time, there was an exceptionally close interaction between cinema and the built environment. In their form and function, the largest movie studios resembled, and were often described as, cities in themselves, being part and not part of their surroundings. Their growth and decline was measured in a large historical arc – the 1910s and '20s witnessing simultaneous enlargement of the studios and the city, the 1930s mutual stagnation, and the 1940s and '50s decline of the studios in contrast to the city's renewed expansion. At the same time, the physical evolution of both Los Angeles and the studios was characterized by waves of demolition and reconstruction of buildings and infrastructure whose frequency and intensity was matched only by the erecting and striking of movie sets.

Meanwhile, the complexity and innovation of Los Angeles architecture was very evident. The presence of the film industry helped make the city a leader in the construction of lavish movie palaces, homes of the stars, and industrial buildings such as soundstages and studio management offices while, in their *mise en scène*, films made in Los Angeles played a key role in popularizing historical and modernist architectural styles among American and international audiences. Motion pictures proved effective at disseminating architectural idioms not necessarily unique to Los Angeles but which achieved a distinctive regional form there: craftsman bungalows, streamlined moderne offices and public buildings prior to the Second World War, and 'California cool' thereafter.

In cinematic form, representations of Los Angeles' built environment were remarkable for at least two tensions. In the first, the vertical and horizontal – commonly associated with New York and Los Angeles, respectively – were often at odds in a city whose suburban expanse made it known for a supposed flatness and in films that sometimes involved high-rise, but more often low-lying, structures and planes. In the second, a tension was evident between monumental buildings such as civic offices, public memorials and bridges, which were relatively few, and commonplace, transient ones such as bungalows, gas stations and drive-in restaurants, which were ubiquitous and remain so to this day. These tensions underpinned the city's cinematic image and its physical reality, and they had self-perpetuating effects upon attitudes to Los Angeles in the city, the United States and abroad.

To focus the analysis of Los Angeles' landscapes, geography, urban planning and architecture, and my interpretations of their cinematic expression, each chapter in this book is structured around one key spatial motif: 'the trace', 'navigation', 'the simulacrum' and 'geopolitical pressure point'. I argue that each of these predominated in a particular kind of film set or shot in Los Angeles during a particular phase of its history, and each was emblematic of the actual city's development at that time. These motifs are not imposed upon the cinema or the place but naturally arise from careful viewing of the large numbers of films that were made there in the light of the historical growth of the city and its studios. These motifs also allow a fruitful interaction between the close film analysis, cultural geography, and film and urban history that make up the book as a whole.

In chapter One, entitled 'The Trace', traces of the past in the modern urban landscape provide an illuminating route for contemplation of the residual pre-modernity of Los Angeles at the turn of the twentieth century. Its emergence as a metropolis was predicated upon the fading history of Native American, Spanish and Mexican California, and their cinematic representation in Edison actuality films, short fiction films by D. W. Griffith, and the first feature film made in Los Angeles in 1914. These accelerated and widely disseminated the imagining of the region as a kind of Eden by Spanish and Mexican settlers, and as a 'Land of Sunshine' by their Anglo successors. The utopianism for which that part of the world was known continues today in its popular associations with beauty, romance and wealth, but for early filmmakers it lay in the city's distinctive landscape and climate, its distance from the oppressive monopoly of the New York-based Motion Picture Patents Company, and civic boosters' promotion of Los Angeles as a place of industrial and creative opportunity. Today the frequent bombast of early twentieth-century Los Angeles and its film pioneers contrasts with the relatively scant traces they have left behind, their haphazard memorializing and the shifting sands of urban archaeology.

The fragility of our historical understanding of the city echoes the fragility of celluloid itself.

In chapter Two, I propose that Los Angeles and its cinematic image in the 1910s and '20s can be fruitfully interpreted in terms of various modes of 'navigation' at a time of rapid growth. The distance between Los Angeles and other major cities gave rise to a distinctive geographical distribution of creative, managerial and technical personnel in the so-called 'Hollywood' film industry, and to new interactions between people in the East and on the West Coast. What was arguably then the most important of Hollywood film genres, slapstick comedy, was marked by the fact that many of its exponents were recent migrants to Los Angeles whose films incorporated that city's distinctively novel landscapes in their quotidian modern chaos. Chaplin, Lloyd, and Laurel and Hardy frequently made use of location shooting in downtown Los Angeles, Edendale and Culver City. They described peculiarly auto-mobilized and decentred urban and suburban environments, and often featured high-speed chases on wide and elongated streets, in a manner that aided the narrative integration of Hollywood cinema at that time. But this same geography also entailed changes in the spatial organization of the Los Angeles film industry until the coming of sound. The major film studios fuelled the city's exceptionally dynamic real estate market, they relied heavily on automobiles and set new motoring trends, and they desired association with the growth of a prosperous suburban order.

In chapter Three, I use the concept of the 'simulacrum' to characterize the internal appearance of Los Angeles' movie studios and the design and promotion of the largest as semi-autonomous cities. While the film industry made a substantial contribution to Los Angeles' economic growth, it was most visible on the ground in the huge areas of real estate, which contained a heterogeneous mix of shooting stages, technical workshops, administrative offices, and outdoor sets depicting far-flung geographical and historical locales. Many movie studios were built by means of a peculiarly temporary kind of urban planning, but their buildings were architecturally significant for their historicist styles or their modernist construction in iron, steel, concrete and glass. Like movie palaces and homes of the stars, the design and construction of the studios exaggerated features of the real Los Angeles while foreshadowing Disneyland and other theme parks. At the height of the studio era a variety of publicity films, comedies, melodramas and musicals, shot mostly within the studios' walls, illustrated their internal and external relations, sometimes with notes of critique but mostly overlaying Los Angeles' existing utopian mythology with ethereal new conceptions of the 'dream factory' and the 'silver screen'.

In chapter Four, I focus on Los Angeles and its cinematic image as a 'geopolitical pressure point' in the 1940s and '50s. Increasingly reliant on location shooting, film noirs often explicitly named Los Angeles as an exemplar of the physical, social and moral crises of the modern city in general. Iconic settings such as beaches, bungalows, movie studios, the Hollywood Hills and the Sunset Strip were used to expose the underbelly of Southern California's especially intense American Dream. This dystopian turn was shaped by the decline of the studio system and by that of downtown Los Angeles and Hollywood as physical and commercial centres wounded by the building of freeways and newer suburbs further afield. However, the dystopian turn also took place just as Los Angeles was gaining new geopolitical importance because of the Second World War and the ensuing Cold War. Splitting their action between New York and Los Angeles, a small but significant number of film noirs shed light on the younger city's distinctively dispersed and privatized urban form and its historically turbulent labour relations, which exploded in the Hollywood strikes between 1945 and 1947. These gave Los Angeles a leading role in the globally influential reorganization of American economic and political life that was taking place at that time, generating a charged interaction between the real and imagined city of a kind arguably never seen before or since.

Each of the chapters in the book is intended to open a window onto a certain conjuncture of time and space in the real Los Angeles and its representation. But while my focus is the first half of the twentieth century, I am interested also to find evidence of the beginnings of the process by which modernity and industrialism were displaced in that city – in my view, earlier than in other cities – by the seeds of a post-industrial economy and postmodern extended city, which Los Angeles today is so frequently said to epitomize. Such evidence lies in the ways in which that earlier moment in Los Angeles anticipated many of the features of the world in which we currently live.

In the period with which I am explicitly concerned, Los Angeles and its cinema were already notable for an intense interaction of art and commerce and a distinctive balance between artisanal and industrial production. Los Angeles was an especially narcissistic city, self-referential and self-promoting, economically and ideologically driven by the production and consumption of images, but also deeply self-conscious of its novelty and youth. It was remarkable for a relatively early displacement of the central city by a multi-centred network of suburbs, a process then underway in many cities but particularly pervasive in Southern California and accelerated by motion pictures. The rapid physical fluctuation of Los Angeles' built environment, its monotony and heterogeneity, its transience and lack of history were already critiqued by residents and visitors in the 1920s and '30s. And Los Angeles was a disciplinary society, outwardly democratic but often segmented, exclusive and unjust, underwritten by the soft power of capitalism and the hard power of the police. By keeping these traits in focus, I hope to present not simply an account of the past but a means to a fuller understanding of Los Angeles and its cinema now.

In recent years, a substantial amount of literature has been published on cinema and the city, some of which has shed valuable light on aspects of Los Angeles' history as a filmmaking centre.[2] This book focuses on the interaction between cinema and Los Angeles in the first half of the twentieth century, when their close relationship came into being and was arguably at its height. I concentrate on the Hollywood film industry, arguably the world's most popular and influential for nearly one hundred years, offsetting a cultural paradigm against an urban one, Los Angeles, one of the world's largest urban agglomerations in size, population and economy, as well as in cultural reach and cutting-edge social and physical change. At the same time a prominent place is given to the close analysis and interpretation of individual films in terms of their content (especially the natural, urban and suburban landscapes of the region), their form (*mise en scène*, cinematography, editing, narrative and sound), and their production and reception. This leads me to delineate a body of films geographically connected by place rather than genre, star, director, decade or style. And from this combination of industrial and urban history with film analysis, I propose an explicitly spatial history of Hollywood cinema that insists on the specificity of the real places in which films were made rather than describing them in terms of an abstract diegetic space or as a broadly American or global phenomenon.

This approach has led me to draw upon a variety of research resources. Studio records and correspondence feature prominently, as do film reviews and industry reports. I gain invaluable information, and an established narrative against which to define my own, from historians of American cinema such as David Bordwell, Janet Staiger, Kristin Thompson, Thomas Schatz and Janet Wasko. But my interest in the studios' built spaces and geographical distribution, and in the shaping of the films by the city, requires me to also draw on sources of a kind less often used to understand the cinema. These include official urban planning reports, architectural or construction industry magazines, aerial photographs and maps.

Such sources ground the subject in the specifics of real places, something I also do by drawing upon the urban sociology and geography of the so-called 'Los Angeles School', whose members include Mike Davis, Michael Dear, Edward Soja and Allen J. Scott. My investigations convince me more than ever of the veracity of their arguments for the distinctively post-industrial and postmodern character of Los Angeles, and its status as an exceptional urban paradigm in whose image more and more of the world's urban landscapes are being re-shaped every day. I rely on historians of Los Angeles such as Robert M. Fogelson, Greg Hise and William Deverell, who have emphasized the roots of Los Angeles' contemporary condition in much earlier times. And I have been informed by the arguments of Dolores Hayden, Norman Klein, Dana Cuff and Richard Longstreth, for whom place has a continuing importance in Los Angeles notwithstanding generalized critiques and popular prejudices about its monotonous placelessness. If film theorists and historians of Hollywood cinema have not paid enough attention to that city, I also find myself thinking that geographers and historians who know Los Angeles well have not fully acknowledged cinema's decisive role in shaping the city's past, its present, and its future.

One of the most notable features of life in Los Angeles in recent years has been an explosion of institutional and grass-roots interest in the history of the city, and an increasing rejection of the long-standing prejudice that it is a place of little substance or depth. A small but significant proportion of the city's output of motion pictures – for example, *Magnolia* (Paul Thomas Anderson, 1999), *Crash* (Paul Haggis, 2004) and *Little Miss Sunshine* (Jonathan Dayton, Valerie Faris, 2006) – has examined Los Angeles' consumerist excess, media spectacle, social fractures, hypermobility and sprawl. Notable too, though less well known, has been a wave of locally published studies of cinema's interaction with Los Angeles neighborhoods and streets, which testifies to a real appetite among its residents for a knowledge of their city's history on the screen.[3]

The real city's history – and the fact that it is much deeper than has often been allowed – has also been evident in the growth of organizations such as the Los Angeles Conservancy, whose walking tours and campaigns for architectural preservation have contributed to an increased attachment to the fabric of the city's past. Los Angeles' presence has also become virtual, disseminated in online databases and exhibits, scholarly websites, blogs and Google maps in which one can visualize not only the city in general but user-made maps of settings and locations used in Raymond Chandler novels and their screen adaptations, to name just one example.[4] Indeed, to this list we can add the current plan of the Academy of Motion Picture Arts and Sciences to finally build a museum – the Academy Museum of Motion Pictures – in cooperation with the Los Angeles County of Art.[5]

While never losing sight of the ways in which Los Angeles has abused and destroyed, disappointed and enraged many of the people who have lived in or known it, my hope is that this book will also make a contribution to the multiple reflections that Los Angeles has and will continue to inspire.

one

The Trace

Today the Los Angeles urban region has a population of eighteen million, its economy is the second largest in the United States and sixth largest in the world, its physical footprint is the eighth largest, its society among the most diverse and fractured, and its strategic location in the southwestern corner of the United States allows it to play a globally decisive cultural role not only in North America but in Europe, Latin America, Asia and the Pacific. For the last 100 years, a particularly important factor in Los Angeles' growth and visibility has been its role as the home of the largest motion picture industry in the world – and, more recently, music, television and digital media industries as well. Understanding the sheer presence of such a city is a challenge, and explaining cinema's contribution to it even more so.

From the turn of the twentieth century to the mid-1910s Los Angeles emerged as a city of national importance and a magnet for filmmakers whose activities would lead to 'Hollywood cinema'. Films of Los Angeles from that era have the special ability today to act as traces of times and places long since erased. But, paradoxically, when they were made and first shown, those same films had the effect, and sometimes the aim, of erasing the traces of previous societies that the modern era had decided were redundant. Four short actuality films by the Edison Company between 1897 and 1901, and three narrative films – *Ramona* (1910), *The Unchanging Sea* (1910) and *The Squaw Man* (1914) – are among the earliest extant films in which Los Angeles and its region are recorded. They also demonstrate that early cinema actively shaped and structured Los Angeles' history and appearance. This process may be understood by counterpointing the sense of human mortality and the contingency and loss of the past, which the early films convey today, with the long utopian tradition that once imagined Los Angeles as an Eden forged by the heroic struggles of men.

In 'Some Motifs on Baudelaire', Walter Benjamin refers to Marcel Proust's *A la recherche du temps perdu*, whose narrator was reminded of his childhood in Combray when he happened one day to bite into an ordinary *madeleine* (a soft butter cookie beloved of children in France) and found that the taste 'transported him back to the past'.[1] For Benjamin, the *mémoire involontaire* described by Proust typifies the way people in the modern world relate to the past, which often eludes deliberate efforts to remember but comes upon one fleetingly and movingly from time to time:

> It is the same with our own past. In vain we try to conjure it up again; the efforts of our intellect are futile . . . [It lies] somewhere beyond the reach of the intellect and its field of operations, in some material object . . . , though we have no idea which one it is. And whether we come upon this object before we die, or whether we never encounter it, depends entirely upon chance.[2]

Early motion pictures of Los Angeles conjure up things beyond our control, which no longer exist and have long been forgotten. However, in contrast to Proust's evocation, the past in these films is not one we have experienced ourselves: most viewers of films of Los Angeles are not natives and have little or no memory of it at all. Rather, as we watch them, that city and the traces of *its* past emblematize a relationship that each of us has with the city in which we live and have lived *our* past. This connection between cinema and the urban past is exceptionally intense in Los Angeles where the movie camera has a long and widespread history.

Before Hollywood

The sheer presence of Los Angeles today is, in large part, the expression of a long history of utopian investment that has gained currency there and worldwide because of Los Angeles' ubiquity as a place in which images are made. The geography and history of this utopian investment, whose apotheosis is 'Hollywood cinema', is like a Russian doll, four utopias one inside the other: the American West encompasses California, which contains Los Angeles and Hollywood in turn. From the region to the state, the city, and the district, each was defined in roughly chronological order. Beginning in 1769, what the Spanish called 'Alta California' became the site of an ambitious archipelago of Catholic missions running from San Diego north to San Francisco, from which Jesuits and Franciscans spread out to evangelize Native Americans with the zeal of the soldier-saint or the pacifist-pantheist. Indeed, in the early seventeenth century California had been literally mapped as an island off the western edge of the continent, typical of utopias in general in appearing a remote and imaginary place.[3]

With the establishment in 1781 of El Pueblo de Nuestra Señora la Reina de los Angeles de Porciúncula – in present-day downtown – Los Angeles became a walled colonial city and soon the largest civilian community in Spanish California. After Mexican independence, accounts by visitors were often anything but utopian: in 1842 the English Captain George Simpson described it as 'the noted abode of the lowest drunkards and gamblers of the country'.[4] But a rhetoric emerged that saw local supporters lavish the city with high praise: in 1845 Leonardo Cota, a member of its *ayuntamiento* (city council), declared that Los Angeles 'is beginning to show its astral magnificence and brilliance . . . it will be a Mexican paradise.'[5] This ascent continued after the Mexican-American War (1846–8), which saw Alta California ceded to the United States, and the California Gold Rush of 1848, from which Los Angeles profited by supplying miners in the northern part of the state.[6]

Subsequently, as Los Angeles became the most important end-point for westward migration in the United States, the city grew rapidly with the expansion of agriculture, oil drilling and refining and, later, aircraft and automotive industries. Becoming a capitalist growth utopia, its population rocketed from 11,333 in 1860, to 33,000 in 1880, 170,000 in 1900, and 936,000 in 1920.[7] Despite this, however, so-called 'boosters' – civic and business leaders such as Harrison Gray Otis and the board of the Los Angeles Chamber of Commerce – frequently sought to promote Los Angeles on the national and international stage by means of Edenic iconography. This emphasized the Mediterranean climate and pastoral fertility of the city and its hinterland – and, by implication, their morality and social order – sometimes evoking the classical beauty of ancient Greece and Rome or the region's Arts and Crafts architecture and design.[8] While characterizing high-density, urban-industrial centres in the East and Midwest as over-populated, ugly, polluted and dangerous, Los Angeles' boosters pretended its growth left Nature intact, blending urbanism and Arcadia, the modern and the timeless.

The presence of Los Angeles today can be thrown into relief by speculating counter-factually on what it might have become if 'Hollywood cinema' had not flourished. As James Miller Guinn explained, '[s]cattered at intervals along the highway of California's march to wealth and progress are the ruins of enterprises that failed'.[9] Until the last third of the nineteenth century, the raising of cattle was the only industry in Southern California, carried out on vast ranches by the long-established families known as *californios*. Their activity was fuelled by the Gold Rush but then blighted by drought and famine in the 1860s, after which the *californios* declined and their ranches were subdivided. A series of business experiments ensued but disappointed one by one: cultivation of silkworms failed because the farmers who took it up were too widely dispersed and lacked a sufficient local market; cotton growing collapsed when the African Americans brought in to work the fields moved away for better pay; and efforts to specialize in sheep, tea, coffee and beans died out for a lack of irrigation and Wall Street money. Instead, in the 1880s, these efforts and their traces were erased by a new economy of citrus fruit cultivation, which encouraged a new iconography of Los Angeles as a 'Land of Sunshine' that would define the city's local and national identity for generations as an ideal place for investment, work and leisure. Agricultural success and self-publicity were aided by the completion of the 'Sunset Route' of the Southern Pacific Railroad from New Orleans (1882) and the founding of the Los Angeles Chamber of Commerce (1888).

Los Angeles grew, although many business leaders continued to worry that it lacked industrial potential because of its low population, physical isolation and need for speculative finance. As late as 1908 a spokesman for the Southern California Edison Company argued to the California Railroad Commission that 'Southern California will remain largely an agricultural country. We can't expect any extraordinary development in manufacturing except such as may be for home use – for local consumption.'[10] However, such concerns were gradually displaced by boosters' descriptions of Los Angeles' growth in terms of a monumental harnessing of Nature and individual heroic achievement. For example, in *Sixty Years in Southern California* (1916), Harris Newmark presented an epic memoir of his eventful life from his arrival in Los Angeles by ship from Prussia in 1853 to 1913 when he wrote at eighty

21

years of age.[11] One of Los Angeles' original boosters, Newmark was an important real estate developer and owner of a large grocery concern, who co-founded the Los Angeles Chamber of Commerce, the Los Angeles Board of Trade, the Los Angeles Public Library, the California Club, the Los Angeles B'nai B'rith Jewish synagogue, and the nearby city of Montebello. Newmark was also an associate of Phineas Banning, the stagecoach and shipping magnate who founded the Port of Los Angeles, and in Montebello he collaborated with the civil engineer William Mulholland, designer of the Los Angeles Aqueduct, which facilitated the city's massive expansion after 1913. Newmark's memoirs exemplify the Herculean rhetoric often deployed by boosters to describe the city's foundation. When he first arrived, it was 'a sleepy, ambition-less adobe village with very little promise for the future' but 'the spirit properly called "Western"' ensured that 'within this extensive area it builded [sic] great cities, joined its various parts with steel and iron, made great highways out of the once well-nigh impassable cattle paths, and from an elemental existence developed a complex civilization.'[12] Because of this westward destiny and its now large population and economy, Newmark concludes portentously:

> I believe that Los Angeles is destined to become, in not many years, a world center, prominent in almost every field of human endeavor; and that, as nineteen hundred years ago the humblest Roman, wherever he might find himself, would glow with pride when he said, 'I am a Roman!' so, in the years to come, will the son of the metropolis on these shores, wheresoever his travels may take him, be proud to declare, 'I AM A CITIZEN OF LOS ANGELES!'[13]

Los Angeles' growth was a function of visualization as well as physical effort, as it became a centre of fine art and photography well before motion pictures. Beginning in the 1880s, nearby resort towns such as Santa Barbara and Laguna Beach attracted *plein-air* painters such as William Wendt to their sublime views of nature and their romantic Spanish and Mexican ruins. These provided subjects for a picturesque impressionism in oil, pastels and watercolours in which the defining element was the play of plentiful sunlight on the shapes and textures of the land and sea – and the human figure, to a lesser extent.

This work was extended by an explosion of commercial and artistic photography that was often notable for formal and technical innovation. In the 1870s photographers such as Carleton Watkins produced clear and detailed landscape views of immense canyons, mountains and lakes, captured by the camera on very large negatives and from distant points of view. Although often beautiful, according to the art historian Joel Snyder these were intended primarily as 'disinterested reports', often being made on commission for railroad, mining and lumber companies as advertisements of the West aimed at investors.[14] Photographed during construction of the railroad line from San Francisco to Los Angeles through the Tehachapi Pass, Watkins's images of iron tracks in the wilderness implied an ideal balance between nature and industry that would be echoed in the first motion pictures of the region by the Edison Company in 1898.

As William Alexander McClung and Jennifer Watts have explained, a flood of somewhat softer but still boosterist photographs was subsequently produced for local, national and international consumption that foregrounded Southern California's favourable climate, physical beauty, abundant flora, and its Spanish and Mexican romantic antiquity, emblematized by its historic missions.[15] Amateur photographers, the first Kodak cameras, cheap picture postcards, and half-tone printing in newspapers and magazines allowed even those of modest means to participate in a new visualization of the land. High-end publications too used photographs to assert the city's coming greatness. Harry Ellington Brook's *Southern California: The Land of Sunshine*, a booklet sponsored by the Los Angeles Chamber of Commerce for the Chicago World's Columbian Exposition of 1893, was followed by *The Land of Sunshine* magazine in 1894, edited by Charles Fletcher Lummis. And Lou V. Chapin's boxed set of photographs *Art Work on Southern California* (1900) presented Los Angeles as a sequence of immaculate parks and park-like residential streets. In such work it might be said that Los Angeles was becoming cinematic before the fact, the reproduction and dissemination of photographs of the city fundamental to its everyday life.

In the first fifteen years of the twentieth century, Los Angeles also became one of the most important centres for fine art photography by Alvin Langdon Coburn, Edward Weston and others who extended into Southern California the 'pictorialist' principles and aesthetics of the Photo-Secession, led in the East by Alfred Stieglitz. In their work panoramic views predominated, often presented in slightly soft focus or in the natural haze of the sun to emphasize the subjective perception and symbolic value of landscape while disavowing any advertising function.[16] With the First Los Angeles Photographic Salon held in 1902, Weston's arrival in 1906, and the foundation of the Camera Pictorialists of Los Angeles in 1914, this tendency was almost exactly contemporaneous with the opening of the first motion picture studios in the city.

There was variation in the degree to which these visual representations and their creators were committed to boosterist agendas but, cumulatively, the images encouraged a new self-assurance in Los Angeles and its promotion far afield. By 1915 the iconography had become standardized in content and form – for example, in the sumptuous brochure *Los Angeles Today*, in which the Los Angeles Chamber of Commerce presented a detailed and hyperbolic textual narrative accompanied by plentiful photos in full colour.[17] Intended to capitalize on the Panama-Pacific International Exposition at San Francisco and the Panama-California Exposition at San Diego, both held that same year, the brochure proposed that people travelling by train between those two cities should stop off in Los Angeles. There they would discover 'one of the most enterprising business communities of the world . . . the Wonder city of the United States [and] the most talked of city on the continent'. Los Angeles was said to be first among all California counties in the value of its farms, first in output of lemons and dairy produce, and second in oranges, olives, walnuts and poultry. Los Angeles had a more complex and efficient 'interurban electric railway' than most other American cities but was already 'the paradise of the owner of the motor car'. In a typical boosterist tactic, a list of impressive statistics was provided: Los Angeles had 796 miles of improved streets, 1,036 miles of track, and about 50,000 of the 120,000 cars in California. These, together with its transcontinental railroads, steamships, banks and manufacturers, were said to drive Los Angeles' exuberant growth, represented in page after page of captioned photos of busy downtown streets, oil derricks, the Los Angeles Aqueduct and Los Angeles Harbor. These were matched by an equal number of romantic photos of Westlake Park, Arts and Crafts bungalows, alfalfa fields, orange groves and the Sierra Nevada Mountains.

Although produced in 1915, *Los Angeles Today* makes no reference to motion pictures, suggesting the film industry did not yet command recognition as one of the city's key features. It indicates that Los Angeles could not yet take for granted its ascendancy over San Diego and San Francisco, two cities that it overtook in population and economic and political weight in the 1880s and 1920s, respectively.[18] The brochure typifies the promotion of Los Angeles' supposedly ideal balance of urban, suburban, and rural space and function, and the city's integration of the best of Nature and engineering. It also demonstrates that, quite apart from motion pictures, Los Angeles was already mass producing visual imagery for consumption at home and abroad. It described the city as a 'paradise' suited to 'artists of every kind':

> The architect finds here conditions such as his fancy might have pictured as necessary to the full expansion of his talent, but hardly hoped to see. Owing to favorable climatic conditions, embellishments of great delicacy and color schemes and forms of structure impossible in more rigorous climates are here altogether practicable. Marine painters find here within easy reach a dozen beaches, with all the life and action of the seaside resort. In the winter and early spring from the whole coast of Southern California may be seen the extraordinary combination of green wooded foothills, surmounted by snowy peaks.[19]

Benevolent climate and variety of landscape were two key factors that attracted artists and photographers to produce picturesque landscape views of Los Angeles and its region. Boosters combined them with images of an industrious built environment, placing the ancient and modern, natural and manufactured, in a deliberate constitutive tension that would be stretched as the city grew out of all proportion. The coming of motion pictures to Los Angeles accelerated its physical growth and visual repetition, especially as the medium was technically improved and industrialized in the Hollywood studio system.

Short actuality films of Los Angeles and its region were among the first taken by film crews employed by Thomas Edison to tour the United States in the late 1890s, and they were among the first films shown commercially in Los Angeles. The earliest screening we know of was 'Blizzard Scenes in New York', which opened in 1896 at Thomas Tally's Kinetoscope Parlor on South Spring Street, the city's first purpose-built facility of its kind.[20] That venue surely also presented the first films of Los Angeles, which were made the following year when a unit of the Edison Company, which had filmed many scenes en route from New York through Philadelphia, Chicago and San Francisco, finally arrived in Los Angeles on the Southern Pacific Railroad.

The street scene filmed by a camera strategically placed at eye level at a busy intersection, looking towards a vanishing point to the left of the centre of the frame, was a common feature in Edison actuality films. The version filmed in Los Angeles is the earliest moving picture made there, dating from 31 December 1897 and known simply as *South Spring Street, Los Angeles*. Twenty-eight seconds long, this presents five successive teams of horses pulling buggies and coaches full of passengers, and an electric streetcar, travelling south on Spring Street towards the camera (which looks north) and out of the frame to the right. Like many films of its type, the sequence is fleeting, yet dynamic and rich with detail for those who care to look. Telegraph poles and advertisements clutter the sidewalk, occasional pedestrians cross from left to right, and a few seem to look or wave at the camera. Here is as much frisson as was ever made by the conjuncture of cinema and the city.

Yet to compare *South Spring Street* with Edison films of other downtown scenes is to reveal something of the specific texture, volume, density and appearance of the Southern California metropolis. Always seeking to maximize visual interest and topicality, the Edison Company declared of *The Corner of Madison and State Streets, Chicago*, made in June or July that same year, that it depicted 'the busiest street corner' in the city.[21] This film, of roughly equal length, opens on a passing streetcar but is dominated by a sea of pedestrians waiting and then walking slowly across the street on a myriad of individual routes, while the film's only horse stands in front of the camera waiting for a break in the traffic. On the other hand, the film of *Herald Square* (New York), 11 May 1896, is a relatively restricted composition: a large building occupies the middle ground, confining human activity to the foreground where pedestrians at an intersection are directed by a policeman and streetcars move laterally in the frame.

We should not read too much into three urban scenes out of scores produced by one company among many in one of the most urbanized

Three frame enlargements from *South Spring Street, Los Angeles, California* (Thomas Edison Manufacturing Co., 1897).

Three frame enlargements from *The Corner of Madison and State Streets, Chicago* (Thomas Edison Manufacturing Co., 1900).

Three frame enlargements from *Herald Square* (New York) (Thomas Edison Manufacturing Co., 1896).

societies of its day. But even in this earliest moment, Los Angeles displays characteristics for which it later became well known. The buildings are generally lower, there are gaps in the skyline, perhaps vacant lots in the distance, and the sky has a much greater presence. The pedestrians are fewer, the street less crowded and, although only the Los Angeles film shows bicycles, the traffic is faster moving. This urban scene already seems more open and fluid, perhaps lighter and less hard-edged, than those of older cities.

Appropriately, other Edison films of the Los Angeles region are natural or rural in setting, albeit disrupted by modern engineering. *Sunset Limited, Southern Pacific Railway*, made in mid-January 1898, depicts the Southern Pacific Railroad junction at Fingal about 90 miles east of Los Angeles and fifteen miles west of Palm Springs. Through this area of then undeveloped prairie ran the so-called 'Sunset Route', from San Francisco via Los Angeles to New Orleans, opened in 1891 and promoted as one of the greatest railroads in the nation. The Edison Company assisted by describing the benefits of the route in its film catalogue of 1898:

> The Southern Pacific Company ('Sunset Route') offers special inducements to winter travelers, by reason of its southern route, thereby avoiding the extreme cold of the winter months. Its course lies through a section of the country that presents a variety of beautiful and picturesque natural scenery. It is also the direct route to the popular resorts of Southern California, thereby

Three frame enlargements from *Sunset Limited, Southern Pacific Railway* (Thomas Edison Manufacturing Co., 1898).

making it a favorable route for tourists. The following subjects were taken by our artist while traveling over the very extensive lines of the Southern Pacific Railroad Co., to whom we are indebted for many courtesies, and without whose co-operation we should not have been able to bring before the public these animated photographs of interesting and novel scenes.[22]

The assistance of railroads by motion pictures is evident again, but with a twist, in *Going through the Tunnel*, which was made in Santa Monica slightly earlier, in January 1898. This presents the point of view of a camera looking forward from a locomotive on a section of the Sunset Route known as the Santa Monica Canyon Line, which was noted by the Edison catalogue for 'beautiful and picturesque natural scenery'.[23] However, the film begins with an image of a cluttered railroad depot, criss-crossing tracks, freight cars, a tunnel, an overhead bridge and what seems to be a winch. This is not wilderness but technology – it is only halfway through the 52-second film that the camera and train clear the depot and head north along the coast, the track stretching into the distance between Santa Monica's famous bluffs on the right and the ocean barely visible on the left. This constitutive tension is revealing. The title of the film points to a man-made structure and its first setting is industrial. But the catalogue's description of the film, like the Sunset Route's promotion, emphasizes Santa Monica's natural aspect, implying its already-established reputation as a seaside resort with famous beach, pier and funfair, and sublime ocean views from Palisades Park. The root of this juxtaposition lies in a history almost lost without a trace, which *Going through the Tunnel* illuminates but does not explain.

One of the causes of the rise of Santa Monica after the Mexican-American War was the appeal of its setting and climate, which drew day-trippers from Los Angeles and holidaymakers from further afield, many arriving by stage coach. However, industrial plans arose too.

Colonel Robert S. Baker, who had come west with the Gold Rush and later moved south to farm sheep, bought thousands of acres from the *californios* that he sold to US Senator John Percival Jones. Determined to make Santa Monica an international port, Jones and other local businessmen built a railroad and a wharf for ocean-going ships only to be bankrupted by price-cutting by Southern Pacific when it connected its Los Angeles & San Pedro branch to the first transcontinental line in 1876. Southern Pacific founder Collis P. Huntington took over the local interests, tearing down the wharf and building a new one, almost one mile long, which carried railroad tracks and depots for passengers and freight. Opened in 1893, this too was ruined by a rival bid for federal funding by the Port of Los Angeles at San Pedro to the south, the Santa Monica wharf surviving as a sightseer's curiosity until it was demolished three decades later.[24]

In the Edison film, the wharf remains off-screen to the left but its surroundings come to life. The train begins a few hundred yards from its landfall, at Colorado and Ocean Avenues, underneath which the tunnel was located. From there the train proceeds north on the route of today's Pacific Coast Highway, whose six lanes of traffic generate very different visual and emotional effects. This is a place that continues to exist, but a time which does not and a landscape which has utterly changed. The film exemplifies the ability of early moving pictures to allow reflection on Los Angeles' lost past, although its origin as a promotion for the railroad reminds us it was made to intervene in what was then the future of the city.

In the *Pacific Historical Review* of June 1937, Edna Monch Parker noted the different impacts of railroads upon American urbanization: 'In the East settlement promoted railroad construction. In the West railroads promoted settlement.'[25] Indeed, Parker argues that railroads actually *caused* the 250 per cent increase in the population of Southern California during the 1880s. The Southern Pacific, which quickly became the most extensive and powerful railroad in the region, had

Three frame enlargements from *Going Through the Tunnel* (Thomas Edison Manufacturing Co., 1898).

been granted by the US government more than ten million acres of land that had to be developed but lacked a large local market:

> There was little to support a railway in southern California in the [eighteen] seventies . . . Even Los Angeles was really nothing more than a country town . . . Populated by Mexicans, Indians, and Americans, it boasted three hotels. Three banks served the community. The town had no paved streets; sewers, without outlet, existed in only part of the district; gas street lights were erected at a few of the main street crossings. The first street railway was completed in 1872.[26]

To the Southern Pacific, the Los Angeles region was a space that had to be filled. As if anticipating the strategies of the Hollywood studio system, the railroad 'advertised Southern California to the outside world' through a decades-long campaign in billboards, books, pamphlets and articles, distributed to prospective residents, businesses and investors across North America and Europe.[27] Hence, Edison Company films of the Southern Pacific not only typified early cinema's fascination with the railroad as a modern spectacle, they did so in a way specific to Los Angeles, where they called for modernization of a 'new' part of the world.

Much the same can be said of *Building a Harbor at San Pedro*, a slightly later film made by the Edison Company early in the construction of the Port of Los Angeles. Like the earlier films, this also projects infrastructural and industrial growth. That the building of the harbour was a historic event was marked by the crowd of 20,000 who gathered for its opening in April 1899 and to whom was read a congratulatory telegram from President McKinley himself. A speech by US Senator Stephen M. White emphasized the transcendence of time and space by engineering:

Three frame enlargements from *Building a Harbor at San Pedro* (Thomas Edison Manufacturing Co., 1901).

We are here to celebrate the commencement of a work destined to last when we and ours are gone – the benefits of which only one endowed with prophecy by divinity can for a moment attempt to enumerate . . . The undertaking is certain to culminate in a harbor not only fitted for local commerce or coast-wide trade, but also suited to the needs of all merchant vessels, and to our warships and those of friendly powers, plying in these waters, needing for the time being a haven where they may ride without fear. Nor is this all: the United States has made great strides in her foreign trade.[28]

Given this hyperbole, it is striking that *Building a Harbor at San Pedro* shows not a grandiose public event (although Edison crews filmed those elsewhere) but a rather unstable and understated moment in a vast process of which the film presents us with a four-minute fragment. Indeed, the film's effect is somewhat off-putting. The camera, mounted in a small boat that we cannot see, presents a long shot of a temporary timber wharf on which is mounted a steam-powered winch, to the left of the frame, which repeatedly lifts huge boulders from the wharf, pivoting over the side, and dropping them into the ocean. As each rock announces itself with an enormous splash the viewer can almost hear it despite the film's lack of sound. Repeatedly, workmen tie each boulder by chain and rope to the crane before jumping clear as the boulder is lifted away. Their small human scale, set against the wharf, crane, water and sky, conveys a sense of the magnitude, ingenuity and bravery of the project. But the viewer is also struck by the wild rocking of the camera in the boat as if the waves might wipe them out in an instant.[29] The Port of Los Angeles is one of the largest in the world today, but the boulders in this film disappear without a trace as if the ocean were swallowing them for all time. The effect is enhanced by the film's repetitive action and open ending, the slinging of the rocks evoking David and Goliath and the insignificance, as much as the importance, of man-made things.

Origins of the Studios

The Edison films' concern with transport helps to explain the migration by filmmakers from the East that gave rise to a film industry ten years later. However, the films' emphasis on monumental construction contrasts with the transience of Los Angeles' early studios. With the first tentative forays being made after 1907, and then more surely after 1910, film companies such as William Selig Polyscope, the New York Motion Picture Company (NYMPC), and Biograph, followed quickly by Lubin, Kalem and Nestor, initially rented makeshift facilities but soon planned to use Los Angeles as a permanent base.[30] By 1912, in Charles Clarke's estimation, approximately 3,000 people were employed in 73 film companies around Los Angeles and its hinterland, although many only 'made a picture or two and then faded into obscurity'.[31] The early studios were not only numerous, and often obscure, but they frequently changed name and address. A film industry arose in Los Angeles at a time when the city was rising rapidly as a demographic and economic centre and at a moment in American history when manufacturing was shifting from downtown to suburban districts. These factors combined with a good degree of happenstance to shape the geography of film in the city.

The earliest film industry in Los Angeles was dispersed over a large urban, suburban and rural area, about twenty miles from east to west, which encompassed downtown Los Angeles, Edendale, Glendale, Hollywood and Santa Monica. However, quite quickly in the mid-1910s, Hollywood emerged as the most important concentration – especially at the intersections of Sunset Boulevard and Gower Street and Hollywood Boulevard and Vine Street – with secondary concentrations to the south in Culver City and in the lower San Fernando Valley to the north. And it was within this general pattern that the industry would gradually consolidate in its 'classical' era from the First World War to the late 1950s, especially around the eight major studios – Paramount, Fox, MGM (Metro-Goldwyn-Mayer), Warner Bros, RKO (Radio-Keith-Orpheum), Columbia, United Artists and Universal – which were at its core. However, within this general geography, it is not always easy to piece together a specific record of who did what, where and when, especially in the earliest days. Scholarship, the press, biographies and original documents provide a wealth of detail that is sometimes confusing and contradictory, and which requires excavation. This reminds us of the industry's contingent roots and the partial indeterminacy of all historical knowledge of the modern city, especially such a shifting one as Los Angeles.

Most accounts agree that the first film studio in Los Angeles was a makeshift facility downtown, in the back of a Chinese laundry near

Seventh Street and Olive Street, estsablished by the Chicago-based Selig Polyscope Company, although the date given is autumn 1907, spring 1908, or January or March 1909, depending on which source one consults.[32] Most accounts suggest this venue was used by Francis Boggs to shoot interiors for *The Count of Monte Cristo* (1908), whose production began in Chicago but was finished on the West Coast because of the attraction of the coastline for exteriors. Here too, however, opinions differ as to whether those were shot in Santa Monica, Venice Beach or Laguna Beach 60 miles south.[33] That film then became the first narrative film completed in Los Angeles, while Boggs's next production, *The Heart of a Race Tout* (1909), was the first made there entirely, both at the studio and on location at the Santa Anita racetrack and various city streets.[34] On the other hand, another account suggests that film's exteriors were shot at Santa Monica, another that Boggs first completed *In the Sultan's Power* (1909) in a rented mansion at Eighth and Olive Streets, and another that the first film made behind the Chinese laundry was *Across the Divide* (1909). Still others vary as to the location of that studio – between Seventh and Eighth, between Seventh and Ninth, or not on Olive but on Hope Street nearby.[35] We then have relatively certain knowledge that the Selig company left downtown for a new purpose-built studio at Clifford and Alessandro Street (now Glendale Boulevard) in Edendale, although the date of the move is given as August or November 1909 or 1910, depending on the source.[36] Other important filmmakers who used downtown as a base included D. W. Griffith, who arrived from New York with Biograph in 1909, filming parts of *Ramona* in Chutes Park before returning to make *The Unchanging Sea* on location in Santa Monica the following year. During this time, Biograph used temporary studios there at 312 California Avenue, at Grand Avenue and Washington Street downtown and, in 1911, at 906 Girard Street nearby (site of the present Los Angeles Convention Center).[37] In 1908, Hobart Bosworth, who had worked for Selig, set himself up independently in a studio in the Bradbury Mansion at 406 Court Street, which would later be occupied by the producer and director of comedies Hal Roach and his Rolin Film Company.[38]

Kalem and Vitagraph are also said to have filmed in Santa Monica after 1908, while Essanay filmed in Santa Monica Canyon in the summer of 1911 before setting up a permanent base in Niles, California, 300 miles north.[39] However, as much as oceanside locations appealed for filming scenes of certain kinds, they were not enough to generate a permanent

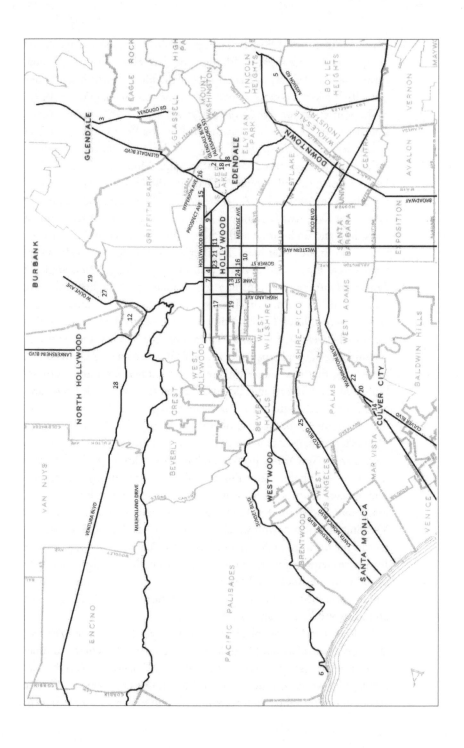

Map showing sites of the most important motion picture studios in Los Angeles, 1910s–40s.

Key
Studios are numbered in chronological order by year of their first founding; studios founded in the same year are ordered alphabetically. Asterisks indicate the headquarters of the eight major studios at the height of the studio era. See text for more detail.

1 Bison (1909), later part of Mack Sennett/Keystone Company Studios; 1719 Alessandro St, Edendale

2 Selig Polyscope (1909/10), later William Fox, and Garson Studios; 1845 Alessandro St, Edendale

3 Kalem (1910); 400 N. Verdugo Rd, Glendale

4 Nestor (1911), later Universal; northwest corner of Sunset Blvd and Gower St, Hollywood

5 Selig Zoo (1911); Mission Road, near Eastlake Park (present-day Lincoln Park)

6 'Inceville' (1912); Santa Ynez Canyon, Santa Monica

7 Jesse Lasky Feature Play Company (1912), later Famous Players-Lasky; southeast corner of Selma and Vine, above Sunset Blvd, Hollywood

8 Mack Sennett/Keystone Company Studios (1912); 1712 Alessandro St, Edendale

9 Kinemacolor (1912/1913), later Reliance-Majestic, Fine Arts, and Tiffany Productions, aka 'the Griffith lot'; 4500 Sunset Blvd, corner of Sunset and Hollywood Blvd, Hollywood

10 William H. Clune (1913), later Tec-Art Studios; 5300 Melrose Ave, Hollywood

11 Thomas Dixon Studio (1915), later William Fox; southeast corner of Sunset Blvd and Western Ave, Hollywood

12*** Universal City (1915); Lankersheim Blvd, Burbank

13 Metro Studios (1915–16); Romaine St/Eleanor Ave, southeast of Santa Monica Blvd and Vine St, Hollywood

14*** Triangle Studios (1916), later Samuel Goldwyn Productions, and Metro-Goldwyn-Mayer; 10202 Washington Blvd, Culver City

15 Vitagraph (1916), later part of Warner Bros; Prospect Ave and Talmadge St, Silver Lake

16*** Robert Brunton (1917), later United Studios, and Paramount Pictures; 5555 Melrose Ave, Hollywood

17 Charles Chaplin Studios (1917), later Kling Studios, and A&M Records; Sunset Blvd and La Brea Ave

18 Norbig (1918), later Bronx, Reague, and Westwood studios; 1745 Alessandro St, Edendale

19*** Jesse Hampton (1919), later Pickford-Fairbanks, and United Artists; Santa Monica and Formosa Ave, Hollywood

20 Thomas Ince (1919), later Cecil B. De Mille, Pathé, David O. Selznick; 9336 Washington Blvd, Culver City

21 Warner Bros (1919), southeast corner of Sunset Blvd and Bronson Ave, Hollywood

22 Hal Roach (1919–20); 8822 Washington Blvd, Culver City

23*** Cohn-Brandt-Cohn (1920), later Columbia Pictures; southeast corner of Sunset Blvd and Gower St, Hollywood

24*** Robertson-Cole (1921), later RKO (Radio-Keith-Orpheum); northeast corner of Melrose Ave and Gower St, Hollywood

25*** Fox Hills, aka Fox Movietone City (1923–8); 10201 W. Pico Blvd, Westwood

26 Walt Disney (1926); 2719 Hyperion Ave, Silver Lake

27*** First National Pictures (1926), later Warner Bros; W. Olive Ave, Burbank

28 Mack Sennett Productions (1927), later Republic Pictures Corporation; Ventura Blvd, Studio City

29 Walt Disney (1940); Riverside Drive, Burbank

concentration of studios, only two of which existed by the ocean for any length of time. At Sixth and Alamitos Streets in Long Beach, the Balboa Film Company opened in 1912 but was demolished in 1925. At Santa Ynez Canyon, north of Santa Monica, Thomas Ince founded the legendary 'Inceville' for the NYMPC, a 460-acre lot primarily used for westerns such as *War on the Plains* (1912).[40]

More important for early film studios than either downtown or the coast was the territory in between. At Glendale, studios were relatively far removed, including Kalem's first temporary facility eight miles north of downtown at Verdugo Canyon and its later, permanent studio nearby at 400 North Verdugo Road. However, most studios congregated on Alessandro Street in the somewhat less peripheral Edendale, which no longer exists as such but encompassed what are known as Echo Park and Silver Lake today. In 1909, at 1719 Alessandro, Fred J. Balshofer opened studios for the Bison company, producing westerns, according to the *Los Angeles Times*, with 'rough-riding cowboys, Indians and actors experienced in Western interpretations'.[41] Around the same time, Selig built studios a few hundred yards north, at 1845 Alessandro, where Francis Boggs made westerns with an authentic hickory stage coach and 'dozens of mettlesome steeds'; these studios were later leased to William Fox, and then Garson Studios, before Selig's business collapsed after the First World War.[42] In 1912 the Keystone Company of Mack Sennett, Charles Baumann and Adam Kessel moved into 1712 Alessandro, later expanding to incorporate Bison and the block across the street, and becoming the most important studio in Edendale until the coming of sound changed it completely.

In Hollywood, meanwhile, it is generally agreed that the Nestor Studio was the first, opened in October 1911 by the comedy filmmaker Al Christie on behalf of the brothers David and William Horsley, who had been involved in motion pictures in Bayonne, New Jersey. On the northwest corner of Sunset and Gower, Nestor took shape in a defunct hostelry, Blondeau's Tavern, strategically located halfway between Los Angeles and the San Fernando Valley.[43] In 1912 this site was taken over by the new Universal Film Manufacturing Company, while Harry Revier established a studio two blocks west on Selma Avenue, adjacent to orange groves that would give way to the legendary intersection of Hollywood and Vine.[44] This property was subsequently leased by Jesse Lasky and Cecil B. De Mille to shoot interiors for *The Squaw Man* (1914), often regarded as the first feature film completely made in

View of Mack
Sennett's Keystone
Film Company studios,
Alessandro Street (now
Glendale Boulevard),
Edendale, late 1910s.

Los Angeles. The rapidly expanding Jesse Lasky Feature Play Company
bought out adjacent lots, including Revier's, to establish an acreage
bounded by Selma Avenue, Sunset Boulevard, Vine Street and El Centro
Avenue to the north, south, east and west, which would become headquarters for the company later known as Famous Players-Lasky and
Paramount Pictures.

In the mid-1910s these studios were joined by an assortment of
others within a mile of Hollywood and Vine but stretching up to two
miles east to Edendale. In July 1915 William Horsley established a studio
in a lemon grove at Melrose and Bronson Avenues where Donald Crisp
made a feature-length version of *Ramona* (1916).[45] In 1916 the Vogue
Film Company opened on the northwest corner of Santa Monica and
Gower, and the Lone Star Film Company at 1025 Lillian Way, where
Charlie Chaplin would be based for his Chaplin-Mutual films that year
and the next. Meanwhile, on the district's eastern edge, Vitagraph relocated from Santa Monica to Hollywood Boulevard and Talmadge

Street. Fine Arts Studio set up at 4500 Sunset, which had previously belonged to the Kinemacolor Company and Reliance-Majestic film companies, and which became known as 'the Griffith lot' for D. W. Griffith's use of it for *The Birth of a Nation* (1915) and *Intolerance* (1916).[46] Finally, in 1916, William Fox relocated from Edendale to a purpose-built 30-acre studio at Sunset and Western, which would remain his headquarters until 1928.

The history and geography of Los Angeles' early film industry is striking for its rapidity and flux, close analysis revealing a process less random than the collision of atoms but not inevitable or orderly either. Commentators have certainly varied in explaining why a film industry was founded in Los Angeles at all. Among notable chroniclers of the city after the Second World War, Ralph Hancock argued that because it had the makings of a metropolis from the outset, 'Nothing [was] more appropriate than that the movie industry . . . should have located here. Its emphasis was all on energy, "creativeness", and grandiosity, and it found not only the sun but its spiritual home.'[47] In contrast, Remi Nadeau emphasized the provincialism and conservative values that dominated there in the early twentieth century, contending that 'Almost in spite of itself Los Angeles became a cultural capital with a more powerful impact on the life of the nation than that of any other city.'[48]

In 1911, the *Los Angeles Times* was in no doubt about Los Angeles' suitability to the new industry:

> Los Angeles, as is natural, has drawn the leading moving-image manufacturers of the world, as with a magnet, to establish permanent studios for the developing of the reels of film which are displayed in the various places of amusement in every quarter of the globe. Few of us realize what a great and prominent industry this has become, or the enormous amount of money expended by the various companies in the fitting up of their studios, their rehearsal theaters, and in the general plants involved.[49]

On the other hand, the geographer Allen J. Scott has recently argued that, while the Hollywood film industry may have endured because of a 'recursive relationship between place and industrial performance' – that is, a clustering of filmmaking and ancillary businesses and their development of lasting local roots – that clustering 'might have sprung up virtually anywhere in the United States'.[50]

If the *Los Angeles Times*' explanation was overblown, Scott's is perhaps too sceptical. Early filmmakers were hardly immune to the magnetic power the American West then possessed as a destination for migration and investment, nor to Los Angeles' bombastic but effective self-promotion, and their artistic responses to its climate, light and landscapes informed much early cinematic form and content, arguably in unique ways. One of the most common explanations for the agglomeration of film studios in Los Angeles, rather than in another city, has been the supposed desire of independently minded filmmakers in New York, Philadelphia and Chicago to escape the monopoly of the Motion Picture Patents Company (MPPC), of which Thomas Edison was the leading light. This explanation, which Scott dismisses as 'much repeated but surely improbable', does involve urban legend but is not necessarily unfounded in fact.[51] Marc Wanamaker, in 'The Historic Film Studios' (1976), explained that early Los Angeles studios were referred to as 'blanket companies . . . because the assistant cameraman would throw a blanket over the camera if an agent showed up in the vicinity'.[52] In *Early Filmmaking in Los Angeles* (1976), Charles Clarke, who worked as a cinematographer, technician and editor for D. W. Griffith and Harry Revier, insisted that many early filmmakers liked Southern California partly because they could flee to Mexico with their unpatented cameras when challenged by the MPPC, although Clarke admits, 'I have never heard of a case where this was done . . .'.[53] At the height of the studio era, William C. De Mille provided a classic account of the situation in his memoir *Hollywood Saga* (1939):

> The [MPPC] had an amusing habit of using deputy marshals, detectives, or, it is alleged, just plain strong-arm men to seize and destroy any motion picture paraphernalia which had not been licensed by the patent holders. The independents established their Hollywood studios, surrounded them by high board fences and lookouts, and at the first sign of approaching trouble the illegal cameras were bundled into fast motor cars and were off for Mexico, where they reposed quietly until the danger had subsided.[54]

De Mille presented his view without irony, although contending that larger companies such as Jesse Lasky's were not attracted to the region for extra-legal reasons. Interviewed in 1938, William Selig similarly made special mention of the negative pressure generated by law suits that

Edison had taken against him, and which were documented in records that Selig offered to a museum for posterity.[55] Yet, in an essay on 'The Structure of the Motion Picture Industry' (1926), the editor of *Motion Picture News*, William A. Johnston, made no mention of the MPPC.[56] And Remi Nadeau emphasized that Selig, Kalem, Essanay and Biograph were themselves members of that organization.[57]

Striking a balance between these views, Anthony Slide has argued that 'harassment' by the MPPC was a decisive factor *even though* many of the film companies in Los Angeles were members.[58] However, he has drawn a distinction between the attitudes of the MPPC and independent companies: moves to Los Angeles by the latter were often bigger and more long-term, more innovative in business strategies such as the promotion of movie stars, and their executives more complimentary towards Los Angeles as a place for new beginnings. These characteristics were evident in Carl Laemmle, founder of Universal, and in William Fox, who relocated their film production from the East to Los Angeles in 1915 and 1916.

The westward movements of film companies have also been related by Eileen Bowser to a peripatetic tendency that early American filmmakers inherited from theatrical touring companies.[59] In the late 1900s and early 1910s, film crews regularly travelled south in the autumn and winter from New York (where Edison and Vitagraph were based) and Philadelphia (the home of Lubin), while companies from Chicago (such as Essanay and Selig) were the first to go west in search of sunlight, long days and landscapes. Indeed, in 1910 Vitagraph opened a studio in Paris, while Selig had companies in Mexico and Japan. As late as 1912, however, and despite its vigorous denials at the time, the MPPC used private detectives to monitor members and rivals as they travelled, in response to which Southern California offered the greatest freedom to the filmmaker within the continental United States.

There is irony in the likelihood that many of the earliest filmmakers who moved to Los Angeles long-term first saw moving pictures of the place in Edison Company films, and that many of them travelled west on the Southern Pacific Railroad, another powerful monopoly that often collaborated with Edison. And yet the MPPC's negative role in the rise of a Los Angeles film industry must be matched by attention to the other two most frequently mentioned factors – climate and landscape. In comparison to the East and Midwest, the Los Angeles' climate provided better light and more bright days for shooting, and a variety of landscapes, including not only the coastline but modern urban and suburban streets, the San Fernando Valley and Griffith Park for rural scenes, and Spanish missions for archaic ambience. Large amounts of undeveloped land were available for shooting as wilderness or the construction of studios, and it could be leased or purchased at affordable rates. As investment in studios increased, and the business became more industrial, Los Angeles' reputation as an 'open shop' in which labour organizations and labour law were weak, and wages relatively low, also encouraged film companies to move there and stay.[60]

Questions of real estate and labour – which will be the subjects of chapters Three and Four respectively – were rarely publicly highlighted by filmmakers or studio executives, who preferred to cite climate and landscape in the kinds of terms already evident in boosterist literature and the visual arts.[61] In April 1911 the *Moving Picture World*, published in New York, noted that one of the greatest strengths of 'Los Angeles as a Producing Center' was that it benefited from 320 shooting days of good light in a typical year.[62] That December, the *World* noted optimistically that David Horsley had written to the magazine 'praising the climate and scenery and saying that he has decided to permanently locate there'.[63] Local voices amplified the rhetoric, with the *Los Angeles Times* in January 1912 ascribing the arrival of the film industry to 'Constant, shadow-slaying sunshine day after day, summer and winter – how it gladdeneth the heart of the man who makes drama by the yard, and swelleth the days wherein he may labor with profit'.[64] The newspaper's implication that sunshine was good for business and the soul was a standard doctrine of boosters. Arthur W. Kinney, Industrial Commissioner for the Los Angeles Chamber of Commerce, declared in 1918 that 'too much cannot be said with regard to the factor of climate as determining where manufacturing can be carried on most economically and successfully'.[65] In the previous year, Kinney stressed, Los Angeles had enjoyed a mean temperature of 62.8 degrees and mean sunshine of 75 per cent, with only nine days in which there was none.

William Selig explained that he and others shooting in Southern California in the late 1900s had noticed that 'the light was softer and the results better' than back east.[66] William C. De Mille explained that his brother Cecil was motivated by a romantic response that he conveyed when returning from Los Angeles to New York where the brothers were then based:

[Cecil] spoke in familiar terms of covered wagons and the good old days of the Spaniards, and told me at length what to do on the desert when my water gave out. He alluded to the Atlantic as 'a nice, little ocean' and turned on me with scorn when I remarked the day was nice and sunny. 'Ha!', he snorted. 'Call that little black ball up there a sun? Why I can't see it without my glasses; wait, my boy – just wait till I get you out in California; then I'll show you a SUN.'[67]

In somewhat gentler, but still idealistic, terms, Jesse Lasky Jr recalled the childhood he spent in Hollywood with his famous father:

Hollywood has variously been referred to as 'a state of mind', 'a dream factory', and 'entertainment capital of the world' [but] to me it was, quite simply, a home town. I bicycled through its pepper tree-lined streets, trapped rabbits and skunks in its then-wild hills, and resided somewhat impressively near the top of La Brea in a palatial old house with a billiard room and a projection room over the garage. Hot languid California summer, with skies breeding the drone of insects, and heat waves you could actually see. The dry eucalyptus clashed saber-like leaves. Sunflowers nodded enormously in the empty fields of weeds.[68]

In such explanations, climate and landscape were inseparable. De Mille invoked heritage and raw nature while Lasky suggested only light touches of modernity. This is not surprising: as late as 1912 large parts of the American West awaited incorporation into the United States, with Arizona and New Mexico being granted statehood that year. Exterior scenes in early films shot in Los Angeles frequently exploited the landscape's pre-modern aspect, as well as its adaptability.

The Unchanging Sea (D. W. Griffith, 1910) was filmed entirely on the beach below the bluffs at Santa Monica, although it does not identify the geographical setting of its action, other than to state in an opening caption that the film is based on Charles Kingsley's poem 'The Three Fishers', which concerns the lives of fishermen and their wives 'away to the west'. The narrative takes place, and is filmed, on the sand under partly sunny and partly misty skies. The landscape is especially prominent because the restless ocean and the crumbly rock of the bluffs separate the drama from the outside world, and because long and medium shots outnumber close-ups. The activity and equipment presented are traditional. Small timber rowing boats and hand-made nets are handled by men in heavy overalls who smoke pipes while their wives wait on them diligently, maintaining humble homes in what, somewhat incongruously, appear to be actual Santa Monica bathers' beach huts standing in for cottages.

The use of Santa Monica also involves a temporal dislocation. Long shots are matched by long takes as the wives stand lonely and forlorn on the shore while their husbands row out to sea. The incessant rhythm of the waves and subtle changing of the light meet the human routine of going out and coming back that seems to have shaped this place for generations. The sense of timelessness is reinforced by naming the lead roles 'The Husband' and 'The Wife', and by intertitles suggesting an immutable social order, 'For men must work and women must weep'. These features, together with the imagery, invite comparison with Robert Flaherty's later film *Man of Aran* (1934) and Luchino Visconti's *La terra trema* (1947), although Griffith's film is much more sentimental. When the bodies of three fishermen are washed up after a storm, The Husband is presumed missing at sea, leaving The Wife with a newborn baby who, by a series of large narrative ellipses, grows to be a young woman and falls in love, while her mother grows old and infirm, still vainly looking out to sea for The Husband. However, unknown to

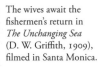

The wives await the fishermen's return in *The Unchanging Sea* (D. W. Griffith, 1909), filmed in Santa Monica.

them, but known to the viewer, The Husband has survived all the while, somewhat improbably living with amnesia nearby on the shore. When he happens to pass by on the daughter's wedding day, an intertitle tells us, 'Familiar scenes restore his memory', leading The Husband and Wife to a concluding embrace that mixes grieving and joy. The extreme condensing of the narrative underlines its setting outside ordinary time and space, while its implausibilities and those of its *mise en scène* highlight the film's status for modern viewers as an artefact of a past that is difficult to trace in Los Angeles today.

Most early films made in Los Angeles were less geographically abstract. Clifford M. Zierer, professor of geography at the University of California Los Angeles, and one of the first people to study the effects of the film industry on the landscape, argued in 1947 that '[i]f the industry had not gone through its "outdoor" and "western" stages of development, it is more than likely that it would never have left the eastern half of the country'.[69] Indeed, notwithstanding costume dramas such as *The Count of Monte Cristo*, the majority of the early films of Selig, for example, were westerns such as *On the Warpath* (1909) and *Across the Plains* (1910), mostly filmed in Edendale. An article in the *Los Angeles Times* in 1912 presented that locale as a replica of the Old West, curious but enchanting to visitors from back east.[70]

Similarly, in Hollywood, which was 'a thinly occupied subdivision' in those days, the Nestor studio also produced mainly westerns, including *The Sheriff's Mistake* (1911) and *Cupid and the Ranchman* (1912):

> The Santa Monica Mountains (known locally as the Hollywood Hills) bordered the community on the north, and the ocean lay a dozen miles to the west. Hollywood and Sunset Boulevards were the two main roads extending from east to west, and along them lay scattered wood bungalows, groves of citrus trees, and open fields. Sunset Boulevard was the favorite roadway between Los Angeles and the Santa Monica beaches.[71]

At this time, Hollywood's past as an untamed wilderness was plainly in view. Gregory Paul Williams reminds us that it had been little more than 'hard earth and aromatic scrub brush' in the 1870s: 'Large impenetrable patches of cactus, some growing seven feet tall, were scattered across the plain. Wild sunflowers bloomed near Highland Avenue. A grove of alders filled the area between Gower Street and Ivar Avenue,

Hollywood Boulevard, 1904.

providing a bit of shade from the hot sun.'[72] The early film industry's special emphasis on westerns echoed the historical layering of Hollywood's landscape. Originally inhabited by the Shoshone tribes called Gabrielinos by the Spanish, the area had become known as the Cahuengas, a territory strategically positioned on the north–south route of El Camino Real, which connected the Spanish missions along the California coast. Having been parcelled out by Charles III of Spain, after Mexican independence in 1821 the region was reorganized to form the cattle ranches of the *californios*, of which Rancho La Brea and Rancho Los Feliz spread east and west from the present El Centro Avenue, one block east of Gower Street where Nestor and Columbia Pictures later built their studios.

By the 1880s, after California's accession to the United States and Anglo-American appropriation of the land, powerful landowners such as John and Henry Hancock and Colonel Griffith J. Griffith came to own much of what would become the modern Hollywood, although contingency shaped its emergence. For Hollywood initially vied with a now-forgotten neighbour, Colegrove, for the support of the larger

45

urban region. Subdivided and promoted by Harvey and Daieda Wilcox, the former ran north half a mile from Sunset to Franklin Boulevard, and from Gower Street west to Whitley. The latter, developed by US Senator Cornelius Cole, ran south from Sunset to Santa Monica Boulevard on either side of Vine. In competition for business, Hollywood gradually prevailed because it was better served by water and rail, and better promoted to tourists.

Incorporated in August 1903, the origin of Hollywood's name seems destined to remain obscure. In *A History of California and an Extended History of Los Angeles and Environs* (1915), James Miller Guinn put forward a now widespread explanation that Hollywood was christened by Daieda Wilcox after a rural retreat near Chicago, which she had heard about by chance on a train journey to her native Ohio.[73] In his municipal history *Los Angeles: City of Dreams* (1935), Harry Carr proposed that during one of the first auctions of lots for home building, 'a Mexican boy came up with a burro loaded with California holly', thereby suggesting the name.[74] Whichever account is more true, Hollywood might never have been known for cinema had many of its early residents not been conservative Methodists: Blondeau's Tavern, in which the Nestor film studio first opened, had previously been a thriving French-owned business but became available for rent in 1910 when the newly incorporated town banned liquor. By this time, however, both Colegrove and Hollywood had reached the limits of their growth: being agricultural and suburban, neither had a sufficient population to fund its own sewers or water supply and both were subsumed in the City of Los Angeles with such modern amenities in mind. Colegrove officially disappeared in 1909, and in the public memory soon after, while Hollywood was annexed in 1910 but became more famous as a part of Los Angeles than it had ever been alone.

Throughout the 1910s Hollywood remained somewhat premodern. For William C. De Mille, it was 'a sleepy little town in which motion pictures had not yet become important, except as a possible menace to the peace and good name of its citizens'.[75] The general population viewed 'all moving-picture people, without exception, as a band of irresponsible gypsies . . . throw[ing] our colony upon its own resources, and [giving] a certain *esprit de corps* which is bound to develop among members of an expeditionary force in a foreign land.'[76] Anita Loos, the celebrated screenwriter who had her first success with *The New York Hat* (D. W. Griffith, 1912), recalled that Hollywood was then 'a dilapidated suburb' and the landmark Hollywood Hotel 'a rambling edifice painted the same dun color as the hills, with a veranda where elderly seekers after sunshine, mostly from the Middle West, sat in big red chairs and rocked their uneventful lives away'.[77] On the other hand, Catherine Parsons Smith has recently argued that Hollywood became a focal point for practitioners and devotees of the arts precisely because it allowed for a utopian belief in their interconnection with Nature, a belief that led to the founding of the Hollywood Bowl in 1922.[78]

Los Angeles and its surroundings were well known for their variety of natural and man-made settings that could be easily deployed in films by creative minds. In 1911 *Moving Picture World* emphasized this adaptability:

> Twenty miles to the west [of downtown Los Angeles] lie the pleasure beaches with a score of high class beach resorts within a forty minutes' trolley ride to the city . . . There may be taken resort comedies with an Atlantic City or Coney Island background. Within the same radius on the same beach were taken the marine dramas made famous by the Selig and Biograph companies. Here were taken such pictures as 'The Unchanging Sea' (Biograph), 'A Tale of the Sea' (Selig), 'Fisher Folks' (Biograph), 'The Buccaneers' (Selig), 'A Message of the Sea' (Bison), the sea scenes from 'The Padre', a recent Selig release, and others . . .[79]

While the city of Los Angeles was notable for modern streets, beautiful parks and fine residential neighbourhoods, antique effects could be achieved at the San Gabriel and San Fernando missions or the old town of Pasadena, while a convenient train ride to the San Bernardino Mountains would provide 'the ideal location' for 'Western and Indian films [in] rolling country cut up by foothills, treacherous canyons and lofty mountain ranges . . .'. Such characterizations added to the myth of the 'Land of Sunshine' a new sense of the region's plasticity.

The western *The Squaw Man* demonstrates the propensity of early filmmakers to shoot outdoors and Los Angeles' appearance in the guise of other places. The film's interiors were shot in the Revier studio in Hollywood while, according to Clarke, its exteriors were mostly shot at upper Bronson Avenue, below the present-day location of the famous Hollywood sign.[80] Other sources contend the main location used was at Chatsworth, in the San Fernando Valley, twenty miles northwest of Hollywood, where until the mid-1960s thousands of westerns, science fiction films, dramas and television series would be made at the Iverson Movie Ranch. However, inspection of certain scenes in the film that feature what appear to be real mountains, pine trees and snow suggests that the San Bernardino Mountains may also have been used. Our uncertainty as to the film's locations reflects the diversity of its settings, in contrast to Griffith's *The Unchanging Sea*, whose narrative space was strictly confined. *The Squaw Man* begins in England with Henry, a cowardly officer who embezzles funds from the war widows' benevolent fund of his regiment, before blaming the crime on his cousin Jim, whom he suspects of having an affair with his wife. As Jim is forced to board a schooner for America, where he eventually arrives in Wyoming, the Los Angeles area is made to stand in for two locations that were even more far-flung then than they are today.

In the opening scenes, England is represented in interiors at a regimental dinner party, where eight men in dinner jackets and surrounded by servants jovially drink a toast, and exteriors of a horse race that might be the Derby, with crowds in formal dress, and light-hearted humour at the expense of bettors who back the wrong horse. This is

The filming of the first scene of *The Squaw Man* (Cecil B. De Mille, Oscar Apfel, 1914) at the Lasky Feature Play Company studios, Hollywood.

Photo by J.A.Ramsey
Dingman Studio
L.A.

followed by another dinner indoors, after which the wives take the air outside while the men smoke cigars amidst a rich Victorian decor of statuettes, heavy curtains, a suit of armour, and a stag's head mounted on the wall. These scenes are not equally convincing: the horse race sequence uses actual footage of a race meeting in what looks like England, complete with a convincing bobby, while in other exteriors palms and pine trees have a less than English feel.[81] Later, action on the ship at sea is followed by a sequence set in New York, which includes a brief cut-in of actual footage of Times Square at night. When a stranger encourages Jim to 'Come out West', Jim relocates to the town of 'Maverick' where the train stops just feet from the door of the saloon, a rudely furnished timber shack rendered with an unconvincing set, in which rough-hewn cowboys greet him with some bemusement, dressed as he is for an English hunt. As Jim settles down, wearing britches, a muslin shirt and neckerchief, and buying the Lone Butte ranch, the film encompasses diverse exterior sequences: a campfire on the chaparral; the local teepee village of Chief Tabywana; Jim's informal marriage to the squaw Nat-U-Rich; and her rescue of Jim when he is snow-blinded in the mountains and nearly dies in a sulphur spring. The diversity of the settings is melo-dramatically underlined in the closing sequence: when Henry and his wife arrive from England, Jim determines to send his young son back for a proper education, but against the wishes of Nat-U-Rich and driving her to kill herself in despair.

While idiosyncrasies in staging can be forgiven, the diversity of settings unintentionally draws the modern viewer's eye to the slippage between space and place that cinema increasingly caused and which became a staple of Hollywood cinema. The ability of filmmakers to find a location in or near Los Angeles that could stand in convincingly for almost any real place in the world became one of its most publicized attractions. In 1929 the *Los Angeles Times* described Southern California as 'The Land of Many Lands . . . a vast stage upon which to enact a monumental pageant interweaving the history of all nations in all ages . . .'.[82] Within a day's drive could be found a 'duplicate' of any location on earth: Las Turas Lake had played Sherwood Forest in Douglas Fair-banks's *Robin Hood* (1922), the Portuguese Bend on the Palos Verdes Peninsula had become the Red Sea in *The Ten Commandments* (1923), San Pedro was New York in Emil Jannings's *Sins of the Fathers* (1928), Guadalupe near Santa Barbara was the Sahara in Bebe Daniels's *She's a Sheik* (1927), and Lake Tahoe acted as Switzerland in Adolphe Menjou's

Service for Ladies (1927). Not only did this demonstrate the suitability of the region to a globally dominant industry but, the *Times* suggested, not entirely ironically, the sum of its parts made Los Angeles better than all these real places combined. Fred Harris, head of the location department at Paramount Pictures, managed a reference collection of 75,000 photographs of 'houses, trees, rivers, mountains, street corners, roads, towns [and] nearly every cactus bush and fir tree within a thousand miles of the studios'.[83] He had once travelled avidly around the world, in every continent except Australia, but no longer did so very often.

The slippage between place and space included a more sinister denaturalizing and re-naturalizing of the landscape according to the demands of a new regime. While the history of the Los Angeles region had been Native American, Spanish and Mexican, by the time Hollywood cinema emerged it was dominated by white, Anglo-Saxon Protestants, and masqueraded as other parts of the world more often than it was asked to be itself. Moreover, in those few films in which it *was* itself, previous historical eras and regimes were delegitimized while the dominant culture was upheld. Meanwhile, Los Angeles' boosters sought to differentiate it from older cities back east, erasing, suppressing or appropriating other histories and peoples despite their prior claims. Indeed, an image of Los Angeles as white and racially pure was promoted, notwithstanding its history and its actually increasing Chinese, Japanese and Filipino populations. Charles Fletcher Lummis declared in *The Land of Sunshine* in 1895, 'the ignorant, hopelessly un-American type of foreigner which infests and largely controls Eastern cities is almost unknown here.'[84]

Non-Anglo peoples did not feature prominently in the Edison films made in Los Angeles, and Griffith's *The Unchanging Sea* remade the coastline at Santa Monica, once the preserve of the Gabrielinos, into a fishing village of Anglo-Saxon Christians.[85] However beautiful their representations in other respects, these films testify to a normalization of racial exclusion. Still, Native Americans and Spanish Americans *were* represented in the second film that Griffith made in the region, but as mythical ciphers of its past rather than participants in its ongoing formation. Subtitled *A Story of the White Man's Injustice to the Indian*, Griffith's *Ramona* (1910) was an adaptation of Helen Hunt Jackson's bestselling novel, published in 1884, which concerned a doomed love affair between Ramona, a young woman of partly Native American descent, and Alessandro, a Native American servant who works on her wealthy family's estate. In the film they elope, against the wishes of her family, the Morenos, and despite her pursuit by a Mexican suitor, Felipe. They try in vain to establish a home on land that is taken from them by aggressive Anglo settlers, who also raze Alessandro's tribal village, and their newborn baby dies when they are destitute in the wilderness. Jackson's book originated as a criticism of conditions for Native Americans in California under Anglo rule, and a plea for federal improvement of Indian rights. However, its primary effect was to intensify the romanticization of the region's Spanish mission heritage within the terms of an ascendant Anglo boosterism.

By the time Jackson's book was published, the missions had fallen into disrepair. By the time of Griffith's film, the *californios* too had been weakened by droughts and Anglo immigration, which altered the balance of power. In this context, the film became the first to explicitly acknowledge its Southern California setting – pinpointing in its intertitles 'Camulos, Ventura County, California, the actual places where Mrs Jackson placed her characters in the story' – and intensifying a wave of tourism initiated by Jackson's book that continues to this day. This naming of place sets it apart from *The Unchanging Sea* and *The Squaw Man*, which were shot but not set in the region, and from the Edison films, which named places in a documentary way.

Consistent with the Edenic image of the region in painting and photography, much of the action of *Ramona* takes place in the gardens of the Moreno home, which Griffith filmed on location in the actual Rancho Camulos, about 50 miles northwest of Los Angeles on the El Camino Real. The opening scenes present a young woman sewing in the shade of palm trees, a small timber chapel half open to the elements, rich vegetation and the verandah of an adobe house, all bathed in bright sunlight. In the gardens, Alessandro timidly introduces himself to Ramona, Ramona turns down the love of Felipe, Alessandro plays the mandolin, he and Ramona embrace, and she pledges her love to him before they elope. The cinematography in these scenes is dominated by tightly framed close-ups and medium shots, presenting faces, torsos or full figures against a backdrop of trees, bushes and a low wall. The narrative of assignations is facilitated by the layout of the Rancho Camulos in connecting courtyards, gardens and verandahs typical of large residences in Spanish and Mexican California as well as the missions themselves.

Subsequently, however, the safety of the garden is thrown into relief when Alessandro and Ramona begin a new life outside, where a vast wilderness seems to promise opportunity but is also fraught with danger. Here the staging and camerawork become more spectacular but also more open and anxious, especially in three long shots: looking steeply downhill at Alessandro's village, which has been attacked by gauchos and is shrouded in smoke and flames; looking across an empty mountainside as the couple discovers their baby's death; and at a high elevation, where an Anglo landowner shoots Alessandro, Ramona lights his funeral pyre, and Felipe arrives *deus ex machina* to return her to the domestic fold.

Eileen Bowser has plausibly suggested that the long shots of landscape in *Ramona* demonstrate that filmmakers shooting outdoors in Southern California tended to produce a 'freer positioning of cameras and the movement of actors and horses' than they did in New York and New Jersey. Out of reach of East Coast managers who might have discouraged experimentation, they used panning shots more frequently, less constrained framing and less centring of human subjects in the shot.[86] In publicity material, Griffith highlighted his innovative long shots and the technique was praised by reviewers in the press. However, the modern viewer is likely to feel that the innovation might have been even greater if the landscape was allowed to speak more clearly for itself: in many shots, its prominence is undercut by the wildly fluctuating bodily movements and theatrical facial expressions of the actors (Mary Pickford and Henry B. Walthall) as they run bewildered to and fro.

As Chon Noriega has argued, viewing these scenes simply in terms of technical innovation misses their ideological purpose.[87] In the narrative progression from the rancho to the high chaparral, the film initially presents Ramona as an active subject only to disenfranchise her when she loses her home, her husband and her child in a land that is never rightfully hers. Moreover, the screen adaptation undermines the book's critique: where the book was set specifically between California's independence from Mexico in 1848 and its accession to the United States two years later, Griffith's film insists the Morenos are 'Spanish', displacing the action back in time and erasing the history of Mexican California. The film ignores the fact that, in the book, Ramona established friendships with certain Anglos who were poor, thereby adding a critique of class to the indictment of racial injustice. The portrayal of Alessandro as hysterical and weak serves to justify the demise of his people for the Anglo male audiences to whom the film was primarily addressed. And the helplessness of Ramona, together

Garden and wilderness in *Ramona* (D. W. Griffith, 1910).

with her final salvation by Felipe, weakens the book's female point-of-view, and its critique of the masculine will to power.

These modifications demonstrate that what Noriega has called 'the progressive ideology of Social Darwinism' was prevalent in cinematic representations of Los Angeles and its region, just as in Los Angeles boosterism as a whole.[88] Hollywood would create further screen adaptations of *Ramona* in 1916, 1928 and 1936, while in 1920 Fred Niblo's *The Mark of Zorro* would give life to an even more popular film legend of Mexican California, also remade in 1925, 1937, 1946 and 1949. In the 1910s, however, very few cinematic representations acknowledged settings in Los Angeles or its region, and those that did tended to impose a racial order in which Native Americans, Spaniards and Mexicans were noble but now outmoded, a cause for nostalgia at best.

Los Angeles and cinema came to shape each other not only in myth and representation but also in their economics and physical growth. The centre of gravity of the American film industry shifted to Los Angeles in a fairly compressed phase from about 1907, the earliest date given for Selig's arrival, to about 1915, when Universal and other major studios emerged. In his geographical history of Los Angeles, *The Fragmented Metropolis*, Robert M. Fogelson does not examine motion pictures, but he does emphasize the immense concentration of decisive events that took place in those years: plans for the Los Angeles Aqueduct were approved in 1907, construction ended in 1912, and it opened the following year; the city's annexation of San Pedro and the Port of Los Angeles was approved in 1906; and its streetcar and local railroads reached their maximum extent in 1910.[89] The coming of motion pictures was not so monumental, but it had significant effects.

Newspapers and film industry journals spoke enthusiastically about the nascent industry as early as 1911. The *Los Angeles Times* exhorted the citizenry to 'realize what a tremendous advertisement this must mean to the city of Los Angeles and to the whole of Southern California as each picture taken here is exploited and broadcast throughout the civilized world'.[90] Acting, as Charles Clarke has put it, as a 'silent Chamber of Commerce', the film industry was said to allow a new connection between the local and the global that not only made the city better known but integrated its parts and helped it to grow.[91] This was the case in Edendale where studios were said to have driven investment, construction, and communications:

> There is naturally great rivalry amongst the different [film] companies, which is a very good thing for Edendale and Los Angeles in general, as they are vying with each other in their building operations and employing a great number of workmen. Many new stores are springing into being to cater to the growing wants of the people connected with this industry, and Edendale is fast becoming a busy thoroughfare, and is likely to become more so as several other eastern companies are heading this way with the view of establishing permanent studios in this home of perpetual sunshine.[92]

A *Times* article entitled 'Los Angeles: Great Backdrop for the World' presented Edendale as the epicentre of a network of film production, distribution and exhibition, which was reaching twenty million people per day.[93] This network encompassed the United States but was also 'advertising Americanism outside of American boundaries' in 'Canada, Mexico, South America, Australia, the countries of Europe, Japan, and the Philippines', thereby implicitly allowing Los Angeles to compete with older influential cities.

Suggestions of Los Angeles' new global prominence were often overblown. In 1910 its population (319,000) was very significantly lower than that of London (7,256,000), New York (4,767,000), Paris (2,888,000), Chicago (2,185,000), Berlin (2,071,000) or Philadelphia (1,549,000), and it would not begin to compete with the largest of those cities until the 1960s.[94] But that it might have *seemed* as if Los Angeles was competing is understandable: its population grew 212 per cent in the 1900s and 81 per cent in the 1910s, outstripping the population growth of every other American city except Detroit.[95] As Fogelson has explained, 'immigrants were the dynamic component' in Los Angeles' emergence at this time.[96] William Selig, Hal Roach, Mary Pickford and Cecil B. De Mille were pioneers in the art and business of the movies, but in the demography of Los Angeles they were simply numbers, possessed of special gifts and more famous but not entirely unlike farm labourers, railroad workers, shop girls and other immigrants who made up the statistical majority.

It was in January 1911 that the *Moving Picture World* sent its first dedicated correspondent, Richard V. Spencer, to cover the West Coast, where he wrote the ground-breaking article 'Los Angeles as a Producing Center'.[97] That and the series of reports 'News of Los Angeles and Vicinity' had the effect of habituating readers to the city's name while addressing them as if they were unlikely to have heard of it before.[98] Spencer explained with excitement:

> The Selig forces lead the California rush, and thither they have lured the rest of the colony. More Eastern producers are known to be making preparations to come this year, and eventually Los Angeles, by reasons of the several advantages above set forth, will become known to the world, not as the second largest picture producing center, but the largest, bar none.[99]

The sense of Los Angeles as distant yet becoming increasingly hard to avoid was also evident in the account of a trip there, in October 1915, by the 64-year-old Philadelphia-based moving picture pioneer Sigmund Lubin. Having visited in his youth, Lubin arrived by train for the first time in forty years and, as if he were Rip Van Winkle, was struck by Los Angeles' transformation from 'a scattering of low wooden buildings, with farms surrounding it on all sides'.[100]

In such reports, the film industry was identified with 'Los Angeles', but not yet with 'Hollywood', although the terms 'Southern California', 'California', 'West Coast' and 'Pacific Coast' were also frequently used. These made clear the transcontinental and intercontinental ramifications of the rise of motion pictures in Los Angeles at a time when the great national cinemas of Italy, France and Britain still held their own in competition with the United States, but would not do so for long. By 1915 motion pictures were considered in the same breath as other exportable goods manufactured in Los Angeles, such as leather products for South America and oil refining machinery for England, and the Industrial Bureau of the Los Angeles Chamber of Commerce was compiling its first roster of motion picture companies.[101] The following year, the actress Louise Glaum proposed that all films produced there should carry the credit 'Made in Los Angeles'; Jesse Lasky, D. W. Griffith and David Horsley met with Mayor Charles E. Sebastian to discuss the film industry's benefits to the city; and the opening of the new Triangle studios in Culver City for Thomas Ince and the NYMPC was an 'elaborate affair' attended by Mayor Sebastian, Chief of Police Snively and District Attorney Woolwine, as well as 'five hundred well known figures in the local photo play world'.[102] And yet the extent to which films emanated from 'Los Angeles' was open to debate. Edendale and Hollywood were in the City of Los Angeles, but Santa Monica, Glendale and Culver City were not, although all were in Los Angeles County. As a film producing centre, Los Angeles had a complex geography that defied simplistic naming but provided a focus for increasingly ambitious claims.

Remembering the Early Studios

Press reports in the late 1910s estimated that between 75 and 80 per cent of all motion picture production in the United States took place in and around Los Angeles, which, according to Arthur W. Kinney of the Los Angeles Chamber of Commerce, provided conditions for filmmaking 'which cannot elsewhere be duplicated on this terrestrial globe'.[103] And yet, despite such hyperbole, neither individuals nor studios in the early industry were without their mortal coil. Indeed, their history is marked by frequent discrepancies between high hopes and failed efforts, dreams of immortality and the passing of real time. These discrepancies bring to mind Percy Bysshe Shelley's romantic poem in which 'a traveller from an antique land' encounters in the desert what remains of a statue of 'Ozymandias, king of kings'. The statue carries the inscription 'Look on my works, ye mighty, and despair', but of those works now 'Nothing beside remains: round the decay / Of that colossal wreck, boundless and bare, / The lone and level sands stretch far away.'

No doubt, this characteristic of the early film industry is a function of its exceptional flux, but it is also a characteristic of man-made landscape in general, which Sharon Zukin has described as 'a social, cultural, and political product of creative destruction . . . a fragile compromise' between the natural human tendency to develop attachments to place and the opposite tendency of market forces to require constant movement.[104] It can also be explained by what Norman Klein has called Los Angeles' distinctive 'history of forgetting': a collective amnesia, persisting even in the late twentieth century, that arose initially from the efforts of the Anglo majority to suppress or determine the histories and experiences of other racial and ethnic groups.[105] And, in the absence of an authoritative institutional history such as an official film museum might provide, surely a third factor is that the Hollywood film industry has preferred to reflect on its past through sporadic shows of nostalgia such as those luxuriant montages of famous faces, voices and movie scenes accompanied at each year's Oscars ceremony by a sentimental orchestral score.

No studio better embodied the hubris of the early industry than the Universal Film Manufacturing Company. On 18 June 1914 it set a precedent that would be followed by all of the major studios by beginning construction on an expansive suburban tract of purpose-built studios, offices and workshops housing a myriad of specialized functions from casting, marketing and writing to carpentry, editing and costumes, and a variety of exterior sets.[106] The 230-acre Universal lot, on Lankersheim Boulevard in the Cahuenga Pass four miles north of Hollywood, was arable farmland bought for the then-unprecedented amount of $165,000 from the developer Stanley Anderson, who was also active in founding Beverly Hills.[107] When it opened in 1915, it typified the sheer physical scale of the largest studios, in which respect it was not unlike other major industrial sites of that time, such as the automobile manufacturing plants of Henry Ford in Detroit.

Richard Koszarski has written evocatively of the remarkable gala send-off organized by Carl Laemmle for the chartered train that carried Universal executives, employees and the press from Grand Central Station in New York (where Universal's corporate management was based), via Chicago and Denver, to Los Angeles. Filmed for the Universal Animated Weekly newsreel, the journey was augmented by local Universal agents who arranged for the train to be greeted by jubilant crowds at each town in which it stopped, and by a crowd of 20,000 people who attended the train's arrival on 15 March 1915.[108] The state-of-the-art facility known as 'Universal City' incorporated two 300-foot-long outdoor stages, to which were soon added three more and two indoor stages as well, and it employed 500 people, some living on the site. Bisected by the newly constructed 'Laemmle Boulevard', it was recognized

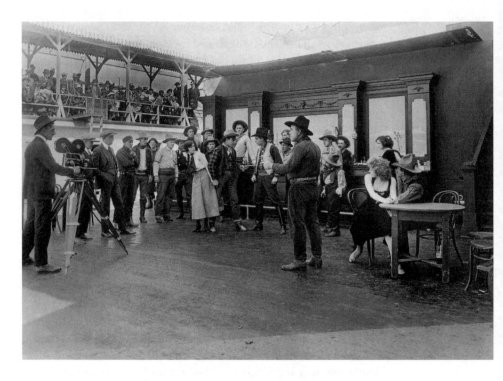

Universal City, filming of a western in progress on an open stage, in front of a live audience, 1910s.

as a municipality by the County of Los Angeles with its own post office and voting district status. Addressing Laemmle at the opening ceremony, Universal City's chief of police, Laura Oakley, identified the executive power of the movie mogul with the creation of an urban domain: 'Mr President, acting for the west coast studios, I am pleased to present you with this golden key, a key which will permit you to open the gates of this wonder city.'[109]

Universal's launch embodied the industry's future. Among the train's passengers were M. H. Hoffman, Universal's distribution manager and future founder of Tiffany Productions, Joe Brandt, Universal's general manager and future head of Columbia Pictures, Jack Cohn, co-founder of Columbia, and Ned Depinet, future president of RKO. Universal's pageantry continued Los Angeles' tradition of mobilizing crowds for marketing purposes. Thirty thousand people were said to have amassed for the opening of the Los Angeles Aqueduct in November 1913, and 20,000 for the inauguration of work on the Los Angeles Harbor in April 1899.[110] In July 1875 the 2,000 dignitaries, investors and citizens who showed up for the opening of Santa Monica's first railroad and wharf were described by the *Los Angeles Daily Star* as 'the largest crowd of people ever seen together in Southern California'.[111]

Universal City today not only remains in place but has grown, its 415 acres including the Universal CityWalk entertainment complex and attracting eight to ten million visitors per year.[112] But other early film companies have been forgotten, and the places they occupied razed or allowed to decay. For example, a film studio in Edendale, at 1745 Alessandro Street, was occupied by the Norbig Company from 1918 to 1922, then by the Reague Production Company for two years, and later by Westwood Productions, though none of these is much remembered today. Chaplin's Lone Star studios, at 1025 Lillian Way in Hollywood, were used by that company in 1916 and 1917 before being taken over by B. A. Rolfe Photoplays, then by Metro Pictures in the early 1920s. The studios of the Robertson-Cole Company, established in 1921 at Gower Street and Melrose Avenue, were rebranded the Film Booking Offices of America the following year, and again when that concern was absorbed into the newly founded RKO in 1928. Famous Players-Lasky left its first studios at Sunset and Vine in 1926, upgrading to grander premises at 5555 Melrose, which had previously been home to Robert Brunton and United Studios, the original facility subsequently being demolished. The studio founded by William H. Clune at 5300 Melrose in 1915 became home to Tec-Art, which, along with Brunton, United and Hollywood General Studios, was one of many 'rental studios' – compartmentalized offices and shooting stages leased out to several companies short-term, sometimes one feature film at a time. Lowly in the public eye and little known to history, the rental studios embodied the early industry's transience and mobility in extreme form.

These traits were evident in another way at Inceville, the studios opened by Thomas Ince in 1911 on leased and undeveloped land in the Santa Ynez Canyon five miles north of Santa Monica. Quickly becoming the largest studio lot, and expanding to 18,000 acres, *Motion Picture World* explained that it contained 'an administration building, a restaurant, a commissary, a wardrobe building, a property building, a scene building, 200 dressing rooms, an arsenal where weapons, ammunition, and explosives are kept, a power house furnishing light for stages and buildings, a reservoir furnishing fresh water, six stables and corrals and a number of other structures'.[113] In addition there were four stages (the largest enclosed in glass and measuring 360 by 160 feet), as well as outdoor sets representing 'a Spanish mission, a Dutch village with a genuine canal, an old windmill, and a Japanese village with jinirikishas, an Irish village, a Canadian village, an East Indian street and a Sioux camp'.[114] In 1916 *Picture Play* reported that Inceville had been 'recognized by the United States government as a town, for it has its own post office. Everything required for the making of gigantic motion pictures is contained here.'[115]

But just at that time, Ince was already preparing to relocate to the Triangle studios in Culver City, at 10202 Washington Boulevard, and in 1919, in turn, he left Triangle to set up independently in new studios a half-mile north at 9336 Washington, while the Triangle studios were bought out by Samuel Goldwyn and later became home to MGM. Five years later again, Ince was dead at 45 and his studios occupied by William C. De Mille. Today, the absence of Inceville could not contrast more strongly with the presence of Universal City. Its former site, which fell into disuse shortly before Ince's death, is occupied by the intersection of two of the region's busiest thoroughfares, Sunset Boulevard and the Pacific Coast Highway, flanked by a gas station, supermarket, seafood restaurant, desert brush and the secluded upscale homes of Pacific Palisades.

Inceville, Santa Ynez Canyon, Santa Monica, 1914.

Reflection on the heyday of Los Angeles' film studios was especially intense in the 1970s, following the studio system's demise. In the midst of what Marshall Berman characterized as a dual economic and emotional recession, commentators noted that both the early studios and the filmmakers who had known them were aging and passing away. In 1976, when *Taxi Driver* vied at the box office with *All the President's Men*, the recently retired 77-year-old cinematographer Charles Clarke published *Early Filmmaking in Los Angeles* as an honorific record of 'hardy souls with vision who had an idea for a new form of entertainment and, despite all the difficulties, steadfastly pioneered the way'.[116] Local historians Marc Wanamaker and Bob Birchard asserted in *American Cinematographer*:

> There are few cameramen living today who remember the studios on Alessandro, Melrose, or Sunset. It is most important that more information be saved for the future. It was these studios and the men who worked in them which made the film industry's history in Los Angeles an important milestone in the development of filmmaking as an art and of Los Angeles as the film center of the world.[117]

At a time when the film industry in Los Angeles had given way extensively to television and the music industry, and was about to be challenged by home video, the early film studios were minutely described in text and photographs with an acute sensitivity to the overturning of the real landscape in which films had been made.[118] For example, the Chaplin Studio at 1416 La Brea, in which *The Kid* (1921) and *The Great Dictator* (1940) were filmed, had been sold by Chaplin in 1953, becoming a rental studio, then a television studio for the Kling company and CBS, before being acquired by A&M Records in 1966.[119] The Ince Studio, built in Culver City in 1919, had been taken over by De Mille in 1926, then by Pathé, RKO-Pathé and David O. Selznick, before becoming a television studio for Desilu, home to *Batman* and other productions until 1968, but falling into disrepair in later years.[120]

In a 1979 issue of *Los Angeles Times Magazine*, Ray Herbert wistfully contrasted the legendary names and celebrity of the studio era's greatest stars with the lack of public interest in the buildings that had housed them. Most were now dilapidated or demolished because 'the region's growth, economic conditions and changing demands', including an increase in filming on location, had made them 'unproductive [and] expendable'.[121] In 1961 Twentieth Century Fox, whose original studio site at Sunset and Western had long since been turned into offices, had taken an influential step by selling its 260-acre flagship property on Pico Boulevard. This was redeveloped into the commercial and retail complex known today as Century City, with Fox leasing back 80 acres for film production. MGM studios in Culver City, which had comprised seven distinct lots in its heyday, retained only Lot 1, which housed its offices and stages. The other six, which had been used for exteriors and exterior sets, had been sold for residential use, with a development of townhouses on Lot 3 being named 'Raintree' in memory of the Civil War costume drama *Raintree County* (1957), which Edward Dmytryk had directed there. However, while realtors repackaged the past, the Los Angeles Cultural Heritage Board listed only 'a handful' of film industry buildings among the 226 cultural-historic monuments on its books, although the Chaplin Studio was one of them. The Los Angeles Conservancy, newly founded in 1978, was now campaigning for preservation of the last remaining studio buildings of the silent and early sound eras, focusing on Culver City because it contained the best assortment of original structures.

The city's quite casual disregard for preservation did not only affect film industry buildings – preservation remains a problematic and vexed issue in Los Angeles. But it seemed a poignant and cruel index of a general tendency, given the sense of an epochal break in motion picture history that prevailed in the 1970s. In truth, however, the remembrance of people and places associated with filmmaking had been evident almost since the industry's inception, although highly selective and shaped by crucial moments of change. In July 1967, for example, a bronze plaque had been installed at the entrance to MGM studios by the Native Daughters of the Golden West to commemorate Ince's construction of the first studios in Culver City more than fifty years before.[122] Coming just two years before MGM was bought and restructured by the leisure industry entrepreneur Kirk Kerkorian, the event reunited survivors of that era, including Mrs Thomas Ince and some of her husband's former colleagues, with current MGM executives, Mayor Dan Patacchia of Culver City, and members of the Culver City Chamber of Commerce. Speeches recalled that the 175-acre site had been part of the La Ballona ranch under Mexican rule.

'Fox to Develop a City for 37,000 on Studio Land in Los Angeles', announcement of the Century City commercial real estate development, *Los Angeles Times*, 8 January 1958.

In 1962 *The Dolphin Guide to Los Angeles and Southern California* demonstrated the sense of a new era because 'Today at most of the Hollywood studios the main action on the sound stages is created by the television film makers'.[123] A decline in film production in Los Angeles after the Second World War, the rise of 'runaway' productions filmed on location around the United States and abroad, and the proliferation of apartment complexes and commercial developments where studios once stood, was fuelling efforts to memorialize the film industry's past. The Hollywood Walk of Fame, proposed in 1953 and inaugurated seven years later, already included 1539 commemorative plaques in the sidewalk on Hollywood Boulevard. According to the *Guide*, planning was well underway for a Hollywood Motion Picture and Television Museum, intended by the Los Angeles County Board of Supervisors for a site near the Hollywood Bowl, although the project never came to fruition.

On occasion, the death of an especially important early filmmaker could prompt reflection on the gulf between the studios' heyday and the here-and-now. In October 1958 local newspapers and motion picture trade journals marked the death of William Horsley, co-founder of the Nestor Film Company, who was later responsible for the design and construction of Universal City into which Nestor was absorbed.

His death elicited explanations of the humble origins of many Los Angeles film pioneers, obituaries tracing his childhood working in coal mines in his native England, his emigration to Connecticut where he worked for a company making boilers, and his first involvement in motion pictures with his brother David in New Jersey in 1907.[124]

On Sunday, 22 September 1940, the Los Angeles Junior Chamber of Commerce had unveiled a bronze memorial to mark Horsley's foundation of Nestor Studios at Sunset and Gower in Hollywood on 27 October 1911, an event that was said to have inaugurated Los Angeles' film industry. James Stewart, Jean Hersholt, Hedda Hopper and some of Nestor's earliest stars, including Mary Carr and William Farnum, attended the unveiling. By this time the site, which had initially produced one one-reel western, comedy and drama per week, was owned by CBS, who had bought it from Universal in 1935 for its West Coast radio headquarters. The *Los Angeles Times* noted wryly that when the Nestor studio was first built, orange groves had covered the land. One

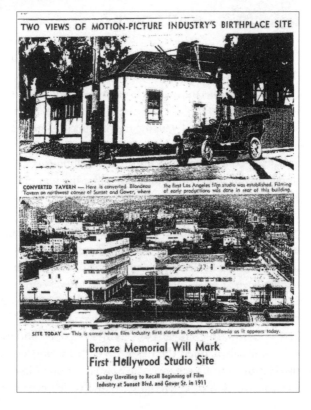

TWO VIEWS OF MOTION-PICTURE INDUSTRY'S BIRTHPLACE SITE

CONVERTED TAVERN — Here is converted Blondeau Tavern on northwest corner of Sunset and Gower, where the first Los Angeles film studio was established. Filming of early productions was done in rear of this building.

SITE TODAY — This is corner where film industry first started in Southern California as it appears today.

Bronze Memorial Will Mark First Hollywood Studio Site
Sunday Unveiling to Recall Beginning of Film Industry at Sunset Blvd. and Gower St. in 1911

'Bronze Memorial Will Mark First Hollywood Studio Site', *Los Angeles Times*, 25 September 1940.

veteran recalled having to be 'constantly on guard against coyotes that would wander down from the Hollywood hills and ruin a scene by frightening the leading ladies'.[125]

The death of William Selig in July 1948 at 84 years of age prompted an even larger retrospection. Indeed, Selig was presented as a point of origin for everything that the film industry had become, with sorrow expressed by Louis B. Mayer, Samuel Goldwyn, Lionel Barrymore and Cecil B. De Mille.[126] It was recalled that Selig had come to Los Angeles for his health while a young man in 1893, before establishing himself as a theatrical producer in Chicago and becoming known as the manufacturer of the Selig Standard Camera and Selig Polyscope projector. He had returned to Los Angeles in 1909 and established the city's first permanent film studio in Edendale, produced the first motion picture serial, *Adventures of Kathleen*, introduced Tom Mix in *Ranch Life in the Great Southwest* (1910), and opened a famous menagerie at Eastlake Park (now Lincoln Park), providing animals for the movies and a zoo for the local community. In 1947, a year in which the studio system was thrown into crisis by the investigations of the House Un-American Activities Committee, Selig was presented with a Special Academy Award for his pivotal role.[127]

In contrast to William Horsley, who outlived the studio he founded, Selig was outlived by his buildings. In January 1963 *Los Angeles* magazine reported on the threadbare remnants of the Selig Zoo, which had become a much-loved local landmark:

> Only the gateway remains today, a crumbling relic of another age. Between a pair of entrance arches richly carved but suffering from falling plaster, a pack of once proud, loudly trumpeting elephants now stands practically tuskless, their steel skeletons exposed to the view of passers-by, few of whom either know or remember what they represented.[128]

This unintended memorial contrasted starkly with other traces left behind. Dead stars were often remembered grandiosely, no doubt partly to counteract the early prejudice that film acting was a frivolous business, but also because the devotion of fans and the studios' publicity machines coincided to make bizarre spectacles of their deaths, funerals and tombs. Popular books suggest that Hollywood movie culture was tinged with an increasing sense of mortality. For example,

Los Angeles, Hollywood, and the Southland at a Glance, was published in
Hollywood in 1943 with support from the Los Angeles Chamber of
Commerce, the major studios, and local aircraft manufacturers and
banks. It devoted an important section to Rudolph Valentino, the silent
star who had died from pleurisy in 1926 and was described as 'the
Valentino, who will never die', his memory preserved by a modest nude
male statue in Hollywood's secluded De Longpre Park.

More sensationally, *Life and Death in Hollywood*, published in
Cincinnati in 1950, without support from Los Angeles or its studios,
suggested that a morbid fascination with the mortality of stars had
always underpinned the interest of fans. It emphasized the public hys-
teria to which Valentino's death gave rise. Riotous crowds had formed
outside the New York funeral parlour where he lay in state, three
women had allegedly committed suicide out of unspeakable grief, and
a mysterious woman in black was said to visit his tomb in the Hollywood Memorial Park Cemetery on each anniversary of his death.[129]
Jean Harlow, who had died from uremic poisoning in 1936, while
filming *Saratoga* with Clark Gable, was entombed at Forest Lawn
Memorial Park in Glendale 'in her finest gown and placed in an all-
glass coffin pumped full of embalming fluid'.[130] And D. W. Griffith
had spent his final years forgotten by the industry and the public, 'a
lonely and embittered man . . . taking long walks through the streets
of Hollywood' in a double-breasted suit and cane. In July 1945 he had
been found unconscious in the hotel room where he lived following a
cerebral haemorrhage, his funeral at the Hollywood Masonic Temple
attended by Chaplin, Goldwyn, Sennett, Richard Barthelmess and
Cecil B. De Mille.[131]

Such funerals contributed to the now long-established tradition
in Los Angeles whereby tourists make pilgrimages to the sometimes
modest, sometimes vulgar tombs and headstones of the stars. They also
extended a habit of rooting motion pictures in the past, despite the
transience of the medium and the shape-shifting of the city. Special
acts of remembrance, which served to mythologize the early industry,
took place even in the 1920s. In March 1925 it was announced with
sadness by the *Los Angeles Times* that the former Balboa Studios in Long
Beach had been demolished by 'unimaginative workmen' who had
caused to '[pass] out of existence the cradle in which many cinema
stars, past and present, first pantomimed their way into the hearts of a
not-too exacting public'.[132] The studio, which had been opened in

D. W. Griffith walking in Beverly Hills, undated photograph (probably early 1940s).

1913 to make comedies, had over-produced and gone bankrupt three years later, being bought out by an oil producer, its contents sold off, adjoining buildings torn down, and the land subdivided into stores, apartments and a bungalow court.

On 29 June 1928 a ceremony was held to mark the redevelopment of William Fox studios at Sunset Boulevard and Western Avenue in Hollywood. This was forward-looking in breaking ground for the new Fox Movietone sound laboratory, but it also remembered the studio's inauguration in 1915. What had previously been 'thirteen and one-half acres of citrus groves and alfalfa patches' was fondly recalled by 'a gathering of civic, cinema, club, scientific, social, religious, and educational representatives'.[133] Fred W. Beetson, Hollywood representative of the film industry umbrella organization, the Motion Picture Producers and Distributors of America (MPPDA), was master of ceremonies; Dr Rufus B. von KleinSmid, the president of the University of Southern

California, made a special address; and guests of honour included Raoul Walsh, whose *The Honor System* (1917) was the first feature film made at the studio, and Henry Lehrman, director of its first comedy, *The House of a Thousand Scandals* (1916). As a mark of the event's importance, and the longevity the film industry was expected to enjoy, a corner-stone was laid into which 'parts of these two first films' were placed for some future generation to unearth.

Such events were the earliest efforts to reflect upon, and preserve something of, the temporary life of the motion picture in Los Angeles. But they were not numerous and reflection was not the industry's main concern. Instead, as Hollywood cinema achieved a global currency not known by earlier kinds of art or entertainment, its most striking new form, and the industry's bedrock until the early 1930s, was very focused on the present and the future. The narrative and action of slapstick comedies presented a headlong rush *away* from the past and into thoroughly modern urban spaces. These films will form the focus of chapter Two.

two

Navigation

From the mid-1910s to the early 1930s Los Angeles quadrupled in size. Championed by its boosters, it self-consciously pretended to the rhetoric, and actually assumed some of the functions, of the cosmopolis. And yet the process of putting Los Angeles on the map was drawn-out and contentious, and its image was overshadowed by the sense of a great distance between it and other places, especially New York. Daily navigations between those two cities were a fact of life and shaping influence while the studio system grew to maturity, generating grandiose characterizations of Hollywood's ascent in the world.[1] One was the famous logo of Universal Pictures – a revolving planet Earth – which seemed to propose that cinema from Los Angeles provided the basis for a new global culture. As such, Los Angeles and its film industry extended what the geographer Denis Cosgrove has described as the historical tendency of exceptionally influential cities to organize the world around them in their own image.[2] Examining the evolution of maps, this is a tendency Cosgrove especially identifies with Rome, which presented itself as 'urbis et orbis' in the classical and medieval eras.

Meanwhile, slapstick comedy, arguably the most fundamental of all Hollywood film genres, took as one of its key subjects the internal navigation of Los Angeles and its environs. Many of the films of Charlie Chaplin, Harold Lloyd, and Laurel and Hardy were concerned with the comical efforts of citizens to orient themselves in the city's increasingly large, complex and fast-moving landscape despite its frequent hazards. These films provided revealing descriptions of the shape of Los Angeles, its parts and their relations. But, predating the widespread use of the aerial view that would become notable in film noirs, these earlier films only occasionally presented what Cosgrove calls an 'Apollonian gaze . . . a divine and mastering view from a single perspective'.[3] More often, they involved multiple ground-level perspectives, describing the geography of the city in a partial and contingent way reminiscent of the medieval maps known as *portolanos*. Those flourished, before the adoption of the scientific system of latitude and longitude, as 'a logical extension of deckboard observation and recording' by sailor-explorers who produced graphic representations of the meandering coastlines of unknown lands from 'written lists of locations and compass bearings'.[4]

In so far as they were recently arrived in Los Angeles, slapstick comedy filmmakers were in a real sense exploring unfamiliar terrain that was rapidly evolving before their eyes and those of moviegoers far and wide. And in an imaginary sense, the protagonists of their films were often akin to Cosgrove's 'heroic navigator [who] is also a vulnerable mortal on a flimsy craft'.[5] But Los Angeles was not *terra incognita*. Though undergoing expansion, it had been seen and conquered long before, and slapstick comedies selectively used – and, thereby, intervened in – the city's real and complex geography. Their imaginative mappings were ideologically biased by gender, race and class, and skewed in favour of an accelerated free-market capitalism. Such biases also decisively shaped the city's rapid expansion, as a quantitatively and qualitatively new suburbanization demanded that filmmakers and film studios periodically adapt their activities to Los Angeles' changing shape, navigating and re-navigating it, especially with the coming of sound.

Putting Los Angeles on the Map

By 1922 Los Angeles was responsible for 84 per cent of all film production in the United States.[6] New York continued to have some importance, for example, because of D. W. Griffith's relocation to Mamaroneck in 1920, and the studio maintained by Famous Players-Lasky in Astoria until 1932. But it was mainly in corporate management and distribution that the East Coast retained its importance. Biograph operated a studio and film laboratory in Los Angeles by the spring of 1911, but shipped its completed prints to New York, while Selig's were processed in Chicago and Nestor's at Bayonne, New Jersey.[7] Film industry executives, including Carl Laemmle, Adolph Zukor and William Fox, were represented in Los Angeles by their deputies, Irving Thalberg, Jesse Lasky and Sol Wurtzel. Umbrella organizations such as the National Association of the Motion Picture Industry and the Society of Motion Picture Engineers, and trade papers such as *Motion Picture News* and *Film Daily*, were also based in New York.

The *Motion Picture Studio Directory* of 1918 displays the geographical split in the industry. It listed 117 film studios in the United States, of which 50 were headquartered in New York and New Jersey, and 34 in Southern California, with the remainder in various cities, mostly in the east or industrial Midwest.[8] The vast majority of companies specializing in technical equipment and expertise were also in those regions, many advertising in the *Directory*: Craftsmen Film Laboratories, Erbograph Co. producers and film developers, Victory Film Manufacturing Company, and Motion Picture Apparatus Company, all in New York City; Cooper-Hewitt Electric Company, Hoboken, New Jersey, and Commonwealth Pictures Corporation and Essanay Film Manufacturing Company, both in Chicago.

On the other hand, the *Directory* demonstrates that by 1918 creative personnel were already based almost exclusively in the Los Angeles area. Advertisements for film stars, character actors and singers usually consisted of little more than a photograph, the person's name, the company to which he or she was contracted and, rather than a specific mailing address, simply the name of the city or town in which they could be reached: 'Clifford Bruce – Leads' of 'Hollywood, Cal.'; 'Donald McCallum, Sennett-Paramount Comedies Production Staff, Los Angeles, California'; 'Eddie Lyons and Lee Moran' of 'Universal Film Mfg. Co., Universal City, Cal.'[9] A publicity still of Roscoe 'Fatty' Arbuckle placed him in 'Long Beach, Cal.', while a full-page 'postcard' sending greetings to 'the Rest of the World' carried the caption 'With best wishes from . . . Thomas H. Ince Studios, Los Angeles, California', the place name in prominent type and accompanied by portraits of the actresses Sylvia Bremer and Enid and Marjorie Bennett.[10] Occasional small ads highlighted migrants from overseas. The Italian 'Alfred E. Gandolfi, Cameraman, Diando [Film Corp., Glendale]', for example, had worked for the film studio Cines in Rome, and Itala Films in Turin, before taking up employment with Pathé, who transferred him to the United States; there he found work with Oscar Apfel for the Jesse Lasky Co., then for Morosco-Pallas and the Fox Otis Turner Company. Gandolfi advertised that he was 'the first man to use a foreground reflector in California and invented the double exposure sunshade which is now almost universally used'.[11]

Overseeing these indications of a new film capital to the west was the editorial authority of the *Directory* and its parent *Motion Picture News*, which strongly identified itself with New York. A two-page editorial, 'The Story of an Institution', sought to impress the reader with its expertise and wide readership, as well as its ability to amass information from geographically widespread sources and disseminate it with efficiency and know-how:

> The first mail is caught at six o clock in the morning. Thereafter until twelve noon sacks of copies for each state are rushed to specific trains in order that every subscriber to *Motion Picture News* shall have his magazine at the earliest possible moment. To give a concrete idea of the careful precision of the schedule, copies for Southern and Northern California leave on different trains and from different depots in New York City. Many copies go out special delivery. The foreign delivery reaches the following countries: Australia, British Guiana, China, Denmark, Dutch East Indies, England, France, Haiti, India, Ireland, Italy, Japan, New Zealand, Norway, Russia, Scotland, Siam, South Africa, South America, Spain, Straits Settlements, Sweden, Switzerland, Wales, West Indies . . . The pages of all the copies printed in 1917 would stretch end to end from New York to Bombay, India, via London . . . Branch offices are maintained in Los Angeles with four employees and Chicago with three employees.[12]

In this ambitious recitation of nations, cities and regions, the *Motion Picture News* spoke in the heyday of newspaper publishing in the early twentieth-century United States, and presented New York City as the focal point of an information network that was global. Indeed, the list of places suggested that the older networks of the imperial powers of Europe were being transcended by those of the United States. In this new regime, however, 'Los Angeles' had a relatively small role, just one point among many, and 'Hollywood' had virtually none.

That men and women in the film industry had a sense of the distance and difference between New York and Los Angeles is clear from correspondence of the day. For example, telegrams between Adolph Zukor and Jesse Lasky, president and head of production, respectively, for Famous Players-Lasky, reveal the sometimes competing interests of the East and West Coasts. Such correspondence very rarely refers to 'Los Angeles', preferring 'California' or 'Hollywood' instead, the latter having been incorporated into the City of Los Angeles only in 1910 and evidently inspiring a greater loyalty among people who did not think of themselves as Angelenos.

On 2 July 1921, on company letterhead marked 'Lasky Studio, 1520 Vine St, Hollywood, California', Lasky wrote to Zukor at Famous Players-Lasky Corporation headquarters, 485 Fifth Avenue, New York City:

> I have been here [in Los Angeles] now for two weeks, and I think I can safely report that I have put over everything I came out to accomplish . . . [cutting salaries of workers, directors, and artists during] a period of reorganization and great stress . . . Our people here have responded splendidly, and I really feel that we have the situation well in hand, so that we can safely count on about a twenty per cent reduction in the cost of our product without hurting its quality. After studying the situation, I feel sure we made a wise decision when we decided to close the New York studio [Astoria]. We can take care of all the work here, and with an organization drawing reasonable salaries from top to bottom, we will have a comparatively low overhead. This, plus the enthusiasm we have renewed, and the competition among the directors to show that they can make pictures at reduced cost as good as the next fellow, is going to bring the result you expect.[13]

Lasky's text evokes the then widespread sense that Los Angeles was little more than an outpost, although his conviction that there is little future for film production in New York is a sign of Hollywood's drive for autonomy and exudes confidence in the benefits of working in Los Angeles, which echoes boosterist rhetoric. Cordiality laced with a sense of competition was evident in other correspondence that summer. On 28 May Lasky urgently requested the sizeable amount of $137,257 from the Finance Committee in New York to add roofs to two 'California Studios' [open stages] so that they could stay in full production through the coming winter.[14] On 11 July Zukor replied that such improvements would have to wait for lack of cash and that Lasky should rent space for the winter from Brunton or Robertson-Cole. Remarking that 'our main object in closing the Eastern studio was for the purpose of curtailing the cash outgoing', Zukor indicated that he had not entirely discounted the possibility of reopening it in the future, to which Lasky replied disappointedly a week later not only that the improvements were essential but that the need for them had been acknowledged when the New York studio had been closed.[15] Lasky elaborated on the problem of the 'rainy season' in Southern California, which caused delays and cost overruns in production, advising Zukor that 'we will lose a good deal more than the amount in question from lost time during rain, and from damage to sets that have to be repainted and mended after each rain storm'. Subsequent letters indicate that in 1928, even after the Astoria studio reopened, Lasky continued to champion West Coast over East Coast production, arguing that the New York studios were too small and technically limited to make them viable for shooting feature films with sound.[16]

By 1923 the *Motion Picture Studio Directory* carried not one list of all film studios in the United States but two separate lists of 28 'Eastern Studios', most of which were then past their prime, including Edison and Biograph, and 120 on the 'West Coast'. Three of these were in San Francisco, one in San Diego, ninety-two in 'Hollywood', twelve in 'Los Angeles' (four downtown and seven in Glendale), ten in 'Culver City', one in 'Burbank' and another at 'Universal City' (actually also in Burbank but listed as a separate place).[17] The *Directory* was still headquartered in New York and its 268 pages of lists of actors, actresses, directors, producers, cinematographers, writers and agents were roughly equally split between that city and Los Angeles, though with fewer based in third cities than in 1918. The 1923 *Directory* demonstrated the consolidation of Los Angeles as a permanent base for film production, although the fact that the proportion of companies and studios established there was greater than that of individuals would seem to suggest that individuals were slower to move from New York. At the same time, the vast majority of advertisements for individuals and companies based in Los Angeles specified 'Hollywood' rather than Los Angeles as such. Indeed, where the 1918 edition had explained that *Motion Picture News* had branch offices in Chicago and 'Los Angeles', its 1923 edition stated that those were in Chicago and 'Hollywood'.[18]

Notwithstanding this slippage, however, by the late 1920s, whether they preferred to refer to Los Angeles or Hollywood, film industry commentators began to speak of something established rather than new. William Johnston of *Motion Picture News* wrote:

> The center of production today is Hollywood, California, and it has been for a number of years. Sunlight and scenery attracted here the pioneer producers. These advantages are not such pronounced

factors today. Florida, for example, has both. But the production industry has become settled in California and around it have been established studio supplies of all kinds, labor, facilities, and, of course, the important element of professional talent.[19]

Geographical inertia was an increasingly evident feature of an industry that had now reached critical mass and was clearly there to stay.

Evidence of this was also to be found in film industry professional organizations. The Society of Motion Picture Engineers (SMPE) was based in New York but met biannually, usually in April and October, in a wide range of cities from Boston, New York and Washington, DC, to Chicago, Philadelphia and Pittsburgh. By 1927 it had even met in Montreal and Ottawa, but never in Los Angeles, although that would soon change. In April that year, at a meeting in Norfolk, Virginia, a prominent member declared that 'In spite of its isolation, the wealth of Hollywood is such that people, important people, gravitate to it from every corner of the world.'[20] Another delegate pointed to a superciliousness he had detected among filmmakers on the West Coast:

> I have been in Hollywood several times and know that out there they consider themselves as about nine-tenths of the whole entire thing. I once listened to one of the big directors setting forth his views as to the relative importance of Hollywood and the rest of the United States. I gained the impression that outside of Hollywood only very small potatoes grew.[21]

Pressure increased to recognize Los Angeles by meeting there, although regret was expressed for the great distance between the film industry's 'chemists, physicists, engineers, and opticians' in the East and creative personnel on 'the Coast'.[22] Expressing the view that regular meetings held in Hollywood might also forestall the founding of rival organizations, a representative of Eastman Kodak from Rochester, New York, reported news from Los Angeles of a new film industry body, presumably the Academy of Motion Picture Arts and Sciences which was officially launched in May 1927.

The first meeting of the SMPE in Los Angeles was held in Hollywood in April 1928 and attended by industry heavyweights Douglas Fairbanks, Fred Niblo, Louis B. Mayer and Cecil B. De Mille, all of whom were founders of the Academy. De Mille reached out to the visiting technical personnel of the SMPE by declaring in his opening address that 'There is no industry more dependent than we are today upon science.'[23] Dr C. Mees, for Eastman Kodak, outlined plans for a greater collaboration between film studios and technical companies. Fred Beetson, Vice-President of the MPPDA, informed the audience of a new film research laboratory in Hollywood. And W. B. Cook, of Kodascope Laboratories, New York, and president of the SMPE, made the case, presumably aimed primarily at the gathered creative personnel, that 'No artistic conception of the author, scenario writer, or director, can be given to the public except through the application of chemical, mechanical, and electrical engineering.'[24] By 1930 the Society had established two branches outside New York – one in London, as a base for all of Europe, and another in Los Angeles to 'keep . . . in direct touch with the directors and cameramen in the field'.[25] Though perhaps a little condescending, as if Los Angeles was a place for safaris, such declarations showed a growing recognition of its new economy, based on the creation of images, and its difference from the heavy industrial base of New York.

New ways of thinking about the relationship between old and new economic centres and activities was also demonstrated by attitudes in the film industry to the bastion of American industrial capitalism, Wall Street. By 1920 not only Carl Laemmle and Jesse Lasky, but also Louis B. Mayer, Sam Warner, Harry Cohn and other movie executives had relocated from the East to the West Coast. As Neal Gabler has convincingly explained, the Los Angeles movie studios constituted for them 'an empire of their own' which they, as Jewish entrepreneurs and mostly first- or second-generation immigrants, invented as a business and cultural alternative to the entrenched industrial and financial interests of East Coast WASP elites.[26] Dislike of Wall Street on the West Coast was often actively expressed. In his memoirs, Charlie Chaplin asserted that he was 'opposed to Wall Street having anything to do with my work'.[27] In 1919 he had rejected a $4 million dollar investment in United Artists from the leading investment bank Dillon Read and Company, which financed the expansion of the Dodge, Chrysler and Goodyear automobile industries. Two years later, James William Dixon, president of First National Pictures, declared in a telegram to Chaplin's business partners, Douglas Fairbanks and Mary Pickford, that they ought to be 'determined more than ever before not to have business dominated by Wall Street interests'.[28]

Nonetheless, Wall Street money was heavily invested in motion picture studios and Wall Street financiers held seats on many of their executive boards, especially given the industry's self-evident profit potential. In 1921 and 1926 the American Bankers Association held its annual conventions in Los Angeles, its *Banker's Magazine* reporting enthusiastically that the city's bank deposits grew from $500 million to $986 million in the five intervening years and that, by 1926, the city was 'now more metropolitan and certainly more cosmopolitan' than at any time in history.[29] Indeed, the movie industry was an important influence on banking at this time. No less a bank than Bank of America originated as the Bank of Italy, which became the first California-wide chain in 1918 and was the first to cultivate the motion picture industry. Janet Wasko has explained that Bank of Italy provided 'a radical departure from traditional banking policies, constantly challenging the Eastern financial establishment'.[30] Its top executives, especially its president A. H. Giannini, shared seats on the boards of banks and film studios with Hollywood moguls such as Joseph and Nicholas Schenck, Cecil B. De Mille and Samuel Goldwyn, and socialized with them too.

By the late 1920s, with the coming of sound, the film studios' increasingly massive capital investments indebted them to the banks even more. The *Film Daily Year Book 1927*, published by *Film Daily* newspaper, described Famous Players-Lasky Corporation as 'the United States Steel Corp. of the motion picture industry' and pointed out that the largest studios, such as Loew's, had now become 'complete producing, distributing, and exhibiting organization[s]'.[31] In bullish tones typical of what was then a confident business environment, the *Year Book* used an impressive list of statistics to emphasize the growing value of the motion picture industry to investors: the seven largest film studios listed on Wall Street constituted 'a $1,500,000,000 business' owned by 60,000 shareholders, and their films attracted 130 million people to the cinema every week at 20,300 theatres across the United States.[32] In this context, senior film executives based in New York fraternized equally with major players in traditional industries. In January 1928 *Arbitration News*, the journal of the American Arbitration Association, documented a meeting of heads of New York industry at which Adolph Zukor took a lead in discussions that sought to encourage arbitration as a means to the resolution of business disputes. A photograph of Zukor flanked by Charles M. Schwab (Bethlehem Steel Corporation), Lee J. Eastman (Packard Motor Car Co.) and Alfred H. Swayne (General Motors) suggested that the leading lights of what had once been an upstart enterprise had become elder statesmen.[33]

Los Angeles mounted another challenge to the dominance of the New York stage. Robert McLaughlin has explained that the rise of motion pictures was inversely proportional to the collapse of the touring dramatic companies that had been a feature of American life for decades.[34] Many of the earliest feature films to enjoy success in the United States were adaptations of stage plays, including *Queen Elizabeth* (1912, starring Sarah Bernhardt), *The Prisoner of Zenda* (1913), *Tess of the D'Urbervilles* (1913) and *A Good Little Devil* (1914), in which Mary Pickford starred in both the play and the film. However, the motion picture industry in Los Angeles, generating mass audiences and salaries unimaginable in the theatre, soon began 'a talent raid that in many respects has never ceased'.[35] Where Broadway paid its stars a maximum of $600 per week, the Hollywood studios could offer up to $1,500 for good actors and $5,000 for top stars. This made a long-term move irresistible even to those not naturally inclined to go, in an era when lingering distrust of motion pictures made it commonplace to refer to New York as the home of 'legitimate' theatre. In June 1920 the New York-based theatrical trade paper *Pantomime* reported that the actress Marjorie Rambeau, then starring on Broadway in the Shubert brothers' comedy *The Goldfish*, had 'purchased 100 acres' near Fresno, California, for use as 'a ranch home between theatrical engagements', at which the columnist quipped, 'So long as you didn't buy the land in Hollywood, Marjorie, we'll forgive you.'[36] In July of the following year, while writing to Jesse Lasky about studio finances, Adolph Zukor pointed out that the celebrated Broadway star Thomas Meighan, who had made his film debut in 1915, was still not enthusiastic about his relocation. In March 1923, on the other hand, Fox made an announcement, one of many of its kind, that it had contracted three new female stars – Jean Arthur,

Adolph Zukor with Charles M. Schwab, Lee J. Eastman and Alfred H. Swayne, *Arbitration News* magazine, January 1928.

Ruth Dwyer and Peggy Shaw – to migrate from Broadway to Hollywood, and had optioned plays by the Broadway producers John Galsworthy, William Anthony McGuire and David Belasco.[37]

Even some of the biggest names in the film industry remained ambivalent for years to come. Although he made some of the most important early films there, D. W. Griffith never settled in Los Angeles, returning to Mamaroneck to found his own studio in 1920. From the account of Anthony Slide, it is clear that his geographical and psychological frame of reference was defined by the East Coast, where he spent most of his life and career, and the Deep South and Britain in which *The Birth of a Nation* (1915), *Hearts of the World* (1918) and *Broken Blossoms* (1919) were shot or set.[38] Charlie Chaplin, born and raised in London, first visited New York City with an English vaudeville company before moving to Los Angeles for Keystone in 1914, where he lived and worked until the early 1950s, apart from brief stints elsewhere. In his early memoirs, he was impressed by the size and range of American cities:

> New York, where the buildings were ten, twenty, even thirty floors high, and the sky blazed with enormous signs in electric light; Chicago, where the tinned meat came from . . . The number of American cities seemed endless to me . . . I had imagined a broad, wild continent, dotted sparsely with cities – New York, Chicago, San Francisco – with wide distances between. The distances were there, as I expected, but there seemed no end to the cities. New York, Buffalo, Pittsburgh, Cincinnati, Columbus, Indianapolis, Chicago, St Louis, Kansas City, Omaha, Denver – and San Francisco not even in sight yet![39]

When Mack Sennett suggested Chaplin should move to Los Angeles, Chaplin was 'confounded' and 'did not see the connection between California and the cinematograph'.[40] Once working there he complained of working 'thirteen hours in a mask of grease paint under the blazing heat of the Southern California sun'.[41]

Implicit in many commentaries was a sense that Los Angeles was preposterously remote, inexplicably large, and unjustifiably grand in its aspirations. In 1927 the *New York Times* opined:

> Los Angeles, at first glance, is not quite real. The traveler from the East, after rolling over many leagues of picturesque but not

especially fertile desert, has to pinch himself to be sure that this sudden congestion of buildings and humanity, multiplying and transforming themselves almost under his eyes, is not a mirage. What business have thirteen hundred thousand people . . . out here on the edge of things, so far from what are commonly considered the centers of population? Here is a metropolis without visible means of support – that is to say, without means visible to those who think of cities as chiefly dependent upon coal and iron . . . Los Angeles, essentially, is homes – single-family homes, square miles of homes, homes with palm trees in the front yard, homes of all degrees of architectural charm and hideousness, but always homes.[42]

In such opinions, Los Angeles was suggested to be inherently lacking in substance, almost defying the laws of physics by existing. This was reinforced by a popular conception of the frivolity and vulgarity of the movies, generating vast material wealth by making mere moving pictures. To the journalist, historian and socialist Carey McWilliams, Los Angeles was 'a harlot city – gaudy, flamboyant, richly scented, sensuous, noisy, jazzy . . . [with] the aspect of a three-ring circus'.[43] Its population was dominated by the 'middlewestern banker or farmer' who sought 'to escape the barrenness of [his] own intellectual incompetence' by means of beach clubs, golf, mysticism, Spanish legend and innumerable movie palaces, which were 'brothels of ill taste' to which its 'mob-mad' people were devoted. At the same time (a subject to which I will return in chapter Four), the Protestant work ethic, which had driven the expansion of frontier settlement and industry in the nineteenth century, continued to fuel a distrust of motion pictures that exploded in vitriolic debates about the morality of the film industry during a series of sex scandals in the early 1920s and at later points in the studio era.

In contrast, some voices sought to make positive claims for Los Angeles' modernity. Dr Robert A. Millikan, Nobel Prize-winning physicist and Chairman of the Executive Council of the California Institute of Technology, announced the establishment there of an Atheneum, a forum for 'philosophers, poets, scholars, and educationalists', which was destined to make Southern California a centre for the 'diffusion of culture', like Athens, Rome, Constantinople and Versailles in former times.[44] Rockwell D. Hunt, professor of history at the University of Southern California, proposed that that university's first

PhD graduates and the recent opening of the University of California Los Angeles at Westwood were creating a 'City of Destiny' in culture and education.[45] Both men implied that Los Angeles' coming greatness was partly due to its new organization of urban space. Millikan explained that 'whereas men [in the ancient world] traveled by foot and ox carts, today they travel by motor and airplane. Thought shares the modern swift transit fever. Contacts are quicker and easier.' Hunt evoked 'the teeming metropolis of the entire Southwest . . . a place unsurpassed by any in the world in the number and proportion of its happy homes under the blue skies of this happy land.' McWilliams did this too, but with a notable sense of irony, arguing that the main compensation for Los Angeles' 'lack of culture' was its unusual landscape: 'the surging life of Los Angeles, its very crowds . . . Its plain of lights at night – jewels on the breast of the harlot – and its jauntily designed houses and foothills . . . the indolent languor of its noondays, its dawn by the sea, and the lush, warm radiance of its nights.'[46]

Silent Comedy and the Shape of Los Angeles

From 1910 to 1930 the City of Los Angeles grew from a population of 319,000 to 1.24 million, and from the seventeenth to the fifth largest city in the nation, while the population of Los Angeles County also quadrupled, from 504,000 to 2.21 million.[47] At this time, Richard Longstreth has explained, downtown Los Angeles was 'one of the most extensive business cores of any American city', although distinctively low-rise suburban development characterized the region as a whole.[48] Indeed, the physical area of Los Angeles increased more rapidly than its population, almost by a factor of five, from 89.6 to 441.7 square miles, making it not only 'the world's largest city in area' but also 'perceptually'.[49] At this time too, the idea took hold that Los Angeles embodied a new balance between the progressivist vision of the United States as technological, modernizing and capitalist, and the Jeffersonian vision of its expansive and bountiful nature.[50] This balance was most visible in its suburbia, where a proliferation of single-family homes, unprecedented in American history in numbers and extent, was coming to embody what Reyner Banham would later call 'the great bourgeois vision of the good life in a tamed countryside'.[51] Los Angeles was surrounded by mountains to the north, desert to the east, and ocean to the west, but it was centred on a large and fairly flat central basin – what Banham calls 'the Plains of Id' – stretching roughly 50 miles inland and 60 miles from north to south. Across this space, urbanization was dispersed, firstly by streetcars and then the automobile, while boosterist discourse emphasized the open space ready for 'improvement', to use the loaded term favoured by business interests.[52]

Dominated by a large and powerful white Anglo-Saxon Protestant middle class, the growth of Los Angeles was also driven by conflicts – of a kind known in all cities but more acute – between business interests, real estate developers, city planners and community groups. On the one hand, Los Angeles grew out from downtown, as older cities had done, but in an exaggerated way that included aggressively annexing adjacent land in anticipation of future population increases. On the other hand, Los Angeles grew in a new way, as a constellation of dispersed and often competing municipalities, including the City of Los Angeles, Glendale, Santa Monica, Culver City, Beverly Hills and dozens of others. As early as 1909, Los Angeles claimed to be the first American city to introduce land zoning, seven years before New York and St Louis, but urban planning was slow to gain acceptance before the late 1920s. Instead suburban sprawl between downtown Los Angeles and the coast, up and down the coast, and into the near desert of the San Fernando Valley, began to create what Richard Weinstein has called an 'extended city' in which downtown Los Angeles was important in population, economics and politics, but less important than the downtown was to older cities such as New York, Chicago, London and Paris.[53] And, from a symbolic point of view, this man-made topography, in which downtown was surrounded by an increasingly large expanse of low-rise and low-density development, combined with the city's relative lack of central planning to ensure that Los Angeles lacked monumental structures equivalent to the Brooklyn Bridge, Union Station, Trafalgar Square or the École Militaire. Moreover, the openness of this man-made landscape, and the concept of opportunity that it was supposed to express, belied its social injustice. In addition to its white Anglo-Saxon majority, Los Angeles encompassed large communities of African Americans, Chinese, Japanese, Mexicans and Filipinos, the majority working class or working poor. The social geography of the city was marked by a rigid separation between ethnic and racial groups, reinforced by restrictive covenants designed to exclude minorities from suburban developments and by the fixing of prices for property to minimize the mixing of socio-economic groups.[54]

While much filmmaking took place in studios, and westerns used its rural hinterland, the real Los Angeles was used extensively for location filming by slapstick comedies, cheaply produced in large numbers, primarily for mass urban audiences, and arguably forming the bedrock of the industry. Thriving upon the chaos of the modern city, its dynamic physical and social environment, sensory stimulation and constant hazards, the films of producers Mack Sennett and Hal Roach, and stars such as Charlie Chaplin, Harold Lloyd, Stan Laurel and Oliver Hardy, responded to Los Angeles by structuring their narratives around a variety of complex and often high-speed navigations. Chaplin's films for the Keystone and Lone Star studios were shot primarily in Edendale and downtown, on the streets of Hollywood, in the rural Hollywood Hills to the north, and at the seaside resorts of Venice and Santa Monica. Lloyd filmed in Venice, Culver City, Palms and Hollywood, although he too made some of his most noted films downtown, including *Safety Last* (1923), arguably the best-known comedy of the silent era and one that foregrounded the city centre dramatically. And Laurel and Hardy filmed in Beverly Hills, Edendale and Culver City, where their producer, Roach (for whom Lloyd also worked), based his studios after 1919. Given the extensive description of Los Angeles and its locales that their films provided de facto or by design, geographical detail is essential to any full interpretation of them, although most critical studies of slapstick comedy have ignored the specificity of their settings and locations.[55]

Much of the content of slapstick comedy films was locally specific to Los Angeles and was either already or becoming iconic. This included a flatness in the terrain, exceptionally bright and even natural light, the striking presence of the sky, bucolic seasides, palm trees and semi-arid scrubland subdivided for construction or, sometimes, peppered with oil derricks. Equally characteristic were broad streetscapes affording long lines of sight and a remarkable mobility by streetcar (rather than subways or elevated railroads) and by automobile (to a greater extent than in other filmed cities at this time). The low-rise suburban architecture that made up the majority of the films' built environment included commercial strip developments such as service stations and street-front markets, and single-family homes, many of them bungalows of California's 'Craftsman' style, or pastiches of Spanish, Mexican, English Tudor and Italianate traditions, with relatively few of the brick row houses or timber Queen Anne-style homes typical of the Northeast and Midwest.

Whether or not audiences were encouraged to dwell upon them by the narrative or cinematic style employed, and whether or not critics remarked upon them in reviews, these features were present – indeed, readily visible and persistent – in the majority of slapstick comedies. Therefore, they were present in a remarkably large number and proportion of all American films for almost twenty years from the mid-1910s, at a time when urbanization was in full flow across the industrial nations of the world – and suburbanization increasingly too – and when American film comedies were a dominant force in world cinema, and cinema the most popular pastime known to man. In this sense, the films may be said to have provided an 'apprenticeship to a specific culture', to borrow a phrase used by Fredric Jameson to describe the role of more recent Hollywood cinema in globalization.[56] Indeed, the films not only apprenticed audiences in what the city should *look* like but in what it should *feel* like too.

As Tom Gunning has explained, in the late 1890s the first slapstick comedy films typically concerned a mischievous gag at the expense of an individual in authority, but were often less than one minute long and filmed by a stationary camera without elaboration of the setting.[57] Subsequently, the 'theatrical display' and 'direct stimulation of shock or surprise' that characterized this 'cinema of attractions' was gradually displaced by a cinema of 'narrative integration', in which 'unfolding a story or creating a diegetic universe' became the filmmaker's main concern.[58] This process was especially evident in the chase sequence – 'the original truly narrative genre of the cinema' – in which gags were strung together continuously in diegetic time and space, and which became a staple of slapstick comedies.

The process had already begun in films made in Paris, London and New York, but its most decisive phase coincided with the years in which most American film production moved to Los Angeles. Gunning identifies 'the *true* narrativization of cinema' with the period 'from 1907 to about 1913', while Kristin Thompson argues that classical narrative first appeared in 1917 but achieved 'relative stability' only in the mid-1920s.[59] It was midway through this chronology, in 1913, that Mack Sennett permanently relocated from New York, where he had made a variety of films with Biograph, to focus exclusively on slapstick comedies in Los Angeles.[60] There his films with the Keystone Cops and Chaplin were the first to present what Siegfried Kracauer called 'motion at its extreme' – a characteristic also identified by Kracauer with Harold

Lloyd and Buster Keaton and best expressed through the 'un-staged reality' of location filming, which could reveal 'transient material life, life at its most ephemeral'.[61]

Hence, many slapstick comedies were geographically specific both in their content and form, exploiting the distinctive expanses of Los Angeles in *mise en scène* and narrative structure. A minority of films used downtown Los Angeles as a location, implicitly recognizing the social and economic importance it then had and presenting an image of a modern city with a centre like so many others. But the action of many more films took place in individual suburbs such as Edendale, Venice and Culver City, and perhaps the most emblematic of all involved *travel between* two or more places, from downtown to the suburbs or, more often, from suburb to suburb. In this way, the process of narrative integration found a city especially conducive to it because of its exceptional horizontality. Indeed, the motion inherent in these films became increasingly extreme – in his films of the 1910s, Chaplin moved about the city almost exclusively by walking or running but, in the 1920s, Lloyd and Laurel and Hardy used streetcars, buses or automobiles (especially the latter), and older modes of transport like the horse were often singled out for mockery. Moreover, because so many slapstick comedies ended in a car wreck or similar calamity, Los Angeles not only facilitated the continuity of the chase but enhanced the films' anarchic play with the principle of progress toward an ending so important in classical narrative. In other words, the emergence of narrative in early cinema, which has been theorized in terms of the increasingly sophisticated arrangement of actions in time, can also be understood as a function of space and place. In those years, American filmmakers were not only learning a new medium of representation but a new kind of urban environment, Los Angeles, then one of the more rapidly evolving and unusual cities in the world.

A number of cultural historians have convincingly argued for an active conception of the role of motion pictures in the making of the modern urban subject. In the 1930s, Walter Benjamin argued that the regulated and repetitive actions demanded by technologies such as the still camera, telephone and traffic signal had 'subjected the human sensorium to a complex kind of training'.[62] This was enhanced by motion pictures in which 'perception conditioned by shock was established as a formal principle'.[63] More recently, Giuliana Bruno has detailed the historical continuity between cinema and earlier panoramas, view paintings, landscape gardening and maps. In a world of increasing mobility, which could be both stimulating and unnerving, these presented the spectator with 'a moving chain of views' and fostered an understanding of space as a 'product of edited images'.[64] Lynn Kirby has argued that parallel editing and multiple points of view in early cinema ushered in 'a changed temporal consciousness – an orientation to synchronicity', 'panoramic perception', and the routinization of shock.[65] The latter was especially evident in cinema's fascination with train and automobile wrecks, which were not simply spectacular but spoke to the intolerable pressurization of public and personal life in modern cities. And Stanley Corkin has demonstrated that filmmakers such as Edison and Griffith sought to act as 'guardians of middle-class culture', using cinema to aid scientific knowledge or construct convincing historical worlds through 'clarity of the image, the rhythm of scenes, and the recurrence of motifs and formulas'.[66] These could 'smooth over ruptures in American social life' arising out of the settling of the West, the Civil War and the inequalities of modern urban life.[67]

Recognition of the role of place can be added to such arguments that film form and content habituated audiences to new perceptions and experiences of lived space and time. In most slapstick film comedies, the spectator was not only watching a film but Los Angeles, understood as a distinctive set of cinematic landscapes. These surely played a role in shaping the unconscious attitudes, and conscious tastes and expectations, of film audiences far and wide. For context, however, it is important to note slapstick comedies made in Los Angeles but not set there. Among Chaplin's films, for example, *A Burlesque on Carmen* (1915) was set in eighteenth-century Spain; *The Immigrant* (1917) on board a ship arriving in New York; and *Shoulder Arms* (1918) in the trenches of the First World War. Others had modern city settings but took place indoors – for example, *Charlie's Recreation* (1914) in a dance hall and *Work* (1915) in a Queen Anne-style mansion. And, as Alan Dale has explained, the *mise en scène* of another group, including *Police* (1916), *Triple Trouble* (1918) and *The Kid* (1921) 'emerge[d] from the London of Dickens', as did both Chaplin and the character of The Tramp.[68]

Particularly interesting here is *Easy Street* (Charles Chaplin, 1917), in which The Tramp began as a vagrant before being reformed in bible class and finding work as a policeman in a tenement district. This looked much more like The Five Points in Manhattan or Chaplin's native Lambeth than Los Angeles.[69] Its narrow and unpaved street was flanked by sombre four- and five-storey brick buildings, rows of dull windows, and laundry hanging out to dry, its one-room flats were crammed with hordes of children, and it housed a variety of pedestrian street life from a fresh fruit stall to crowds of drunken fighting men, with not an automobile in sight. The contrivance of the setting was underlined by the way in which it was filmed: the one-street set was shot from limited camera positions and almost always frontally so that the edge of the frame was marked by the walls of the buildings. The frenetic action, in which Chaplin was forced to confront a local thug, was entirely contained within the set, with the exception of a remarkable culminating chase in which the action broke away, Chaplin running around the corner and off the set, and the film cutting to a real street filmed on location. There Chaplin ran past a painted sign whose large real letters read 'LA City W[ater Company]', briefly disclosing the film's real place.[70]

By contrast, many of Lloyd's films had generic small town settings in Middle America – for example, 'Magnolia Meadows' in *Dr Jack* (1922)

Charlie Chaplin as a policeman, with back to camera, in a production still from *Easy Street* (Charles Chaplin, 1917).

and 'Little Bend' in *Girl Shy* (1924) – or settings in New York: for example, *Bumping into Broadway* (1919), in which Lloyd was an aspiring but impoverished playwright; *An Eastern Westerner* (1920), in which Lloyd was a wealthy youngster wasting his time at Broadway dance halls; *Among Those Present* (1921), in which he played a hat-check boy at the 'Ritz-Waldorf' hotel; and *Speedy* (1928), in which he tried to save his grandfather's taxi business from bankruptcy, and which was exceptional for its Manhattan locations, although mixed with a chase evidently shot in Culver City.

These New York settings illuminate the representation of Los Angeles in Lloyd's *Safety Last* (Fred C. Newmeyer, 1923), one of the most famous slapstick comedies made in that city, and one of a small but significant number in which Los Angeles appeared as a modern central city – which it then still *was*, if not with the density or verticality of New York. In that film, Lloyd plays a naive but ambitious country boy who moves to the metropolis where he becomes mixed up in a stunt to publicize the department store where he works as a clerk. This requires him to climb all the way up the exterior wall of the building – perhaps a dozen floors – with a large crowd, his boss and his sweetheart looking on, and an angry cop chasing him all the way. Even though it was made in 1922, *Safety Last* displays some residue of what Noel Burch calls the 'primitive externality' of early cinema.[71] The opening scene, for example, is a visual gag that frames Harold against iron bars to make it seem he is imprisoned until a reverse angle reveals that he is saying goodbye to his family at the gate of a train station before departing for the city. In this, and subsequently in the department store manager's office, props and actors are arranged laterally in the set in keeping with theatrical fourth-wall conventions.

A more dynamic sense of action in space is created in the film's extended exterior scenes filmed on location in downtown Los Angeles. These have all of the frenzy expected of a city film of the day – chance encounters, heaving throngs, high-speed driving shots and, because it is slapstick, a myriad of crashes, bumps and falls.[72] But what is exceptional is the sheer verticality of the *mise en scène*, which sets the film apart from most others of the era and from the predominant horizontality of Los Angeles. The climbing sequence is eighteen minutes long, cleverly exploiting the three-dimensional possibilities of the medium and its potential for vertiginous effects with various low- and high-angle shots of Harold's ascent and the crowds and traffic below. In his autobiography, *An American Comedy* (1928), Lloyd explained that *Safety Last* was 'our

Harold Lloyd copes
with the metropolis
in *Safety Last* (Fred
C. Newmeyer, 1923).

first thrill picture depending upon height for its effects, and . . . original with us as far as I know'.[73]

Although the naming of Los Angeles and its parts was not common in films at this time, close inspection of signage in the background suggests a California location: we see large painted advertisements on distant gable walls identifying 'Blackstone's – California's Finest Store' and the 'Los Angeles Stock Exchange Bldg'.[74] But the city in which the film is set is never purposely specified for the viewer. Instead, Los Angeles is allowed to resemble New York or Chicago, and must have done for most American audiences who were concentrated in the East and industrial Midwest. For foreign viewers too, those cities, rather than Los Angeles, were axiomatically associated with the skyscraper. Indeed, Lloyd remarked that he was 'overawed by New York's high hat' on his first visit to Manhattan in 1918.[75]

Because Harold is eventually successful in his climb, and thereby impresses his boss and gets his girl, *Safety Last* celebrates the American metropolis, capitalism and romantic love, while depending upon a utopianism of the skyscraper that had been widespread in the United States since the late nineteenth century. That form of building was not unknown in Los Angeles – indeed, department stores were among the tallest and most imposing structures on Broadway, then the city's commercial backbone, and they played a more important role than any other building type in determining the activity, function and growth of downtown as a whole. Like the fictional 'De Vore' store in the film, real department stores such as Hamburger's, Bullock's and The Broadway were notable as centres of urban life and in their physical mass.[76] *Safety Last* emphasizes this in its displays of luxury goods and the hectic buying and selling that goes on, and in a number of long shots of the building that underline its monumentality and metropolitan ambience.

At the same time, however, the high-rise building was never as prevalent in Los Angeles as in other American cities, at least until the development of Bunker Hill and mid-Wilshire in the 1960s and later. At just 150 feet, the maximum height allowed for buildings in Los Angeles was higher than that in Boston (125 feet) or Washington, DC (130 feet), two cities with prominent historic cores, but it was much less than the limit in other cities that prioritized modernization – just over half that allowed in Chicago and much less than that in New York where there was no absolute height limit at all.[77] In this light, the verticality so evident in *Safety Last* should be considered only as part of its total geography. Horizontality is present too in significant ways.

While the climbing sequence in *Safety Last* traces a vertical movement up from one point, it conceals a horizontal movement that was actually made by the cast and crew as they shot the film. In order to achieve a sense of height, the climb was filmed on the walls of a succession of buildings along Broadway's southeast–northwest axis, nearly always looking north, and the sequence was edited so that the natural height of the buildings and the action was enhanced by the foreshortening of the perspective in each shot.[78] This displacement is readily noticeable in a close viewing of the background of the shots and adds to its vertical description a horizontal mapping of Broadway at a crucial moment in its history.

The concentration of department stores that dominated Broadway was dramatically affected by Los Angeles' decentralization in the 1920s, which was especially marked to the west of downtown given that the ocean lay in that direction, but also because of downtown's constriction by Bunker Hill to the north and by railroads, lowlands and light industry to the south and east. Department stores contributed to downtown's growth because each new store was built several blocks from those already there. But as early as 1914 Broadway's status was challenged by the founding of the Robinson's department store several blocks west on Seventh Street between Hope and Grand. This development anticipated the emergence of Wilshire Boulevard as the most important thoroughfare in the region and a key agent of its sprawl to Santa Monica. Robinson's was also the first department store to incorporate an underground parking garage for commuters and visitors from the suburbs, foreshadowing the branches of department stores in mid-Wilshire and other outlying areas that sprang up in subsequent years.

What Longstreth describes as the 'locational tugs-of-war' by which Los Angeles department stores sought to gain a business advantage in a rapidly evolving city are barely evident in *Safety Last*.[79] But decentralization is hinted at in the early, and less noted, sequence in which Harold, waiting outside the department store before it opens, accidentally finds himself locked into the back of a laundry van and driven for thirty minutes to a distant suburb – in fact, Hollywood – from which he has to struggle to return downtown by streetcar, automobile and ambulance, to clock in without getting fired for being late. Only five minutes long, this horizontal navigation is not as prominent as the climb, but it is arguably a more accurate description of Los Angeles then, and certainly of its future.

Most of the time the film concentrates on generating a sense of centralized activity, especially in the prominent place that it gives to crowds. As Walter Benjamin observed in relation to Berlin, Paris, London and Moscow, these were a feature of modern urban street life that had been seen since the mid-nineteenth century as a key expression of civilization but also 'essentially inhuman' and a cause of '[f]ear, revulsion, and horror' to the increasingly isolated and insecure individual.[80] But *Safety Last* is a Hollywood feature film that prefers entertainment to critique and liberally mixes reality and simulation. The first crowd we see is fake, an implausible mass of men in suits who struggle for places on a streetcar on an otherwise quiet suburban boulevard where Harold has been stranded. The next is real, seen in several brief but evocative long shots of downtown streets as Harold races through them in the ambulance. These show that downtown Los Angeles was indeed busy with pedestrians, but the third crowd is another simulation, a mob of caricatured middle-class ladies shopping in a frenzy for fabrics who over-run the department store, a studio set. The fourth and largest crowd, which watches Harold's climb, is rendered by mixing long shots of real people on location – presumably workers who have taken a break to watch the making of the movie – and medium shots of a stage-managed group of smartly dressed men and women who stand in elevated rows as if for a group portrait. Indeed, the apparently different class profile of the real and simulated crowds may be more than accidental given what we know of the efforts of Hollywood film studios at this time to appeal to middle-class audiences, although the comic characters in the fictional crowd – Harold's roommate, a newspaper boy, a drunk and a cop on the beat – recall the working-class sympathies and origins of the slap-stick genre.

The watching crowds derive a momentary frisson from the possi-bility that Harold might fall, but also cheer and applaud as he progresses to the roof. Moreover, because the department store is the cause of their presence, they too represent the energy of the capitalist metropolis, and Harold's climb exemplifies the increasing distinction of the 'hero' identified by Benjamin as a central feature of mass culture.[81] When struggling with pigeons and other obstacles as he climbs, Harold's repet-itive movements typify the ritualization of risk and 'continually starting all over' that Benjamin argued was central to life under capitalism, and which he illustrated by evoking the automated movements of the factory worker and the gambler playing cards.[82] And yet *Safety Last* denies or defuses alienation with humour and the happy ending.

Finally, the specificity of *Safety Last* also lies in its architecture. As Benjamin observed, the department store was a decayed form of its forerunner, the Parisian arcade, whose glass roof and contiguity with the street had softened the line between indoor and outdoor space, facilitating the strolling, sitting, reading and watching that allowed the flâneur to make himself at home even though he was out and about. The department store, on the other hand, represented the flâneur's 'last promenade', its space entirely private and commodified, cut off from the street by its use of windows for the display of goods rather than the ex-change of light and air.[83] Los Angeles department stores were especially notable in this respect as they set international trends in orientating themselves not only to the automobile but also to the concept of self-service. For Longstreth, that concept originated in Los Angeles precisely as an extension of its reliance on automobiles, and it transformed the places in which shopping occurred from gas stations and drive-in markets and restaurants to the shopping centres and malls of today.[84] Self-service is not yet visible in *Safety Last*, where the shopping experience is heavily mediated by plentiful sales staff and *politesse*. But it became increasingly prominent during and after the 1930s, and is foreshadowed in the film's point-of-view shots from moving vehicles that created a visceral identification between spectator and filmed image and accentuated the already well-established American value of self-determination.

At the same time, despite its iconic status, *Safety Last* is anomalous in so far as most slapstick comedies in Los Angeles had suburban locales, and were increasingly shaped by motor cars and individuals rather than pedestrians and crowds. A sense of the dispersal of Los Angeles can be detected in much earlier short films by Chaplin such as *Kid Auto Races at Venice*, *Mabel's Married Life* and *Making a Living*, all made in 1914, the first year in which Chaplin was contracted to Sennett's Keystone studios. Of these three films, which are typical of a much larger number in which Chaplin starred, the first two were filmed on location in actual suburbs of Los Angeles – Venice and Edendale, respectively – while the third involves a variety of settings and locations in downtown and suburbs and is, therefore, especially significant for its visualization and narrativization of the city as an urban region.

Chaplin, Lloyd and Buster Keaton made numerous films at the seaside resorts of Venice, Santa Monica and Wilmington, between fifteen and twenty miles from downtown.[85] Quintessential modern environments of the early twentieth century, these were favoured locations, crammed with day-trippers and fairground attractions, from roller coasters to penny arcades, which held innate spectacular interest and, fittingly, had also been early sites of kinetoscope parlours. In the eleven minutes of *Kid Auto Races at Venice* (Henry Lehrman, 1914), which was the first film in which Chaplin starred as The Tramp, he seeks to interfere with the filming of a go-kart race by getting in the way of the camera, the threadbare simplicity of the narrative indicative of its relatively early date. Indeed, the film exists halfway between fiction and actuality. On the one hand, it presents a story in which Chaplin is the star, filmed in medium shot or close-up, and engaging in scuffles with the increasingly annoyed director who is filming the race but who is played by Henry Lehrman, the actual director of the film in which Chaplin is starring. On the other hand, made entirely on location and outdoors, the film is effectively a documentation of Venice as a place, and the race as a real event, in which Chaplin is absent from many shots but the racers, spectators and nearby buildings and streets, filmed in long shot, form subjects in themselves. Chaplin is alternately present and absent in the frame as he is pushed out of the way but keeps coming back, so that the film remains on the cusp between the 'primitive' (early) and 'institutional' (classical) modes of cinematic representation theorized by Burch. Moreover, the tension between reality and fiction is heightened by another between mobility and fixed position. Despite being filmed on location and concerning a race, the film's action is tightly concentrated in a few hundred square feet, its protagonist and nearly everyone else is on foot, and the 'autos' involved have no motors, the race being a soap box derby in which we see both the gravity ramp from which the cars are launched and young men working hard to push them to the top.

A comparable tension between shooting *en plein air* and spatial fixity is evident in the many silent comedies made on location in public parks just a few miles from downtown.[86] These presented early film companies with easy-to-manage and ready-made 'sets', free of crowds and traffic but laid out in a variety of pathways and open spaces that lent themselves perfectly to comic movements and encounters. In *Mabel's Married Life* (Charles Chaplin, 1914), for example, Chaplin visits the park with his wife (played by Mabel Normand), leaves her alone for a few minutes to have a drink in a nearby bar, and returns to find her being molested by an over-sized local ruffian (played by Mack Swain). After some intrigue, Chaplin returns to the bar while his wife returns to their apartment with a boxing dummy she buys to practise self-defence. The authenticity of the film's exterior locations in Echo Park is evident

Charlie Chaplin as The Tramp in *Kid Auto Races at Venice* (Henry Lehrman, 1914).

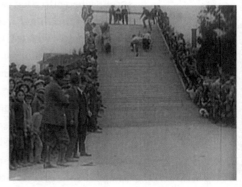

Echo Park and an apartment set in *Mabel's Married Life* (Charles Chaplin, 1914).

in the wind that moves the branches and leaves in the background of many shots, and in the views of the lake and white-arched bridge, which were local landmarks and became cinematic icons by repeatedly appearing in films by Chaplin and Lloyd. Like *Kid Auto Races at Venice*, the effect is a detailed portrayal of place although, unlike that film, the setting is not named and features no mechanized transport or crowds. Indeed, when the action shifts to the couple's domestic space, the movement is achieved simply by cutting to the interior set rather than depicting walking; the artificiality of the space is evident in its heavy Victorian furnishings and hardwood-panelled walls; and its privacy highlights the danger inherent in public interaction in the park, firstly, when the men who deliver Mabel's dummy find her in her pyjamas and, secondly, when the drunken Tramp returns to find his wife alone with the dummy and thinks it is another man.

In *Making a Living* (Henry Lehrman, 1914), in which Chaplin has a run-in with a newspaper reporter when he steals the affections of his sweetheart and puts him out of his job, the *mise en scène* and geographical description of the city is more expansive because the film presents repeated movement between downtown and the suburbs while remaining almost entirely outdoors. This quality creates an exceptional tension between the film's documentation of the real city by filming on location and its status as a fiction film about a con man who pretends to report the news. The setting of the opening scenes, in which Chaplin first encounters the reporter on a sidewalk and asks him for spare change, exemplifies the suburban residential street that was a common feature of slapstick comedy shot in Los Angeles, the street being broad, the houses and lawns quite new, set back from the street but not fenced off, the curbsides lined with palm trees, and neat concrete paths to each

neatly planted porch.[87] Although the action of the figures should be
our main interest, because each sequence is quite long and the camera's
point of view fixed with tree trunks marking the edges of the frame, our
attention is inevitably also attracted to the ground in which these two
men-about-town are situated yet somehow out of place. Indeed, the
ground is especially evident given the absence of other pedestrians,
automobiles, street furniture and cables.

Upscale suburbs and downtown Los Angeles in *Making a Living* (Henry Lehrman, 1914).

The prominence of the suburban home is typified in the subsequent sequence in which Chaplin happens upon a well-to-do mother and
daughter, and their butler, outside a characteristic, if relatively affluent,
Californian timber bungalow fronted by an ornamental stone porch,
pillars and steps. Typical of architecture of that era and type, which – as
in the work of Charles and Henry Greene or Irving Gill – was low-set
and striking for its horizontal lines, the house draws attention to the
lateral dimension of the frame, an effect which is also in evidence when
Chaplin is framed on the wide sidewalk overhung by palm fronds with
porches and lawns repeated down the street behind him. As Chaplin
flatters his way into the ladies' company, the action is split between the
grass in front of the porch and the driveway to the right. Each of these
naturalizes suburban architecture by transforming it into a performance
space akin to the traditional stage, a tactic especially evident in the
repeated use of the porch, whose set-back relationship to the lawn and
shadow relative to its light made it an ideal ready-made background for
action in many Chaplin films of this era.[88]

More than simply a formal device, however, the suburban home
is subject to disruption that reinforces its status as private property and
the importance of the property line. As the reporter arrives to present the
daughter with an engagement ring but finds she has just agreed to marry

Chaplin, a fight ensues among potted plants and sculpted hedgerows on the driveway, and Chaplin is kicked out by the butler. The subsequent action, however, takes place in a markedly different location downtown when the indignant reporter recounts to a typographer his experience of Chaplin, the con man, so that the story may be published. The interiors of the newspaper offices and printing press make for a curiously industrial counterpoint to the suburban gardens presented previously. Here too the narrative involves not the abuse of private property but the theft of personal identity as, in another unexplained coincidence, Chaplin also arrives downtown and takes up work as a reporter at the same place. The metropolitan locale is established by shots of the actual *Los Angeles Times* newspaper building, complete with real newspaper boys waiting outside in a dirty, brick-walled alley, and a hilltop panorama of the city in front of which Chaplin and the reporter come to blows while ant-like pedestrians cross distant intersections.

But the downtown qualities of these settings are countered by intervening sequences in other suburbs – firstly, on a winding dirt road near the ocean where a speeding automobile careens down a hillside in long shot; and, secondly, in another, relatively modest, residential district, perhaps Venice or Santa Monica, in which a young woman washing laundry on the balcony of a shared house is disturbed by Chaplin and the reporter who chase and fight their way across the city, followed by the Keystone cops. Throughout there is a discrepancy between the wide range of settings and locations and the way movement between them is achieved: the two men quite implausibly negotiate the distances involved on foot, and mechanized transport is mostly absent except at two strategic moments. In the first, the film satirizes newspaper sensationalism in an image of a wrecked automobile whose driver is pinned in agony underneath while the reporter takes photos and makes notes – a comic anticipation of similar themes by Andy Warhol and J. G. Ballard decades later. In the second, at the end of the film, after Chaplin has stolen the reporter's camera and notes to pretend he covered the story himself, he and the reporter run frantically down Broadway before being carried away, still fighting, on the front of a passing streetcar. Preferring comic anarchy to resolution, this final shot *in medias res* defies the classical narrative structures that were still in formation at this time.

The narratological instability of *Making a Living* is, therefore, a function of its geography of Los Angeles and of the tension between continuity and disjuncture in American cinema circa 1914. The frantic running within each scene is facilitated by the length and breadth of the city's thoroughfares and has a natural, if hyperactive, flow. But travel between the evidently disparate settings is indicated simply by cutting, and with a technical roughness likely to strike viewers as 'primitive' today. This is also an expression of the disjointedness of Los Angeles at this time. If the entire film is a chase across many places in one city, it is a chase, and a city, full of spatial gaps. In this it reflects Los Angeles' multi-centred development and the unusually 'porous' quality of its landscape, to borrow the term Benjamin used to explain the fact that Naples seemed haphazardly pockmarked by holes in the urban fabric that could throw up telling contrasts between the new and old, the modern and ancient, the man-made and the natural.[89] This porosity is evident in the film's alternations between built-up and natural space, and in whole spaces elided by the montage. It is also evident in *Safety Last* and other films, in undeveloped suburban lots awaiting housing or other construction, temporarily left behind in the city's race to expand.

As Los Angeles was emerging as a metropolis and its film industry was growing apace, its business and civic elite, and homeowners, became concerned that it should avoid the high-density, mixed-use and congested patterns of development of older cities. Gordon G. Whitnall, founder of the Los Angeles City Planning Association, declared in 1924:

> We find ourselves in the peculiar position of being a community in its inception, and yet with a fair realization of what the future holds. This knowledge places upon our shoulders an obligation to prevent the recurrence of those mistakes which have happened in the growth of metropolitan areas in the east . . . We still have our chance, if we live up to our opportunities, of showing the right way of doing things. It will not be the west looking back to the east to learn . . . but the east looking to the west to see how it should be done.[90]

In truth, Los Angeles' 'inception' of new patterns of development dated back to the 1880s, following which four decades of expansion in the city's road and streetcar network had facilitated the growth of many urban centres and unprecedented subdividing. Realtors deliberately pandered to a prevalent anti-urban attitude in advertising homes, as did Los Angeles Chamber of Commerce publications such as *Los Angeles Today* (1915):

The rare beauty of the grounds surrounding the attractive homes of Los Angeles is a constant theme of admiration on the part of Eastern visitors. The mildness of the climate permits the most delicate plants and trees to flourish in the open all through the winter. A majority of the residences stand in spacious grounds, a lot of 50 × 150 feet being the smallest occupied by a house of any pretension . . . One of the most attractive features about a home in this section is the wonderful rapidity with which vegetation of all kinds grows, so that, instead of having to wait years for a new residence to assume a settled and homelike appearance, the owner has to wait only a few months until his house is surrounded with thrifty plants and climbing.[91]

Characterizations of the Los Angeles home often placed more emphasis on the space around it than on the building itself, reflecting the influence of the Arts and Crafts and Garden City movements.[92] Those had been shaping international urban design since the mid-nineteenth century, although the forms, lifestyles and values that they encouraged were predicated on a perpetual mistrust of urban modernity and a strongly retrospective and privatizing mood especially strong in Southern California.

Emblematic here were tens of thousands of private lawns, each of which represented what Richard S. Weinstein has called 'a subjugation of nature to the rule of civilization'.[93] That was already underway at the time of *Making a Living* but it was in the 1920s that the building of houses peaked, and not just in Los Angeles. In 1922 Herbert Hoover, future President, but then US Secretary of Commerce and chairman of the Better Homes in America organization, declared: 'One can always safely judge of the character of a nation by its homes. For it is mainly through the hope of enjoying the ownership of a home that the latent energy of any citizenry is called forth.'[94] A new national record was set in 1925 when 937,000 new housing units were constructed, though Los Angeles played a special role given that attached homes and multi-storey, multi-occupancy dwellings were much rarer there than in other cities.[95] By 1930 it had the highest percentage of single-family homes in the nation: 93.9 per cent, in comparison to Philadelphia (91.6 per cent), San Francisco (88.3 per cent) and Washington, DC (87.9 per cent), and the largest cities, New York (52.8 per cent) and Chicago (52 per cent), which had far fewer structures of that type.[96]

In the Harold Lloyd film *I Do* (Hal Roach, 1921), what Hoover called 'latent energy' is both celebrated and made fun of. Unlike *Making a Living*, Lloyd's film is set in one suburban location and does not involve movement across the city although, like the Chaplin film, its narrative does begin with a chance encounter by pedestrians on a quiet residential street. At the opening, Lloyd and Mildred Davis walk past recently subdivided lots and newly built modest timber homes, wheeling a baby carriage that one assumes contains a baby, and for which a local pastor congratulates them. However, suburban propriety is quickly shown to be false. To the pastor's horror, the 'baby' turns out to be a wrapped-up jeroboam of liquor – Prohibition having come into force in 1919 – and the couple scurry away to a bungalow at which dozens of people arrive with prams that they push through the front door empty and out again with a new load of alcohol. Here the uniformity of suburbia is in evidence, though not really critiqued, in the repetition of identical houses on the landscape, which is flat, in the constant stream of people filmed in long shot, and in the implication of a population boom even if the babies are bottles. Moreover, the film later speaks directly to the expectation that young suburban couples should procreate – firstly, in an extended comic intrigue in which Lloyd is entrusted with the care of two young children in a nearby Italianate mansion and, secondly, at the end of the film, when Davis admits to Lloyd she is pregnant and they soon will be parents for real.

Although both had long careers, a key difference between the comedies of Chaplin and Lloyd from the mid-1910s to the mid-1920s, when each was in his prime, is that Chaplin navigated the city almost entirely by walking or running whereas Lloyd, whose stardom came slightly later, did so more often by mechanized transport. Occasionally Chaplin used other means: in *His Musical Career* (1914), filmed on Broadway, he and another man attempt to load a piano on a mule-drawn cart; in *His Favorite Pastime* (1914), he jumps a streetcar to follow a young woman in an automobile to whom he has taken a fancy; in *The Fireman* (1916), he works with a horse-drawn fire tender in Hollywood; and in *A Day's Pleasure* (1919), exceptionally, he takes his family from their bungalow for a scenic drive by car. But motorized vehicles are relatively rare or, when present, rarely under his command. Lloyd's films, on the other hand, suggest that by the early 1920s Los Angeles well exceeded the mechanization of movement in Paris, where carriages had long since, in Benjamin's words, 'scorned to recognize pedestrians as rivals'.[97]

A pastor congratulates The Boy (Harold Lloyd) and The Girl (Mildred Davis) on their new 'baby' in *I Do* (Hal Roach, 1921).

High-speed motorized chases and races against the clock had a new prominence in Lloyd films, whether by streetcar or, increasingly, by automobile, as in *Number, Please?* (1920), *Get Out and Get Under* (1920), *Girl Shy* (1924) and *Hot Water* (1924), as well as *Safety Last*. These were more simply intent upon entertainment than the Chaplin films, which contained a stronger class critique.[98] But in their depiction of the experience of the city, they nonetheless illustrate Benjamin's observation that moving through 'traffic involves the individual in a series of shocks and collisions. At a dangerous intersection, nervous impulses flow through him in rapid succession, like the energy from a battery.'[99]

Number, Please? (Fred C. Newmeyer, Hal Roach, 1920) is set in Venice, like many other films of the era, but concerns the relationship between it and inland residential suburbs. Venice is rendered through scenes of bathers, parasols and the promenade colonized by coconut shies and stalls selling orange punch. The inland suburbs are described when The Boy (Lloyd) and another young man, The Rival (Roy Brooks), engage in a race to contact the mother of The Girl (Mildred Davis) to ask her permission to take her daughter on a romantic ride in a hot-air balloon. Within Venice, there is much conventional slapstick: when The Girl's dog gets loose, The Boy chases it through the funfair, is bashed on the head by a man wielding a mallet in a test of strength, and is mistaken for a pickpocket and chased by police. Hence the film presents a myriad of local movements by means of cameras on a roller coaster, long shots of The Boy running on the busy boardwalk, close-ups as he sprints to keep pace with a carousel, and shots from the carousel as it revolves.

Most interestingly, however, in the race to find the mother the film relies on a contrast between staying in place and travelling by car. The Rival hops into his roadster and speeds through wide and nameless streets lined with bungalows and pineapple palms, while The Boy (who does not own a car) ducks into a telephone booth where his efforts to put through a call to the mother are comically frustrated by other callers, operators and overloaded switchboards. The automobile proves even faster than telecommunications. Like *Mabel's Married Life*, there is also a strong architectural contrast between exterior locations and studio-bound interiors. The pier and boardwalk are constructed in white timber beams and criss-crossing iron struts, places of sensation replete with billboards, yet close to Nature and filmed in the strong light of the sun. The interiors of the mother's home are over-stuffed with ornate Victorian furniture and fabrics, which heighten the opposition between private and public space, and the liberating value of the youthful, modern city outdoors.

A similar contrast, which is surely even more intense for viewers today than it was in that era, is important in *Get Out and Get Under* (Hal Roach, 1920), in which Lloyd races across the city to take part in a Shakespearean costume drama. Like *Making a Living*, this film foregrounds private ownership. Opening at a typical subdivision where Lloyd keeps in a garage a shiny new car he has bought by instalments, a dispute about property rights arises when unwanted junk he throws out of the window lands on the head of his neighbour who is gardening next door. A series of further actions transgress the line between them – the neighbour provocatively leans his implements against the garage and sprays his hose through the window, while Lloyd clumsily puts his car in reverse and shoots through the gable wall onto his

Number, Please (Fred
C. Newmeyer, Hal
Roach, 1920), mostly
filmed in Venice.

neighbour's land. Here the automobile is a desirable commodity, proudly cleaned and admired by Lloyd, but it is also a nuisance to existing residents and uses of the land.

The rest of the narrative enacts an anarchic but celebratory engagement with the city's public spaces in which the vehicle enhances the self-determination of suburban life in general. An increasingly symbiotic relation between the car and human body is proposed. When the vehicle breaks down, Lloyd restarts it with difficulty but then must sprint as it runs away unmanned. At a busy intersection, his driving forces other cars to swerve out of his way, scattering police and a civic parade, but later he becomes adept at jumping out of the moving car to perform some other action before catching up and retaking his seat to drive on. This technique also allows him to evade capture by the police when he moves a roadworks sign to throw them off his trail. The porosity of the landscape is again in evidence as much of the motorized action takes place on Los Angeles' still rural fringes, while the backgrounds in suburban districts display a mixture of smart-looking homes and undeveloped lots covered in dirt or long grass. This is the city as construction site – indeed we also see a road being laid, a billboard advertising the 'Pyramid Investment Company . . . Will Build to Suit Purchaser', and a moving van of the 'California Fireproof Storage Company' in which Lloyd hides his car until pursuing police speed past.[100]

Get Out and Get Under
(Hal Roach, 1920).

Similar motifs were repeated in subsequent films by Lloyd, although extended to feature length, as in *Girl Shy* and *Hot Water* (both Fred C. Newmeyer and Sam Taylor, 1924). These recycled many of the ingredients of the earlier films but further normalized their action and *mise en scène*. In the former, Lloyd is chased by police as he uses automobiles, a horse, a streetcar and a motorcycle to race to stop the arranged marriage of his sweetheart to another man. In the latter, Lloyd plays a happily married husband who delights his wife and neighbours by buying a new car but is chased by police for speeding when he takes the family for a spin. In both films, one witnesses technical improvements in the cinematic representation of motorized motion and an increasing modernization of the locale by commercial strip developments. Like *Safety Last*, *Girl Shy* and *Hot Water* make dramatic use of then-innovative point-of-view shots from cameras mounted on vehicles and rapidly moving forward through traffic-laden streets where earlier films rendered motorized movement by shots of the vehicle and driver from the side, the front or the rear. Both films feature streets now lined not only by homes but by the many automobile-orientated businesses in whose innovation Los Angeles played a leading role, especially auto service stations and street-front drive-in markets such as the Cahuenga Public Market, a local landmark of the day seen in both films. Both present the new domination of Los Angeles by the automobile as a necessity, perhaps even a pleasure.

In *Hot Water*, before he buys a car, Lloyd makes an arduous journey home by streetcar with his arms full of heavy groceries. A wall of automobiles blocks him as he tries to board while his own automobile later goes out of control, speeding along sidewalks, panicking strollers and holding up a horse-drawn fire tender. In *Get Out and Get Under*, Lloyd veers into a rail depot, up a ramp, and onto a flatbed carriage before thugs in the railroad's employ chase him and his car away. Both films suggest a struggle for the right to use the streets, playing out the age-old American theme of the modernizing landscape expressed by Leo Marx's metaphor of 'the machine in the garden'.[101] But they also articulate struggles specific to Los Angeles in the 1920s when streetcar use peaked, automobile ownership exploded, and pedestrians, horses and trains were increasingly a thing of the past.

Moreover, these films suggest that historical accounts of Hollywood slapstick comedy ought to be punctuated not only in terms of the evolution of narratology or performance but in terms of regimes of traffic

Automobile-oriented businesses in *Hot Water* (Fred C. Newmeyer, Sam Taylor, 1924).

control on Los Angeles' streets. They and innumerable other films of the era are marked not only by a superabundance of chase sequences and motorized transport but by technologies designed to control and shape movement in a city undergoing exceptional physical growth and increases in the speed of everyday life. These are most evident in run-ins between drivers and police officers whom we see directing traffic by hand in an era just before the widespread use of automatic traffic signals, and in the new ubiquity of the now iconic Southern California screen character, the motorcycle highway patrolman.

During the 1920s Los Angeles' streetcars were still widely used but increasingly seen as inefficient.[102] *The Los Angeles Plan*, which was sponsored by the City of Los Angeles in 1922, celebrated 'the wonder city of the world . . . a city of splendid industrial structures and beautiful homes . . . the capital of the film world and as such . . . the best advertised city on earth'.[103] But it was mainly concerned to improve the usability of the city for motorists, seeking solutions to 'constantly increasing traffic congestion problems' caused by narrow streets and sidewalks, and dangerous grade crossings, which were responsible for an 'appalling list of fatalities that has placed Los Angeles at the head of all cities for its traffic dangers'.[104] Because of 'reckless driving in crowded streets' the number of recorded accidents had doubled in the previous two years to over 4,000 per month, with a fatality rate of 27.9 per 100,000 people, over twice the national average of 11.5, and higher too than Chicago's 20.3 and New York's 18.8.[105] Automobile registrations in Los Angeles County had shot up from 16,000 in 1910 to 110,000 in 1918 and almost 430,000 at the time of the *Plan*.[106] This represented one automobile for every 3.6 Los Angeles residents in contrast to one for every 30 in Chicago and one for every thirteen nationwide.[107] By 1929, when Laurel and Hardy succeeded Chaplin and Lloyd as the most popular slapstick comics, there were 777,000 automobiles registered, a more than five-fold increase since 1919 and way ahead of the already remarkable doubling in population in that time.[108]

Given these orders of magnitude, the *Plan* cited the exhortation of Daniel H. Burnham, proponent of the City Beautiful and originator of the Chicago Plan, to 'Make no little plans; they have no magic to stir men's blood'.[109] The *Plan* called for 'increased street area' while the subsequent and more detailed *Major Traffic Street Plan for Los Angeles* (1924), prepared by the prestigious landscape design firm of Frederick Law Olmsted (Jr), elaborated on several proposals.[110] These included the regulation of turning and signalling, restriction of on-street parking and the elimination of dead ends. Major routes were to be improved, the widths of streets standardized, narrow passes in the Hollywood Hills widened, and hills downtown removed. Also recommended were road designs to separate types of traffic, replacement of busy intersections with overpasses and the creation of parkways.

While the dispersal of Los Angeles had its roots in the rapid expansion of its streetcar system, by the early 1920s, real estate developers no longer relied on proximity of streetcars when choosing new sites for construction and increasingly built in places accessible only by car. Indeed, private investors often laid roads in outlying areas well ahead of other construction in order to add value to their land. Hence, road-building was a means of creating demand rather than merely responding to it, although the largest thoroughfares were built by Los Angeles City or County using public funds. The availability of space was joined by the climate in contributing to automobile use, as the *Major Traffic Street Plan* reported:

> The place of the automobile in the transportation problems of Los Angeles is far more important than in the East. There is no day when it is impossible or even uncomfortable to ride in an open car. The widely scattered population, and the almost universal housing in detached single family dwellings, situated on lots large enough to admit of housing automobiles, encourage their use.[111]

In this sense, one of the key features of Southern California that led to its rise as a motion picture capital also led to its emergence as a peculiarly automobile-reliant society. By 1930 Los Angeles was the fourth largest metropolitan area in the United States by population, standing at 2.3 million in comparison to New York's 10.9 million, Chicago's 4.4 million and Philadelphia's 2.8 million.[112] However, it had a physical footprint that was larger than Chicago or Philadelphia, if not quite New York; it was tenth in the nation in population per square mile; and the ratio of the population of its central city to that of its suburbs was the lowest of any major urban centre.

It was clear, as Fogelson has put it, that 'the structure of greater Los Angeles differed radically from that of the typical American metropolis'.[113] At the time of *Safety Last*, the busiest intersection in the city was already well outside downtown, at Wilshire Boulevard and Western Avenue, and downtown was becoming increasingly unfriendly to users because of its congestion.[114] From 1920 to 1924 the volume of automobiles entering downtown during peak hours increased tenfold from 22,000 to nearly a quarter of a million, while the *Los Angeles Times* predicted that shopping and movie-going in that district, two of its most important activities, would become 'a thing of the past'.[115] A few years before *Safety Last*, the City had instituted a ban on most kinds of on-street parking downtown during daytime and this was later reinforced by new street markings to discourage stopping or waiting by cars, laws against jay-walking, and the installation of traffic lights on major routes.[116] Outside downtown, on the other hand, free movement of automobiles appeared to be the order of the day, giving rise to a qualitatively new and positive driving culture, evident in Harold Lloyd's enjoyment of his motoring despite its risks. Official plans considered congestion as a practical problem to be solved but welcomed the automobile per se. Slapstick comedies recognized its intrusion but acclimatized the people nonetheless.

Indeed, although it would be two generations before Jean Baudrillard would describe Los Angeles and postmodern culture in terms of hyper-mobility, that city's officials in the 1920s already argued for a unique utopian synergy between Los Angeles and the automobile.[117] The report by Olmsted and Bartholomew, *Parks, Playgrounds, and Beaches for the Los Angeles Region* (1930, hereafter the Olmsted-Bartholomew report) explained that '[p]robably nowhere else in the world does highway recreation form so large an element in the lives of the people as in

Southern California'.[118] Gordon Whitnall, now director of the City Planning Department, proposed in futuristic terms that 'Here for the first time in history, the efficient travel radius of the individual has been stretched . . . So prevalent is the use of the motor vehicle here that it might almost be said that Southern Californians have added wheels to their anatomy . . . that our population has become FLUID.'[119]

Missing from such discourse, and from most slapstick comedies, was an acknowledgment that fluid mobility was contingent upon gender and race. Notwithstanding the comic ineptitude of the characters played by Chaplin and Lloyd, and the occasional assertions of the women played by Mabel Normand or Mildred Davis, most slapstick comedies of the era relied upon decorous romantic relations and a gendering of narrative space in which the city was navigated by men while women waited to be wooed and were often confined to the home. Indeed, this was increasingly the case: Chaplin's films predominantly ended in anarchy or pathos while those of Lloyd more often concluded with the (re-)uniting of a loving couple. This trend was also a function of the automobile's social role. In Lloyd films, not only is the car the means by which the protagonist gets the girl, but crises while driving are frequently sources of male embarrassment – as in *Hot Water*, where the wrecking of the car with Lloyd at the wheel and his family looking on leads to the loss of the vehicle and a consequent loss of his patriarchal authority in a lengthy interior sequence at their home.

Earlier Chaplin films displayed a similar, though less authoritative, arrangement of male/female and public/private space. In Chaplin's *Caught in a Cabaret* (Mabel Normand, 1914), the organization of cinematic space is also racial, if not explicitly racialized. Like *Making a Living*, it alternates between suburbs and city, cutting between the richly planted gardens of the home of Normand and her parents and a downtown restaurant where Chaplin is a waiter overworked and bullied by his boss. In the suburbs, Chaplin poses as the ambassador of Greece to win a young lady's heart at her coming out party, while downtown is signified by interior shots of the crowded restaurant and exteriors of its urban setting. The latter were filmed on location amid the unpaved streets and dilapidated buildings of Los Angeles' real Chinatown, where the city's Chinese minority was concentrated in a slum to the east of the historic core, on a site cleared for Union Station in the 1930s. This navigation of the city produces a double exclusion. In the suburbs, Normand and her family emblematize an ascendant, home-owning,

Anglo-Saxon middle class while, after the party at home, she and her friends go on a 'slumming party' to the city centre. There, Chinatown is used as a generic built environment, the real location identified only accidentally, if the viewer pays attention, by a doorway painted with Chinese characters and a cluster of tenement residents standing forlorn in the distance.[120] Although this and other Chaplin films contain a critique of class, *Caught in a Cabaret* acquiesces in a marginalization of impoverished racial minorities that was all too unfortunate a characteristic of the real Los Angeles at this time.

In his book *Hollywood: The City of a Thousand Dreams, the Graveyard of a Thousand Hopes* (1928), the writer Jack Richmond was typical of many literary commentators who downplayed Los Angeles' racial minorities, asserting that '[t]here are no slums in Los Angeles, excepting the Mexican Quarters – heritage of the early village days of Los Angeles – and a certain small area known as the "Black Belt".[121] While Mexican characters or extras appear to have been largely absent from representation, many later slapstick comedies conform to what Jacqueline Stewart has compellingly characterized as the general tendency of American silent cinema to 'treat Black figures as complex and contradictory reflections of white anxieties about Black mobility and visibility'.[122] The films of Harold Lloyd provide a telling example. Merrill Schleier has pointed to the manner in which in *Safety Last* Harold's heroic climb is prefigured by a number of scenes in which African American characters are depicted in terms of cowardice, weakness and incompetence.[123] The problem is evident too in other films by Lloyd and always in

Charlie Chaplin on location in Apablasa Street, Chinatown, in *Caught in a Cabaret* (Charles Chaplin, Mabel Normand, 1914).

conjunction with some challenge to the fluid movement of the white male protagonist across the city's terrain.

In *Get Out and Get Under*, a relatively innocuous instance occurs in the little black boy who appears at the roadside when Harold's automobile breaks down in the district of Palms. This likeable, curious and diminutive figure provides a comic foil for Harold as he seeks to repair the engine, knocking Harold's tools to the ground, tripping him up with a discarded banana peel, and dropping a scoop of ice-cream on his head. But the boy is simply a boy, one of many comic hazards Harold encounters, and he disappears across the street when he is scolded. In *Number, Please?*, on the other hand, the callers on the line who interrupt The Boy's phone call to the mother of The Girl are not simply neutral others. Rather, the operator mistakenly puts Lloyd's character through to a Jewish man, an African American mother and a Chinese worker, who are caricatured and presented surrounding The Boy in a split-screen effects shot. This unites diverse constituencies artificially by means of cinema and telephony but re-enacts the de facto segregation of such people in Los Angeles at the time. In *Girl Shy*, finally, Harold encounters a black man whose underprivilege becomes a joke. Racing to the church to stop the marriage, Harold steals a car that turns out to be full of bootleg liquor, and he is chased by police down a narrow dirt road. Here he comes bumper to bumper with another car driven towards him by a black man, each gesticulating at the other to get out of the way until Harold instead suggests they trade cars on the spot so that each can turn around and be on his way. The suggestion flabbergasts but quickly persuades the black driver, whose own car is a jalopy while Harold's is a smart new saloon, but it also leads to his undoing as the black driver reverses on to the highway only to be stopped and arrested by the police.

The Film Industry and Suburbanization

Given the prevalence of automobiles in the films, it is hardly surprising that the motion picture industry was also a major contributor to the automobilizing of real life. The *Los Angeles Times* reported as early as 1915 that, in a city which was increasingly automobile-reliant, among those most likely to own their own vehicles were film industry personnel. The 5,000 people in the studios' employ owned 2,000 automobiles worth $2 million in total, while each of the studios had a fleet: 200 at Inceville, 100 at Lasky, 50 at Universal and six at Keystone. What was then a still new technology was shaping the way movies were made:

> Many long tours are made by the picture people . . . One director at one of the largest studios in the city said last week that the automobile and the camera were of first importance in the picture industry and that the directing did not matter much.[124]

A report in 1919 observed that the common sight of automobiles at movie studios reflected the popularity of the 'automobile pursuit race', which 'most emphatically registers an essential to the successful film – action, rapid action, and plenty of it'.[125] The automobile was ubiquitous, diverse and adaptable:

> In Southern California, in the movie towns that are near or a part of Los Angeles, nearly every studio in the business operates an automobile department larger than the average city garage. In the movie world's motordom virtually every make of machine is used in the wide variety of work that the motor vehicle is called upon to perform. Stars have their limousines, directors their chummy roadsters, magnates their top-notch touring cars, comedians their 'flivvers', while the mechanical departments move mostly in the more ponderous vehicles such as buses and trucks.[126]

The interpenetration of movies and car culture was also evident in business dealings by leading film industry figures. Hal Roach owned a controlling interest in the Clippinger-Kincaid chain of Chevrolet dealers based downtown.[127] Will Hays, who became president of the MPPDA in 1922, teamed up with a local realtor and car dealer to establish a Los Angeles-based national chain of auto service stations.[128]

The Olmsted-Bartholomew report was commissioned to assess the detrimental effects upon Los Angeles' natural spaces of urbanization and the automobile. The report declared that the number and condition of parks, beaches and playgrounds fell so 'far short . . . of the minimum recreation facilities of the average American city' as to constitute 'a crisis in the welfare of Los Angeles'.[129] While the city's climate never dissatisfied, its scenery was increasingly apt to cause 'surprise and disappointment' because of the 'pressure of growing masses'.[130] Rapid population growth, a 'fondness for the single family detached house' and under-investment in public facilities had led to a lack of communal leisure space.[131] This had been exacerbated by a prevalence of motor cars, which 'sharply distinguished' Los Angeles from 'the age in which older cities developed', and because of which it suffered from 'monotonous urban surroundings'.[132]

Although the report does not discuss the film industry, its enumeration of problem areas makes clear that, by 1930, the beaches and parks of the region – which had been essential film locations for Edison, Griffith, Chaplin and Lloyd – were increasingly threatened. The beaches of Santa Monica and Malibu were now about 90 per cent screened from view by private homes and other structures and accessible to the public only along 'short, disconnected stretches'.[133] One of the worst-affected areas was near Santa Ynez Canyon, the former home of Inceville where urban development was said to have destroyed lines of sight and picturesque vistas. The mountains and canyons north of Hollywood and Glendale, which had long been used for shooting westerns, were 'fast being subjected to subdivision and cheek-by-jowl cabin construction' while roadsides were 'disfigured by signboards, shacks, garages, filling stations, destruction of trees, and multiplication of poles and wires'.[134]

In a contemporaneous report in the *Los Angeles Times* location managers complained that urbanization was making it more difficult to film:

It's almost impossible to find roads on which to run stage coaches for western scenes nowadays . . . They are now selling lots for a thousand dollars a front foot where we used to make our western pictures ten years ago. Bill Hart chased many a villain through what is now Carthay Center, and we used to have the Indians scalping the whites nearly every day in the valley near Beverly Boulevard and Vermont Avenue. Both of these locations are now fashionable residence districts.[135]

Roads had been straightened and levelled by surveyors and modern steam-shovels; regulation of motorized and pedestrian traffic curtailed shooting on location downtown; and filming had been banned in Echo Park because filmmakers were said to have damaged the grounds.[136]

Restriction of location filming around the city was matched by a redistribution of film studios – a complex process, involving both geographical inertia and pressures to move. Universal was unusual in opening on 230 acres in Burbank and then staying put throughout its history, as was Thomas Ince, who established first at the outlying 460-acre Inceville before moving to the more conveniently located, but much smaller, 11.5-acre Triangle site in Culver City.[137] But most studios started in more central locations, then moving outward as they grew. In Hollywood, the earliest studios, such as those of Nestor and Francis Ford, were typically about half an acre in size. By the 1920s Columbia Pictures owned eight acres, Jesse D. Hampton ten, United Artists thirteen, Robertson-Cole twenty and Paramount 26.[138] Fox, who had relocated from less than two acres in Edendale to 30 acres in Hollywood in 1916, acquired 108 acres in Westwood in 1923.[139] First National/Warner Bros outgrew its ten acres and decentralized from Hollywood to 62 acres in Burbank in 1926.[140] Other studios, including the two most important sources of slapstick comedy, followed a similar pattern. Hal Roach's Rolin Film Company, which had first rented studios downtown and then in Edendale, moved to a 14.5-acre lot in Culver City in 1920.[141] Mack Sennett's Keystone studios moved from its 25 acres in Edendale to a lot of similar size but more modern and further out, in Studio City in the San Fernando Valley, in 1927.[142] And many studios also owned or leased undeveloped land for exteriors. Jesse D. Hampton leased 100 acres behind the Beverly Hills Hotel on which a western street set was built. Paramount-Famous Lasky owned the Hollingsworth ranch of 500 acres in the San Fernando Valley, gradually buying adjacent land, before leasing it to Warner Bros and buying another ranch five times bigger nearby.[143]

When the first studios were established in outlying areas from Santa Monica and Burbank to Hollywood and Culver City, land zoning appears to have been arranged locally between industrialists, developers and civic leaders.[144] However, the consolidation of the film industry coincided with the formalizing of city planning. Los Angeles was one of the first American cities to professionalize zoning in 1908, when it distinguished between industrial and residential areas, and in 1913, when a City Planning Commission was established and land was further categorized into commercial, light industrial and heavy industrial zones, and single- and multiple-family residential areas.[145] All land not zoned industrial was declared residential by default, although film studios were zoned 'light industrial'.[146] Conventional factories, which were few before 1918, were their heavy equivalents, although clustered quite tightly in the so-called Central Manufacturing District, just south of downtown, where the proximity of railroad terminals facilitated shipping raw materials and manufactured goods for companies such as Goodyear Tire and Rubber.[147]

Population growth and pressures on land came face to face with the need of the studios to grow in response to their success but at a time when zoning was expanded and refined.[148] Hal Roach, who leased an empty lot on Olive Street downtown as late as 1918, was ordered to relinquish the premises for reasons of fire safety. In Edendale and Glendale, the opening of new studios became impossible and the growth of existing ones more difficult, a problem that also affected Hollywood as time passed. Hence, the film industry became a leading agent of industrial decentralization as studios looked to Culver City, Westwood and the San Fernando Valley for fresh expanses of land.

Although Fogelson has likened film studios at this time to steel furnaces in Torrance, oil refineries at El Segundo and aircraft factories in Santa Monica, they were really a special case.[149] Not only were they among the first to settle in outlying areas, but they were unlike other industries in so far as their choice of such areas was dictated by their unique desire to reproduce the world on film – by using the given landscape or recreating it on stages or sets that required large amounts of space. William Johnston of *Motion Picture News* remarked in 1926 that '[m]any visitors at Hollywood marvel at the extensive ground space of the large studio plants. As a matter of fact, expensive as the land is, it pays the large producing companies to have plenty of stage floor space so that there will be no delays while heavy payrolls are going on.'[150]

The studios' appetite for space was part of an emerging decentralization of American industry in general in the late nineteenth and early twentieth centuries.[151] In his study of Albert Kahn, the German-born chief architect to Henry Ford, Federico Bucci has explained the evolution of Ford's conception of the factory, and of Kahn's designs, in terms of increasing size and rationalization. From Ford's first major purpose-built plant at Highland Park (1909–18) to that at River Rouge (1921–39), then the largest factory in the world, this process entailed the development of the first assembly lines, but also a shift from manufacturing in multi-storey buildings in urban settings to manufacturing outside cities in sprawling sites of extensive low-rise structures.[152] The imperatives of demographic growth and industrial rationalization fuelling decentralization also dovetailed handily with the ideological motivations of the white, middle-class male entrepreneurs who drove it. In December 1921, Will Hays, US postmaster-general and former national chairman of the Republican Party, was invited by the film studios to form the industry regulatory body, the MPPDA, in response to the national public scandals that surrounded the alleged rape of Virginia Rappe by the slapstick comedian Roscoe 'Fatty' Arbuckle and the murder of the director William Desmond Taylor.[153] Historians have demonstrated that this move had two main aims: to improve public perceptions of the morality of the industry and its stars, for example, by regulating the labour and lifestyles of naive young 'extra girls' who might fall prey to sexual exploitation; and to reform the morality of Hollywood films by a codification of acceptable representations, which would become the Production Code.[154] However, the MPPDA and subordinate organizations that it sponsored, such as the Central Casting Bureau and Hollywood Studio Club, were also part of a larger strategy that sought to reconstruct the film industry as a rationally planned community. Just over one week after Hays was appointed, Thomas G. Patten, Hays's West Coast representative, addressed the Hollywood Chamber of Commerce and Los Angeles Realty Board, the early date of the meeting an indicator that the motion picture and real estate industries took each other seriously:

> Mr Hays' idea is to reconstruct the movie headquarters to make it somewhat like model industrial towns such as, for instance, Gary [Indiana]. Mr Hays wants to do for the workers in the motion picture industry what Henry Ford has done for his automobile

workers . . . Nothing was said about morals. The word 'industrial' was stressed. A 'model industrial community' is what Hollywood is to be under the new scheme of things.[155]

This agenda extended into the film industry the distrust of central cities and preference for suburbs that was central to Henry Ford's philosophy and the industrial organization of Fordism. Ostensibly guided by a belief in the healthfulness and conviviality of suburbs, Ford declared in his memoir *My Life, My Work* (1922): 'There is something about a city of a million people which is untamed and threatening . . . The modern city has been prodigal, it is today bankrupt, and tomorrow it will cease to be.'[156]

That moral reform and the reorganization of urban space went hand in hand was subsequently evident in the attitudes of film stars and executives who were active in the community. The entrepreneurial and civic elite who made up the 161-member Citizens' Committee convened to oversee the Olmsted-Bartholomew report included eight prominent film industry personnel: Cecil B. De Mille, Douglas Fairbanks, Samuel Goldwyn, Carl Laemmle, Sol Lesser, Fred Niblo, Mary Pickford and Joseph M. Schenck, as well as Bank of America president A. P. Giannini and the Hollywood realtor C. E. Toberman.[157] Mary Pickford became especially influential because she was one of 24 members of the Executive Committee and because she advocated City Beautiful design. Speaking to the Los Angeles Chamber of Commerce in 1926, she explained that she always advised visitors from Europe or the East 'to get off [the train] in Pasadena . . . never downtown'.[158] She hoped that any new railroad station would be built in 'an attractive part of the town, surrounded by a park with fountains. The first impression of Los Angeles would be a beautiful one and the last one something that they can carry away instead of going through packing houses.'[159] This (somewhat snobbish) desire formed part of her larger interest in 'the staging of a city'.[160]

Notably and tragically, given its vitality in the films of Chaplin and Lloyd, in the late 1920s commentaries critical of downtown became increasingly visible. A distrust of its alleged deviance, danger, and crime, which would persist for the rest of the twentieth century, took hold especially among social conservatives. For example, in *Hollywood: The City of a Thousand Dreams, The Graveyard of a Thousand Hopes*, Richmond singled out its most famous public space as an emblem of the degenerate city centre:

The human material displayed in Pershing Square is surely abominable enough either to be pitied or despised, if not condemned, depending on whether you belong to the 'soft-minded' individuals or to the 'tough-minded' ones. Pershing Square is the meeting place of the creatures that once were men, the never-were, the incapacitated and the retired human mules. The disillusioned and the visionary, the super-emotional, the religious-pervert and the crank – they all find ready listeners in the blazing sun on the hard and dry benches in Pershing Square. The shallow atheist and the stupid emissary of Jesus; the half-baked socialist and the ardent communist, they all peddle their wares there, noisily and violently. Now and again large groups are formed, voices are raised and hands gesticulate to the amazement and amusement of passers-by.[161]

Inflation in land values further drove decentralization as film studios and the city grew, congestion combining with the potential for profits to encourage a search for cheaper land. In 1922 Al and Charles Christie declared that the value of their studio in Hollywood 'has so increased that the investment is not compatible with picture making'.[162] Instead, using the site as collateral, they had arranged with the Janss Investment Company, one of Los Angeles' leading land development firms, to relocate to a new site of 230 acres in Westwood, of which they would use 40 acres for a studio while developing the rest as a business venture through their own Christie Realty Corporation. The following year, Fox explained that it would relocate to Westwood partly because 'the present Fox studio [in Hollywood], which was bought only six years ago, for $185,000, is now valued at $1,250,000'.[163] Such cases demonstrate that studios' desire to acquire more space for increases in film production dovetailed with their desire to realize the increased value of the land on which their original studios were standing. This was spelled out in a telegram from Jesse Lasky to Adolph Zukor that also recognized strategic location as an important consideration as Famous Players-Lasky looked for a new site on 13 June 1923:

I have realized for some time past the probability that in a very short time we would be forced to change our studio location to less thickly populated section where land is not so valuable and where we would not be so congested and cramped for room.

Stop. Several pieces of property have been called to my attention at various times which I have not seriously considered but yesterday I looked at acreage which impressed me very much because of its location, topography, and traffic and street car facilities. Stop. Proposition submitted by owners of the land would work out so that land would cost us practically nothing in the end and the sale of our present studio property will go long way toward providing money for new buildings. Stop.[164]

In a city that was rapidly growing, not only did movement and displacement become prominent in the form and content of films, they characterized the geography of the studios as well.

Decentralization of commercial activities in Los Angeles was almost non-existent in 1900, except for grocery stores, meat markets and drug stores, but by 1910, just before the first film studio was opened in Hollywood, it had become significant with many larger stores, for example, selling hardware and furniture to new homeowners outside downtown. By 1920 there were ten or more centres of significant commercial activity in which branch banks and other new businesses were found, although none rivalled downtown. Most of this development took place in the vicinity of streetcar lines, for example on Hollywood Boulevard. However, in the following decade, Longstreth has explained, downtown's 'hegemony over the commercial life of the region was broken' and Hollywood, in particular, emerged as one of a number of 'Aladdin cities' several miles from downtown that pretended to be self-sufficient.[165]

Its population growing from 5,000 in 1910 to 36,000 ten years later and 235,000 ten years after that, by 1922 Hollywood was already named in Regional Planning Commission literature as one of four major residential, commercial and industrial nodes surrounding Los Angeles' core (the others being Pasadena, Inglewood and Laguna).[166] Construction of stores, offices, apartments and film studios in the district was sufficient for the Los Angeles Realty Board to monitor its building activity distinctly and for press reports to speak of it as an economic and demographic engine of its own.[167] Held up as an ideal example of how benevolent decentralization could be, Hollywood benefited from a unique strategic location, halfway from downtown west to the ocean and a bridgehead into the increasingly important San Fernando Valley to the north. Its promotion emphasized not only film production but its credentials as a place to live and work, attracting mainly affluent white middle-class families to settle in proximity to its convenient streetcar routes and, increasingly, in the Hollywood Hills to the north, where only automobiles could go.

Hollywood was known for its greater sophistication and range of amenities than Glendale or Pasadena and by the late 1920s, when it was home to the famed Schwab's drugstore, Dyas department store and General Electric (GE) showrooms, its promoters claimed that one no longer had to go downtown for most activities or needs. The presence and activity of the film studios enhanced the magnetism of the place, while the opening of movie theatres such as Grauman's Egyptian, Grauman's Chinese, the El Capitan and Pantages, earned Hollywood a reputation as a spectacular home of movie premieres rivalled only by Broadway in New York. Mary Pickford and other stars participated in Christmas pageants and other promotional events by the Hollywood Chamber of Commerce. A gradual centralization of film laboratories and other technical services added to Hollywood's light industrial base.[168] And movie executives and stars invested in local real estate ventures.[169]

On a smaller scale but, unlike Hollywood, actually an autonomous municipality, Culver City arose from barley fields after 1913, quickly becoming such an important motion picture centre that it was only when the Culver City Chamber of Commerce proposed to rename Culver

Hollywood Business Center, c. 1931.

City 'Hollywood' that Los Angeles City Council fixed the latter's boundaries and recognized it as a district.[170] Culver City exemplified the synergy between film industry growth and entrepreneurial capitalists not only because the first major producer to settle there, Thomas Ince, was one himself but also because of the city's founder Harry H. Culver, extensively publicized in mythical terms as an adventurer and self-made man. Culver, a former newspaper reporter in the Philippines and agent for the US Treasury who arrived in Los Angeles with limited resources, was said to have been inspired by a day-trip by streetcar from downtown Los Angeles to Venice Beach to invent a new community at a strategic point roughly midway along the route. Described in 1915 as 'a progressive embryo of a town', Culver City had a population of 15,000 within ten years and embodied the suburban spirit of Better Homes in America as well as anywhere else in the region.[171]

However, three film studios underpinned the success of the venture: in addition to Ince, who arrived in 1915, Culver also sold land to Hal Roach in 1916 and again to Ince in 1919 when Ince went independent, leaving his previous studios to Samuel Goldwyn, and subsequently MGM. Initial reports stressed the risk of trying to do business in outlying areas. The *Los Angeles Times* ventured that 'Hollywood was the center of film endeavor and it seemed suicidal to build a studio anywhere else'.[172] While building his studios, Roach found that Culver City only had one shared phone line to the outside world and was charged long-distance rates for calls to Los Angeles. He also had to build his own generator because the regional electricity provider could not guarantee sufficient supply for his studio's needs.[173]

Nonetheless, an advertisement of 1923 billed Culver City as 'The City of Opportunities', inviting investors, business owners and home buyers to visit the place on one of the Company's complimentary guided tours.[174] These drew attention to its pleasant climate and cleanliness, its school, churches, country club and large residential tracts, and its picturesque setting against the backdrop of Baldwin Hills. Also highlighted were its modern utilities, streets, commercial district and low taxes. The greatest emphasis was placed on the ease of circulation afforded by being '[d]irectly in the path of Los Angeles' rapid growth to the Ocean'. This was 'the hub of a wheel with fourteen spokes – each representing an artery of travel' and served equally by the 'best street car service in Southern California' and 'the most cosmopolitan thoroughfare in the United States – Washington Boulevard'. The latter, it was claimed, allowed an average of 250,000 people and 35,000 automobiles to pass through Culver City each week.

More remote again, but creating a growth spurt of its own, was Burbank, five miles to the north of Hollywood and much slower to develop because of the intervening canyons and hills. The extent to which Universal City broke new ground by establishing there may be gauged from the fact that in the early 1910s utility companies such as Southern California Edison and Sunset Telephone would extend service to businesses there only after extensive negotiations, the payment of a large deposit and a guaranteed monopoly on the company's account for a number of years. Such arrangements were also made in 1926 when First National studios (later Warner Bros) opted to use Burbank as its base, an event described in one report as the most important in Burbank since its founding forty years before.

Accounts of the new studios' construction emphasized that, in contrast to Hollywood and Culver City, this was fairly unspoiled land, presenting before and after photographs of its 'native scenery' and artist's impressions of the buildings that would blend into the landscape:

> A beautiful natural setting for the studio is afforded by the Holly-wood foothills against which it is built; wooded Griffith Park on the east; Lakeside Country Club on the west; the expanse of San Fernando Valley and beyond it the high peaks of the Verdugo range and the Sierra Madres on the north.[175]

However, urbanization soon followed, the studios' construction contributing to a 60 per cent increase in the total value of buildings in Burbank in one year.[176] This was accompanied by a marked increase in subdividing, and in demand and prices for tracts, construction of a Junior High School, Public Library and offices for the Chamber of Commerce, and a two-thirds increase in Burbank's annual payroll.[177]

Shortly after, what would be called 'Studio City' became the last of the new zones in which film industry growth pulled the expansion of the city in its train. Also in the San Fernando Valley, but to the west of Burbank, it emerged in 1927 and was built during the coming of sound. That summer Mack Sennett was preparing to vacate the Edendale lot he had occupied since 1912, but whose 25 acres and 1,800 feet of frontage on the busy Glendale Boulevard was now 'so valuable that it is imprac-tical from a production standpoint to operate a motion-picture studio

here any longer'.[178] Planning to redevelop the original site for offices and bungalow courts, Sennett's relocation was the heart of 'one of the most extensive programs of studio construction ever experienced in the film capital of the world'.[179] Development of the 503-acre Studio City, which would include homes and other businesses at a total cost of $20 million, was to be coordinated by the Central Motion Picture District, Inc., a syndicate of private investors that included Sennett, executives Milton E. Hoffman and B. P. Schulberg of Famous Players-Lasky, and the actor Wallace Beery. Sennett's new studios, which would anchor the whole initiative, would comprise twenty acres, eighteen buildings in a Spanish Revival style, and 44,000 square feet of stages, for a substantial $1 million.[180] And they were joined by a new lot for the Christie studios, other smaller studios, and the adjacent ranches of Famous Players-Lasky, MGM and Cecil B. De Mille.[181]

Significant collateral urbanization also took place. The Pacific Electric railway agreed to build one and a half miles of new track from an existing route. Southern California Telephone and Southern California Edison extended service to an area they had not served before. The City of Los Angeles widened the major route of Ventura Boulevard and dredged the Los Angeles river, removing a natural ravine and setting its banks in concrete.[182] It extended the new San Fernando Valley sewer system in a move reported to be 'the most important public improvement the valley has obtained'.[183] And it announced the construction of two new major roads – south to Hollywood through the Cahuenga Pass and into downtown north of Griffith Park – which would become freeways in years to come and key agents of Los Angeles' growth as a city of global proportions.[184]

'Time is Ripe to Buy Property in Studio City', advertisement by the Central Motion Picture District, Inc., *Los Angeles Times*, 4 September 1927.

Naturally, Studio City attracted residents, banks, drug stores and markets.[185] But especially notable was the *way* in which it did so, exploiting its association with the movie business not just in its name. A plan of beautification to make Studio City 'a Southern California show place' was led by the director Irving Cummings.[186] Reports about home-building in adjacent suburbs highlighted residents with movie connections such as Joseph Van Meter, an official at the Chaplin studios, who constructed a home in well-to-do Toluca Lake Park.[187] Advertisements evoked the aura of motion pictures, which would presumably rub off on anyone who bought in the area: 'Cameras will soon be clicking, sun lights glaring, megaphones resounding and thousands of workers and actors hustling in unison to meet the demands of picture production.'[188] By 1929 the total value of the construction of homes at Studio City, at $20 million, exceeded the $15 million invested in new studios.[189] The area's new pretensions were marked when the nearby district of Lankersheim renamed itself 'North Hollywood' and when the San Fernando Valley was said to be the source of over two-thirds of film production in the entire Los Angeles region.[190]

The extension and evolution of Los Angeles by the end of the 1920s is evident in the slapstick comedies of Laurel and Hardy, whose heyday began shortly before the coming of sound and continued well into the 1930s. As in the cases of Chaplin and Lloyd, not all of the films they made were set in Los Angeles, but the many that were demonstrate a further normalization of suburban navigations and landscapes.[191] For example, one of their earliest films, *Putting Pants on Philip* (Clyde Bruckman, 1927), is typical of the numerous shorts they made on the streets of Culver City and provides evidence of what such places were

J. Piedmont Mumble-thunder (Oliver Hardy) and his nephew Philip (Stan Laurel) explore Culver City in *Putting Pants on Philip* (Clyde Bruckman, 1927).

really like. The film concerns the efforts of J. Piedmont Mumblethunder (Hardy) to host a visit by his dim-witted and womanizing Scottish nephew Philip (Laurel) who sails in on the ss *Mirimar* wearing a kilt, which causes hilarity and shock among the locals. Taking Philip on a tour of Culver City, Piedmont determines to make his nephew wear trousers while having to constantly intervene to stop his lascivious pursuits of young women. Although downtown Culver City actually consisted of little more than ten city blocks of one- or two-storey buildings, with only one of greater height (the six-storey Culver City Hotel), the film does its best to generate a metropolitan milieu, for example by carefully framing Laurel and Hardy in medium shots and close-ups as they walk past a series of shop fronts.[192] However, the relative underdevelopment of this 'city' is evident most of the time, especially in numerous long shots of Main Street, whose exceptional width is opened up by bright sunlight while large amounts of sky and oil derricks on the horizon emphasize the low-rise nature of the surroundings. Because one can see in the background of many shots that pedestrians were few and automobiles numerous in the real Culver City, one's sense of its low density is heightened by the crowds that appear round Philip and his kilt spontaneously and seemingly from nowhere. A running joke in narrative terms, these create notable juxtapositions between an open field of vision and the masses.

Should Married Men Go Home? (Leo McCarey, James Parrott, 1928) is also notable for a striking counterpoint of closed and open space, being one of several films in which Laurel and Hardy routinized the theme of the hen-pecked suburban husband desperate for a break from his marriage.[193] The normalization of suburban landscapes is evident in the way in which the setting is effectively conveyed with a few simple opening shots: Mr Hardy (Hardy) and his wife sitting in the bay window of their bungalow's living room, framed against drapes and the street outside; Stan (Laurel), a lone pedestrian walking down the street to visit them, its concrete sidewalks apparently recent, undeveloped adjoining lots, and a sky marked only by telephone poles and a smattering of one-storey commercial buildings in the distance.

Similarly, the middle-class preoccupation with privacy is quickly mocked: Mr and Mrs Hardy snuggle on the couch for some quality time alone, their irritation at Stan's arrival heightened by alternating point-of-view shots looking out of and in through the window. Stan, dressed for golf, leaps nimbly over their white picket fence on his way to the front

A balance of vertical and horizontal action in *County Hospital* (James Parrott, 1932).

door, but Hardy stumbles and collapses the fence when he tries the same thing moments later (a joke about his weight, of course, but also perhaps a mockery of the build quality of many hurriedly constructed homes). The film elaborates on the property line much recognized by Chaplin and Lloyd but with a greater habituation to it because in this and other Laurel and Hardy films one or both of the pair is already a married property owner. This is underlined by the focus of the rest of the film on a chaotic game of golf, the archetypal suburban hobby that spawned many clubs in Los Angeles. Leaving Mrs Hardy at home, the two men make up a foursome with a couple of flappers although, this being a Laurel and Hardy film, little golf is actually played and the round degenerates into a comedy of lost balls, loose divots and a mud fight. In this extended action, a counterpoint to the suburban street is offered by the sheer expanse of the fairways while the real oil derricks in the background combine with the mud that is centre stage to make the golf club resemble an oil field, another archetypal Los Angeles landscape of that time.

By contrast, *County Hospital* (James Parrott, 1932) is one of many films the comic duo made after the coming of sound that seem to retreat from exterior locations in favour of interiors and an intensified simulation of urban life. Reorganizing the balance of horizontal and vertical action in *Safety Last*, the film begins at the high-rise County Hospital where, after an accident, Ollie (Hardy) has his leg in traction in a room on an upper floor. When his visitor, Stan (Laurel), accidentally drops out of the window the heavy weight restraining Ollie's leg, the rope pulls Ollie's doctor out the window, dangling him high above the street. This section of the film intercuts studio sets and location shots of Culver City's real City Hall, which stands in for the hospital but was really only two storeys high. The film tries even harder than *Putting Pants on Philip* to make Culver City more urban than it was: painted flats depict high-rise buildings that simply were not there; and the 'hospital' is given artificial height by a low upward shot of the face of a much higher building and a high downward shot of a metropolitan street busy with people and cars.

Subsequently, in an extended sequence shot partly on location in Culver City, but mostly with rear projection, Stan attempts to drive Ollie home despite having sat on a syringeful of sedative and being only just about conscious. The exterior location shots here demonstrate a real lack of significant buildings and Culver Boulevard disappears to a distant horizon marked only by a water tank and telephone poles. Hence, it is confirmed that slapstick comedies often enhanced Los Angeles' horizontal and suburban aspects with a vertical and metropolitan look and feel. Most significantly, however, as the automobile careens through busy traffic, movement *along* the street is presented by unnaturally fast and disjointed rear projection, which compresses images of a fuel truck, streetcars, gas stations, drive-in markets and billboards with a degree of excess surely designed for effect. As if, by this time, filmmakers felt obliged to acknowledge that audiences were well-used to the motorized slapstick chase, the vehicle appears to defy laws of physics – at one point, facing backward but moving forward – and we lose any sense it has any traction on real roads. Indeed, the finale cuts to a location shot in which the speeding car spins on water or oil at an intersection before being crushed between two streetcars and thoroughly decommissioned. This is the *ne plus ultra* of slapstick navigations of Los Angeles: Stan attempts to comply with a furious policeman's order that he pull over to the side of the road but the car has been bent in a right angle and can only drive in circles, a conclusion that anticipates the absurd automobiles of Jacques Tati or Jean-Luc Godard.[194]

In subsequent years, slapstick comedy remained popular but the coming of sound brought greater reliance on studio recreations of the city while prompting a standardization of the comedy feature at the expense of the comedy short. These developments were evident in *Sons of the Desert* (William A. Seiter, 1933) in which Laurel and Hardy showed great skill in the comedy of the domestic interior, a setting with understandable appeal in the early days of sound when sound recording on location was often uneven in quality. In such films, exterior locations were few, although Los Angeles was sometimes present in details – either implicitly, for example, in that film's regionally typical white stucco bungalows with mock Tudor timber doors or, explicitly, as in the headline from the 'Los Angeles Bulletin' that announces the duo's drowning in a disaster at sea.

The concentration of film production in the studio occasioned by the coming of sound was matched by a slowing of decentralization in the industry as a whole. Hollywood's pivotal role was reinforced by its increasing importance as a base for technical companies such as Western Electric and RCA (Radio Corporation of America), while Fox and Warner Bros, who had planned to dispose of their Hollywood lots, kept them for redevelopment as sound labs.[195] Then both the studios and the city were engulfed by the Depression. The City Beautiful plans of Olmsted-Bartholomew were shelved;[196] Hollywood's residents petitioned the city to rezone old studios for homes;[197] Mack Sennett was bankrupt and Hal Roach Studios went into decline;[198] and the Central Motion Picture District was enmeshed in corruption scandals.[199] In this climate, navigations of the real city were gradually displaced by a new emphasis on the structures and textures of the studios and the space inside their walls.

three

The Simulacrum

There's Paramount Paris and Metro Paris and, of course,
the real Paris. Paramount's is the most Parisian of all.
Ernst Lubitsch, c. 1926[1]

While location filming involved many slapstick comedies in the city's
sprawl, a significant number of films were made about the film industry
that tended in the opposite direction. As I will explain in this chapter, *The
Extra Girl* (F. Richard Jones, 1923), *A Star is Born* (William Wellman,
1937) and many other less well-known films created and identified with
'Hollywood' an exaggerated sense of place that often meant pretending
that the rest of Los Angeles was not really there or did not count. This was
especially the case in the first fifteen years after the coming of sound when
studio-based filming was predominant and the studio system was at its
height. As movies about the movies made clear, the major studios often
explicitly claimed the status of cities, replicating their physical and social
characteristics in their design and construction, and asserting a semi-
autonomy of the real city in which they were located and upon which they
relied. Because of these characteristics, and their reproduction and amplification of the real world on movie sets, each of the studios came to resemble
what Jean Baudrillard called a 'simulacrum' – that is, a product of 'the
generation by models of a real that is without origin or reality'.[2] What
might be called the simulacral 'effects' of the movie studios spilled out across
the urban landscape and, by a kind of osmosis, made *it* simulacral too.
Movie props, homes of the stars and movie theatres embodied qualities
similar to the studios themselves, if on a smaller scale, while movies about
the movies disseminated the simulacral disposition even more widely.

Baudrillard's idea of the simulacrum provides a tool with which to describe and critique these phenomena. It encourages a view of the shift toward studio-bound film production as a backward step, given the filmmaker's greater engagement with real life outdoors in earlier years. It is useful in countering what the studios tended to present as an always-productive symbiosis between capital and culture. And, throwing into question the difference between the real and imagined, it suggests a nearly seamless relationship in which the real city and the studio were constantly remaking each other. This is a two-way process I hope to explain by organizing this chapter into two sections on 'movie studios as cities' and 'the city as a movie studio'. Their analysis side by side lends weight to Baudrillard's identification of Disneyland as a prototypical simulacrum:

> Disneyland exists in order to hide that *it* is the 'real' country, all of 'real' America that *is* Disneyland . . . Disneyland is presented as imaginary in order to make us believe that the rest is real, whereas all of Los Angeles and the America that surrounds it are no longer real but belong to the hyperreal order and to the order of simulation.[3]

Disneyland, however, was founded in 1955. The simulacral tendency that Baudrillard found it to portend had a prehistory in Los Angeles as far back as the mid-1910s.

Movie Studios as Cities

The increasing role of the motion picture industry in Los Angeles' growth was particularly evident from the 1910s to the 1930s in the architecture and planning of the movie studios, a subject that has been remarkably neglected.[4] Technically detailed and ideologically sensitive studies of important building types in the city's history are a relatively recent phenomenon. Richard Longstreth's histories of gas stations, supermarkets and shopping centres have proven that what were long considered banal expressions of design had deep social and cultural influence in Los Angeles, across the United States and abroad.[5] Like such buildings, movie studios prioritized utility, efficiency, profit, and methods and materials specific to industrial and commercial construction. However, unlike retail architecture, which tended to be dispersed across the urban landscape, movie studios were monumental structures commanding it, yet separate and removed.

In this respect, Dana Cuff's history of housing projects is also useful. Proposing Los Angeles as an exemplar of 'the provisional city', Cuff ascribes its tendency to constantly destroy and remake itself to its exceptionally intense modern history of large-scale land development for homes.[6] Always utopian, this was first evident in capitalistic terms when Harry Chandler, the owner of the *Los Angeles Times*, purchased and improved 50,000 acres of the San Fernando Valley between 1903 and 1909. And it continued in a collectivist vein during the Depression, the Second World War and the Cold War, when the priority was housing migrant workers, war veterans and the poor. Cuff draws on Rem Koolhas's typology of S[mall], M[edium], L[arge] and XL [Extra Large] buildings to characterize the housing project as an Extra Large intervention in the fabric of the city that tends to 'structure and dominate the fine-grained interstitial matter. The dominant places are sited upon others that have somehow lost their value in the city. And the new inhabitation comes into being convulsively, sometimes violently, leaving little trace of what it evicted.'[7] As such, the Extra Large building tends to undermine the sense of linear growth that has long been central to histories of the American city, in contrast to which Los Angeles has developed by rupture and disturbance.[8]

Aerial photographs of William Fox Studios, at Sunset Boulevard and Western Avenue, Hollywood, 1918 and 1928, showing growth.

There are obvious differences between housing projects and movie studios in the type, function and arrangement of the buildings involved, but movie studios also had utopian aspirations and an Extra Large presence in the landscape. Like retail architecture and public housing, the city's film studios have often been taken for granted, their history as urban environments barely written. And yet their siting, complex construction and frequently enormous scale surely had significant effects. Downtown Los Angeles and Santa Monica were important before the first filmmakers arrived, but Edendale, Hollywood, Culver City and the San Fernando Valley were not. And many of the studio buildings that appeared in those places shared what Cuff calls the 'fugitive' quality of much Los Angeles architecture, its lightweight, inexpensive and modular solutions, which became increasingly common during the 1920s because of the population boom and forgiving climate.[9] This quality was especially evident in the first makeshift studio buildings, but it remained as the studios invested in increasingly large and expensive shooting stages and administrative blocks designed for the long term. At any given moment, a large part of the man-made environment of a studio consisted of myriad low-grade workshops and storerooms, and extensive outdoor sets of a more or less temporary nature. Moreover, the industry's rapid growth to global prominence, combined with frequent technological change, caused the studios to

adapt, enlarge, demolish or rebuild whole buildings and sites again and again.

Estimates of the size of the film industry in Los Angeles, and the measures used to quantify it, vary. In 1927 the investment firm Halsey Stuart estimated bullishly that 350,000 people were employed in the film industry's various branches nationwide (that is, production, distribution and exhibition) and that the box office gross for that year was at least $750 million.[10] However, Mae Huettig, in *Economic Control of the Motion Picture Industry* (1944), cautioned that, despite its thriving box office and high profile, viewed

> as part of our national economy, the motion picture industry is not a major bulwark. There are forty-four other industries, out of the total of ninety-four industrial groups enumerated by *Statistics of Income* (Bureau of Internal Revenue), that reported a larger gross income in 1937 than did the combined motion picture producing and exhibition corporations.[11]

The film industry contributed 92 per cent of the net income of what Huettig called 'amusement corporations', approximately 1 per cent of the total earnings of all corporations in the nation. But it was surpassed by laundries, hotels, restaurants, loan companies, investment trusts, tobacco and liquor.

However, neither Halsey Stuart nor Huettig was especially interested in the economic importance of the film industry to Los Angeles, nor did they observe that the nation's motion picture industry, unlike most others, with the exception of automobiles, was so strongly identified with one particular place. There the emerging studio system was very significant and it was growing. In 1918 the Los Angeles Chamber of Commerce claimed there were 100 film companies in Los Angeles County employing 10,000 people.[12] In 1922 it was reported that 15,000 people were employed full-time, plus up to 15,000 extras on call, on a total payroll of $30 million per year.[13] By 1926, according to the Chamber of Commerce, the film industry was 'the fourth largest industry in the world, and stands at the head of thirty-five great basic industries in California'.[14] At that time, it was said to employ 35,000 people on an annual payroll of $65 million.[15] In 1928 it attracted weekly attendances of 65 million at the US box office.[16] By the mid-1930s, when its total employment stabilized at around 30,000, the industry was estimated to have an annual turnover between $150 million and $200 million and to produce films worth $170 million each year.[17]

The film industry was also significant relative to others in the region. In 1928 it produced goods (i.e. finished films) worth $225 million in comparison to the whole manufacturing sector in Los Angeles, whose output was valued at $903 million and which had an annual payroll of $130 million.[18] While Los Angeles had a relatively small industrial base, from 1921 to 1929 it tripled in output as the city's large commercial and services sectors, and small industries such as machine shops, slaughterhouses, publishing houses and lumber mills, were joined by the film studios, oil drilling and refining, and automobile-related factories.[19] In 1920, for example, its tyre industry consisted of Goodyear, Firestone, Goodrich and US Rubber plants employing 5,000 with a total output worth $56 million.[20] In 1923, when the oil industry in Southern California produced 20 per cent of the world's crude oil, Los Angeles County had up to 400 wells employing up to 20,000 people and producing 700,000 barrels per day.[21] And, by 1928, Los Angeles took a leading role in aircraft manufacture, becoming home to 25 companies, including Douglas in Santa Monica and Lockheed in Burbank, and producing more than one-third of commercial aircraft in the US.[22] Like the motion picture companies, the aircraft plants originated in small family-run firms that operated out of rented or converted workshops. However, by the mid-1930s, when Los Angeles County became the fifth most important nationally in industrial output, they employed roughly as many people as the film industry (i.e. 33,000), and became the region's largest manufacturing industry during the Second World War, when 120,000 people were employed.[23]

Recognition of the film industry was mixed but gradually grew. In 1915, in an article on 'Business Conditions and the Outlook', H. S. McKee proposed that while Los Angeles had significant commercial activity and small-scale manufacturing, it had little of that

> more important kind of business, which consists in carrying on, in any particular place, some large industry characteristic of that place . . . which produces a product far beyond local needs for sale and export to other localities, and which brings, in return, to that locality, a large gross income, employs and pays an industrial army, and yields a net income to the proprietor.[24]

The film industry would come to serve such a function in Los Angeles but did not yet, although Chaplin and Keystone, for example, had made numerous films in the city by this time. The Los Angeles Chamber of Commerce mounted extensive nationwide campaigns to promote Los Angeles as a manufacturing base, especially in the late 1910s when it persuaded Firestone and Goodyear to open plants.[25] When reflecting on 'the healthy industrial condition of the city' in 1920, the *Los Angeles Times* listed construction of new facilities by the Los Angeles Union Terminal, United States Compressed Inner Tube Company and United Dry Cleaners, but gave special attention to construction of the Standard Film Laboratories in Hollywood, which represented a remarkable $200,000 investment by a consortium of Eastern financiers and would bring 'the latest inventions for the production of fine photographic work'.[26] In October 1921, for the first time, the Manufacturing Committee of the Chamber of Commerce undertook a tour of Goldwyn studios in Culver City, its members admitting that 'while they realized the motion picture industry leads in Los Angeles they did not know the full meaning of the business to the city's interest until making the tour of inspection'.[27] In that year, and in 1926, the American Bankers Association held its annual convention in Los Angeles, although it included no mention of the film industry in its annual reports.[28] The notable, and otherwise encyclopedic, three-volume account by William A. Spalding, *History and Reminiscences: Los Angeles City and County* (1931), was full of detail on the lives and achievements of Los Angeles civic and business leaders, not including people from the movie business, although it did acknowledge the film industry's contribution to the city's economy by means of impressive statistics.[29] On the other hand, in April 1928 the film studios prominently contributed to civic life when Fred Beetson of the MPPDA, Louis B. Mayer and Howard Strickling of MGM, other studio executives and Sid Grauman formed a committee with responsibility for a 'mammoth City Hall dedication parade' when the city's landmark government building was first opened.[30] In the following decade, a column in the *New York Times* regularly referred to Hollywood as 'the cinema capital' and tours of the movie studios were a highlight of US visits by royalty from Europe.[31]

While Hollywood cinema's box office and movie fan culture thrived, there was always disagreement as to whether it was an industry in the usual sense. David James has suggested that the classical

Workers in the film processing department at Metro-Goldwyn-Mayer, Culver City, 1939.

filmmaking of the studio era tended to erase the traces of production in films, presenting them as reified images only, almost the result of a magical process.[32] This may have been true of the studio system once it was substantially in place, especially after the coming of sound, but it was less true in the 1910s and '20s when the technological and organizational complexity of the studios' construction was everywhere visible in the press and in the studios' self-promotion. In Los Angeles the mechanics of the film industry were often front-page news and a sense of the labour behind the illusions of the silver screen was routine. For example, a *Los Angeles Times* report on the opening of the new Melrose Avenue studios of Famous Players-Lasky acknowledged that, 'While the magic of actual filmmaking is in progress with famous stars gesturing before the cameras to thrill millions, there will be a toilsome complement, too, of grime-covered men in overalls attending to their share of the tasks demanded by the screen.'[33]

The now-standard use of the term 'studio' to denote a place in which movies are made predates the film industry in Los Angeles and 'studio' was not the only term in use. A report on Thomas Edison in 1908 made a distinction between the 'vast plant' at Orange, New Jersey, where 4,500 people were employed, many in what we would now call post-production, and the 'studios' in the Bronx where the films were actually shot.[34] Once the film industry was established in Los Angeles, commentaries sometimes mocked it as just another of California's 'canning industries'.[35] Sometimes the term 'factory' was used in conjunction with other wording that softened it – for example, in headlines such as 'Studios: Fun Factory Builds New Quarters' or 'Palatial Studio Building to be the Most Complete Cinema Factory in Existence'.[36] The film studios were zoned light industrial and included in Los Angeles city and county assessments of industrial employment and output. William Johnston of *Motion Picture News* stressed in 1926:

> The least understood fact about the motion picture business is, strangely enough, the large and basic one that it is an industrial machine. From manufacturer to consumer it functions exactly like the industries of automobiles, clothing, food products, or of any manufactured product. The machine works with regular economic rules and under economic laws.[37]

As if hedging its bets, when the US Bureau of the Census introduced the designation 'industrial area' in 1929, figures for Los Angeles County were reported in two separate columns, one including and one excluding the film industry. Throughout the period, as Taylorist and Fordist principles were implemented to organize production (in so far as that was possible in an industry whose product was a commodity *and* an art), another term emerged that was second only to 'studio'.[38] That was 'city'.

One of the earliest reports on the building of a permanent studio in Los Angeles, in the *Los Angeles Times* in 1915, announced Mack Sennett's new Keystone company in Edendale with the headline 'New City For Movies To Be Built At Once'.[39] Thomas Ince's 'Ince-*ville*' had already pretended to be a bona fide town in 1911, a hyperbolic gesture trumped by the opening of 'Universal City' four years later. During the 1920s, the new Famous Players-Lasky studios were called 'a small industrial city exclusively for the films', while William Fox declared of the new Fox Hills studios in Westwood that 'The walled city is a dream come true'.[40] Descriptions emphasized that the studios were spacious and carefully laid out. Johnston of *Motion Picture News* continued:

In the earlier days of feature production there were many producers. To-day the business is largely consolidated and the large, modern studio plant is a complex affair of many departments and heavy current expense. The most recently built studio in Hollywood [First National] cost $2,000,000 and comprises twenty-three buildings with over 350,000 feet of floor space. In addition, there are bungalows, sheds, and minor buildings. A large administration building houses the production chiefs, the supervisors, directors, writers, business and casting offices. To the rear are the carpenters, metal and plaster shops, dressing rooms, property and wardrobe departments. Then the large stages themselves, and about them open spaces, with streets and a variety of structures for outdoor 'locations'. The streets are concrete paved. Forty-eight acres of land are utilized. The stages, measuring 240 by 135 feet, are equipped with great overhead tramways, for handling the arc and mercury vapor lights; the floors are heavy enough to support trucks. The electrical plant has space for twelve huge generators. Twenty billion candle-power is available, sufficient to supply a city of 10,000 population.[41]

At the meeting of the Society of Motion Picture Engineers in Hollywood in 1928, W. B. Cook of Kodascope Laboratories conveyed an even stronger sense of conscious design, implying something akin to a Fordist production line:

> Then, suppose we proceed to the studio or lot. First of all, the economical lay-out of that lot, the arrangement of the studio buildings, the laboratories, the projection rooms, and everything connected with the production of the picture depend on the engineer called a 'studio manager', but he had to have the essential knowledge of the civil engineer to lay it out.[42]

While Henry Ford was an acknowledged inspiration for the managerial reform and suburbanization of the film industry, Cook's language is as close as one gets to an explicit recognition of Ford's influence on the internal architecture of the studios. These were dwarfed by the heavy construction of Ford plants: the River Rouge site at Dearborn, Michigan, encompassed eight key buildings in its heyday, including the Foundry Building (1921), Glass Plant (1922), Cement Plant (1923),

Walt Disney Studios,
Burbank, *c.* 1941.

Power House (1925), Open Hearth Building (1925), Administration Building (1927), Tire Plant (1931) and Press Shop (1939). These contained a total of 1.9 square miles, or 1,200 acres, of floor space, and the plant included an elevated production line three-quarters of a mile long.[43] However, on a smaller scale, Los Angeles' film studios recapitulated Ford's practice of housing a specific function in each building, with an administration building typically fronting the street, shooting stages behind it and centrally located on the lot, technical buildings peripheral to them, and a back lot behind everything else, built on only with exterior sets. This was not as linear an arrangement as Ford's, but it was hierarchical and designed for efficient production.

The Walt Disney studios, which produced animated rather than live action films, and whose work process was therefore more linear, did adopt a Fordist design when it outgrew its original studios on Hyperion Avenue in Los Feliz and moved to Burbank in 1941. According to *Transactions of the Society of Motion Picture Engineers*, its new facility was 'a small city' equipped with many of the utilities 'with which modern cities are equipped', including streets, storm drains, sewers, an independent electricity supply, fire hydrants, a sprinkler system, private telephone exchange and public address system.[44] The arrangement of the studio's twenty buildings on 51 acres was 'a smooth and efficient . . . picture assembly line' from the Animation Building to the Inking and Painting Building, the Paint Laboratory and Process Laboratory, the Camera Building, the Cutting Building, and from there to the outside world.[45] In fact, what was described was far more carefully

138

planned than most modern cities in being designed on a *tabula rasa* as a streamlined and synthetic whole. At the new Disney studio, an innovative and custom-designed air conditioning system by GE permitted total 'control over atmospheric humidity' essential to the water-based paint animation process and to 'the simple need for comfort' of workers in buildings where the temperature was a constant 74 degrees.[46]

Disney's Burbank studio was exceptionally functional – indeed, arguably, disciplinary in a way that would later invite the critiques of Disneyland made by Baudrillard and others.[47] In the 1910s and '20s studios were rough around the edges, a fact evident in promotional films, some of which remain only in fragments and are just a few minutes long. Most of these consist of little more than a rapid succession of smiling movie stars' faces, identified with intertitles, and brief glimpses of studio buildings here and there. For example, *Universal Studios and Stars* (1912–27) shows Hoot Gibson, Laura La Plante and Reginald Denny, and a panning shot of Universal Pictures office buildings; *William Fox Studios and Stars* (1915–27) presents a brief establishing shot of the Fox 'West Coast Studios' accompanied by Tom Mix, Bessie Love and Fox himself; and *A Trip to Paramountown* (1922) records several casts and crews working on the set – for example, William C. De Mille directing Conrad Nagle in *Nice People* (1922) and Sam Wood directing Gloria Swanson in *Her Gilded Cage* (1922) – but these are spliced together in an arbitrary order with little sense of the studio lot as a whole.[48]

By contrast, a smaller number of films provide proper mappings. The earliest seems to be the six-minute long *Behind The Screen: A Tour of Universal Studios* (1915), which proceeds from the entrance to the scenarios department, make-up and costume department, properties room, a Middle Eastern street scene, and the studio cafeteria packed with happy workers and stars.[49] However, the fourteen-minute long *MGM Studio Tour* (1925) presents a more detailed anatomy – this time of 'Culver City, Calif. – The Metro-Goldwyn-Mayer Studios, a city within itself . . . its 45 buildings, including 14 big stages, . . . connected by 3 miles of paved streets' and its powerhouses, generators and substations 'sufficient to light a city of 8000 homes'.[50] The film begins with a high angle panning shot of almost 360 degrees, which establishes the scale and general arrangement of the studio buildings, before cutting to a point-of-view shot from a vehicle that enters through the main gate in the studio's famous neoclassical facade, before driving straight to the shooting stages at the centre of the lot. This is followed by footage of the script department, dressing rooms, costume department, carpenters' workshop, art department, properties room, camera repair shop, film laboratories, publicity department, studio hospital, restaurant and executive offices, where Louis B. Mayer and Irving Thalberg are working at their desks. This order does not precisely reproduce the geography of the buildings on the actual lot but the film's intertitles do explicitly point to the script department, which is the first we visit, and the executive offices, which are the last, as the two most important aspects of the business that frame the rest. Moreover, the film ends with cans of finished film being packed and loaded onto a truck for distribution to 'Metro Goldwyn Dist. Corp'n', 1014 Forbes Street, Pittsburgh'. With the clear suggestion that this is just one

MGM Studio Tour (1925).

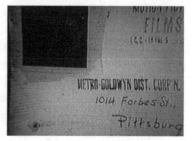

Table 1. Total value of assets of the major studios, and value and proportion of assets in the form of land, buildings and equipment in the United States, 1925–6, in millions of dollars[51]

Studio	Total assets	Land, buildings, and equipment	%	Land	Buildings and equipment
Famous Players-Lasky	76	32	42		
Loew's Inc.	79	38	48	14	24
Fox Film Corporation	26	8	31		
Universal	15	v	27	2 (land and buildings)	2 (equipment only)
Warner Bros. Pictures, Inc.	11	3	27	1	2
Total	207	85	41		

destination among many, the final shot shows the truck leaving through the back gate.[52]

Another interesting aspect of *MGM Studio Tour* is its presentation of a new shooting stage under construction, where we see a large scaffold surrounding a steel frame, roof beams being winched into place, and rows of men busily nailing down wooden battens for the floor. This makes explicit the engineering and labour that underpinned the studios' growth and implies pride in their contribution to Los Angeles' growth as well. As Table 1 shows, land, buildings and equipment accounted for between one-quarter and one-half of the total value of each of the major studios in the mid-1920s. The proportion was higher for companies such as Famous Players-Lasky and Loew's (MGM), which were already 'vertically integrated' – that is, owning significant nationwide chains of movie theatres as well as production facilities. The proportion was lower for Fox, Universal and Warner Bros, which were not yet vertically integrated and whose fixed assets were, therefore, more concentrated in Los Angeles.

As Table 2 shows, in the 1930s, when most of the majors were vertically integrated, the importance of land, buildings and equipment was even greater, between one- and two-thirds of the total value of

Table 2. Total value of assets of the major studios, and proportion of assets in the form of land, buildings, and equipment in the United States, 1933–4, in millions of dollars[53]

Studio	Total assets	Land, buildings, and equipment	%	Land	Buildings and equipment
Warner Bros. Pictures, Inc.	168	116	69	n/a	n/a
Paramount	150	85	57	n/a	n/a
MGM (Loew's Inc.)*	45 (131)	18 (92)	40 (70)	4 (26)	14 (66)
Fox Film Corporation (General Theaters Equipment, Inc.)*	45 (130)	11 n/a	24 n/a	n/a n/a	n/a n/a
RKO	68	52	76	20	32
Universal	13	8	62	4 (land and buildings)	4 (equipment only)
Columbia	8	2.5	31	0.5	2
Total	668	485.5	73	n/a	n/a

At this time, MGM and Fox Film Corporation were film production subsidiaries of Loew's Inc. and General Theaters Equipment, Inc., respectively. n/a = data not available.

each company. Not surprisingly, some of them dedicated subsidiaries to real estate management – for example, the Paramount Land Corporation and Fox Realty Corporation of California.[54] Some of the property they managed was in New York, where each had its corporate headquarters and some owned studios: Paramount and Fox, for example, built production facilities there for $2.5 million each in 1920.[55] Much of the rest of the property was movie theatre chains, and these were large investments: Fox Theater Corporation, for example, spent over $100 million on such properties from 1926 to 1929, including $26 million for the Poli chain of twenty theatres, two construction sites and three hotels in New England.[56]

But theatre chains were, by their nature, dispersed. Los Angeles was home to the studios' largest concentrations of land, buildings and equipment, and these were one of the most important ways in which the film industry made its presence felt. Los Angeles' phenomenal growth was evident in the remarkable expansion of the city's construction industry (see Table 3), which seemed to be immune to national economic downturns such as the 'sharp depression' of 1920–21.[57] The leading construction industry periodical, *Southwest Builder and Contractor*, noted optimistically that Los Angeles 'held third place among the cities of the United States' in building for September 1921, with a total value of contracts of $8.3 million, beaten only by New York's $35.6 million and Chicago's $12.3 million.[58] Annual investments in construction in Los Angeles, and the number of building permits issued, grew frantically until 1923 when they dipped slightly but remained high in national terms. In November 1925 Los Angeles set a new record of $8.6 million for the total value of buildings constructed in one month. In December

Table 3. Growth of the construction industry in Los Angeles, 1919–28[59]		
Year	Total investment in construction in millions of dollars	Total number of building permits
1919	28	13,000
1920	60	25,555
1921	82	37,000
1922	121	47,000
1923	200	62,548
1924	150	51,134
1925	152	44,000
1926	123	37,000
1927	123	37,655
1928	101	33,195

Table 4. Typical large investments in the construction of new industrial facilities in Los Angeles, 1916[60]

Film companies		Other companies	
New York Motion Picture Company	$500,000	American Tron Corporation	$750,000
Famous Players-Lasky Company	$175,000	American Can Company	$500,000
Keystone Film Company	$175,000	General Petroleum Company	$220,000
Universal Film Company	$150,000	Linde Air Products Company	$200,000
Balboa Amusement Producing Company	$130,000	Globe Grain and Milling Company	$150,000
David Horsley Studio	$60,000	California Food Product Company	$100,000
Pacific Film Company (laboratories)	$25,000	Firestone Tire and Rubber Company	$50,000
Selig Polyscope Company	$12,000	Southern California Fish Company	$25,000
Rolin Film Company	$6,000	Los Angeles Packing Company	$10,000
Vitagraph Film Company	$5,000	Burbank Canning Company	$10,000
Christie Film Company	$5,000	Hamilton Decorative Tile Company, Culver City	$5,000

1926 the previous twelve months were said to have seen a record annual investment of $112.8 million.[61] And these developments were part of a national construction boom: June 1928 'witnessed the greatest volume of construction work ever carried on in the United States during a single month'.[62]

As early as 1916, of a total of $13.75 million spent on construction by all Los Angeles industries, $1.2 million was invested by the motion picture business – or, put another way, within half a dozen years of first settling there, motion picture companies were contributing nearly 9 per

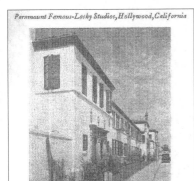

Paramount Famous-Lasky Chooses In-Vis-O

THE NEW studios of the Paramount Famous-Lasky Corporation are among the most modern in Hollywood. Quite naturally, they are screened with In-Vis-O Disappearing Roller Screens. Whether you are planning a huge institution, an elaborate mansion, or merely a simple cottage, you can insure your clients the same beauty, convenience, and ultimate economy. The coupon below will bring you full details.

IN-VIS-O Rolls up and down like a roller shade. Out of sight, out of the way, out of the weather when not in use. Permits full freedom of vision when in use. Ideal for casements or double-hung sash. Used in thousands of homes costing under $10,000.

Inviso
ROLLER SCREEN

Disappearing Roller Screen Company
1260 Temple Street   Los Angeles, California

16 pages of valuable technical data on screening modern windows. THIS COUPON WILL BRING YOUR COPY

IN-VIS-O Disappearing Roller Screen Company
1260 Temple St., Los Angeles

I shall be glad to receive for my files a copy of your manual on screening modern windows.

NAME..

ADDRESS...

Advertisement for In-Vis-O Disappearing Roller Screen Company, 'among the most modern in Hollywood', c. 1927.

cent of the total annual investment.[63] A *Los Angeles Times* review of expenditures on construction that year listed 60 manufacturing companies and eleven motion picture studios, making clear, as in Table 4, that film companies' investments were among the largest individually and as a group. The investment of the NYMPC, presumably for work on the Triangle studios in Culver City, was one of the three most significant.

In certain years, heavy industries spent exceptionally large amounts that the movie studios did not match – as in 1919, when the Goodyear Rubber Company announced a $6 million factory employing 35,000 people, and in 1923, when the Pan-American Petroleum Company built a refinery for $18 million near Los Angeles harbour and Shell built another for $10 million.[64] However, the film industry planted roots in many more low profile ways. *Southwest Builder and Contractor* carried numerous announcements of relatively mundane projects such as high schools, churches, bungalows and packing plants, among which were often listed film-related construction, for example a 'Moving Picture Plant' for the Art Studios Company at 219 East Broadway in Glendale, a 'Studio Building' for the Robertson-Cole Company at 780 North Gower Street in Hollywood, and a 'Picture Studio' at 3700 Temple Street for the Cosmosart Picture Art Corporation.[65] Many of these were contracted to important local architectural and construction firms such as the Milwaukee Building Company, Baker Iron Works and the Austin Company of California.[66] And stylish advertisements in *Pacific Coast Architect* sought to capitalize on specialist manufacturers' work for the movie business: in 1927 an advertisement for the In-Vis-O Disappearing Roller Screen Company of Los Angeles displayed the new studios of Paramount Famous-Lasky Corporation, which, because they were 'among the most modern in Hollywood', were declared to be 'quite naturally . . . screened in with In-Vis-O Disappearing Roller Screens'.[67] Others advertised heating systems and doors in similar ways.[68]

There is a paucity of reliable information on the construction of the very earliest studios about 1907 to 1910. Most were makeshift, adapting existing commercial premises – typically rented space at the back of street front properties. On his first visit in 1914, Charlie Chaplin was not very impressed by the Keystone studios in Edendale:

> It was an anomalous-looking place that could not make up its mind whether to be a humble residential district or a semi-industrial one. It had small lumber-yards and junk-yards, and abandoned-looking small farms on which were built one or two shaky wooden stores that fronted the road. After many enquiries I found myself opposite the Keystone Studio. It was a dilapidated affair with a green fence around it, one hundred and fifty feet square. The entrance to it was up a garden path through an old bunga-low – the whole place looked just as anomalous as Edendale itself. I stood gazing at it from the opposite end of the road, debating whether to go in or not.[69]

The opening of the first studios was sporadically reported in the press until 1915 when public attention increased. That year, the first temporary wooden structures at Keystone were replaced by 'modern

Office of the Keystone and Broncho Film Companies, 1712 Alessandro Street (now Glendale Boulevard), Edendale, 1912.

and attractive buildings of reinforced concrete, hollow tile and brick construction', designed by the local architect Harold Cross, and including an administration building, a cafeteria, and an open air stage measuring 60 by 160 feet (9,600 sq. ft), the whole place at a cost of $100,000, not including the price of the land.[70]

By the mid-1920s, according to one of its own press releases, the Keystone Studios lot was 'one of the largest on the Pacific Coast', extending over thirty acres, of which one acre was dominated by four stages comprising 66,640 square feet of useable space.[71] In addition, the lot contained: three office buildings, twelve women's and 24 men's dressing rooms, a planing mill, two property rooms, a plaster works, a paint shop, a carpenter's shop, a paper hanger's shop, a blacksmith's shop, two film laboratories (one for motion pictures and another for still photography), a garage housing fifteen automobiles, a restaurant, a screening room, a swimming pool 30 feet long and 16 feet wide, and living quarters for bears, cats and Teddy, the Wonder Dog. A range of technologies for the creation of cinematic illusions included three wind machines, three panoramas and a cyclorama, said to be 'the only one of its kind in any of the studios', which measured 25 feet high, 109 feet in diameter, 321 feet in circumference, and was surrounded by a platform 20 feet in width 'on which eight horses can race side by side'. Power was provided by a 500 horsepower generator 'large enough and powerful enough to furnish light and power for a town of 15,000 population'. One hundred and fifty people were employed on the studio's payroll with actors and production divided into four companies making 50 comedies per year.

Keystone's growth shows that the emergence of the film studios was quite sudden, intense and well publicized. As Janet Staiger has explained, in 1911, shortly before Inceville was founded, Ince first made films for NYMPC at a studio in Edendale that was 'a converted grocery store: one stage (without even a muslin overhang), a scene dock, a small lab and office, and a bungalow which served as a dressing room'.[72] By October 1915 *Moving Picture World* reported that Inceville had four stages totalling 104,100 square feet.[73] Then, early in 1916, he relocated to the studios of the new Triangle Film Corporation in Culver City, a venture he had formed with D. W. Griffith, Mack Sennett and the NYMPC.

In January 1916 the near completion of this 11.5-acre facility, the future home of MGM, was reported as evidence of 'the miraculous stride of the motion picture industry in Southern California', press reports emphasizing that its thirty new buildings were 'permanent'.[74] Five of eight planned shooting stages had been finished, each measuring about 8,000 square feet, while Inceville was kept in operation as an additional lot for shooting.[75] The Culver City facility already possessed many of the buildings presented in MGM *Studio Tour*, including the famous neoclassical administration building and facade, scenario, property, carpentry, plumbing and costume departments, a restaurant and 300 dressing rooms, the entire design and construction by the Milwaukee Building Company for $250,000.[76] Not only were the studios visually and technologically impressive, but their layout no doubt facilitated Ince's pioneering scientific management of film production. This included his development of the continuity script, a hierarchical division of labour, and the splitting of production into multiple film units, each headed by a director and assigned to one of the more or less identical shooting stages.

Following the break up of Triangle in 1917, Ince temporarily leased much smaller studios from Mack Sennett in Hollywood and the former Biograph studios on Pico and Georgia downtown, before commissioning his own eleven-acre facility in Culver City, which was begun in June 1918 and completed seven months later.[77] This $250,000 development, also by the Milwaukee Building Company, was expanded in the mid-1920s when Cecil B. De Mille took it over after Ince's premature death. Leasing 42 acres of adjacent undeveloped land, De Mille constructed two new stages, one of nearly 45,000 square feet (315 × 142 × 40 ft), which was described as 'the largest film stage in the world. Eclipsing in size the former record studio stage, one of the buildings in the great UFA studios in Berlin.'[78]

Developments in Hollywood were often on a smaller scale and less reported. Some of the most important studios, such as Fox and Vitagraph (later taken over by First National), established there in 1915 and 1916, but subsequent growth was dominated by a large number of companies who were initially relatively small. Metro studios, for example, completed three stage buildings, stars' dressing rooms and an administration building, on Romaine Street in January 1919.[79] That June, Hollywood Studios, Inc. began four shooting stages and other structures on fifteen acres at Santa Monica and Seward, with designs in the Spanish Revival style by the Milwaukee Building Company and worth $250,000.[80] And in September, on Santa Monica Boulevard,

The Newest of Southern California's Great Moving Picture Centers.

MAMMOTH FILM PLANT
IS NEAR COMPLETION.

New Quarter-million-dollar Motion Picture Establishment at Culver City Comprises Over Thirty Buildings and Covers Twelve-acre Site — Fronts Seven Hundred Feet on Washington Boulevard.

'Mammoth Film Plant
is Near Completion',
report on the Triangle
Film Corporation (later
MGM) studios, Culver
City, *Los Angeles Times*,
9 January 1916.

Jesse D. Hampton built three shooting stages totalling 14,400 square feet as well as administrative and technical buildings on ten acres, also for $250,000 – a property that would become home to United Artists.[81] In September 1920, on a site that would later house RKO, Robertson-Cole Studios Inc. contracted the Milwaukee Building Company (again) to build an administrative building and 1,300-foot-long neoclassical facade on thirteen acres on Gower Street together with eight stages, each 14,000 square feet.[82] Fred J. Balshofer built two stages on Gordon Street, each of 7,200 square feet, and the Studio Leasing Company announced plans to build ten studios at the intersection of Sunset and Santa Monica boulevards on Hollywood's eastern edge, effectively in Los Feliz.[83] That two of these – Hollywood Studios, Inc. and Studio Leasing Company – were rental studios rather than producing companies confirms the relatively high density, high overheads and high cost of land that companies and studios in Hollywood had to deal with. Indeed, the *Los Angeles Times* reported that 'production space is at a premium in Hollywood . . . thirty companies desirous of making pictures have been unable to do so'.[84]

The geographical evolution of the Fox Film Corporation demonstrates that pressures of space were encouraging some studios to move out of that district. In March 1923 Fox began a search for a new site and planning to redevelop its fifteen acres in Hollywood for apartments or commercial buildings. That autumn, it purchased the 108-acre site named Fox Hills in Westwood, where it set out to construct an El Dorado for the movie business on a scale that Hollywood could never have accommodated. Initially projecting costs of $2 million, the company stressed its plans to build 'a mammoth new studio which will surpass in size, modernity, and utility any motion-picture producing plant now in existence'.[85] It envisaged a range of ancillary facilities in which roominess was also a feature:

> a spacious restaurant . . . equipped with modern utensils and appliances similar to those in the best hotels . . . Dressing-rooms . . . with spacious sitting-rooms and separate for maids; toilet and bathrooms equipped with every convenience . . . A fully equipped gymnasium, tennis courts, and handball court . . . lounge, reading, writing, and rest rooms in which the artist may find comfort, recreation, and rest.[86]

Triangle had landscaped lawns and gardens in front of its shooting stages, and Robertson-Cole even had 'a garden for every star', but Fox Hills suggested the ambience of a spa or country retreat removed from the city altogether.[87] Development of the site took an unusually long five years, however, its construction being sporadic and overtaken by events. The coming of sound not only caused a reorganization of cinematic narrative and representational procedures, and a redoubling of its dependence on capital. It also brought a significant expansion of the size and presence of the film industry in Los Angeles as existing studios were overhauled and new ones opened.

In the spring of 1926 reports continued that Fox intended to vacate Hollywood once Fox Hills was completed, and the new lot was officially opened in August.[88] However, little was actually built on it other than some electrical plant, stables and large outdoor sets, while, by contrast, new construction was undertaken at the Hollywood site, including an administration building, wardrobe building, three stages and landscaped gardens, completed the following March.[89] Meanwhile, Fox first seriously committed to investing in sound with the formation of the Fox-Case Corporation in July 1926, deals with GE, RCA and Western Electric that winter, and trade previews of the first Fox films with sound in February 1927.

It was only after Fox's premiere of F. W. Murnau's ground-breaking sound feature *Sunrise* the following September, its rolling out of sound equipment across its movie theatre chain, and its decision to make only sound features in future, that the studio wholeheartedly commenced construction of permanent buildings, including the first stages, at Fox Hills.[90] Beginning in June 1928, both it and Fox studios in Hollywood were overhauled to cater for its proprietary Movietone sound system. At the older site, which was redeveloped for a modest half million dollars, destruction had to precede rebuilding:

Aerial photograph of the Twentieth Century Fox 'Fox Hills' studio, Westwood, looking north (Pico Boulevard runs east–west at bottom), *c.* 1930.

During the last week workmen have been razing the former publicity and casting offices and this work, together with dismantling of the adjacent gardens, will be completed Tuesday. The offices being torn down, together with the gardens, will provide a site 75 × 130 feet on which the new structure will rise.[91]

Investment in Fox Hills quickly dwarfed expectations, by the time of its opening in October 1928 gobbling up $3 million for land, $3 million for 25 new buildings, and $4 million for equipment. Four of the buildings were sound stages, just under 35,000 square feet each, by the Baker Iron Works. A report in the *Los Angeles Times* took the rhetoric of studio construction as city building to new heights:

> Into this walled city go 2,202,712 feet of lumber, 400,000 square feet of floor area, 2,100,000 feet of reinforcing steel, including thirty-six great trusses weighing ten tons each, 240,000 square feet of pavement for streets, 660 tons of cement, 32,000 tons of rock, 24,000 tons of sand, 51,200 pounds of nails, 45,000 feet of water and sewer pipe, and 6,200 feet of carpet.[92]

As if Fox executives and financiers had to convince not only the public but themselves in the face of such expenditure, and after the very recent Wall Street Crash, it was reported in 1930 that the so-called Fox Movietone City was 'the largest talking-picture studio in the world', costing $25 million and incorporating natural features such as a ravine and a park as well as 39 buildings:

> Administration, five sound stages, scenic studio, scenario studio, bungalows, test stage, music studio, dressing rooms, cutting rooms, generator plant, school, property receiving and rental buildings, mill, canvas shop, blacksmith and tin shop, wardrobe, plaster shop and yards, miniature shop, grip department, sound-device building, electric lamp docks, garage, police and fire department, gate and timekeepers' office, camera repair shop, publicity building, greenhouse, parking station, ten additional vaults, additional electric research, laboratory, and Café de Paris.[93]

With some temerity, 36 more buildings were planned for construction in 1931.

The Fox case is exemplary of the manner in which, in perhaps half a dozen years, the major studios, which were already embarked on massive infrastructural investment, were quickly obliged by the coming of sound to undergo another round of expansion and retooling before the Depression took hold. While the new studio's opening ceremony was a major public event, attended by 50,000 people and broadcast on the radio, it contributed to weakening the company's finances and to the ousting of William Fox in 1930. MGM also ramped up investment in response to exceptional growth and technological change. By 1925 it had become owner of the Culver City studios formerly of Triangle and Goldwyn, spending $5 million on six new sound stages and the remodelling of five existing ones.[94] In January 1926, First National announced plans to relocate from the Vitagraph studio in Hollywood to Burbank, where its initial 62-acre site was purchased from the Los Angeles Creamery Company at a cost of $1.5 million. There it intended to construct 40 buildings, including ten stages, each about 35,000 square feet. By 1930 Warner Bros, which shortly absorbed First National, had invested a total of $13 million.[95] Universal, which had at least 266 permanent buildings at Universal City by 1927, invested $1.5 million in three new sound stages, three projection rooms, laboratories, props, drapery, dressing rooms, garages and an arsenal.[96]

Through the late 1920s, major investments were also made by other studios in Hollywood. RKO spent $6 million on buildings and $3 million on equipment, while also purchasing a 500-acre ranch in the San Fernando Valley for locations.[97] Paramount paid $5 million for the former United Studios on Melrose Avenue, and $22 million for improvements, including a school for 70 children, and a further $2 million for 2,670 acres off Ventura Boulevard.[98] United Artists invested $2 million in studios on Santa Monica Boulevard and $700,000 in an additional Culver City lot.[99] Working on a smaller scale, Columbia Pictures, one of the so-called Poverty Row companies, built its first studio at Sunset and Gower Street on eight acres, with two stages about 40,000 square feet each, and two administration buildings, for a grand total of $250,000.[100] Pathé Studios, Tiffany Productions, Tec-Art Studios, Charlie Chaplin and Metropolitan Studios also made investments.[101] According to Harry E. Jones, president of the Hollywood Chamber of Commerce, the total value of buildings in Hollywood grew from $5 million in 1910 to $180 million twenty years later, with $100 million of that invested between 1926 and 1929. Perhaps with delusions of grandeur, Jones declared, 'Hollywood now ranks as the fourth building center of California, with only Los Angeles, San Francisco, and Oakland, all incorporated cities, exceeding the screen capital.'[102] James L. Davis, Real Estate Editor of the *Los Angeles Times*, estimating the grand total of investments in new studios required by the coming of sound to be $110 million, asserted that not only had the investment been beyond all expectations but it 'will permanently anchor the studios to this section for years to come'.[103]

Because of the Depression, there was a dramatic slowdown or stoppage in construction from 1931 through to 1935, at which point Paramount, Fox and United Artists added new buildings, though with more modest aims.[104] Larger projects were commenced by Warner Bros, which sought to add nine more stages to the nine it had in Burbank so that it would have 'the largest stage floor area in the industry'.[105] Disney began its high-tech facility nearby. United Artists built an additional sound stage on Santa Monica Boulevard, and NBC Radio City opened in Hollywood at Sunset and Vine, a facility that would play a major role in a later technological revolution as one of the region's first television centres in 1949.

Of all the buildings on the typical studio lot, the shooting stages were often the largest and most numerous. They were central to film production and, like the medium and the industry as a whole, they went through rapid and substantial change. However, because no handy inventory of shooting stages was produced and they have been little studied since, today one has to compile what evidence remains from various documentary, photographic and cartographic sources.[106] In the silent era, stages were notable for their lightweight and temporary character. The very first examples were essentially open-air timber plat-forms surrounded by timber posts over which were suspended sheets of muslin to diffuse the sunlight about twenty feet above the ground. These 'open' stages were to be found at all of the studios until at least 1919 – some of them small, as at the William Horsley and Francis Ford studios in Hollywood or Bronx studios in Edendale, and some, such as those at Universal, exceptionally large. Typically, larger studios also had some so-called 'closed' stages for shooting interior and exterior scenes indoors under artificial light. Sometimes referred to as 'light' and 'dark' stages, the two types stood side by side at Fairbanks, Brunton and Bulls-Eye studios in Hollywood, at Universal City, and at Mack Sennett's in Edendale, where there were three open stages and one closed.

Open stages at the
Famous Players-Lasky
studios, Hollywood,
late 1910s.

The lightweight character of the open stages was in keeping with the
dominant tendency in industrial construction in Los Angeles at this time.
In 1918 Arthur W. Kinney, Industrial Commissioner of the Los Angeles
Chamber of Commerce, pointed out that because of the favourable
climate, factory construction costs were typically 'about 60 per cent'
of what they would be in the East: 'Heavy construction and massive
foundations are here unnecessary. Water, steam, and gas pipes do not
have to be buried deeply and elaborate heating systems are unnecessary.
Factory operation here is not retarded by reason of frozen water mains
or through electrical disturbances caused by thunder storms.'[107]

No architectural solution better embodied the tension in the
movies between art and industry, aesthetics and engineering, than the
glass shooting stage, which became common at the larger studios. For
example, Selig Polyscope, on Alessandro Street in Edendale in 1911,
possessed a studio building 'entirely composed of glass', which was said
to be 'the largest of its kind in the world'.[108] When the Triangle studios
opened in Culver City in February 1916, the heart of the property was
occupied by five glass stages each 50 by 150 feet (i.e. 7,500 sq. ft) and
possessing concrete floors and steel frames with 'elaborate devices for the

regulation of light and shade'.[109] Thomas Ince had an even larger stage enclosed mostly in glass at Inceville, 360 by 160 feet (ie. 57,600 sq. ft), which was built some time before October 1915. And when he left Triangle for his own studios in Culver City in 1919, it had two glass stages each 90 by 180 feet (i.e. 16,200 sq. ft).[110] Hollywood Studios, Inc. built four stages in steel and glass with concrete floors in 1919; and in 1921, when the Lasky Studio made the urgent investment to add roofs to two muslin-topped 'California Studios' so as to allow them to stay in full production through the winter rainy season, it used glass, despite the considerable expense of $99,000 for one roof.[111] Reports in *Southwest Builder and Contractor* remarked that these buildings stood out because they were of a type new to Los Angeles, not simply utilitarian, open or semi-open to the elements, and made with newer materials such as steel and glass in contrast to brick, plaster and shingles.[112]

The 1910s witnessed a whirlwind of international experimentation with glass as a building material in combination with iron or steel.

Production still from *Show People* (King Vidor, 1928), showing Marion Davies (2nd from right) and other stars in Stage No.1 at MGM studios, Culver City.

While the film studios of Los Angeles are not usually thought of as hotbeds of the avant garde, their glass shooting stages, which were to be obliterated by the coming of sound about ten years after they were built, bear out Anton Pevsner's observation that many pioneering developments in early twentieth-century architecture took place in 'structures which were not architecture with a capital A'.[113] Paul Scheerbart, the German utopian thinker, proposed glass architecture as a revolutionary form that had the potential to break open Europe's stultifying cultural, social and political status quo on the eve of the First World War. In his manifesto on the power of glass architecture, Scheerbart passionately declared:

> The surface of the Earth would change greatly if brick architecture were everywhere displaced by glass architecture. It would be as though the Earth clad itself in jewelry of brilliants and enamel. The splendor is absolutely unimaginable. And we should then have on the Earth more exquisite things than the gardens of the Arabian Nights. Then we should have a paradise on Earth and would not need to gaze longingly at the paradise in the sky.[114]

Scheerbart's conviction inspired Bruno Taut's famous Glass Pavilion at the Deutscher Werkbund exhibition in Cologne in 1914, but their experimentation was only the latest crest in a long wave of innovation.

This could be traced back to the glass houses, known as 'orangeries', which became popular among the French aristocracy in the seventeenth century, but in the nineteenth century large-scale structures in glass on iron frames became widespread and were intended for public use.[115] This was evident in Paris, in the Passage de l'Opéra (1823) and other arcades and at the Jardin des Plantes (1833). In London, the Crystal Palace at the Great Exhibition of 1851 was exceptionally large, at 1,850 by 456 feet (843,600 sq. ft), while everyday structures such as St Pancras railway station had mostly glass roofs spanning two or three hundred feet.[116] In the United States, where glass and iron, and glass and steel, were quickly adopted, notable glass houses were installed at Golden Gate Park, San Francisco, in 1878 (67 ft high, 12,000 sq. ft) and at the New York Botanical Gardens in 1900 (90 ft high, 55,000 sq. ft), while Penn Station in New York, completed in 1910, had a glass and steel roof 341 feet long by 210 feet wide (71,610 sq. ft).[117]

Many of these structures were built as part of the City Beautiful movement, whose proponent, Ebenezer Howard, placed a large glass pavilion at the centre of his plans in *Garden Cities of Tomorrow* (1902).[118] His ideal found some favour in Los Angeles in the 1910s and '20s even if it was not much put into effect. By then, however, glass was no longer a material that simply filled the space of a window but, as Brent Richards has put it, was considered 'a "climatic envelope", a membrane that controlled the environment, encapsulated space, and mediated the light'.[119] These characteristics explained the appeal of glass in spaces intended for observation or display, including Monet's studios at Giverny and Thomas Edison's studios in Manhattan and the Bronx.[120] But such structures were more numerous and larger in Los Angeles where, because of their size and advanced engineering, the glass shooting stages of the movie studios compare not unfavourably in historical terms with the more well-known glass houses and railroad stations. This is especially true because, unlike most of them, stage buildings in glass did not contain pillars to support their roofs but allowed for unobstructed lines of sight inside. They embodied both an artistic devotion to natural light and a usefulness to Taylorist and Fordist production.

Hence, they can also be compared with what Reyner Banham characterized as 'a rapprochement between creative designers and pro-ductive industry' in early twentieth-century factory design.[121] In 1913 Hermann Muthesius of the Deutscher Werkbund, praising glass and iron architecture, argued for the engineer as an architect, against the decoration of *art nouveau* and *beaux arts* neoclassicism, but in favour of the 'overwhelming monumental power' of the leading industrial buildings of Germany and the United States.[122] From Peter Behrens's AEG Turbine Factory (1909) in Berlin, through the heyday of the Bauhaus (founded in 1919), modern architecture saw a gradual dis-pensing with solid walls in favour of a supporting steel skeleton – a trend Frank Lloyd Wright called an increasing 'etherealization'.[123] And the establishment of the production line system by Henry Ford also depended upon what Giancarlo Consonni has called 'the search for wide covered spaces liberated from weight-supporting features'.[124]

Such design principles found fertile ground in Southern Califor-nia. Timber frame houses had long been appreciated for the open-plan living they permitted in a warm and sunny climate.[125] Frame construc-tion was valued over traditional walls for its greater earthquake resistance.

And in commercial buildings, such as the supermarkets that became ubiquitous and increasingly large in the 1920s and '30s, it was favoured for ease of display and navigation in the shopping space.[126] Partly for these reasons, Southern California became known for a distinctively minimalist modern architecture made famous by the steel-framed Lovell House (1929) by the Austrian-born architect Richard Neutra, though Neutra acted as his own construction supervisor on that project because the construction industry at the time thought of steel as a material for industrial and commercial construction, especially skyscrapers, rather than for homes.[127]

Early shooting stages in Los Angeles had wood truss roofs on wood columns. Slightly later, steel truss roofs on steel columns were employed, as in the most spectacular glass stages at the Triangle studios. But the low-rise, low-profile, lightweight and open forms that the latter embodied, and which mediated the tensions between art and industry, the man-made and natural environments, were suddenly displaced – and in most cases literally demolished – when the studios were re-engineered for sound. Concrete now came to dominate, not only for floors but for walls, and a new importance of studio over location filming was evident that marked a shift in the relationship between filmmaking and the real world – indeed, a withdrawal from it. For Charlie Chaplin, sound made for 'a cold and serious industry . . . It was all very complicated and depressing.'[128] Press reports on studio construction, however, were more ambivalent. A report about Universal City in the *Los Angeles Times* carried a tinge of regret, explaining that a 'new arrangement of buildings and stages necessitates the clearance of many of the old buildings – dressing rooms of stars of bygone days, the property room with its accumulation of years'.[129] However, this was justified because the new buildings' air conditioning system would 'repel dust-laden air which is a menace to films in the process of developing and printing'.[130] Other reports accepted the new development as inevitable:

> Just as an infant progresses from crawling to walking and then to talking, the motion picture industry is in the throes of another transition as important as the evolution of silent drama from the prototype, the nickelodeon. Silent drama is about to be silenced forever, if one will note the activity of Fox, Metro-Goldwyn-Mayer, Warner Brothers, United Artists, Christie and Sennett.[131]

A slight hint of nostalgia was evident in the choice of words but the main intention was to assert the progressive modernization that sound required. The report noted that it called for 'the novel construction of sound stages, recording buildings, and other paraphernalia'.[132] At MGM, the Scofield-Twaits Company was employing 163 men, two steam shovels, five cranes and three concrete mixers to construct '[f]our hundred tons of structural steel, more than 1200 cubic yards of concrete, doors that weigh more than two tons each, and apparatus so delicate it can register the footsteps of a fly'.[133] The reader today, however, cannot help but be struck by the degree to which this effort was intended to create a cocoon:

> All buildings are constructed of concrete walls eight inches thick set upon vibrationless pillars which go down into the earth sixteen feet to strike sand. All buildings have floors sixteen inches deep, consisting first of a six-inch sand cushion, on which is set a slab of four-inch concrete and on this, on top of three inches of cork, is set a double wood floor, making the structure absolutely sound-proof. Within the eight-inch concrete walls are inner walls composed of acoustic plaster which absorbs sound so that echoes are not possible. A 'dead' space between the two walls insulates the interior from the outside world so far as any sound is concerned.[134]

Similar techniques were employed at all other studios, although soundproofing was more modest at smaller companies: at Columbia Pictures, for example, the Austin Company of California employed timber-framed stud-and-stucco construction padded with layers of fabric to minimize 'objectionable noises'.[135]

In one sense, the concrete sound stages, even more than glass shooting stages, embodied what Pevsner called the 'approval of the un-adorned surface' typical of modernist architecture.[136] In another sense, however, in leading to the standardization of entirely enclosed steel and concrete construction, the coming of sound required architects to diverge from the main trajectory of modern architecture in the US. From the late 1920s through the 1960s, this was a trajectory *away* from heavy structures and opaque surfaces towards steel frame and glass buildings for all sorts of purposes from bungalows to skyscrapers. Indeed, even Albert Kahn, who was sometimes critical of the European modernists' use of glass and sometimes reduced its use in his own designs to minimize

A new sound stage
under construction at
MGM studios, Culver
City, 6 August 1930.

heating costs caused by Detroit's harsh winters, continued to build with
skeletal steel and glass long after the Hollywood studios turned their
backs on the outside world, reaching a pinnacle in his Chrysler Corporation, Dodge Division, Half-ton Truck Plant, at Warren, Michigan
(1937).[137]

The studios did use glass for technical buildings in the 1930s:
in 1935 Warner Bros constructed a new 'crafts' building described as
'the largest studio building in existence' at 126,000 sq. ft, or 3.5 acres,

under a steel and glass roof.[138] But the trend towards concrete was overwhelming and accelerating. Speed of construction had always been a concern given the studios' pressurized finances and production schedules. In 1916 the NYMPC demanded of contractors at the Triangle studios that construction be 'rushed along in whirlwind order'.[139] Occasionally a long time would elapse from planning to completion, as at Fox Hills, but a rapid pace was more typical. Curiously reversing the usual process, at Fox and other studios, outdoor sets were built before indoor stages, craft shops and administration buildings, so that shooting could get underway and costs could be recouped as soon as possible.[140] Construction contracts frequently involved tight deadlines: the Austin Company built the 40 buildings of First National studios at Burbank in 74 working days and was contracted to build 22 buildings for Mack Sennett in Studio City in 100 days, but completed them in 75.[141] A contract agreed by RKO with Consolidated Steel Corporation of Los Angeles in November 1929 called for the construction of various buildings, including what was called 'the largest structure in the world exclusively devoted to the filming of talking pictures'.[142] It was stipulated that 'actual construction is scheduled to begin the 12th inst. and the completed building is to be ready for operation not later than midnight February 20 [1930]'.[143]

Where the architecture of shooting stages moved from the ethereal to enclosure from the outside world, their construction was marked by increasing compression of time. Prefabrication implied a further shift from artistry and craft towards industry and mechanical reproduction. The Crystal Palace in London had been innovative for its use of glass but also because it pioneered prefabricated construction and was taken down from its original site and relocated to Sydenham for more permanent use in 1854. This practice was also employed at Los Angeles film studios such as MGM, which moved stages to make room for new buildings, and at Famous Players-Lasky, which dismantled, moved and rebuilt three stages when it relocated from Sunset and Vine to Melrose Avenue.[144] With concrete, however, prefabrication became much more common, beginning when Albert Kahn and his brother Julius pioneered the world's leading method in the Packard Motor Car Company Building, no. 10, in Detroit in 1905.[145] With the coming of sound, concrete, which had previously been used only for floors in film studio buildings, and which had been cast *in situ*, became the dominant material for walls and roofs. This was aided by so-called 'tilt-up' construction, first used in California by Irving Gill in building houses in 1912, in which pre-cast concrete panels were simply tilted up from the ground and fitted to an awaiting steel frame.[146] In the aftermath of the Second World War, when it was valued for its low cost and low requirements in skill and manpower, tilt-up concrete construction became standard, although it was said to be especially typical of the West Coast.[147]

Four key trends are, therefore, identifiable in the construction of movie studios in Los Angeles from the late 1900s to the Second World War: larger lots, more buildings, larger stages and more of them, higher densities of buildings and filmmaking on each lot. After the coming of sound especially, one notes an increasingly explicit desire to manage space in rational ways: for example, it was planned that a series of stages at Fox Movietone would be arranged in a circle around a central collection of dressing rooms, carpentry, plaster and paint shops, and an 'immense control room' for sound recording equipment.[148] On the other hand, as a function of innovations in steel and concrete, stages for sound filming would be larger and more adaptable: the stage RKO commissioned in 1929, and which was said to be the largest in the world, cost $600,000 and measured 90 feet in height with a floor 500 by 200 feet (100,000 sq. ft); this was useable as one space or subdivided in four, and it included an overhead monorail system to allow for the efficient moving of sets.[149]

Such developments pointed to a diminishing interest in engaging cinematically with the real world outside the walls of the studio and even outside of the shooting stage. This was certainly a function of the fact that sound recording technology was not as reliable out of doors, at least in the early days. However, the sheer magnitude of infrastructural investment, and the fact that much of it preceded the coming of sound, suggests that it was not simply that sound technology forced filmmakers into the studio but that many preferred it there. Correspondence between the leading production designer, Cedric Gibbons, and executives at MGM in the mid-1930s indicates the extent to which shooting in the studio became the natural way of working even where shooting on location might have seemed simpler, not to mention more authentic.

In November 1936 Gibbons sent an internal memo to Al Lichtman, executive producer, analysing the studio's 'need for more stage space' to allow 'efficient operation in producing our pictures'.[150] Listing the total square footage of sound stages at various studios – MGM 306,000, Fox 260,000, Paramount 170,000, Warner Bros 608,000 – Gibbons noted:

The above is comparison only in actual stage space. It is no comparison of methods of operation. MGM's operation, because of our retake policy, requires 50% more stage space than any other producing company. Paramount attempts to overcome its stage space shortage by using its ranch, 30 miles distant, and other locations for entire productions. They are forced into this because their lot permits them no stage expansion. Warner Bros have, for the amount of their production, almost an ideal plant, and Fox are approaching it. Our stage space, for our production needs, is woefully inadequate.[151]

A ship set under construction for *Sea Hawk* (Michael Curtiz, 1940), in the recently built Stage 21 at Warner Bros, Burbank (the stage opened on 21 February 1940).

By 'retake policy', Gibbons meant to refer to the policy then recently introduced by Louis B. Mayer, as a way of speeding up production, which required that each film be shot quickly from its continuity script, previewed, and then a bare minimum of scenes needing improvement be re-shot. But more important is Gibbons's implication that a studio such as Paramount is hard done by having to shoot outdoors at a ranch, as if doing so could have no advantage or appeal. Gibbons makes clear that MGM has been tending in the opposite direction, explaining that '[a]n average production of today requires 30% more stage space than it did four years ago', partly because settings have increased in size but more because the number of settings per film has increased.[152] The scientific management of space is further evident in Gibbons's explanation of the overcrowding of sets at MGM and the minute calculations preoccupying a key figure more often thought of a maestro of style:

> At the present time of low production, we have the *Camille* sets and *After the Thin Man* sets standing for retakes. These two productions take up 25% of our stage space. *Maytime* will take 20% of our stage space. *Parnell*, because of Myrna Loy retakes, will take 20% of our total stage space. *Captains Courageous* will take 10%. The remaining 25% of stage space will be used for B pictures, shorts, and standing sets. Our percentage then of standing sets is totally inadequate to effect any material saving on costs. (It has been our experience that the most effective saving on set costs is the number of standing sets. This, of course, does not apply to costume pictures.) This is as it stands today. The exceedingly expensive juggling of this stage space will begin immediately other productions start.[153]

These comments reveal that 75 per cent of the stage space of even such a large studio as MGM could be taken up by what Gibbons characterizes as a bottleneck of just five productions. The comments also open a window on the manner in which the everyday life of the studio entailed balancing the fates of temporary and long-term man-made structures – that is, sets for a particular production and standing sets that could be used for years:

> There are certain kinds of setting which are continually used and re-used. To strike and re-erect these settings is a costly procedure.

Train sets, hotel suites, lobbies, offices, hotel dining rooms, etcetera, occur in all modern pictures. Any difference in style is unimportant and these sets can be used with no changes, except those required by specific action, indefinitely. A Pullman train set, for instance, at a building cost of $8000, after having been installed eight times at a cost of $1000 for each installation, costs MGM, for that set, $16000. The additional $8000 does not improve the set. It is simply spent on labor and repairs. Such sets should be erected on smaller stages and kept there permanently.[154]

A sense of the waste involved in studio-bound production is palpable in this description, although equally noticeable to our eyes today must surely be the metaphysical denial of reality entailed in the declaration that any train or hotel, lobby or office, is just like another. This is at odds with the specificity of place revealed in silent comedies made on location around Los Angeles and it stands as a historical contrast to the striking return to location filming that would mark film noir in the 1940s. Many films in both of those traditions were made on relatively low budgets by small and mobile casts and crews with a minimum of alteration of the given built environment. By contrast, Gibbons describes the comings and goings of people for each shoot as if he were describing the action in a costume melodrama (though at times too a Keystone comedy):

Sets will be built and assembled in the mill. They will be reassembled on the stage the night before they are shot. Carpenters will be falling over painters and painters will be delayed. Set dressers will be standing by awaiting the painters to clear out. The studio is kept open all night. The commissary is kept open; police are held on duty, and all the rest of the load that goes to keep the studio operating at night. The director will not see the set in time to familiarize himself with it. In consequence, changes will be asked for and discussions taking time directly from production will be had. This most certainly adds at least 25% to the cost of each set. This method will only be used because we have not sufficient stage space for efficient operation. This will increase the element of error 10 or 15%. And some sets will, in many instances, be put up and taken down a dozen times.[155]

The high logistical and financial cost of *not* using given locations outside the studio is not Gibbons's intended meaning but is evident nonetheless, foreshadowing the imperative that would face the studios after the Second World War, when new economic challenges and technologies increasingly favoured location filming. As a partial solution, although not one with much aesthetic appeal, Gibbons notes a recent increase in the use of rear projection to simulate real world environments inside the shooting stage. Joe Cohn, MGM's studio manager, to whom Gibbons sent a copy of his memo, acknowledged in reply that the studio had an especially acute shortage of stage space, and required more retakes, longer shooting schedules and a slower turnover of sets, precisely because of the kind of films that MGM prioritized – *Camille* (George Cukor, 1937), *Parnell* (John M. Stahl, 1937), *Captains Courageous* (Victor Fleming, 1937) and *Maytime* (Robert Z. Leonard, 1937) were all costume dramas and none was set in Los Angeles. While Gibbons's memo appears to have persuaded Lichtman to approve the construction of four new stages at MGM, before they could be built, another memo requested permission to destroy a submarine set from *Born to Dance* (Roy Del Ruth, 1936) and Ziegfeld's bedroom at Hastings and an Austrian restaurant from *The Great Ziegfeld* (Robert Z. Leonard, 1936). Joe Cohn noted simply, 'It is unfortunate that our lack of stage space makes it necessary to destroy these stock sets.'[156] This exchange demonstrates the normalization of artificiality that characterized Hollywood cinema at the height of the studio era, and which devalued its relationship with Los Angeles. It also suggests that production designers and studio managers were something like urban planners, responsible for deciding the fate of places, building and demolishing them, even showing a sense of attachment to them, and an ethical doubt about wiping them out.[157]

That Los Angeles was notable for its fanciful sets was well known. A particularly striking book of postcards, entitled *Making the Movies: A Peep into Filmland* (1920), included richly coloured pictures of a 'Realistic Street Scene of an Irish Village' at Vitagraph Studios, 'Chinatown' at United Studios, 'early California' at Christie Studios, 'a snow scene in tropical California' at Mack Sennett's, and Charlie Chaplin dancing with four 'wood nymphs'.[158] As the studios grew so did their reliance on sets, and not only those indoors. Exterior standing sets on the studios' back lots were less evidently pressurized for space than those which perplexed Gibbons, although pressure did increase with the coming of sound, which required that film units work in isolation where they had worked side by side in the silent days. Spread out over many acres, outdoor sets represented an incongruous multiplicity of historical and geographical locales, which rubbed shoulders in adjoining constructions of timber frame, canvas and stucco. In November 1923, for example, the newly commissioned studios at Fox Hills contained 'a Western street, New England street, Spanish street, old English street, French ruin street, two haciendas, detached farm houses [and] a reproduction of Johnstown, Pa. as it appeared in 1889 when a great flood swept it into oblivion'.[159] Construction of sets generated significant sales of building materials in Los Angeles and was a major source of employment among carpenters, joiners, plasterers, painters and electricians. In 1925 it was estimated that set construction cost as much as $10 million per year.[160]

Commentators often looked at the studios' outdoor sets as a means of understanding Los Angeles' distinctive architectural heterogeneity and mutation, sometimes anticipating the critiques of more recent historians by blaming the ubiquity of sets for the confusion of the real built environment.[161] Dr E. Debries's satirical, but not unaffectionate, study *Hollywood As It Really Is*, published in London and Zurich in 1930, emphasized the strangeness and disappointing lack of quality of the physical landscape to the foreign observer:

> Even to-day we can look in vain round Hollywood for things which the European would consider measures of the degree and value of culture . . . The broad and monotonous streets, drawn as with a ruler, ambitiously called boulevards, and made exclusively for motor traffic, are lined – often at distances of a quarter mile apart – by the most weird buildings. Red-tiled bungalows in the Spanish-Mexican style alternate with the plainest new American types of building. Banks like marble renaissance palaces stand alongside glaringly painted Dutch houses, near which real windmills are turning. The streets of Hollywood are as much a patchwork as the scenery in its studios, and more like an amusement park, and indeed the studios are often better built than the streets. Why should much trouble be taken? It never rains, and with the sun always burning with equal brightness, one can afford to build from the very slightest of materials.[162]

Debries passes judgement on what he sees as a preposterous re-cycling of European originals. But his perspective was shared by many locals. In *Los Angeles: Preface to a Master Plan* (1941), John Parke Young, a Los Angeles native and chair of the Department of Economics at Occidental College, suggested that the city's architectural mélange was a cultural weakness whose root cause was clear:

> Motion picture sets have undoubtedly confused architectural tastes. They may be blamed for many phenomena in this land-scape such as: half-timber English peasant cottages, French provincial and 'mission bell' type adobes, Arabian minarets, Georgian mansions on 50 by 120 foot lots with 'Mexican Ranchos' adjoining them on sites of the same size. A Cape Cod fisherman's hut (far from beach and fish) appears side by side with a realtor's field office seemingly built by Hopi Indians. These buildings are not constructed in adobe, nor in half timber or masonry as they

British journalists on a movie studio lot, probably 1920s.

appear to be, but are built of two by fours covered with black paper, chicken wire, and rittle plaster, or occasional brick veneer, and are crowned with a multitude of synthetically colored roofing materials . . . Whenever a civilization assumes loyalty and responsibility to its own historical moment and level, there is orderliness and clarity for consumers. Whenever it arbitrarily reduces the qualities and forms of production to the innumerably more primitive previous levels and stages, there spreads uncertainty and an unhealthy multiformity which bewilders the natural judgment.[163]

Young's castigation of his home town suggested a preference for modernist uniformity and, indeed, the *Preface for a Master Plan* was one of the most important urban planning documents before the Second World War to propose re-engineering the city with freeways and mass housing. But the recognition of the shaky standing and dubious value of movie sets did not only express mid-twentieth century technocracy. An article in the *Los Angeles Times* in 1916, entitled 'Why is a Movie Studio?', mocked the inadequacy and banality of early production facilities:

A movie studio is an aggregation of walls, floors, and actor people, painted in front and with scaffolding in the back. The outside of a movie studio looks like a class A baseball park, and the inside looks like the remnant sale of a Kansas cyclone . . . The furniture and wall paper houses would be almost unhappy if it were not for the movie studios, for aside from the scaffolding there is little to the studios but furniture and wall paper.[164]

Frank Lloyd Wright Sr, who came to Los Angeles in 1919 to build the famous Mayan-inspired Hollyhock House (1919–21) for the wealthy bohemian Aline Barnsdall, referred to Los Angeles as 'that desert of shallow effects', although, as Thomas Hines has wryly observed, the Hollyhock House was only a few blocks from Griffith's Babylonian palace set for *Intolerance* (1916), which was visible from the street because of its sheer size until it was demolished in 1922.[165] Architecture and set design also directly interacted. The interiors for Hal Roach's American Colonial style home were by set designer Harold Grieve and Cedric Gibbons designed a Spanish Revival style home for Louis B.

Mayer. Indeed, Gibbons even claimed that set design was more 'complicated' than the architecture of permanent buildings because what he called the 'motion picture architect' not only had to understand design and construction but light, colour, materials and human figures as they would appear when filmed by the camera.[166]

The peculiar liminality of the back lot was frequently further evident in stylistic similarities between movie sets and the studios' offices and workshops. Reports of planning and construction for First National, for example, emphasized a conjuncture of modernity and tradition while blurring the imagined and the real:

> The Old Spanish missions that have graced the King's highway [El Camino Real] since many years ago are the models for the new First National studios. On a site in Burbank, out a few miles from one of the oldest California missions and closer still to the Church of the Angels, California's aged and picturesque place of worship, will soon rise the most modern picture plant. Designed entirely along the old Spanish style, the buildings that will comprise these studios will rise and remain active in the Southland's valley for years to come. And within their walls may be filmed from time to time, photoplays symbolic of the olden Spanish regime of California, with the fiestas and the high-combed senoritas with their sparkling eyes and bright-colored mantillas.[167]

This slippage was supported by technical peculiarities that made movie sets un-categorizable as real in conventional terms. Building permits were neither required nor issued for the construction even of large sets, nor was the investment of capital and manpower that they represented recorded in tallies of construction in Los Angeles. And in order to minimize their tax burden at the end of each fiscal year (31 March), the studios would often deliberately time their production schedules so that they could strike standing sets that *were* considered as assets for *ad valorem* taxation by the State of California – a tactic they also pursued by frequently shipping film negatives out of state when the taxman came around.[168] These considerations illustrate that the Hollywood film industry tended towards a 'post-industrial' flexibility many years before that term became well known.

From time to time in their daily routines, many Los Angeles residents no doubt caught sight of movie sets without giving them much thought, although one can speculate on the ontological ramifications for those who did reflect. Georg Simmel, living and writing in Berlin in the 1900s, at a time of unprecedented modernization in that city, proposed that observation of the mutating urban landscape could create in the viewing subject a critical awareness of the nature of modernity and his or her place within it. Simmel's understanding of the city was partly shaped by a fascination with its representation in municipal exhibitions: the 1896 Berlin Trade Exhibition and the 1903 First German Municipal Exhibition in Dresden anticipated those at San Francisco and San Diego in 1915. But what struck Simmel about such displays was not only their commercial and nationalistic promotion but their tendency to recreate various older urban environments: 'Old Berlin' or 'Cairo' at Berlin, 'The Old City' in medieval and Renaissance styles at Dresden. These had the effect of making the actual city what David Frisby calls 'a late nineteenth-century Disneyland'.[169] Simmel's critique of modernity also drew him to the image of the ruin, whose anachronistic presence in the modern urban landscape revealed 'the great struggle between the will of the spirit and the necessity of nature' that drove all city growth.[170] Indeed, Simmel's description of the ruin now seems to evoke the deserted movie set: '[It] orders itself into the surrounding landscape without a break, growing together with it like tree and stone . . . It is the site of life from which life has departed . . . the fact that life with its wealth and its changes once dwelled here constitutes an immediately perceived presence.'[171]

Back lot sets of historical or exotic locations in Los Angeles surely functioned in analogous fashion, especially for those who worked in the studios and could see them everyday, but also for the general public who could often spy them from the street. The exterior set shared physical characteristics with the ruin: anachronistic architecture, incomplete structure, fragility and friability in its materials. And, although some sets were semi-permanent, most shared a temporal characteristic with the ruin: once they had been used to film such and such a fictional world, the shoot itself, and that world's action and time, became part of Los Angeles' past, and the set was liable to destruction at any moment.

The City as a Movie Studio

While the internal architecture of the movie studios was highly artificial, heterogeneous and mutable, many of their characteristics spilled out across the real city, making them simulacra of each other. The studios' most visible aspects were their often elaborate facades, which, like movie theatres and the homes of the stars, often displayed the synthetic qualities of movie sets. Those qualities were evident too in everyday events, on occasions when fire consumed studio buildings, and when the studios auctioned off props they no longer needed. But, above all, movies about the movies were the most widely disseminated form in which audiences, in Los Angeles and worldwide, were habituated to Hollywood's simulacral characteristics and participated in a qualitatively new blurring of the fictional and the real that had widespread currency in twentieth-century popular culture.

Inceville and Universal City sat in open countryside in the 1910s, and the earliest studios in Edendale and Hollywood were surrounded by waist- or head-height wooden fences. But as the studios grew they became increasingly enclosed, cutting themselves off as the city grew around them. At Fox Studios in Hollywood in 1916, for example, one of the glass shooting stages fronted onto the street so that it was theoretically possible to look in a window and see the stars in action. At Fox Hills in Westwood, the most important buildings were set back from the street and the perimeter was composed of chain link fence and walls. The studios were commercial premises, of course, but their enclosures were not only functional – they were unusually prominent in the landscape because of their decorative facades and the semi-magnetic attraction of the magical goings-on inside. If the studios were 'cities', they were more medieval than modern. They also anticipated the theme parks and gated communities critiqued in more recent histories of Southern California.[172]

The promotional film *Behind the Screen: A Tour of Universal Studios* (1915) opens with a slow panning shot from left to right of the long white stucco Spanish Revival style office buildings that were the public face of Universal City in Burbank. The dirt road outside, a castle-like tower behind, and the arid hills of the Cahuenga Pass in the distance evoke California's colonization by Spanish and Mexican priests and generals, while the United States flag flying at the gate lends the aura of an outpost on the American frontier. Historicism was one of the most typical characteristics of studio buildings – pared-down Gothic for Fox Hills, Spanish Revival for Christie Studios and Warner Bros in Burbank, Spanish Revival with a French Rococo twist for Paramount, English

cottage style for Chaplin and, later, streamlined moderne for RKO. Sometimes these aesthetics were evident only in the facade, sometimes in an elegant arrangement of office buildings at the front of the lot, and sometimes in a kind of City Beautiful planning of the whole.

Panoramic photograph of Universal City, Burbank, April 1916.

On Washington Boulevard in Culver City, described in 1915 as 'one of the most beautiful thoroughfares in Southern California', Triangle studios was known for its 200-foot long administration building fronted by Corinthian columns two storeys tall, and extended by an adjacent street-front wall, with matching pilasters and architrave, another 500 feet in length.[173] However, not only was the facing made of plaster and cement, rather than stone as Palladio would have wanted, but immediately behind the main gate was the most banal collection of workshops in wood, brick, concrete and steel, and cluttered by parked cars and telephone lines. This disjuncture, made clear in the film *MGM Studio Tour*, typified the grandiose facadism of studio architecture, outwardly ceremonial but mechanical inside.

All studio lots mixed manufacturing and creative activities, but most also sought to mask their function. Such masking was evident in other industries – as Bucci has explained, Albert Kahn's factory designs for Henry Ford relied on a distinction between 'functionalist essentials for the production departments, and echoes of classicism for the administration and the theorists'.[174] Los Angeles film studios were at least in step with, and perhaps ahead of, the trend. In 1916 the neoclassical facade at Triangle was said to be good for 'hiding the less attractive industrial structures inside'.[175] In 1919, at the nearby Ince studios, there was 'a complete departure in the design from even a semblance of a commercial institution. There will be the usual stages and work buildings, but these will be hidden from the view of the passerby along Washington Boulevard.' Instead, one would see only 'a great Colonial mansion', said to be modelled on George Washington's home, Mount Vernon, and separated from the street by a picturesque tree-studded lawn.[176] Also that year, the neoclassical administration building at Warner Bros on Sunset Boulevard was made in a relatively austere Doric style, but its 300-foot long portico could be colourfully adapted to carry giant advertisements for the latest feature films. In the promotional film *Warner Bros Studios and Stars* (1923–7) the building announces '*Don Juan* Now at Grauman's Egyptian', flanked by two large radio antennae then used for broadcasts by the studio's radio station KFWB.[177]

If the studio facade projected a heavenly aura, the studio gate was the eye of a needle only the privileged could pass through. In 1926, for example, *Bankers' Magazine* speculated on the venue of the American

The neoclassical facade of MGM studios, Culver City, in 1929, originally built for Triangle Film Corporation in 1916.

Bankers' Association conference (which was actually held in Los Angeles that year):

> The motion picture studios of Hollywood and other parts of Los Angeles now closed to the casual visitor, will be thrown open to bankers and their families if the ABA powers-that-be decide upon Los Angeles for the 1926 meeting. The studios and the stars are almost without exception the first things that visitors in Los Angeles wish to see, but admittance is, of necessity, strictly

Aerial photograph of Ince Studios, 9336 Washington Boulevard, Culver City, *c.* 1925.

limited. In the event of an ABA convention, however, the studios will open wide their doors upon the busy and colorful life within.[178]

The studio gate provided security and minimized disruptions to filming, but it also heightened the sense of exclusivity that surrounded the studios, their films, and the stars who passed in and out with ease. This equation was intensified by the coming of sound. In *Overland Monthly* in 1931, Charles Fletcher Scott sympathized with the tourist:

Of course you will want to see [the studios] . . . But now you are asking something very difficult. Ordinarily, since they have had to be so careful with the sound effects, it is hard to get into the studios while they are working. They are so strict you almost have to get a pass from Will Hayes [*sic*].[179]

A tongue-in-cheek article in the *Los Angeles Times* in 1939, entitled 'How Not To "Crash" a Studio', estimated that of approximately 1.7 million tourists who visited Los Angeles that year, half attempted to visit a movie studio and about 300,000 actually tried to enter. However, only 2 per cent succeeded because

a studio where perhaps $1000 to $5000 a minute is being spent can't drop everything and entertain visitors . . . Keeping out un-warranted sounds is a problem so serious that studio guides even observe visitors' shoes. A squeaky pair of shoes, even if you are a privileged visitor, severely limits the range of the rounds you'll be allowed to make.[180]

Occasionally the sanctity of studio walls was publicly overwhelmed in events that tally with Mike Davis's description of Los Angeles as an 'ecology of fear' given to natural disasters in which urbanization and the destruction of ecosystems play a major causal role.[181] Periodic floods had created havoc in the region since the mid-nineteenth century, the most disastrous caused by three days of torrential rain in February 1938, and resulting in 115 deaths and $50 million worth of property damage.[182] However, little harm appears to have been done to the studios, apart from a temporary interruption of shooting and the destruction of some exterior sets in the Hollywood Hills.[183] Much more threatening to the studios was fire, which was taken very seriously as a risk. Even from the earliest days when nearly everything was built in timber, every studio possessed a fireproof vault for storing film, usually quite small but tremendously important to the business, and always made in concrete and steel – materials whose industrial and commercial use had been pioneered in Chicago after the Great Fire of 1871, which destroyed nearly two-thirds of that city. The *Film Daily Year Book* indicates that in a typical year such as 1925, a large proportion of the studios' net worth was in the form of unreleased film negatives and positives: for example, $3 million of Fox's total assets of $26 million, $4 million of Universal's $15 million, and $17 million of Famous Players-Lasky's $76 million.[184]

At Triangle in Culver City in 1916, special attention was given to what was described as

> a large fireproof vault enclosed with masonry. To protect the films stored within from excessive heat as well as flames there has been devised an elaborate sprinkling system by which, in case of emergency, the four walls, floor, and roof of the entire structure may be literally enveloped in sheets of water.'[185]

At the new Famous Players-Lasky studios in Hollywood in 1923 it was explained that 'Fire, the great destroyer of motion picture film, will find no foothold here, for there will be no exposed wood in the building.'[186] At RKO's Hollywood studios in 1929 'fire hazards [were] minimized by the most modern type of sprinkler system'.[187] And in 1930, what had become Paramount Famous Players-Lasky constructed 'seven fireproof vaults with a capacity of approximately 13,000,000 feet of film' (about 9,000 hours).[188]

Nonetheless, a fire at the Hollywood studio of William Fox in November 1916 caused injuries to six firemen and $30,000 worth of damage. Although the studio's films escaped, firemen ventured that the fire, which started in an office, was encouraged by the 'inflammable nature' of buildings on the lot.[189] Forty thousand dollars' worth of damage was caused by a cigarette at C. L. Chester Productions in Hollywood in 1921, the fire spreading to the supposedly safe vaults where reels of film exploded into flames.[190] An unoccupied shooting stage at Metro studios was burned down in March 1926.[191] That August, Century Film Corporation lost $400,000 worth of buildings in a fire worsened by explosions of chemicals, films, gunpowder and blank cartridges that

Landmark of Film Industry Lies in Smoking Ruins

FLAMES RAZE FILM STUDIO

Century Corporation Building Burns and Other Structures in Hollywood Imperiled

'Flames Raze Film Studio', report on a fire at the Century Film Corporation studios, Hollywood, *Los Angeles Times*, 16 August 1926.

'rocked the neighborhood' and destroyed a number of homes.[192] In the summer of 1927, fire claimed a $200,000 stage at the De Mille studios in Culver City.[193] That December in Hollywood, thousands of persons seeing 'the skies illuminated' rushed to a blaze at Metropolitan Studios where quick-thinking film crew aided firefighters by turning spotlights on the buildings.[194] And in 1929, at Famous Players-Lasky, one of the worst fires in the industry's history claimed the life of a firefighter, although others managed to prevent the fire from 'wiping out the entire West Coast studio'.[195]

The boundaries between the fantastic space of the movie studio and the real world of the city outside were also blurred through the exchange of everyday objects between them. As early as July 1917, Strouse & Hull Auctioneers advertised 'Furniture, Rugs, Period Furnishings Consigned from Pasadena, Hollywood, and Wilshire homes, Manufacturer's Samples', and what was described as 'Another Large Consignment from Moving Picture Studios'.[196] The ad typified the manner in which objects from studios were listed routinely with those from real homes. That the items being sold by the studios were emerging from an imaginary realm was evident in auctioneers' assurances that they had 'been used for photographic purposes only, and absolutely in condition like new, not a scratch or mark on the pieces'.[197] In November 1920, following the bankruptcy of David Horsley's Motion Picture Studios, a liquidation sale was announced by auctioneer Charles Kemp. His colourful newspaper ad insisted that 'Covering 7 acres of ground, all buildings must be removed at once' together with a huge assortment of everyday studio equipment, including '50 wild animal skins', a Pierce Arrow Limousine, 20 park benches and '1001 other articles too numerous to mention'.[198] In November 1923 Kemp & Ball Auctioneers sold off the 'Studio, Equipment, Furniture, and Furnishings of the Former Francis Ford Studios', including everything from '14 Twin Broadside Winfield-Kerner Studio Lamps' and '15 Sections Globe-Wernicke Mahogany Sectional Bookcases' to 'a magnificent Italian Renaissance Library Table', 'Antique Mahogany Beds', a 'French Bevel Plate Wall Mirror' and a 'Baldwin Cabinet Grand Piano'.[199] The ad was careful to mention that the furniture had been 'used in the production of many noteworthy screen creations' and invited not only buyers from other studios and from businesses but 'the general public seeking furniture and furnishings for the home.'[200]

Auctions such as these seem to have been especially prevalent prior to the late 1920s when many studios were small and financially unstable. However, it is tempting to think that, in addition to being merely economic transactions, they created between movie studios and the outside world something like an alchemical 'interchanging of atoms', to borrow from Flann O'Brien's description of the relationship between bicycles and their riders in *The Third Policeman*. In that dark comic novel, repeated contact between an object and its owner leads each to become more like the other: policemen, when not riding their bicycles around the Irish countryside, spend their time 'leaning with one elbow on walls or standing propped by one foot on kerbstones', while two bicycles fall in love and disappear without a trace.[201] The bizarre qualities of movie studios' props, and their sale back and forth between studios and other owners, was underlined by a lengthy article

Property room at MGM studios, Culver City, 1930s.

in the *Los Angeles Times* in May 1925, which explained that, among their $2 million worth of antiques, paintings, decorative lights, and wall and floor coverings, the studios also owned

> [a]ll the odd, strange, and curious things of past centuries ... either in their original state or in replica. Suits of armor, worn before firing arms were invented; faro layouts, roulette, snow-shoes, grass skirts for South Sea Island dancers, deer heads, moose, machetes, wooden shoes, throne chairs, helmets, gibbets, uniforms of many nations, grain mortars, canopied beds, bolos and the like.[202]

Some of the properties had come from real homes for use in front of the camera:

> Sitting alongside of [a four-poster bed] in the property room are numerous genuine antiques which were purchased from the William Rockefeller homes on Fifth Avenue and Tarrytown, NY, following his death and the distribution of his estate. And with them are antiques purchased in cities of the Old World.[203]

One studio manager explained that people would often turn up at the studios looking to sell antiques for cash, one woman accepting a below-market price because by selling to a studio she felt that '[m]aybe some time, I can see them in plays'.[204] At the same time, most props owned by studios were reproductions, manufactured but resembling the real. At United Studios were found

> Quaint, hand-carved pieces made by the Chinese, replete with dragons and replicas of mysterious gods; Italian chests and tables delicately inlaid with rare woods; English pieces indicative of the Elizabethan and Jacobean periods, and strange carvings from the French and Spanish Renaissance . . . The studios, like so many of the art shops, are filled with imitation pieces done by old masters, which only the close student of carvings and furnishings can detect from the genuine.[205]

Although the writer was not alive to it, reports like these no doubt confirmed for those with a more avant garde perspective that the studios were bastions of kitsch. The contrivance and inauthenticity of filmed objects was evident to Charlie Chaplin in his memoir *Charlie Chaplin's Own Story* (1916), in which he recounted the uncanny experience of seeing himself become a prop in everyday life after *Dough and Dynamite* (1914), one of his first major successes:

> Within a week half the motion-picture houses in Los Angeles had the only original and genuine Charlie Chaplin parading up and down before them. I grew so accustomed to meeting myself in the street that I started in surprise every time I looked into a mirror without my make-up. Overnight, too, a thousand little figures of Charlie Chaplin in plaster sprang up and crowded the shop windows. I could not buy a tooth-brush without reaching over a counter packed with myself to do it.[206]

The qualitatively new blurring of the real and fictional also encompassed the way Hollywood and Los Angeles were described. In the press, 'Hollywood' was used increasingly to refer to the film industry despite the fact that the industry was dispersed across Los Angeles, which had absorbed the municipality of Hollywood in 1910. For example, an article in *Forum* magazine concerned 'Movieland, that place of studios and bungalows on the edge of Los Angeles, called Hollywood'; *Life* magazine contended that Los Angeles 'lives in the minds of its visitors as Hollywood's largest suburb'; and the *Los Angeles Times* described Hollywood as 'a City within a city'.[207] These descriptions were predicated on an increasingly ironic sense of Hollywood's grandiose self-image and its pretended autonomy from the metropolis of which it was really just one small part.

The blurring of real geography was most evident in the films themselves. Promotional films such as MGM *Studio Tour* described the inside of the studios in detail but ignored the growing city that surrounded them. This elision was also evident in narrative fiction films about the movie business, at least 25 of which were released prior to the coming of sound, and which often concerned a naïve young woman or man from a small town who migrates to seek movie stardom.[208] Such films almost never referred to 'Los Angeles' but frequently identified 'Hollywood' in intertitles and other textual cues. In perhaps the earliest example, the melodrama *The World's a Stage* (Colin Campbell, 1922), a caption explains of the starlet's experience that '[t]he first few months in Hollywood seem to Jo the fulfillment of all her dreams' as she has travelled to do a screen test from 'Mitchelltown – ten hours by rail from Hollywood – a spot that California boosters like to overlook'. In the satirical comedy *The Extra Girl* (F. Richard Jones, 1923), Sue (Mabel Normand) seeks to escape an arranged wedding in 'River Bend, Illinois' by sending a letter and photo, asking for a part, to the 'Golden State Film Co., Hollywood, Cal.'. Travelling by train, an intertitle announces her arrival in 'Hollywood, Any Day', where a madcap automobile chase with stunt men firing pistols is underway outside the movie studio (actually the Keystone lot in Edendale). In the romantic comedy *Show People* (King Vidor, 1928), an opening intertitle informs us that 'To hopeful hundreds there is a golden spot on the map called "HOLLYWOOD"'. The aspiring actress Peggy Pepper (Marion Davies) is chaperoned by her father along what is supposed to be Hollywood Boulevard, but is actually a composite of that street and Washington Boulevard in Culver City. A rapid, and vaguely Eisensteinian, montage from Peggy's point of view shows no fewer than twelve storefront signs in which the place is named, from the Hollywood Boat Shop to the Hollywood Public Market, eliciting Peggy's gleeful exclamation 'It *must be* Hollywood!' A second montage presents the front gate of Paramount Pictures, a driving pan of William Fox studios, the gable walls of First National Pictures, and the neoclassical facade of Goldwyn Studios in Culver City, consolidating for the viewer a misleading sense that 'Hollywood' was a unified place. Later,

Peggy Pepper (Marion Davies), aka Patricia Pepoire, the aspiring actress in *Show People* (King Vidor, 1928).

Hollywood's rising importance is driven home when the boss of the studio at which Peggy becomes a star considers business telegrams from New Orleans, Detroit and Philadelphia, each place name shown in close-up as if to suggest older cities are now subordinate to the new West Coast metropolis: *Hollywood; not Los Angeles.*

These films are typical of many movies about the movies in the 1920s and '30s that presented deliberate journeys to Hollywood by outsiders who are in search of opportunity, excitement and success. Most such films also associate the place with excessive artifice. At the beginning of the slapstick comedy *45 Minutes from Hollywood* (Fred Guiol, 1926) a rustic family of four eat sausages for supper until Mother opens a letter that demands mortgage arrears be paid in person at a Hollywood office. As father and son visit the movie colony partly for the mortgage but mainly for Mary Pickford and Gloria Swanson, they journey from small town 'Coyote Pass' by bicycle and train, their arrival announced by a spectacular effects shot of 'Hollywood – A Quiet Morning'. Aerial footage presents the real Hollywood Boulevard, looking west, on top of which are superimposed the crazy actions of acrobats, a cameraman, a director suspended from a crane, hot air balloons, airplanes, bursts of flame, crowds of people jumping to their deaths from the the tallest building, and actors duelling with swords on a nearby roof.

Because its streets are laden with traffic and pedestrians, and its two tallest structures – in actual fact, banks – stand proudly in a sea of commercial buildings and bungalows, *45 Minutes from Hollywood* makes clear, despite its mockery, that the real Hollywood is dynamic and on the rise.[209] But the line between the real and make-believe breaks down completely when father and son join a guided bus tour, filmed on location in Culver City, during which they catch glimpses of Theda Bara, the Bathing Beauties, and the Our Gang kids, who are presented in what are obviously cutaways to completely different places and times. Suddenly, everyone dismounts to watch a location shoot of a bank robbery, which turns out to be a real bank robbery by a gang pretending to be film actors so as not to draw attention to themselves. When the son naively strikes up a conversation with a female movie star who is actually a male crook in drag, a chase by police ensues whose filming exploits the straight length of the street with an extended leftward tracking shot, presumably from a vehicle-mounted camera, past shop fronts and parked cars. When the police fire their revolvers, the son exclaims,

'Hollywood – A Quiet Morning', the effects shot which introduces the legendary district in *45 Minutes from Hollywood* (Fred Guiol, 1926).

'I didn't know you used real bullets in the movies!', before the action shifts to mayhem in the 'Hollywood Hotel'.[210]

A recognition of Hollywood's contrivance had been evident much earlier in Chaplin's comedy short *Film Johnnie* (1914), in which the Tramp sneaks past the guard at the door of a movie studio, mooches around the busy open stages, and gets in the way of actors, directors and technicians.[211] However, *Film Johnnie* suggests a causal relationship between the simulation of movie sets and of human emotions, the awe-struck Tramp being unable to distinguish between his own feelings and the sentiments generated for the cameras. He interrupts a love scene to declare his affection for the woman, turns his anger on the cast and crew when she rejects him, fires wildly with a stage prop gun, and causes a fire to which real firefighters respond, before an actress tries to strangle him for meddling.

In *Show People*, the line between reality and fantasy is also blurred within the movie lot. Soon after arriving with her father, Peggy visits the studio cafeteria, which is filmed naturalistically but where she stands in line with extras dressed as rabbits, prophets, aristocrats and clowns. In her first day on the job, she unwittingly disrupts filming on the exterior set of a swimming pool with bathing beauties, a tragic melodrama about the suicide of an upper-class woman, and a slapstick food fight between a chef and Billy Boone, a rough diamond who is soon to be her sweetheart. Here again emotion seems changed by the studio. In her first bit part, Billy and the director play along with her story that she is an accomplished actress, rehearsing only briefly before telling her to enter the scene on a certain cue. When Peggy does so, she thinks she

185

is entering a serious drama but is soaked by spray from a soda fountain and driven to break down in tears, the director playing her real emotions for laughs. The action is comical because the viewer finds humour in the gap between reality and expectation, but it also exposes Hollywood as a place of synthetic feeling.

Although Peggy falls in love with Billy, her ascent to stardom as a serious actress depends upon a willed disavowal of her past as a comedienne and country bumpkin. Corrupted by luxury, she changes her name to Patricia Pepoire, shuns her former colleagues in slapstick, and agrees to marry the conceited swashbuckling hero with whom she stars in an overblown costume drama. Her redemption comes only when a cathartic food fight on her wedding day reawakens her love for Billy, of whom she declares, 'He was the only real person and now I've lost him!' Hence, character doubling points to dangers in the artificiality of movies. But the film's critique does not go too far: *Show People* is also one of the earliest films to include cameo appearances: John Gilbert, Charlie Chaplin and Elinor Glyn appear, as well as the director of *Show People*, King Vidor, pretending to direct a different film.

Doubling also features in *The Extra Girl* in which the would-be star Sue finds that the photo of herself she thought she had sent to the studio has been replaced with a much more beautiful one by a rival from her home town who wants to make sure she never comes back. As Sue is forced to take work in the studio's costume department, we are presented with everyday activities on the lot. On the set of an African adventure, Sue dimwittedly mistakes a real lion for a studio dog in a costume, letting the lion loose among the terrified cast and crew. But *The Extra Girl* is unusual in linking the trickery of the movie studio to a narrative of criminal fraud that takes place in the city outside. Although Los Angeles is not named, a conman called Hackett offers Sue's parents an investment opportunity in oil, well known to be one of the city's thriving industries. Panning shots of a real field of mud peppered with derricks, sheds and smokestacks starkly contrast both with the pastoral of Sue's native Illinois and the studio's make-believe. When Hackett runs off with her parents' life savings, Sue struggles violently with the crook to recover them, but then deserts Hollywood and the oilfields to return to Illinois with her parents, having learned the truth in two different ways.

This fairly moralistic representation echoes critiques of Hollywood that were widespread in the 1920s, particularly among Christian conservatives, for whom the industry's exploitation of young women was an outrage. In his book *Hollywood: The City of a Thousand Dreams, the Graveyard of a Thousand Hopes* (1928), Jack Richmond admitted that, while Los Angeles had many advantages, one of its key problems was '[c]onfidence men, go-getters, unscrupulous promoters and all sorts of babbitts [who] find here a lucrative field for their activities'.[212] Chief among these, the Hollywood film industry was governed by 'a very crude and primitive conception of the motives underlying human behavior' and its victims were 'mostly young, inexperienced girls who come there heedless of advice, with nothing in their possession save perhaps good looks and a good dose of optimism'.[213] Led astray 'body and soul' like butterflies attracted to 'the glare of film life . . . Some commit suicide, some end up serving jail terms, while others drag a miserable existence as best they can.'[214]

In *The World's a Stage*, which is comical in its opening sequences, the young actress, Jo, is less naive because she comes to the movies from an impoverished touring theatre company. There she has been struggling with her cantankerous thespian father to bring Shakespeare to rural California, but on arrival in Hollywood she encounters a stricter industrial regime: a studio guard requires her identification in keeping with 'company manager rules', and her director's first instruction is to 'Be on the set tomorrow at eight thirty, made up'. Hence, the industrialized artistry of the movies is contrasted with a romantic characterization of the theatre as a more humane, though obsolescent, mode of expression. This narrative of adjustment becomes increasingly melodramatic when Jo is mistreated in her marriage to Foster, a wealthy citrus grower who turns out to be an alcoholic. His death in a high-speed motoring accident on a stormy night leads to a conclusion that is in tune with the

Los Angeles movie studios and oil fields in *The Extra Girl* (F. Richard Jones, 1923).

moralism of Prohibition but also bleak and lightened only by a suggestion that Jo will have a romance with Brand, the benevolent industrialist who first encouraged her Hollywood career.

More interesting than this didacticism, however, is the inadvertent way in which the film's *mise en scène* suggests that Hollywood and its surroundings are a hotchpotch of spatial types. Both Brand and Foster own mansions that are sites of patriarchal authority, notable for their overbearing Victorian parlours, densely furnished with hardwood arm-chairs, dressers and desks, heavy carpets and curtains, tapestries and vases, ornate lampshades and silver service. Against this interior design, whose origin is neither Californian nor modern, the movie lot is appealingly informal, especially in a scene in which Jo, Foster and Brand eat at a luncheon trailer on an outdoor set, alongside an actor in Union Army uniform who is on a break from the American Civil War. Subsequently, the film moves almost seamlessly between studio sets, the back lot and locations, presenting gradations of real and imaginary space. Jo and Foster honeymoon at the 'Hotel Baghdad', whose Moorish arches and stucco walls were apparently filmed on location, and Jo performs on an Italian Renaissance set in fake moonlight and in what looks like a Victor-ian London tenement in torrential rain. Perhaps uniquely among films of the silent era, the movie set eventually becomes empowering for the actress, an intertitle explaining that '[a]fter the wreckage of her marriage, Jo carries on bravely, hiding her heartache behind a smile and finding an antidote for her sorrow in her exacting work before the camera.'

In *Show People*, settings and locations are used more deliberately to counterpoint the authenticity of slapstick and the falsity of costume drama. In an especially remarkable scene, Peggy is playing a damsel in distress on an outdoor set resembling the Austrian Tyrol when the shoot is rudely interrupted by Billy and his slapstick crew, who are filming a chase on a real dirt road nearby. The image of two film crews side by side provides what Walter Benjamin would have called a 'dialectical image' – a representation whose juxtaposition of elements creates in the viewer a revelatory understanding of history.[215] The flat expanse of the countryside, which the comedians exploit for laughs, contrasts with the vertical enclosure of the costume drama's set, two contiguous spaces constituting two divergent 'realities', Los Angeles and the made-up worlds scattered across it. And what is revealed is nostalgia for the comic short, whose narrative form and preference for locations were increasingly marginalized by studios and classical narrative. Indeed, the nostalgia is heightened by our knowledge that *Show People*, released in November 1928, was one of the very last films of the silent era.

The heterogeneity of the Los Angeles landscape is also apprehended when Peggy, driving to the studios one day, is filmed on location in a tracking shot, speeding past an alternating background of real, affluent suburban homes and undeveloped plots of land overgrown with grasses and weeds. This pattern became typical of the Los Angeles landscape in the 1920s when the headlong rush to suburban development gave rise to a patchwork quilt of residential and commercial buildings, rough ground, paved roads and dirt tracks. The sequence acts as another dialectical image and a reminder of Los Angeles' porous landscape.[216] Similar textural contrasts are also evident in scenes shot outdoors at MGM studios in Culver City. When Peggy explores the lot we are presented with three types of architecture in one frame, each emblematic of an era: a garden with palm trees in the foreground, a Spanish style studio building on the right, and one of the original (and clearly quite beautiful) glass and steel shooting stages commissioned by Thomas Ince for Triangle in 1915. *Show People* is one of the only moving pictures in which these early studio buildings appear, and they were demolished shortly after the film's completion.

The conclusion of *Show People* extends a narrative pattern in which the protagonist is disabused of an illusion: Peggy Pepper renounces her conceited alter ego Patricia Pepoire and reverts to her simpler, better life with Billy Boone. At the end of *Film Johnnie*, the Tramp is contemptuously dismissed but freed from his captivation by the movies; in *The Extra Girl*, Sue quits Hollywood altogether; and in *The World's a Stage*, Jo barely escapes death at her drunkard husband's hands. Only *45 Minutes from Hollywood* closes differently, in the middle of the comic mayhem caused by the crooks who pretend to be actors. All of these films establish connections between real-world deception and the trickery of movie-making, which they poke fun at and sometimes critique. And the deception central to their plots is linked to a shape-shifting built environment in the studio, Hollywood and Los Angeles.

Movies about the movies were only a portion of the total output of the Hollywood studio system, but they were especially symbolic because they portrayed the place in which the movies were made. The simulacral characteristics they displayed were also concentrated in the movie theatres where the films were shown. In Los Angeles, such buildings were especially well-represented across the landscape, and often more cutting edge in design than those in other American cities. Prioritizing artifice over reality in construction, they were also liminal spaces, wormholes, or shortcuts in space and time, from the studios to the city's streets and back.

By 1926 Los Angeles was already home to ten of the most important movie theatres in the US by box office gross, in comparison to New York's sixteen.[217] By 1931, Los Angeles' Broadway was reputed to have the largest concentration of movie theatres in the world, and they became ubiquitous as the city's centre of gravity migrated west to Hollywood and Westwood. Above and beyond routine screenings, David Karnes has explained, the owners of the most prominent theatres collaborated with studio publicity departments and the Los Angeles and Hollywood Chambers of Commerce to ensure that 'the premiere skillfully transferred Hollywood's potent "magic" from the screen to the street . . . Hollywood Boulevard on opening night resembled . . . a sprawling outdoor movie set.'[218] The entrances of the Egyptian Theater and the Chinese Theater, for example, were deliberately set back from the street so as to provide an extended threshold upon which crowds, stars and photographers could assemble, heightening the ceremony of movement from the outside world to the darkened auditorium inside. In the 1920s these entranceways were often a scene of fans' idolatry, disorder, and even scuffles with police, evidence that the emotional fabrication satirized in *Film Johnnie* and *Show People* actually did take place.

Indeed, Los Angeles led the way in defining the movie theatre as a new building type. S. Charles Lee, who had trained in the Beaux Arts tradition at the School of the Art Institute of Chicago, moved to Los Angeles in 1921 where he became the most celebrated, and surely the most prolific, specialist in the design of such structures, his work evolving gradually from historicism to International Style modernism but always with an idea of 'architecture as stage set', as Maggie Valentine has put it.[219] With The Tower theatre on Broadway (1926–7), in which Lee mixed French Renaissance, Spanish and Moorish influences, he created a new type of auditorium that contravened the City of Los Angeles' distinction in building permits between a theatre with a stage and balcony intended for live performance, on the one hand, and a nickelodeon without a stage or balcony intended for motion picture projection, on the other. When complete, The Tower elevated the motion picture theatre in physical scale and grandeur, a new direction extended by Lee in 186 other movie theatres, most of them in Southern California.

In 1927 the professional magazine *Pacific Coast Architect* made an explicit link between the artifice of films on the screen and that of the buildings in which they were shown. It argued that baroque styles were entirely appropriate because '[w]hen a building is erected frankly to amuse people, to divert them from serious work and worry, to house the representation of things which are not as they seem, its purposes can be most truly expressed by the false facade'.[220] However, much of Lee's later work is now celebrated for its pioneering adaptation of the International Style in streamlined moderne movie theatres of the 1930s and '40s, a dramatic functionalist turn in which Los Angeles also led international trends. In an essay of 1948, 'Influence of West Coast Designers on the Modern Theater', Lee argued that movie theatre architects in Los Angeles had a geographical advantage because '[b]eing close to the motion picture studios we are guided a great deal by what the producers, directors, cinematographers, and other creative artists say'.[221] However, such people no longer wanted theatres so ornamental that they overpowered the spectacle of the movies themselves. Instead, the theatre ought to be stripped down to its essential form and opened out to the view of potential customers passing in the street. This was a paramount concern given the shaping of everyday uses of the city by automobiles and plans for a freeway system that were already well advanced. As in Lee's streamlined moderne Academy Theater, Inglewood (1939), and Bay Theater, Pacific Palisades (1949), the theatre ought to be seductive but in a more modern way.[222]

Such movie theatres, like so many today, were frequently located in outlying districts and incorporated large areas for parking and passenger set-down. Richard Longstreth has suggested that Los Angeles movie theatres were tremendously influential in this respect, setting an example followed by supermarket chains such as Ralph's.[223] To a much greater extent than those, however, movie theatres advertised their presence in the urban landscape with large lettering and lights, which took up the building's whole surface, and minimalist sculptural shapes that enhanced its iconic value. As Valentine explains, this made the theatre marquee more prominent and more legible:

> What started as a simple sign announcing a film eventually enveloped the entire facade. The marquee of the Academy, for example, was a seventy-foot semicircle. At the Bruin Theatre [in Westwood], the horizontal band of light wrapped around the

corner and could be seen from all directions. Located in a busy theatre district, the Bruin was distinguished from its competition by a thousand square feet of coordinated light that blinked in harmony. The message constituted the architecture; the walls had virtually disappeared.[224]

This description indicates the dramatic evolution of movie theatre architecture in Los Angeles while suggesting a homology between it and the architecture of studio facades and sets. Homes of the stars too blurred the line between function and form, building and representing. Since the late nineteenth century, Los Angeles had emerged as the quintessence of a supposedly new and better suburban domesticity, proclaiming its comfort, beauty and open space. Hollywood was one of the most important suburban districts but, as the film industry grew, concentrations of stars' homes also arose in the Hollywood Hills, Beverly Hills, Brentwood and Malibu. In their architectural ornament and diversity, these buildings extended characteristics of the movie studios across Los Angeles in physical form and worldwide in photo shoots and feature stories about the ostensibly private spaces to which movie stars repaired once filming and the premiere were done.

In 1935 it was estimated that film industry personnel had a total of $150 million invested in private property in Los Angeles.[225] The biggest stars and producers commissioned grand homes in a myriad of styles in keeping with what Thomas Hines has called a characteristic 'conservative historicism': Italianate (Buster Keaton, Harold Lloyd), Spanish Revival (Louis B. Mayer, King Vidor, Spencer Tracy), English Tudor (Norma Shearer and Irving Thalberg), Regency (William Powell), Georgian (Joan Crawford), American Colonial (David O. Selznick), New England (James Cagney, Merle Oberon) and Greek Revival (Jack Warner).[226] Real estate, promotion and the production of images had been integrally linked in Hollywood since the French painter Paul de Longpré's famous picturesque house and gardens was opened to tourists in 1900. But their relationship intensified with a proliferation of postcards, pamphlets, advertisements and brochures, and through commercial tours of the homes of the stars that began in 1914.[227] And, in the early 1920s, Harry Chandler advertised the housing development known as 'Hollywoodland' with giant letters in the Hollywood Hills, all but four of which remain today as the legendary Hollywood sign.[228]

Exterior and interior
of Harold Lloyd's
'Greenacres' estate,
Benedict Canyon,
built 1926–9.

Certain homes of the stars achieved an exceptional reputation. For example, Harold Lloyd's sixteen-acre estate in Benedict Canyon, known as Greenacres (1926–9), was an Italianate villa clad in clay tiles and stucco and decorated with Renaissance-style carved wood ceilings and wall panels, furniture, tapestries and paintings.[229] Outside reflecting pools, richly planted borders, colonnades of trees and rambling creepers were maintained by sixteen gardeners, who also managed a 120-foot waterfall and a nine-hole golf course on the grounds. Greenacres clearly contrasted with the modest *mise en scène* that dominated most of Lloyd's films, while recapitulating the outward appearance of a movie set and the superabundance of the studios' props. As Simon Dixon has explained, photo shoots of movie stars' homes became an especially popular genre in *Photoplay* and other magazines, the star becoming 'a person condemned to live in a strange luxurious space somewhere between art and life'.[230] Here the distinction between on-screen and off-screen, inside and outside, substance and appearance, broke down almost completely.

Such photo shoots also often blurred the architectural past and present because so many stars opted for a historical vernacular style, at least until the late 1920s when modernism came into favour. This was especially evident in the vogue for Spanish Revival architecture, which movie stars were instrumental in fuelling. Eight years after the foundation of the Bauhaus and four years after the publication of Le Corbusier's *Vers une architecture*, the December 1927 edition of *Pacific Coast Architect* included a telling interview with Mary Pickford. Having previously addressed the Los Angeles Chamber of Commerce on architectural preservation, Pickford was described as a 'Student of Architecture' possessing 'ideas on the subject . . . besides the usual vague or cut-and-dried ones of the layman'.[231] She and her husband, Douglas Fairbanks, were developing a 2,500-acre estate near San Diego in 'the lordly and gracious manner of the old Spanish rancho'.[232] This would complement the couple's already highly celebrated Beverly Hills mansion, Pickfair, described by *Photoplay* as 'an exquisite replica of an 18th century domain' but really looking more like a cross between English Tudor and Arts and Crafts styles with French and Italian interiors.[233]

In *Pacific Coast Architect*, Pickford's interviewer recalled the 'primitive frontier' of early California history, 'whose climate and topography seemed fashioned by a higher wisdom' but whose significance Californians had been 'so blind in perceiving . . . so slow in taking it to ourselves as to a familiar garment, which it is'.[234] Now, thanks to the example set by Pickford and Fairbanks, Spanish-style architecture was recognized as 'something eminently suitable to the creation of a tradition of beauty, utility, and artistry for a growing land and people'.[235] Yet Pickford's interest in architecture also extended to 'the men and women who will live in the cities we are building today', which she criticized for their tendency towards 'a confused, cluttered collection of ridiculous contrasts'.[236] Without a hint of elitism, Pickford and the interviewer agreed that such contrasts were more characteristic of medium and lower income neighbourhoods than of wealthy ones where 'architectural control and conformity' prevailed.[237] Pickford hoped for an end to the congested modern urban landscape, speaking of a future in which traffic would run in tunnels, leaving the ground level for pedestrians and children's play.

This interest in a rather Corbusian urbanization seems to contradict the devotion to historical styles of which the Spanish Revival vogue was part, casting the latter in an even more conservative light. But such a contradiction was perhaps inevitable at that particular moment in time. The emergence of international modernism not only added to Los Angeles' architectural melange, challenging historicism in real buildings and in cinema's *mise en scène*; it also took place as the film industry made its decisive transition to sound.

Reality and appearance continued to be blurred despite the epochal shift. In his book *Los Angeles – City of Dreams* (1935), the newspaper columnist and occasional screenwriter Harry Carr described Hollywood as a 'City of Broken Hearts', which was at once 'an incredible fairyland and the most unhappy city in the world'.[238] A perceived discrepancy between Hollywood and Los Angeles had also become pervasive overseas:

> When I have registered in Europe as from Los Angeles, they have asked me what section of America the place was to be found. Register from Hollywood and three extra bell-hops grab your bags. A friend of mine went into an Irish lace factory and signed the visitors' register 'Hollywood' – and the entire force of girls stopped work.[239]

A wry article in the *Los Angeles Times* argued that, technically speaking, 'No Movie Was Ever Made in Hollywood' because the first film studio was founded there in 1911, one year after it was absorbed by Los Angeles.[240] Nonetheless, and despite the fact it did not have its own train station, port, airport or bank, a letter mailed to 'Hollywood, Cal.' from anywhere in the world would reach its destination. Indeed, Los Angeles had missed 'the biggest bet in the line of advertising that ever came its way when it permitted Hollywood, a town that isn't, to cop all the glory and prestige of the cinema, and failed to grab it off for itself – the city that swallowed the Hollywood that once was.'[241]

The overshadowing of 'Los Angeles' by 'Hollywood' prevailed until the late 1940s when the studio system began to disintegrate and references to 'Los Angeles' became much more frequent in cinema, especially in film noir. Between 1928 and the Second World War, however, at least 65 comedies, musicals and melodramas were released whose action was centred on movie studios, and in which the place name 'Hollywood' was endlessly repeated in dialogue, street signs, newspaper headlines and song lyrics. Twenty-five films included the place in their titles, such as *What Price Hollywood?* (George Cukor, 1932) and *Hollywood Hotel* (Busby Berkeley, 1937).[242] Others dealt with similar subjects, including *The Studio Murder Mystery* (Frank Tuttle, 1929) and *That's Right, You're Wrong* (David Butler, 1939), although the most famous was surely *A Star is Born*.[243] In most of these 'Hollywood' was the centre of attention although references to 'Los Angeles' were made and the real city did appear. This was especially true in the late 1930s when, according to newspaper reports, filmmaking outdoors, which had been 'an extremely difficult, if not almost impossible, feat', was facilitated by 'a perfected system' of sound recording by which film companies 'suddenly rediscovered' the advantages of location filming, although a fuller re-engagement with it would take place after the Second World War.[244]

The degree to which the coming of sound required a concentration of activity in the film studio is evident in *The Studio Murder Mystery*, a whodunit set at 'Eminent Pictures' and filmed entirely on the Paramount lot, in which an extramarital affair leads to the murder of the actor Dick Hardell (Fredric March). While many scenes matter-of-factly depict painted flats, lights, props and rehearsals, the exclusivity of the setting is underlined by shots of Paramount's studio gate and by the narrative importance of the guard who is the only person who may have seen the killer come or go. Because most of the settings are confined to the lot and the action unfolds in 24 hours, the film has a unity of time and space akin to that of a stage play by Agatha Christie. This is especially noticeable when the somewhat comical police call a conference of those involved on the floor of Stage 10, where a closed circle of translucent

Tony White (Neil Hamilton) and Blanche Hardell (Florence Eldridge) are questioned by Detective Dirk (Eugene Pallette) in a production still from *The Studio Murder Mystery* (Frank Tuttle, 1929).

screens has been readied for a production. Perhaps no movie about the movies excludes the real city more, the cordoning off of the crime scene reflecting that of filmmaking in the earliest days of sound. Indeed, in the only two settings outside the lot – interiors of a police station and a prison – it is clear that the settings are sets not only visually but acoustically.[245] At the same time, references to Hollywood in the dialogue are delivered with mild cynicism. When the studio boss explains he wants to protect his business by concealing the murder from the press, the police captain admits 'If someone is bumped off in any other town, they feature the murder. Out here, they'll feature Hollywood and pictures!'

In the comedy *Movie Crazy* (Clyde Bruckman, 1932), made three years later, the place described is also specifically 'Hollywood', although certain scenes are set in other parts of Los Angeles without naming them or it. Reworking the premise of *The Extra Girl*, the film begins with Harold Hall (Harold Lloyd), a star-struck youngster in 'Littleton, Kansas' who listens to radio news from 'Hollywood, the enchanted town'. Sending his photo to 'Planet Studio', he accidentally puts the picture of a much more handsome man in the envelope and is, therefore, invited on false pretences. Stepping off the train, he finds a location shoot in progress at the station where an actress is playing a Mexican señorita and he is immediately given work as an extra. Although the location is not identified, the sequence is shot at the La Grande terminal of the Santa Fe Railroad, which was just east of downtown Los Angeles but no longer exists. Filmed at some length, with depth of field and crane shots, it generates a tangible sense of place heightened by glimpses of real train tracks disappearing into the distance, advertisements for one of the 'Fred Harvey Dining Room' restaurants that used to be famous in Southern California, painted lettering on the neighbouring 'Savoy Auto Park Garage', and the image of a little girl playing on a platform quite apart from the action of the film. However, the vast majority of the subsequent narrative unfolds on a studio lot, as in *The Studio Murder Mystery* but with more exterior scenes. The adobe bungalows of writers and stars, their lawns and the streets they line, create the ambience of a tidy residential suburb but also outdoor shopping malls of recent times. The falsity of the architecture is underlined when Harold steps into a 'Public Telephone' booth but realizes it is just a prop when stage hands wheel it on to an indoor set with him still inside. There, dressed in a summer waistcoat and trousers, he finds himself surrounded by snowy

Harold Lloyd in
Movie Crazy (Clyde
Bruckman, 1932).

mountains, beside a building devastated by war, next to a large wooden
ship and the skyline of Manhattan.

Four years later again, the melodrama *Hollywood Boulevard* (Robert
Florey, 1936) is marked by an increased tension between location filming and characterization of Hollywood as a place apart. Concerning a
has-been silent film star, John Blakeford (John Halliday), who writes his
memoirs for a pulp magazine, a large part of the film was made at several
locations around Hollywood, Malibu and Santa Barbara. Its striking
credit sequence and opening montage rapidly cut between exterior
shots of Hollywood Boulevard, canted angles looking up at buildings
and down at pedestrians, splitting the screen in four, and populating it
with extra girls, movie cameras and streetlights, as well as local landmarks
– the Taft Building, The Broadway and the Brown Derby – accompanied
by a refreshing jazzy score. This strategy recalls the opening of *Show
People*, but with a greater modernist intensity in keeping with the experimental film *The Life and Death of 9413 – A Hollywood Extra* (1928),
which was co-directed by the director of *Hollywood Boulevard*, the French
expatriate Robert Florey.[246] The atmosphere is intensified by scenes
shot on location at Grauman's Chinese Theater, Sardi's cocktail bar and
the Coco Tree Café, which combine to create a wonderland of sophisticated urban living and design.[247] Some settings display simulacral
effects quite clearly. At the real Café Trocadero, Blakeford and the maître

d' are framed against the background of a trompe l'oeil painting of the roofs, domes and spires of Paris. But in another scene Blakeford dances at the 'Pago Pago' nightclub, meant to be somewhere in Hollywood but evidently a studio set with giant indoor palms and Polynesian decor of a kind in vogue in California throughout the 1930s and '40s. These degrees of contrivance are counterpointed with natural locations: at Malibu, the publisher, Winslow, redrafts Blakeford's memoirs while lounging on the beach; and at Santa Barbara, where Blakeford's alienated daughter lives, the coastline, mission and flower gardens provide a touristic antidote to Hollywood's urbane and sordid society.

Lead actor John Halliday and director Robert Florey (both standing) on location for *Hollywood Boulevard* (Paramount, 1936).

The musical *Hollywood Hotel* is likewise focused on the place but uses far less location filming. It also shows greater stylistic restraint, in keeping with the austerity and populism of the Depression and New Deal, which had a sobering impact on the style and moral tone of many films.[248] The opening song is knowing but promises a movie business accessible to all:

> Hooray for Hollywood!
> That screwy, ballyhooey Hollywood,
> Where any office boy or young mechanic
> Can be a panic, with just a good-looking pan.
> And any shop girl can be a top girl
> If she pleases the tired businessman.

This film too is predicated on a journey to Hollywood by an outsider. Ronnie Bowers (Dick Powell) is already an actor and small-time celebrity in St Louis, Missouri, where he begins the film at the airport, given a rousing send-off by well-wishers and a supposedly local big band, which is clearly, in fact, the real Benny Goodman and his Orchestra.

When Ronnie touches down on the West Coast, his Midwestern excitement is comically counterpointed with the jaded repartee of press photographers who ask Ronnie to 'Give us a big smile, one of those "Hello California, I'm tickled to death to be here!" smiles'. However, cynicism is set aside as Ronnie is driven through Hollywood, his gaze satiated by a now conventional montage of footage of the Brown Derby, the Café Trocadero, Sardi's, the Vendome and the Cocoanut Grove nightclubs, a sign for 'Personal Guides to Movie Stars' Homes', and the Hollywood Hotel itself. But most of these are presented only briefly. The film's exterior locations are outnumbered by scenes using rear projection and a couple of large sets evoking Los Angeles landscapes: a night-time song and dance number takes place on a darkened indoor set representing a streamlined moderne diner called 'Callahan's', which closely resembles Santa Monica's real restaurant of that name; and a large dayime exterior set represents a busy downtown intersection flanked by high-rise buildings. There, as if by chance, Ronnie bumps into Benny Goodman and his band, who have come to Los Angeles for a radio show.

In these films, the naming of Hollywood and places in it is not generally matched by a naming of Los Angeles or its other parts, although

Populism and streamline moderne style in *Hollywood Hotel* (Busby Berkeley, 1937).

in the late 1930s the city does feature more often. In the musical *That's Right, You're Wrong*, executives at the ailing 'Four Star Pictures' seek to turn around their business by persuading the big band leader Kay Kyser to bring his band from New York to make movies. Their arrival by train is cued by a sign on the wall of 'Los Angeles Union Station', the real building filmed on location. But a more insistent naming is evident in *Crashing Hollywood* (Lew Landers, 1938), a comedy about gangsters in the movies. At the beginning of the film, a likeable hoodlum, Herman, is released from prison and met by his moll, going straight to the nearest train station where he asks for 'two for Los Angeles, please . . . just one way'. Subsequent dialogue makes reference to 'Westlake Park', 'Brentwood', 'Malibu' and 'Long Beach', as well as 'Beverly Hills'. This distinguishes the film as one of a small group of 1930s crime dramas set in Los Angeles that anticipated film noir in naming or filming the real place: *Blood Money* (Rowland Brown, 1933), *Lady Killer* (Roy Del Ruth, 1933), *Murder in the Private Car* (Harry Beaumont, 1934) and *Bordertown* (Archie Mayo, 1935) did something similar to varying degrees.

Significantly, one of those movies about the movies in which Los Angeles is most consistently acknowledged is also one of the most dystopian. The opening credits of *A Star is Born* roll over a night-time view of Los Angeles and its lights. The would-be movie star Esther Blodgett (Janet Gaynor) leaves her rural roots for 'Hollywood . . . the beckoning El Dorado . . . Metropolis of make-believe in the California hills.' However, myth is counterbalanced by markers of real place: a montage signalling Esther's journey presents the arrival of a bus, a train and an airliner, each emblazoned with the words 'Los Angeles'; Esther is filmed on location seeing the sights at Grauman's Chinese Theater; Esther and her lover, the actor Norman Maine, attend the Academy Awards at the Biltmore Hotel downtown; they watch horse-racing at Santa Anita Park; and their private lives are reported in the 'Los Angeles Daily Press'. As in *Hollywood Boulevard*, Hollywood's narcissism is relieved by pastoral scenes: Esther and Maine honeymoon in the San Bernardino Mountains; their Spanish Revival home in Beverly Hills has immaculate lawns and a pond with swans; and a Malibu beach house provides romantic sunsets in the evening.

Perhaps the most significant element of the film's *mise en scène*, however, occurs when Esther and Maine stand on the terrace of the Café Trocadero after the premiere of the film that makes her a star. Their view of the city stretching to the horizon is one of the earliest cinematic perspectives on Los Angeles from the Hollywood Hills, inviting Esther to compare it to a 'wonderful . . . crazy quilt' and Maine to describe it as 'a carpet spread out' before her. The view is brief, and evidently shot on location, a cutaway from their dialogue, which was filmed in the studio. But it recognizes Los Angeles' distinctive character in a striking way and provides a foretaste of the renewed engagement with the real city that would be notable in film noir, where vistas from the Hollywood Hills would frequently express dislocation (see chapter Four).[249] In *A Star is Born*, Esther and Maine's vision is full of promise but will soon be overturned by Maine's heavy drinking and suicide – the melodramatic ingredients for which the film is renowned.

In the 1930s, however, dark melodramas were less common among movies about the movies than musicals and comedies. Those continued, but also modified, the character doubling of earlier narratives. In *Movie Crazy*, the actress playing the señorita at the train station is an egotistical star, but when Harold meets her later without her make-up he thinks she is a different woman and falls in love. In *Hollywood Hotel*, when Mona Marshall, the leading lady, falls ill, she is replaced by a lookalike waitress, their doubling intensified because the two actresses in the film were sisters in real life. In *Crashing Hollywood*, Herman collaborates with a screenwriter on a crime drama based on his experience as a hoodlum. But, comically, their film turns out to be an incriminating re-enactment of an actual bank robbery in which Herman was involved, and its star is the spitting image of the real gangster for whom Herman used to work, the latter showing up in Hollywood to exact revenge.

In playing with reality and illusion, such films showed less distrust of the movie business than silent-era predecessors like *The Extra Girl*, aiming to demonstrate the industry's democratic openness by championing the right to fame of any boy- or girl-next-door. By extension, the cameo role was even more common. In *Hollywood Boulevard*, Gary Cooper says hello to John Blakeford in a Hollywood bar; in *Hollywood Hotel*, Mona Marshall is interviewed by the real-life gossip columnist Louella Parsons; and three other columnists – Sheilah Graham, Erskine Johnson and Hedda Hopper – make appearances in *That's Right, You're Wrong*.

Views and signs of Hollywood and Los Angeles in *A Star is Born* (William Wellman, 1937).

In *Hollywood Hotel* and *That's Right, You're Wrong*, in fact, the real-life big band leaders Benny Goodman and Kay Kyser, respectively, appear in what are dramatic roles in one sense but extended cameos in another. This is especially true in the latter film, in which Kyser is the protagonist. As we watch Kyser and 'Kyser' simultaneously, the film conflates the person and the performer, seeking to democratize stardom and the artifice of the studio system. Relocating to Los Angeles reluctantly, Kyser and his band fear that Hollywood's affectation may ruin their popularity among the ordinary citizens of places like Toledo, Ohio, and Fort Wayne, Indiana, who are their greatest fans. Kyser is over-awed by the mansion in which the studio expects him to live, relaxing only when he finds that his grandma has also made the trip and is in the kitchen cooking. Self-deprecatingly, Kyser plays up the fact that he is short, bespectacled and goofy, with a heavy Southern drawl, especially when he is comically miscast as Romeo in a Venetian costume drama. And when one of the band dresses in a loud plaid jacket with a buttonhole and beret, Kyser only half-jokingly reproaches him, 'You're the last person I would have expected to go Hollywood!' Hence, the film attempts a humanizing counter-strategy to what were, by the late 1930s, well-established criticisms of the excessive artifice, wealth and vanity of the movie business and its stars.

A parallel recalibrating of the simulacral qualities of Hollywood cinema was evident in architecture and *mise en scène* at this time. Notwithstanding exemplary skyscrapers such as New York's Chrysler Building (1928–30) and Chicago's Board of Trade Building (1930), Los Angeles arguably became the most innovative (if not the most recognized) centre for modern architecture in the United States. This began not only with downtown skyscrapers, such as Walker and Eisen's United Artists Theater Building (1927) and Oviatt Building (1928), but with the Samuel-Novarro House in Hollywood (1928), by Lloyd Wright, and the Lovell House (1927–9) by Richard Neutra. These were followed by a nationwide lull in the early 1930s during which, with the exception of Neutra's Universal International Pictures Building at Hollywood and Vine (1931–2), the Depression held up a more widespread proliferation of modernism until the construction industry began to recover in and after 1935. Then followed new homes for Anna Sten (Santa Monica, 1934) and Josef von Sternberg (San Fernando Valley, 1935), both by Neutra, MGM's administrative Thalberg Building (1938), studios for RKO (1935), CBS (1937–8), NBC (1938–9) and Walt Disney

(1939–40), and the streamlined moderne movie theatres of S. Charles Lee. Indeed, David Gebhard and Henriette von Breton have described a veritable 'Los Angeles School', which also encompassed the design of department stores, supermarkets, gas stations and public buildings.[250] But movie-related commissions were especially prominent and symbolic, their International Style functionality appealing at a time of economic austerity and dovetailing with the film industry's turn towards sobriety after the perceived decadence of the silent era.

In cinematic *mise en scène*, the emergence of modernist architecture coincided with the coming of sound. A few silent films incorporated modernist design, but the vast majority were produced with the new technology.[251] In *Susan Lenox: Her Fall and Rise* (Robert Z. Leonard, 1931), *42nd Street* (Lloyd Bacon, 1933), *Anything Goes* (Lewis Milestone, 1936) and other films, this closely associated sound and modernist architecture in the public mind while ensuring that, in the first half of the 1930s, when few real modernist buildings were built, many *were* constructed in Los Angeles in the form of sets. One notable side-effect was that New York settings achieved an exceptional prevalence and iconic value.[252] As Donald Albrecht has suggested, the desires of Paramount, MGM and RKO to suggest 'undreamed-of possibilities and ways of life' led to a proliferation of modernist hotel lobbies, nightclubs, executive offices, skyscrapers and penthouses whose architectural models were mostly in Manhattan.[253] This created a high point in production design, but it was a technologically determined one, bound by the demands of sound recording and its encouragement of filmmaking indoors.

In movies about the movies, sound and modernist *mise en scène* were similarly intertwined: *Movie Crazy* is one of a very small number of sound films made by the silent-era star Harold Lloyd, whose character in the film fails a screen test because of his unsuitable voice; *Hollywood Boulevard* and *A Star is Born* concern aging stars who were in their prime in the days before sound; *Hollywood Hotel* and *That's Right, You're Wrong* foreground swing bands and the singing voice; and in *Crashing Hollywood* the studio hires Herman specifically to replicate the quickfire slang of hoodlums in the script and actors' intonations. Modernist *mise en scène* was also in those films' sets, and even in some of their locations: in *Movie Crazy*, Harold's screen test takes place on the only modernist set in the film, a smart art deco office; in *Hollywood Boulevard* and *Hollywood Hotel*, the slightly later streamlined moderne aesthetic is evident in hotels, restaurants and nightclubs, though slightly softened in the latter film in which there is also art nouveau. In *Crashing Hollywood* and *That's Right, You're Wrong*, executive offices are especially prominent. And in *A Star is Born*, the International Style makes several appearances in a film director's upscale apartment with plate glass windows and concrete spiral stairs, in the curved concrete wall and strip lights recessed in the ceiling of Maine's bedroom, in the rounded walnut desk and standard lamp in the office of the studio boss, and in the brash white walls, steel and glass of the studio's canteen. All of these films link modernist architecture with the comforts and contrivance of stardom, but with a new aesthetic of efficiency signifying the capitalist success of the studio system at its height.

The endings of these films also contrast with silent-era movies about the movies, which, though mostly light-hearted, were more uniformly critical of artifice. *The Studio Murder Mystery*, the earliest film, is also closest to the silent era morally because the killer turns out to be a director who has killed his leading man for having an affair with his wife, echoing the sex scandals that swept Hollywood in the early 1920s. In later films, however, the movie business is finally redeemed. In *Movie Crazy*, Harold wins a showdown with a rival for the love of the actress, getting the girl and a movie contract in one go. In *Hollywood Boulevard*, Blakeford retracts allegations in his memoirs to save the marriage of one of his former lovers and his own relationship with his daughter. *Hollywood Hotel*, *Crashing Hollywood* and *That's Right, You're Wrong* end with the successful integration of ordinary people in a movie business that is professional, beautiful and talented. Even *A Star is Born*, in which Maine kills himself in Malibu, sees Esther survive and persist with her new career. Hence, 'Hollywood' remains artificial, illusionistic and shape-shifting, but the trickery of the movies is gradually normalized and made safe.

It is ironic, then, that the coming of sound indirectly led to some prescient critiques of Hollywood and Los Angeles in book form. In his memoir, *Hollywood d'hier et d'aujourd'hui* (1947), Robert Florey, director of *Hollywood Boulevard*, documented a wave of migration by French filmmakers, actors and actresses in the early 1930s.[254] This occurred when Charles Boyer, Maurice Chevalier, Jacques Feyder, Ivan Noé and others came to work on sound films made by RKO, Warner Bros and MGM in French for Francophone markets, in an era before dubbing and subtitles.[255] A flourishing of French talent took place that is less well known than that of German exiles in Los Angeles at this time.[256]

The French migration was relatively short, declining when foreign-language production became uneconomical at the end of the decade; it involved fewer people, and they did not leave such a lasting impression on Hollywood films. But it created a spurt of insightful commentaries on Hollywood and Los Angeles at the height of the studio era that emphasized their outlandish built environments and social milieu.

Joseph Kessel was an adventurer and reporter for *France Soir*, the author of the novel *Belle du jour* (1928), which would inspire Luis Buñuel's later film, and of the novel upon which RKO based its First World War romance *The Woman I Love* (Anatole Litvak, 1937). In *Hollywood: Ville mirage* (1936), whose title evoked a contrast between reality and illusion, he saw a heightened opposition in Hollywood between private, interior and public, exterior space, where the former gave a false sense of comfort and the latter was ruled by automobiles:

> On these enchanted roads, one hears not a single child scream, not a single dog bark, one sees no figures in the windows. In these houses, where the indoor comfort is equal to the sumptuous simplicity of the facades, one does not feel life . . . in the largest thoroughfares, there are no passers-by. Automobiles drive, drive one after the other without stopping, like the rings in an endless chain, between deserted sidewalks. Everything is a long way, every-thing is cold, and everything fits automatically, as do beauty and grace, under a sky which seems to dissolve the blood of the newcomer with its mildness. This unreal and inhuman character, this ineffectual affectation, this game without warmth or life is stronger than all wealth and glamour. And it gives to Hollywood the monotony and vanity of an insubstantial dream.[257]

Nonetheless, Kessel proposed that Hollywood was supplanting older cities that were also global symbols but could not compete with its ability to transcend social and political divisions: 'Catholics have the Vatican. Muslims have Mecca. Communists, Moscow. Women, Paris. But for men and women of every nation, of all beliefs, in every part of the world, a city was born a quarter century ago, more fascinating and universal than any shrine. It is called Hollywood.'[258] Paying rela-tively little attention to Los Angeles as such, Kessel evoked Hollywood as a world unto itself, suggesting the compartmentalized nature of the region and that Hollywood was pre-eminent within it:

From the edges of Los Angeles, an immense built-up quadrilateral stretches towards the Pacific, its beaches and its shores. What matter the names which designate the different fragments of this geometric figure: Beverly Hills, Glendale, Santa Monica; there is no solution of continuity between these districts. Have they not blossomed around the stem like secondary roots spread and cling to the earth? Are they not governed by the same forms, the same laws, the same rhythm, the same enchantment? New communities will be able to arise, even more luxurious and more spacious, extending across orchards and prairies Hollywood's aspect of excess. It is the latter name alone which is known by the world, and carries all of its influence and prestige.[259]

This description typifies the tendency of many visitors to inflate Hollywood's reputation for ironic effect. The tendency is also evident in *Hollywood: La Mecque du cinéma* (1936) by the poet Blaise Cendrars, who came as a co-writer of Universal's California Gold Rush drama *Sutter's Gold* (James Cruze, 1936). Describing Hollywood as 'the youngest capital city in the world and the capital of youth', Cendrars satirically noted that passengers landing from ships at San Pedro launch themselves in a headlong race to see 'the latest wonder of the world: the factory of illusions . . . the mysterious city of studios, whose doors are hermetically sealed and whose windows are enigmatically bleached'.[260] Cendrars' account was also concerned with the exceptional economic inequality he saw in Hollywood, where a star could make $10,000 in twenty-four hours. While the 'utopia' of hire purchase schemes dominated its commercial life, its Mexican and Chinese minorities were confined to menial work.[261]

Moreover, Cendrars linked Hollywood's social inequality to what he characterized as its distinctive hedonism, heterogeneity, and spectacle:

> Streets. Streets. Streets. The disorder there is such, and life there is so intense, colourful, and extravagant that it resembles nothing else on earth. Hollywood, which owes something all at once to Cannes, Coney Island, and Montparnasse, is a marvellous improvisation, a continuous and constant spectacle of spontaneity, presented day and night in the street, in front of an American landscape that provides it with a backdrop.[262]

He recounted with frustration that, one night, he was arrested by police while walking home to the Roosevelt Hotel on Hollywood Boulevard because they mistook him for a vagrant. The experience led him to remark that underneath its superficial liveliness Hollywood was 'a forbidden city, and under surveillance to the point where every man who does not move around in an automobile is a suspect'.[263]

Like Kessel, Cendrars here closely anticipates Jean Baudrillard's *America* (1984), in which Los Angeles is new, distant, pretentious, false, spectacular and somewhat sad:

> Dawn in Los Angeles, coming up over the Hollywood Hills. You get the distinct feeling that the sun only touched Europe lightly on its way to rising properly here, above this plane geometry where its light is still that brand new light of the edge of the desert. Long-stemmed palm trees, swaying in front of the electronic billboard, the only vertical signs in this two-dimensional world.[264]

However, the earlier accounts see Los Angeles as a unique place, not yet a symptom of a larger, all-pervasive condition, which Baudrillard would call 'postmodern' and in which Los Angeles would be merely one of the most striking manifestations of simulacral tendencies in Western society in general. In the 1930s Kessel, in particular, retained a clear sense of the utopian potential of mass culture, concluding his book by forgiving, even eulogizing, Hollywood cinema, as a vehicle of 'communal spirit':

> Illusory beauty, illusory paradise, illusory! A large dazzling wheel turns Hollywood, illuminating the world with no more warmth or reality than a fireworks display, delighting and comforting millions of unhappy big children. Sometimes, she throws out a miraculous flash. A good film ascends to the firmament. And it is because film has the capacity to bring back to life this shared faith, and is the only art capable today of doing so, that Hollywood, with its perfect studios, its incomparable workforce, its unlimited resources, its hundreds of writers, musicians, and painters full of talent, would seem chosen for this mission, it is because of all that that I find myself, in these chapters, to have been perhaps too hard on the city of mirages. This is not contempt, nor hate. But rather, in truth, disappointed love.[265]

This utopian note aligns Kessel's perspective with that of the leftist Popular Front, which animated European and American film-making during the mid-twentieth century but came under attack from fascism in Europe and conservatives in the United States. In the late 1940s the latter picked Los Angeles and Hollywood as sites for a titanic ideological struggle in the Cold War that was soon to come. This struggle played itself out with a special intensity in the Hollywood strikes and in film noirs with Los Angeles settings. Those phenomena, and their relationship, will form the focus of chapter Four.

four

Geopolitical Pressure Point

Everybody knows that Hollywood, Cal., is the greatest city
in the United States and Los Angeles, Chicago, New York,
and Washington are its suburbs.
'Hollywood's First Half-Century', *Los Angeles Times*, 13 November
1953[1]

After the Second World War the utopian aspirations that had driven the
meteoric rise of the Hollywood studio system seemed intact initially,
but then suddenly liable to collapse. With weekly attendances at movie
theatres averaging a record 100 million and a total box office gross of
$1.7 billion, 1946 became the industry's most successful year. Quickly,
however, the industry was shaken by the anti-trust 'Paramount decrees'
of 1948 in which the US Supreme Court ordered the studios to sell off
their chains of movie theatres, throwing their long-standing revenue
streams into doubt by breaking their vertical integration. Ownership of
televisions nationally increased from 14,000 in 1946 to 32 million eight
years later, accelerating a decline in annual box office gross, which fell
to $1.3 billion in 1956, and in the studios' profits, which dropped from
$121 million in 1946 to just $32 million ten years later.[2] For the Hollywood moguls, a dream they once had was threatened by industrial unrest,
government regulation and new technology. For workers, the film industry was an increasingly insecure and often hostile place in which to
make a living. And for those on the political right, many of whom had
always objected to Hollywood cinema and the industry on moral and
political grounds, it came to appear as a Communist command post on
American soil.

In a lengthy and spirited defence of the Hollywood film industry in the *New York Times*, in April 1950, Dore Schary, then Head of Production at MGM, contended that many Americans viewed Hollywood as a 'modern Babylon', full of 'white Rolls Royces', 'blonde secretaries', and 'houses full of bear rugs littered with unclad women'.[3] Americans loved Hollywood for its stars on the silver screen but they viewed the real place with mistrust and did not understand it:

> This combination of interest and repulsion inspires attack from every angle. We are accused of being a reactionary town, interested only in a buck; of being enormously extravagant, and of being Communist-controlled. We are attacked for not using the screen to say something and we are accused of being propagandists and of filling the screen with 'messages'. We are viewed as a town tortured by labor strife, and we are told that *of course* there is no labor problem in Hollywood because we have corrupted and suborned the labor leaders. We are called insular, cut off from and oblivious of the world, and we are regarded as a transient community which has never developed any roots.[4]

The encircling of Hollywood by threatening voices stood in contrast to the continuing rise of Los Angeles, the city in which Hollywood was ambivalently based. Like Hollywood, Los Angeles emerged strongly from the Second World War, growing as a result of prioritized investment by the federal government, which had begun under the New Deal and continued with the expansion of the city's vibrant defence, aircraft and automobile industries, and its maritime trade. In 1940 Los Angeles was the fifth most populous city in the United States with 1.5 million people, behind Detroit, Philadelphia, Chicago and New York, the latter having a population of 7.4 million.[5] By 1950 Los Angeles was the fourth most populous. By 1960, when the city had a population of 2.5 million, it was third, exceeded only by Chicago and New York, although it had twice the land mass of Chicago and one and a half times that of New York. And when one considered the population of Los Angeles as a sprawling five-county region, comprising Los Angeles, Riverside, Ventura, San Bernardino and Orange counties, it had a population of 7.75 million putting it in competition with the Big Apple itself. For the majority white population at least, the postwar era was one of economic boom and relatively stable politics, critiqued by Mike Davis as an unsustainable 'Endless Summer'.[6] In that era, the city consolidated its image as an affluent, sunny, healthy and, especially, brash bastion of the American Dream, where life was supposedly enhanced by increasingly abundant domestic goods, shopping malls, freeways, television and Disneyland. At the same time, however, as Edward Soja and Allen J. Scott have argued, one of the main engines of this 'surge of growth' was a series of 'Pacific wars' (Japan, Korea and, later, Vietnam) 'that propelled the Los Angeles region into a primary position within what President Dwight D. Eisenhower would call, warning the people of its power, the American "military-industrial complex"'.[7] According to the United Nations, it was in 1955 that Los Angeles first became one of the top ten largest urban agglomerations in the world, a distinction it would continue to hold until the twenty-first century.[8]

Given these developments, postwar Los Angeles became what might be called a 'geopolitical pressure point', to adapt Fredric Jameson's description of the 'geopolitical aesthetic' of American conspiracy thrillers such as *The Parallax View* (Alan J. Pakula, 1974).[9] Where the exceptional complexity, and partial indecipherability, of narrative space in such films articulated the emergence of late capitalism and postmodernism, film noir emblematized, and sometimes critiqued, earlier paradigms.[10] One of the most remarkable trends in film noir was an increasing proliferation of images and narratives of Los Angeles in which the place was explicitly identified. But this entailed a dystopian inversion of the romantic, comic and fantastical images and narratives that had dominated Los Angeles' earlier representations. It also occurred in response to real-life events in the city that shaped the political, economic and social history of Los Angeles, the United States and much of the rest of the world for decades to come. The most important of these events were the so-called 'Hollywood strikes', which almost crippled the film industry from 1945 to 1947 and became defining flashpoints in the Cold War. Indeed, partly because of them, world-historical processes that continue to shape our present lives were then at least as concentrated in Los Angeles as they were in Washington, DC, Moscow or Berlin. The era was one of exceptional cinematic creativity, but one in which Los Angeles became a testbed for neoliberal economics and neoconservative politics, ground zero in a decisive confrontation between the state, corporations and organized labour, which was predicated precisely upon the distinctive relationship that had been forged there between the individual and the masses in a mediatized and hypermobile environment.

Undercutting Los Angeles' growth, but in tune with the studios' gathering crisis, film noirs from *Double Indemnity* (Billy Wilder, 1944) to *Plunder Road* (Hubert Cornfield, 1957) presented Los Angeles as a disjointed network of nondescript commercial streetscapes, pretty but morally corrupt suburbs, and an increasingly dilapidated downtown as urban jungle. These were described in terms of what Paul Schrader has famously called 'an uneasy, exhilarating combination of realism and expressionism', and through stories of sexual obsession, betrayal, mental breakdown and inevitable doom, frequently with flashbacks and maudlin, introspective voiceovers.[11]

These characteristics have elicited a rich critical literature on film noir, which is surely more extensive than that on movies about the movies, slapstick comedy or even early cinema.[12] For example, studies by Mary Ann Doane, J. P. Telotte, Frank Krutnik and James Naremore have shed light on the relationships between film noir and Freudian psychoanalysis, the female body, classical narrative, the Second World War, gender roles in American society, and postwar popular culture and philosophy.[13] Such studies have historicized their subject, but they have tended to do so in terms of a broad-brush American urban modernity, not closely engaging with the local geography of films' settings and locations. Indeed, the titles of many books on film noir elevate to quasi-mythical status its representation of a certain kind of urban landscape and experience: *Voices in the Dark, In a Lonely Street, More than Night, Somewhere in the Night, Dark City, Shades of Noir, Street with No Name, Black & White & Noir, Noir Anxiety*.[14] These draw attention to the metaphoric power of 'noir', 'night' and 'dark', emphasizing visual opacity, menace and universal moral crisis. They acknowledge the iconic importance of urban space, but usually through reference to an undifferentiated 'street'. Something similar is true of the earliest examinations of film noir by French critics in the 1940s and '50s, whose physical and cultural distance from American cities deprived their analysis of an understanding of the differences within and between them.[15]

Some recent scholarship on film noir has shed a more precise light on the localities of Los Angeles and their architectural and social complexities. Edward Dimendberg has explored the films in terms of a gradual prevalence of 'centrifugal' (dispersing) over 'centripetal' (centralizing) forces in the social and physical evolution of the mid-twentieth century American city.[16] Eric Avila has argued that film noirs express the growing distrust of urban environments by the films' primarily white middle-class audiences in an era of inner city racialization and 'white flight'.[17] Such new directions can be extended by more closely analysing the geographically specific relationship between Los Angeles and film noir in three senses. Firstly, one can assess the prominence of Los Angeles by establishing the proportion of film noirs that were set there, and how that proportion evolved through time. Secondly, one can examine individual film noirs set in Los Angeles for the general character and distinctive features of their landscapes. Thirdly, one can relate the first two issues to the actual redefinition of political life in the United States during the 1940s and '50s, a redefinition in which Los Angeles played an exceptionally important role.

A filmography of film noir, compiled by surveying the most important critical literature, suggests that a total of 518 examples were produced in the United States between 1940 and 1959.[18] As Table 5 in the Appendix indicates, analysis of this filmography indicates that there were two peaks, with 58 films being released in 1947 and 59 films in 1950.[19] The settings of film noirs were predominantly American. Non-US settings featured in English gothic noirs such as *Rebecca* (Alfred Hitchcock, 1940) and in noirs concerning Americans abroad, such as *Gilda* (Charles Vidor, 1946), but such settings became slightly less prevalent in the 1950s. As Table 6 (p. 285) demonstrates, the vast majority of those film noirs with US settings featured cities, no doubt reflecting the significant increase in urbanization which characterized the nation during and after the Second World War. Having collapsed during the Depression, the average annual growth in the proportion of the total US population living in cities more than doubled from 0.7 per cent in the 1930s to 1.3 per cent in the 1940s and 1.7 per cent in the 1950s, a rate higher than at any time since 1900, while the proportion of the total population living in cities increased from 56.7 per cent in 1940 to 64.3 per cent in 1950 and 69.9 per cent ten years later.[20] At the same time, however, as Table 6 indicates, a significant proportion of film noirs in most years also involved small-town or rural settings: for example, *The Lady from Shanghai* (Orson Welles, 1947), *They Live by Night* (Nicholas Ray, 1948) and *On Dangerous Ground* (Nicholas Ray, 1952).

Analysis of the filmography reveals that 110 films included New York City settings and 114 Los Angeles settings, while the next most common city settings were San Francisco in 36 films, Chicago in twelve, and New Orleans in nine. Washington, DC, appeared in four films, Miami and Las Vegas in three, Detroit, Kansas City, Philadelphia and Reno in two each, San Diego, Portland, Atlanta, Raleigh, Boston, Pittsburgh and Atlantic City in one apiece. These simple numbers suggest a genre that was geographically widespread, but they also conceal an important trend. The proportion of film noirs with settings in the American South, Midwest and Northwest was always fairly low: for example, in 1947, which saw the release of 58 films, those regions were represented in three, two and four films, respectively; in 1950, when 59 films were released, they appeared in three, three and eight films, respectively.[21] But settings in those regions were heavily outnumbered by settings in the Northeast and Southwest: the former occurred in seventeen films in 1947 and thirteen in 1950, while the latter featured in fourteen and nineteen films, respectively. These years were part of a larger trend. As Table 7 and Table 8 (pp. 285–6) suggest, the proportion of film noirs with settings in the Northeast declined from 1940 to 1959 while the proportion set in the Southwest increased. Table 9 (p. 286) makes clear that settings in California were also increasingly prominent.

These trends are in keeping with what Kirkpatrick Sale has called 'the Cowboy Conquest', which saw the postwar American West gain a new demographic, economic and political importance at the expense of other regions, especially the Midwest and Northeast.[22] The West outstripped all other parts of the nation in population growth by at least 100 per cent every year from the Depression through the 1960s, and the proportion of the total population living in the West grew by nearly 50 per cent from 10.5 per cent in 1940 to 13 per cent in 1950 and 15.6 per cent in 1960.[23] This was in contrast to a proportionate decline in all other regions, especially the Northeast, which had been home to approximately 28 per cent of total US population from 1900 to 1940 but whose share declined by nearly 9 per cent from 1940 to 1960.[24] Finally, not only were New York and Los Angeles by far the most prevalent settings in film noir but, as Tables 10 and 11 (p. 287) suggest, there was a meaningful pattern to their distribution. In every year from 1940 to 1948, New York was more prevalent, with the exception of 1944 when it and Los Angeles were equally numerous. In those years, New York featured in approximately one-quarter to one-third of all films while Los Angeles featured in very few until 1944 and then became gradually more prominent until 1949. In that and every subsequent year, with the exception of 1952 in which New York made a brief comeback, Los Angeles was more prevalent, featuring in approximately one-quarter to a half of all film noirs from the end of the 1940s through the whole of the following decade. The shift was quite dramatic and significant in its timing, taking place in 1949. Indeed, it was emblematic of a range of fundamental new realities that came into being around that time not only in cinema but in society, culture, politics and economics, and whose coming into being was particularly indebted to, and visible in, Los Angeles. In order to understand the shift, however, it is necessary to first apprehend the distinctive visual and narrative features of film noirs with Los Angeles settings, and their subtle evolution. Film noir was certainly the next most important kind of American cinema to represent that city after slapstick comedy and movies about the movies, but it went further in foregrounding the whole city, its parts and multiple terrains.

The Image of Los Angeles in Film Noir

As in movies of the 1930s, naming of Los Angeles is evident in many film noirs in textual cues such as dialogue, newspaper headlines, headed notepaper and street signs. But the Los Angeles setting is often established from the outset and referred to more habitually. At the beginning of *Double Indemnity*, insurance salesman Walter Neff (Fred MacMurray) stumbles into his downtown office, doubled over in pain from a gunshot wound, to record a confession that begins, 'Walter Neff to Barton Keyes, Claims Manager, Los Angeles, July 16, 1938.' In *The Black Angel* (Roy William Neill, 1946), down-and-out piano player Martin Blair (Dan Duryea) arrives in the city on a 'Los Angeles Motor Coach', while developments in the murder case in which he is entangled are announced by headlines in the 'Los Angeles Bulletin' and 'Los Angeles Sun'. *This Gun for Hire* (Frank Tuttle, 1942), which prefers the 'Los Angeles Tribune', and which is typical of many films whose action begins elsewhere, follows the hitman Philip Raven (Alan Ladd) south from San Francisco by train to the 'Los Angeles Passenger Station'. And in *D.O.A.* (Rudolph Maté, 1950), tax accountant Frank Bigelow (Edmond O'Brien) travels from the small town of Banning to San Francisco where his secretary tells him of 'a phone call from Mr Philips in Los Angeles', thus cueing the viewer for a shift in setting to the south.

In many films, parts of Los Angeles are named with equal frequency. In *Double Indemnity*, as Neff dictates the details of his love affair with Phyllis Dietrichson (Barbara Stanwyck), and their murder of her husband, a flashback presents Neff arriving on a sales call at the

Textual signifiers of place in *The Black Angel* (Roy William Neill, 1946).

Dietrichson home. This, he tells us, is in 'Glendale . . . one of those California Spanish homes everyone was nuts about 10 or 15 years ago', while later he and Phyllis rendezvous incognito at 'Jerry's . . . that big market up at Los Feliz'. In *The Black Angel*, Blair's arrival is preceded by an exterior location shot of the local landmark Gaylord apartment building on Wilshire Boulevard. In *Murder My Sweet*, one of the many screen adaptations of Raymond Chandler novels, PI Philip Marlowe is quizzed by detectives in a shadowy police department while the neon lights of the 'California Hotel' flash outside the window. Later, we learn of a murder at '1206 North Kingsley Drive, Los Angeles' and the address of the heiress Helen Grayle (Claire Trevor) at '962 North Hoover' in Brentwood. Indeed, the film even informs us of her (no doubt fictitious) phone number, 'OL6924', and Marlowe's, 'WH0922', coordinates from an era when the first two letters of American telephone numbers designated specific telephone exchanges and the neighbourhoods or streets where they were based: 'WH' for Whitney and 'OL' for Olympia in West Los Angeles and Beverly Hills. In *Pitfall* (André de Toth, 1948), the insurance executive John Forbes (Dick Powell) has an affair with Mona, visiting her place of work in the locally famous May & Co. department store at Wilshire Boulevard and Fairfax Avenue, and taking her for a romantic spin in a motor boat rented from 'Santa Monica Bait & Tackle'. In *Kiss Me Deadly* (1955), PI Mike Hammer begrudgingly discloses to government agents that he lives at '10401 Wilshire Boulevard, Los Angeles, California'. Such films provide a taxonomy of specific place on the level of the state, city, neighbourhood, street and house. And they do so not only for the sake of ambience but in order to generate a sense of the precise places in which people live their private lives, in which illicit acts of sex, theft and murder take place, and in which police and detectives may apprehend the culprits. This is especially true in *He Walked by Night* (Alfred L. Walker, 1948). As the demented war veteran, thief and cop killer Roy Martin (Richard Basehart) flees through the underground storm drains of Los Angeles, the police close in not only by following him beneath the streets but by identifying and cordoning off the thoroughfares under which he passes, each of which is announced on police radio, from Santa Monica Boulevard and Fuller Street in Hollywood fifteen miles southwest to Venice Boulevard and Garfield Avenue near the ocean.

The distance over which that film's action takes place indicates another key feature of Los Angeles film noirs – a sense of geographic dispersal generated by a diversity of settings and the emphasis placed upon the business of getting around the city, on foot or in a car, a feature that many Los Angeles film noirs share with earlier slapstick comedies. The action of *Double Indemnity* is split primarily between downtown and Glendale. That of *Murder My Sweet* takes place in Brentwood and at Mrs Grayle's beach house by the ocean (presumably Malibu), a remote canyon where Marlowe is taken for a beating by

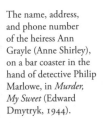
The name, address, and phone number of the heiress Ann Grayle (Anne Shirley), on a bar coaster in the hand of detective Philip Marlowe, in *Murder, My Sweet* (Edward Dmytryk, 1944).

crooks, and the apartment building on Sunset Boulevard where their ringleader resides. In *The Big Sleep*, another Raymond Chandler adaptation, in which Marlowe investigates a case of blackmail and pornography, the action is spread in a wide arc from downtown and Hollywood to the Beverly Hills Tudor mansion of oil millionaire General Sternwood, the hideaway cottage in the Hollywood Hills of the villainous Eddie Mars, the Lido Pier at Malibu, and Art's auto garage somewhere unnamed on the edge of town. In *Kiss Me Deadly*, Mike Hammer's investigations of a murder and the whereabouts of a radioactive suitcase, stolen from the Los Alamos nuclear test facility in New Mexico, lead him from his Wilshire Boulevard apartment to Flower Street and Bunker Hill downtown, a locker at the Hollywood Athletic Club and a dramatic finale in which the suitcase explodes at another Malibu retreat.

It is not only in naming real intersections that *He Walked By Night* emphasizes Los Angeles' physical expanse: the film begins with a montage in which long shots of the city, and dramatic views of the downtown tower of Los Angeles City Hall, are accompanied by a

Downtown at night and Glendale by day in the opening sequence of *Double Indemnity* (Billy Wilder, 1944).

Los Angeles City Hall and police poring over a map in *He Walked By Night* (Alfred L. Werker, 1949).

Steve Thompson (Burt Lancaster) stepping off a streetcar in Bunker Hill in *Criss Cross* (Robert Siodmak, 1949).

voice-of-god commentary that explains that Los Angeles is the United States' capital of glamour, but also its fastest growing city, and its toughest and biggest police beat. Innumerable exterior locations populate the film, mostly shot at night. Anonymous suburban streets and alleys, and the city's disorientating storm drains, are described by the narrator as 'seven hundred miles of hidden highways'. To track down the killer, the police employ the then-innovative technique of building up a composite portrait of his face by bringing together at police headquarters witnesses from various parts of the city whose disparate bits of information are combined. This centralized activity is then linked to the then equally innovative police 'dragnet', a coordinated door-to-door trawling of the city by hundreds of officers, which requires the Los Angeles police to draft in colleagues from Pasadena and Culver City, a step attributed by the narrator to Los Angeles' exceptional size and complex organization. Hence, police headquarters becomes the hub of a sophisticated information network, a direction further popularized by the highly successful television series *Dragnet* (1951–9), and the 1954 feature film of the same name, which *He Walked by Night* inspired. Slightly later film noirs, on the other hand, point to a decline in the importance of downtown within Los Angeles as a whole. As commentators such as Avila, Davis and Dimendberg have explained through analyses of *Criss Cross* (Robert Siodmak, 1949), *Kiss Me Deadly*, and *M* (Fritz Lang, 1951), Bunker Hill, the famous higgledy-piggledy community of late nineteenth-century streets and timber houses, frequently stands in in film noirs for the downtown of Los Angeles as a whole, although it was actually a rapidly declining tenement district whose demolition began in 1955.[25]

In so far as dilapidated downtown settings were a prominent feature of film noirs set in many cities, other settings may be said to have been even more specifically iconic of Los Angeles. As Mike Davis has described it, the middle-class, angst-ridden reaction to urban modernity and the postwar status quo that film noir sought to express found particularly fertile ground in Southern California. That region's long-standing boosterism, emphasizing beautiful landscape, sunshine and opportunity, could be inverted with exceptionally dramatic effect into darkness, perversion and corruption.[26]

Tensions between outdoor and indoor space, public and private life, daytime and its opposite were accentuated in Los Angeles film noirs by the presence of the beach and ocean, whose mythic importance the films understood. Both signified temporary respite from the troublesome urban modernity that the films primarily described. In *Pitfall*, the ocean allows for romantic boating off the bluffs at Santa Monica in the full glare of the sun, while in *In a Lonely Place* (Nicholas Ray, 1950), tough-talking but sentimental screenwriter Dixon Steele (Humphrey Bogart) picnics with girlfriend Laurel (Gloria Grahame) on the beach at twilight. Both are pleasant moments of distraction in relationships doomed to fail. In other films, the beach has the sense of being a terminus in which, perhaps because it is the furthest point west on the continent, the action must come to a head. In *Murder My Sweet*, the Grayles' beach house overlooks romantic but forbidding rocks and breaking waves and is the site of a final shootout in which more than one person is killed; and in *Kiss Me Deadly*, the nuclear explosion on

The nuclear explosion on the beach at Malibu in *Kiss Me Deadly* (Robert Aldrich, 1955).

Laurel (Gloria Grahame) in the courtyard of the apartment building in *In a Lonely Place* (Nicholas Ray, 1950).

the beach at Malibu that concludes the film highlights the symbolic meaning of the sand and waves as a sublime negation of technology right where the city and wilderness rub shoulders. Here is a quintessential Southern California setting, present in cinematic images of the region since Edison and Griffith, but endowed with a menacing meaning.

A parallel deconstruction is achieved in film noirs focusing on the film industry. *Sunset Boulevard* (Billy Wilder, 1950), obviously notable for foregrounding specific place, draws attention to the studios' growing crisis and the weakening of their utopian investment. Its action is concentrated in the magnificent but decaying Hollywood mansion of aging silent screen star Norma Desmond (Gloria Swanson), whose vanity leads her to murder a bankrupt young screenwriter when he declines her romantic attention. In *In a Lonely Place*, Steele is forced to defend himself from suspicion of the murder of a hat check girl after a night in a suave Hollywood club. The film opens with gruesome shots of her dead body dumped in Benedict Canyon, proceeding to a trenchant exposé of the dream factory as a place of egoism and force-fed creativity. The sense of disturbing disjuncture between the ideal and real is driven home by a contrast between the film's style and characterization of the screenwriter. Beverly Hills, where Steele resides and most of the action takes place, is affluent and debonair, filmed occasionally at night but mostly by day with deep focus cinematography and a sedately moving camera. This describes in graceful terms Steele's Spanish-style courtyard apartment building, with classical nude statues, painted tiles,

223

The fictional Mexican border town of 'Hidalgo' in *Borderline* (William Seiter, 1950).

fountain and tropical plants, all shot in a studio, and the ornate stucco headquarters of the Beverly Hills police department, the actual building shot on location, surrounded by landscaped grounds and a sidewalk that is squeaky clean. This pleasant visualization, however, is undercut by occasionally expressionistic cinematography in which canted camera angles suggest the leading characters' disequilibrium, and a remarkably open-ended narrative that leaves the murder unsolved and Steele's innocence in doubt.[27]

Los Angeles film noirs also brought to the fore the nearby presence of the Mexican border, hitherto largely repressed in Hollywood cinema except in adaptations of the Ramona and Zorro legends and rare dramas sympathetic to Mexicans such as *Bordertown* (Archie Mayo, 1935). In Los Angeles film noirs, Mexico cropped up frequently in passing: in *Double Indemnity*, for example, Phyllis Dietrichson wears a perfume bought by her husband in Ensenada. However, a significant number of film noirs concentrated their action near the border. For example, *Border Incident* (Anthony Mann, 1949) exposed corruption in Southern California agriculture by describing an undercover investigation of the exploitation of Mexican migrant labourers or *braceros*. The film uncompromisingly depicted the robbery and murder of people crossing the border without visas, heroically portraying its protagonist Pablo Rodriguez (Ricardo Montalban), a Mexican federal agent, on equal terms with his American counterparts. Using a semi- documentary style, *Border Incident* rendered its rural scenes with a striking combination of deep focus photography and night-time exteriors with very low light. However, it involved no action in Los Angeles as such, while the more famous *Touch of Evil* (Orson Welles, 1958) was shot on location in Venice, California, but used it as a stand-in for a Mexican border town, presumably Tijuana. On the other hand, *Borderline* (William Seiter, 1950) explicitly connected Los Angeles to the border through its narrative of Madeleine Haley (Claire Trevor), a plain clothes LAPD officer sent to Mexico to help smash a Los Angeles-based smuggling ring run by a violent crook (Raymond Burr). However, this film noir had many comic moments as Haley encountered Johnny McEvoy (Fred MacMurray), an undercover US Customs agent, each taking the other for a tourist and inevitably falling in love. Where the border in other film noirs connoted menace, in *Borderline* Mexico comprised sombreroed men sleeping in the sun, the archways of adobe terraces, old women and children in village streets, a large cantina with dancers and maracas, and American day-trippers sipping daiquiris. Humour was derived from MacMurray's incompetent Spanish and a jovial local driving a jalopy whose ramshackle home was a hut with twelve children while his phone line was also used for drying clothes. Not all film noirs, therefore, succeeded in shining a critical light on the border and its meaning – indeed, *Borderline* mocked any suggestion of a link between Mexican poverty and Los Angeles' success: the film's long chase from the fictional town of 'Hidalgo' to the real city of Ensenada, and thence to the border at Tijuana, culminates in a showdown at a monkey cage in Los Angeles Zoo, a police raid and a happy ending.

Hitman Philip Raven (Alan Ladd) on the run from police in a railroad depot in *This Gun for Hire* (Frank Tuttle, 1942).

The increasingly overt geographical description that characterized Los Angeles film noirs was enhanced by what the *Wall Street Journal*, in August 1947, called an 'exodus from Hollywood' in favour of location shooting for all sorts of feature films. The *Journal* ascribed this tendency to an increasing availability of 'fast air travel' for casts and crews, a desire to save money by avoiding the higher material and labour costs of the studio, and 'public demand for more authentic pictures, stemming partly from the war'.[28] Of course, the tendency was not entirely new. In the 1930s the crime dramas *Blood Money* and *Bordertown* had involved notable filming of the real Los Angeles, and *This Gun for Hire*, one of the earliest film noirs, included extensive visually striking location sequences in which the hitman Raven is chased by police through an actual rail depot, its tracks, cranes, locomotives, chimneys and warehouses making a surprisingly industrial scene. By contrast, some of the most famous film noirs were filmed entirely within studio walls, including *The Big Sleep*, which was made at Warner Bros in Burbank despite its narrative's geographical range. Most film noirs, however, involved a mixture of studio and location shooting, with the former more prevalent prior to 1948, both in films produced by the majors – *Double Indemnity* by Paramount, *Murder My Sweet* by RKO, or *The Black Angel* by Universal – and, with much lower budgets, by Poverty Row studios such as Producers' Releasing Corporation (PRC), for whom Edgar G. Ulmer made *Detour* (1945). In later films, location-shot sequences became more prominent. And the fact that later films were nearly always independently produced suggests that increasingly realist representations of Los Angeles were predicated on the demise of the studio system, from *He Walked by Night* (Bryan Foy Productions) and *In a Lonely Place* (Santana Pictures) to *D.O.A.* (Cardinal Pictures) and *Kiss Me Deadly* (Parklane Productions).

Because of the interest in location filming, Los Angeles film noirs were populated by banal commercial architecture and public buildings of a kind that featured in all postwar American cities but were especially abundant there because of the city's sprawl and relative youth, and especially visible because of its relative lack of monumental structures such as the skyscrapers of New York and Chicago. Hence, retail and food outlets were particularly common – supermarkets, department stores, drugstores and roadside diners – as were places of transit that allowed for anonymous movement and interaction in the drama, including train stations, bus depots, parking lots and streets. Especially prominent too were sites of more sensational activity, including hotels, nightclubs, bars, casinos and race tracks. Offices and commercial buildings figured frequently but industrial installations less often; residences included both apartments and single-family homes, though the latter were preferred; police stations, as in *In a Lonely Place*, were ubiquitous and increasingly bright and airy.

In addition, the activity of moving from one part of the city to another was especially prominent at this time. Studio-shot film noir such as *The Big Sleep* often involved walking or driving, but they usually cut efficiently from scene to scene where later film noirs allowed walking or driving to take up more narrative time. *He Walked by Night* is notable for its extended pursuit on foot as is *D.O.A.*, in which the protagonist, Bigelow, chases breathlessly through the art nouveau Bradbury Building downtown and an empty factory full of oil tanks and cranes, where a gunman tries to shoot him. But the cinematography of the latter film is marked by relatively frenetic panning and tracking and an extensive use of depth of field. In one exceptionally striking location sequence, downtown by night is filled with pedestrians, automobiles, streetcars, lights and reflective surfaces as the psychotic henchman Chester abducts Bigelow in his car, warning he will kill him 'nice and slow'. Their dialogue, which is filmed with rear projection, is abruptly 'interrupted' by a location-shot chase as Bigelow escapes, running into a real branch of the Imperial Drug Co. chain, where the ensuing shoot-out scatters customers in the aisles and on the street outside. This exemplifies the new kind of random violence in everyday life for which the most edgy film noirs were known. Similarly, in *In a Lonely Place*, Steele, whose smug exterior conceals a dangerous temper, purges his frustrations by driving frantically through the Hollywood Hills at night; and in *Kiss Me Deadly*, which opens with Mike Hammer cruising a moonlit highway to the strains of Nat King Cole, Hammer's devotion to his convertible Corvette, his mechanic's engine-like catchphrase 'Va Va Voom', and the view of traffic from his Wilshire Boulevard apartment, ensure that automobiles are integral to the landscape.

Critical and public recognition of Los Angeles in such films apparently increased. It was reported as a sign of the times that the cast and crew of *The Street with No Name* (William Keighley, 1948) spent 62 of its 65-day shooting schedule on location, partly in Washington, DC, but mostly in Los Angeles, San Pedro and Santa Ana, California.[29] The shooting schedule for *Pitfall* 'called for 40 separate locations within the

Los Angeles city limits. Director André De Toth decided it was a good idea to shoot the scenes right at home, where they were intended to be.'[30] The *New York Times* attributed the success of *He Walked by Night* to the '"on location" filming procedures followed, which not only contributed more than a modicum of striking realism and authority, but also kept the budget to modest proportions'.[31] The *Los Angeles Times* reviewer of Robert Siodmak's 1949 thriller enthused that 'Angelenos will get a special kick out of "Criss Cross" because much of it was filmed in the city's highways and byways, but the moviegoer in Chicago, Ill. or Hoboken, NJ, will not sit through it unmoved, I'm betting'.[32] And Dan Smith, in the *Daily News*, noted that 'Los Angeles City Hall, Union Passenger Terminal, Bunker Hill, and Angel's Flight are all becoming stars or at least featured players in motion pictures'.[33] This was evidence that 'producers appear to feel that if they get one or all of these elements into a picture, they have definitely stamped their film with a Los Angeles flavor'.[34]

An increased visibility of Los Angeles was also to be found in a significant number of films that presented elevated perspectives on its central basin from the range of hills that flanks it to the north. In *Double Indemnity*, for example, the Dietrichson house in Glendale is introduced by a panning shot taken from the slope on which it sits, the city stretching out in the distance below. This arrangement is repeated in a significant number of films set in one of film noir's favourite locations, the Sunset Strip, in which the natural elevation of Sunset Boulevard as it passes north of Hollywood offers vistas of the city to the south. One of the earliest occurs in *Murder My Sweet* where the villain, Jules Amthor (Otto Kruger), lives in an art deco high-rise apartment building (actually the landmark Argyle Hotel), where large balcony windows on the upper floors provide views that are wide and deep. Amthor proudly boasts, 'On clear days, Mr Marlowe, you can see the ships in the harbor at San Pedro'. Similar perspectives are provided by the wide and curved windows behind the desk of crooked nightclub boss Marko (Peter Lorre) in *The Black Angel*, but the most spectacular are those in *The Strip* (László Kardos, 1951), in which Mickey Rooney plays Stanley Maxton, a Korean War veteran and jazz band drummer suspected of a double shooting by the police.

That film opens with an aerial shot of the Strip accompanied by a Louis Armstrong score and a voice-over narrator who sets the scene by highlighting the city's size and everyday routine: 'Los Angeles, 5am.

Stanley Maxton
(Mickey Rooney,
standing) in the Sunset
Strip office of his boss
Sonny Johnston (James
Craig) in *The Strip*
(László Kardos, 1951).

In another few hours most of the four million people in the County will be going to work . . .'. High-angle shots look down on a police cruiser speeding with sirens blaring to the scene of a crime. The distinctive ambience of the Strip is conveyed by traffic sounds and jazz guitar over a montage of its famous clubs at night: Ciro's, Mocambo, La Rue, Villa Nova, Scandia, and the fictional 'Fluffs Dixieland' where Maxton is employed. This establishes the Strip as a space apart – which, in fact, it was. That particular stretch of Sunset Boulevard to the west of Hollywood became a centre for nightclubs and casinos in the 1920s precisely because it lay outside the boundaries of the city in an unincorporated corner of Los Angeles County where liquor and gambling laws were less enforced. In the upstairs office of club owner and mafioso Sonny Johnston, the floor-to-ceiling plate glass windows give an exceptionally clear view of the city. And yet it is distanced by the art moderne style of the office, which shows the hand of the art director, Cedric Gibbons, and of MGM who lent this particular film noir relatively high production values.

The Strip underlines the reputation of the Strip as a place of lawlessness and loose living. Maxton is suspected of murder when a waitress he tries to romance winds up dead by another man's hands. Like Amthor in *Murder My Sweet*, Maxton resides in an apartment on the Strip, as does the waitress next door, and so many other unattached characters in film noir who become entangled in dangerous love affairs. Despite Los Angeles' preference for detached, single-family homes, a large proportion of its men and women in film noirs live in apartment blocks (Neff in *Double Indemnity*, Mona in *Pitfall* and Hammer in *Kiss Me Deadly*), courtyard complexes (Steele in *In a Lonely Place* and Martin in *He Walked by Night*) and boarding houses (Raven in *This Gun for Hire* and Blair in *The Black Angel*). All of these people are single and stand outside the bungalow-based nuclear families so important in postwar Los Angeles in demographic and symbolic terms. By contrast, the apartment is often a place to which a married person goes for sex with someone other than his or her spouse.

Against this, many Los Angeles film noirs counterpoint the mansions of the wealthy, especially the adaptations of Chandler who carried over into Southern California something of the stratification by class of architectural styles so ingrained in his native England. Hence the enormous Tudor mansion of General Sternwood in *The Big Sleep*, with its oppressive hothouse and the fussy, frilly boudoir of Vivian Sternwood (Lauren Bacall), or the home of Mr and Mrs Grayle in *Murder My Sweet*, which Marlowe sarcastically explains 'wasn't as big as Buckingham Palace'. However, the super-wealthy became gradually less prominent in Los Angeles film noir while relatively mundane middle-class and working-class surroundings came to the fore, especially after the last of the Chandler adaptations in 1947.[35] *The Black Angel*, for example, contrasts apartments and the single family home. Blair's ex-wife Mavis Marlowe, who presumably dumped him so she could meet other men, lives alone in an apartment in Wilshire Boulevard's Gaylord building that is richly decorated with sheepskin rugs, silk drapes and fabric coverings on the walls. But we are no sooner introduced to her erotic domain than she is murdered for the precious stone pendant that hangs around her neck. A rapid montage shows Blair wandering

Suburban breakfast and commuting in *Pitfall* (Andre De Toth, 1948).

hopelessly drunk from bar to bar, his single life, like hers, an epitome of misfortune and vice. Soon he appears to be rescued by Kathy Bennett (Veronica Lake), a happy young housewife whose husband is wrongly accused of the killing. She leaves her bright and airy bungalow with modest floral drapes, joining with Blair to prove her husband's innocence only to discover that Blair did the deed in a drunken stupor that he himself cannot recall – a disorientating turn of events that reunites her with her husband at the end.

In *Pitfall* the route taken by the narrative is different but the effect is broadly the same. At the outset, Forbes and his typical suburban family have breakfast, gentle but not menacing shadow lines running across the kitchen from the morning sun on the palm-tree-lined street outside. Stuck in traffic on the way to his office, which is cramped with small windows, he complains 'Sometimes I get to feel like a wheel within a wheel within a wheel', to which his wife replies, 'You and fifty million other Americans'. The exchange reveals discontent with the conformism of the postwar Californian way of life, but Forbes is soon reminded of the value of his family and their bungalow home: his lover, Mona, kills a psychotic PI in self-defence in her apartment; Forbes shoots Mona's ex-boyfriend Smiley when he breaks into Forbes's home, threatening to reveal his affair to his wife; Forbes goes free but Mona is presumably jailed in a closing twist that is striking today for the double standard in its contrast between wholesome married life and dubious singledom, patriarchy and the deviance of the woman on the side.

Regardless of setting, one of the means by which film noirs undermined the heroic masculinity of more conventional Hollywood films was to construct stories through flashbacks and ellipses that interfered with narrative agency. This strategy had a subtly distinctive aspect in Los Angeles film noirs. In *Murder My Sweet*, Marlowe has two hallucinations when he suffers blows to the head, once in a remote canyon and once leading him to awake in a mental asylum. Both are cued by a shift in the musical soundtrack and a special effects shot dissolving what looks like ink or blood across the film frame. However, in the second episode, which is significantly longer, Marlowe hears voices and sees himself falling, being lifted by big hands, past rows of doors, to a doctor and syringe. When Marlowe comes to, the hospital room restricts his movement and cuts him off from the city. In *The Black Angel*, when Blair blacks out on a drinking binge, his dazed senses register a brawl, his arrest, his detention in County Hospital, its bare walls and its chain link fence. Such hallucinations, which also restrain the field of vision in taking place at night, lend a sense of density and enclosure to the *mise en scène*. This contrasts with the films' daytime exterior locations filmed in the Southern California sun, and with the distinctive vistas of the city from the Sunset Strip. Hence, Los Angeles exaggerates the tension between vertical enclosure and horizontal expanse that was evident in so many film noirs, wherever they were set.

In the 1950s, after *D.O.A.* and *The Strip*, each of which also begins with a flashback, that device and hallucinations became less common, as an emergent rationalism transformed the psychic uncertainty, and displaced some of the expressionism, of 1940s film noir. The potential for this trend was already evident in *Double Indemnity*, most of which takes place at night although, significantly, sunlight is emphasized in the initial happy flashback to the Dietrichson house and in scenes depicting Neff's office routine. In the latter, the open plan arrangement of managers around and above a central court housing secretaries and cleaners indicates the increasing presence in everyday life of a corporate efficiency that is everywhere today but was then relatively new, and which relies in the film on sunlight to function properly. The shapes and surfaces of the office's art deco fittings, its phones and charts, and the letters embossed on its doors are indecipherable in the dark. At the beginning of the film, Neff struggles in pain and in weak lamplight to operate the Dictaphone on which he records his confession, in contrast to his boss Keyes (Edward G. Robinson), an organization man entirely au fait with statistics and the law, who is the first to deduce Neff's wrongdoing. The rationalism of the insurance office is inseparable from the inescapability of the law, and the two are reinforced by the contrast between darkness and light, ever present in film noir but especially acute in its Los Angeles incarnations. This opposition, which is formal and ideological, is increasingly evident in later film noirs, partly because the rise of location filming led to a greater reliance on natural light. But it is also increasingly evident because films such as *He Walked by Night* and *Dragnet* gave more and more narrative and moral prominence to law enforcement agencies as the guarantors of a tough but necessary social order. In the late 1940s and '50s, the police procedural, rogue cop and heist variations of film noir, which became more common, were notable for a gradual decline in chiaroscuro and hallucinations, and a renewal of high-key lighting and linear narrative.[36] Paul Kerr has suggested this resulted from producers' desire to make feature films more suitable for television broadcast at a time when theatrical exhibition was declining.[37] However, it can also be read as part of a political turn to the right centred on Los Angeles.

The working class was always hard to see in film noirs set in that city, despite filmmakers' efforts to capture urban reality by allowing the camera to explore it more fully.[38] Many films featured mid-level professionals who were comfortably off, if not rich – Neff in *Double Indemnity*, Forbes in *Pitfall*, Bigelow in *D.O.A.* – while *He Walked by Night* and others like it, such as *The Crooked Way* (Robert Florey, 1949) and *The Clay Pigeon* (Richard Fleischer, 1949), portrayed lonely veterans who had difficulty adjusting to civilian life and were effectively unemployed. Some films focused on private detectives who were self-employed but hostile to the rich and sympathetic to the man in the street. A few films featured manual workers who also worked alone: for example, auto mechanic Danny (Mickey Rooney) in *Quicksand* (1950) and telephone repairman Jim (Ross Elliott) in *Chicago Calling* (1952). Many depicted the police in terms of a split between middle-class detectives and working-class patrolmen, as in the rapport between the ranks that is prominent in *In a Lonely Place*. At least one film, *Border Incident*, was remarkable for its sympathetic portrayal of exploited farmworkers. And many films featured nameless service workers in casinos, nightclubs and bars. Missing, however, were the working masses in large industrial installations of the kind (automobiles, aircraft, defence) that increasingly led Los Angeles' real economy. The few factories that did appear, as in *This Gun for Hire* and *D.O.A.*, were largely devoid of workers. Instead, the most prominent groups of sympathetic working-class men were the criminal gangs in heist films such as *Criss Cross* (Robert Siodmak, 1949) and *Plunder Road* (Hubert Cornfield, 1957). These were humanized by outlining their personal motivations for rebellion against the economic status quo, but they were also inexorably hunted, trapped and arrested or shot by police.

The Rise of Los Angeles and the Decline of New York

As police procedural, rogue cop and heist films became more common, while expressionism and the murder-mystery declined in relative terms, a new social order was emerging in which cinema played an important role in normalizing the science, firepower and paraphernalia of modern law enforcement.[39] That dual shift carried reactionary political implications and coincided with the relative rise of Los Angeles and decline of New York as real cities and film noir settings about 1949. It may be illustrated geographically by contrasting the relatively open-air, suburban and automobilized *mise en scène* typical of Los Angeles-based films from *Double Indemnity* to *Kiss Me Deadly* with the overbearing, high-density environment of Manhattan-dominating New York film noirs such as *I Wake Up Screaming* (H. Bruce Humberstone, 1941), *Laura* (Otto Preminger, 1944), *Scarlet Street* (Fritz Lang, 1945) and *Force of Evil* (Abraham Polonsky, 1948).[40] Certainly, the contrast is not absolute, but a question of degree. A significant number of celebrated Los Angeles film noirs predate the shift and the *mise en scène* of some of those takes place in downtown environments, as in parts of *Double Indemnity* and *Murder My Sweet*. And New York was not only the scene of some of the most important police procedurals, such as *The Naked City* (Jules Dassin, 1948), but it continued to be an important setting from *Fourteen Hours* (Henry Hathaway, 1951) to *Edge of the City* (Martin Ritt, 1957). Nonetheless, across the large body of films encompassed by the term film noir, we witness a major step in Los Angeles' dramatic ascent to global importance in the mid- and late twentieth century.

Commentators on the macro-geography of American urbanization, such as David Perry and Alfred Watkins, have argued that cities do not coexist in a neutral way but compete with each other for resources and manpower to grow, and constantly develop their social and economic systems to get or stay ahead of competitors. Through a process of 'uneven interregional development', the 1940s and '50s saw the United States make a decisive transition from an industrial economy epitomized by New York to a new form of post-industrial 'capital accumulation' epitomized by Los Angeles, which, like other 'Sunbelt' cities such as Houston and Phoenix, 'was able to assume the mantle of growth leadership'.[41] By 1940 Los Angeles was a major metropolis with a growing industrial base, in the words of a *Los Angeles Times* columnist, 'World leader in motion picture production; first in America in aircraft manufacture; leads America in secondary automobile manufacture and oil refining; ranks second in tire manufacture and fourth in furniture and women's clothing'.[42] New York received less of a boost from the wartime economy than either Los Angeles or Chicago and from 1945 to the mid-1950s saw its industrial employment fall in absolute and relative terms.[43] Chicago's economic performance was sluggish, largely because of its failure to attract new technologies, while New York,

Chicago, Boston and other cities in the Northeast and Midwest lost population in the fifteen years after the Second World War.

New York's response to Los Angeles was not passive. Its civic and business leaders strove to lift the city's economy. As early as 1940, Edwin Schallert reported in the *New York Times*, in a story entitled 'Why New York Will Not Get Hollywood', that New York City Mayor Fiorello LaGuardia had raised hopes of 'a wholesale migration of the fabulous motion-picture colony of Hollywood from the West to the East Coast of America'.[44] Schallert dismissed as a 'phantasm' the idea that the Hollywood moguls would ever seriously consider leaving Southern California.[45] For evidence, he pointed to the motion picture industry's by-now highly developed infrastructure in the region, its established pool of skilled labour, the deep personal roots planted by its employees and the relative affordability of land. The last serious effort by any major studio to invest in East Coast production (First National Pictures in 1923) had been given up after one unsuccessful year in which a lot of money was spent for little return. However, Schallert acknowledged that, for the industry's bosses, departure from Southern California was 'an idea that is worth dallying with just for expediency's sake'.[46] The Hollywood moguls were rumoured to be dissatisfied with California's relatively high corporate taxes and 'the high cost of maintaining executive forces at both ends of the continent'.[47]

But the more important reason for rumours of a move was said to be the ongoing threat of socialism in California, which had been supposedly manifested in the 1934 gubernatorial campaign of the famous muckraker Upton Sinclair, known as EPIC for 'End Poverty in California'. During that campaign, Schallert alleged, 'the film nabobs [the Hollywood moguls] themselves made use of the migration mirage to put the quietus on any wild new political theories. They said that if the California votes were favorable to the disturbing candidate, the movies had no other course but to move to another part of the country.'[48] Although Sinclair achieved by far the highest popular vote in primaries in August that year, the majority of the Hollywood film industry's managerial class, including Louis B. Mayer of MGM and Joseph Schenck of Twentieth Century Pictures, made public statements and raised funds to oppose him and, in the case of MGM, produced newsreels to stoke up conservative fears that immigration and radical ideas could overwhelm the state.[49] Meanwhile, Warner Bros held up a $350,000 investment in new buildings at Burbank in anticipation of the result of the election that November.[50] Although Sinclair was defeated, the radicalism that he represented extended beyond him in widespread labour unrest that swept the West Coast from the longshoremen's strike, which shut down California's ports and led to a four-day general strike in San Francisco and Oakland in the summer of 1934, to the strike that crippled the Hollywood studios in May and June 1937.[51]

Rumours that the film industry might relocate appear to have vanished during the Second World War, but the industry's sense of fragility re-emerged with the return of labour unrest in 1944 and two further strikes that shut down many studios between 1945 and 1947. These were complicated after 1946 by a decline in the box office for Hollywood films occasioned by the Paramount decrees, television and suburbanization. In this context, suggestions of a resurgence of New York as a film producing centre resurfaced. A 1947 *New York Times* story announced that La Guardia's successor, Mayor O'Dwyer, was attempting to facilitate Manhattan investors and realtors by persuading at least one Hollywood major to move to the island, offering a 100,000-square-foot converted building on a seventeen-acre site and promising a skilled workforce, low industrial unrest and a minimum of red tape.[52] In 1950, when United Artists found itself in deep financial crisis and was forced to shut its Beverly Hills office and transfer management to New York, Edwin Schallert expressed concern that 'Elimination of [UA's] West Coast officers and executive staff is causing an increasing stir in Hollywood because no one is yet sure of just what it portends'.[53]

New York remained important to the motion picture industry. It continued to be home to many of the parent companies of the Hollywood studios, the centre of American film distribution and a tremendously important source of financing. Ed Sullivan reported in 1947, for the *New York Daily News*, that Wall Street financiers had approximately $600 million tied up in loans to the studios and independent producers.[54] New York retained an important role as a display window for Hollywood's cutting edge products, such as Cinemascope, which was first shown to the public with great fanfare in September 1953 at the Roxy Theater on Broadway, the largest movie palace in the world. In the absence of feature film production, New York also emerged as the centre of documentary and experimental film in the United States.[55]

But the Hollywood moguls continued to place great value on the relative autonomy of their movie studios from the industrial and financial interests of East Coast WASP elites. Indeed, after the Second World War Los Angeles emerged as the centre of a larger, diversified, mass entertainment industry. In the late 1930s it had begun to rival New York for popular music live and on radio, becoming a major stop on the national touring circuit for big bands such as Kay Kyser's and Benny Goodman's, and encouraging the growth in Los Angeles of music recording labels such as Decca and RCA-Victor.[56] Despite the initial panic it caused them in the 1940s, motion picture companies embraced television in the following decade, Los Angeles then displacing New York as the centre of television production as the medium moved from live broadcasts to a diet of mostly recorded shows.[57] And, as if to add insult to injury, at least one report in the *New York Times* suggested Los Angeles might be emerging as New York's chief rival in theatre because it 'is thickly populated with actors, directors, designers, producers, composers, playwrights, and technicians who hail directly from the New York theater but who are now located in California'.[58]

The relationship between Los Angeles and the other side of the nation had been intensifying since the 1880s because of increasing travel between the two by train, automobile and bus. But cinematic representations of journeys from New York did not become common until the 1930s, at which point they were typically made by train, as in *That's Right You're Wrong* (1939). As early as *Hollywood Hotel* (1937), air travel also became a fact of life, albeit one whose luxury and convenience only movie stars and other notables could afford. The rapid growth of scheduled passenger and cargo air services between the East and West coasts that came with the end of the war heightened the inter-connectedness and rivalry between them. American Airlines began using '[r]emodelled Douglas DC-4s' in 1944 to ship newspapers, magazines, food and clothing from east to west and '[f]lowers, sportswear, and movie films' from west to east.[59] In February 1946 a daily nonstop service with TWA was

Nick Blake (John Garfield) in New York City and on the beach at Malibu in *Nobody Lives Forever* (Jean Negulesco, 1946).

initiated from Burbank to New York with the first eastbound flight carrying 'thirty-five motion picture stars, producers, and writers' and piloted by Howard Hughes.[60] In August 1947 the *New York Times* expanded into the Los Angeles newspaper market, with the first copies being specially delivered to 'Mayor Fletcher Bowron and Los Angeles civic and business leaders and Hollywood motion picture executives'.[61]

The rise of transcontinental air travel was as yet relatively elitist but it was an indication of the growing automobility of Americans and, in particular, Californians, who were the most automobilized Americans of all. Carey McWilliams estimated that 'in 1945 two out of every three people in the state had been born in some other state or nation'.[62] Indeed, he argued that 'Broadway to Hollywood migration' was one of the most important factors in this unique demographic.[63] A small but significant group of film noirs narrativize journeys between New York and Los Angeles, beginning with *Detour* (Edgar G. Ulmer, 1945), *Nobody Lives Forever* (Jean Negulesco, 1946), *They Won't Believe Me* (Irving Pichel, 1947) and *The Man I Love* (Raoul Walsh, 1947), and continuing in the next decade with *The Damned Don't Cry* (Vincent Sherman, 1950), *The Big Bluff* (W. Lee Wilder, 1955) and *The Harder They Fall* (Mark Robson, 1956). Like other Los Angeles film noirs, these films too foregrounded the city and its distinctive landscapes in their plots, dialogue, locations and studio sets. However, they are especially interesting because they recount stories of migration from east to west, beginning with promise but ending in disillusion, and relying on visual contrasts between Los Angeles and New York. Many film noirs were shot on location back east,

The home of gangster Nick Prenta (Steve Cochran) in 'Desert Springs', California, in *The Damned Don't Cry* (Vincent Sherman, 1950).

Eddie Willis (Humphey Bogart) flying from New York to Los Angeles in *The Harder They Fall* (Mark Robson, 1956).

but in most of these films New York is presented in short-hand by establishing shots of Manhattan and its skyline, followed by sequences of action on its streets recreated in a studio with painted backdrops and rear projection. Emphasizing the verticality of skyscrapers, these scenes are usually brief and concentrated early in the film, providing a visual and narratological pretext against which the rest unfolds.

Nobody Lives Forever, for example, opens with long shots of the Manhattan skyline in sunshine. The chirpy voiceover of ex-con man and war veteran Nick Blake (John Garfield) explains his life-long love of New York but also, now that the war is over, his desire to make a clean break in California, 'a great spot, clear away from everything.' Arriving by train at Los Angeles Union Passenger Terminal with the bankrupt nightclub singer Gladys Halvorsen (Geraldine Fitzgerald), he finds the new city to be a bright and breezy place of opportunity. Filmed on location, its Plaza bustles with street life, its beaches are full of bathers, the Sunset Strip is alive with the music of big bands at the club Mocambo, and the picturesque gardens of the Mission San Juan Capistrano are a short drive down the coast to the south. Nick is determined to match his romantic surroundings with a new law-abiding lifestyle, but soon slides back into the criminal underworld through encounters with other ex-crooks who have made the journey west. This leads to a showdown with the rival fraudster Doc in a dirty, light industrial landscape of oil derricks, piers, and timber and corrugated metal huts (perhaps San Pedro or Playa del Rey) where the likeable elderly crook Pop loses his life to Nick's dismay.

Much of this pattern and iconography is repeated in the subsequent films. In *The Man I Love*, lonely nightclub singer Petey Brown (Ida Lupino) quits her job at the '39 Club' in New York to visit her family in Long Beach at Christmas, where she struggles to prevent her brother's descent into a life of crime while romancing a piano player she drinks with at the 'Bamboo Club' and walks with by moonlight on a nearby ocean pier. *They Won't Believe Me* begins with a murder trial in 'the courtroom of the County of Los Angeles' from which a flash-back immediately recalls 'Nick's' basement restaurant on 52nd Street in New York where the man on trial, Laurence Ballantyne (Robert Young), regularly meets his lover until his suspicious and domineering wife insists they move to California. When the young son of Ethel Whitehead (Joan Crawford) is killed by a truck in *The Damned Don't Cry*, she flees her husband and small town home for New York, where she becomes entangled with racketeers. Relocating to 'Desert Springs', a casino town filmed on location in Palm Springs, and full of modernist bungalows typical of postwar Southern California, her flirtation with the top mobster on the 'West Coast' leads his jealous New York-based boss to shoot them both. In *The Big Bluff*, the terminally ill Manhattan heiress Mrs Bancroft (Martha Vickers) is ordered by her doctor to go to Los Angeles for her health. But she declines tours of the Huntington Library and Griffith Park in favour of the Sunset Strip, while living in a large Spanish-style mansion in the Hollywood Hills where a playboy whom she marries tries to hasten her death by replacing her pills with duds. In *The Harder They Fall*, semi-retired sportswriter Eddie Willis (Humphrey Bogart) goes on a nationwide tour to promote an up-and-coming boxer whose ruthless manager has connections to the mob. Flying with American Airlines to Los Angeles, they visit Hollywood's

Al (Tom Neal) makes a long distance call to Sue (Claudia Drake) in *Detour* (Edgar G. Ulmer, 1945).

Knickerbocker Hotel and the Beverly Hilton, and watch a television news report about downtown's Skid Row.

In these films the high-rise and high-density urbanism of New York appears relatively jaded, a cause of the protagonist's restriction, dissatisfaction or insecurity. Settings in and around Los Angeles are novel and optimistic until the promise of the place is undercut when the past that each character flees proves impossible to escape. In some films, travel and communication between New York and Los Angeles seems routine: arriving on the West Coast in *They Won't Believe Me*, Ballantyne finds a job with a brokerage firm dealing with Wall Street by telephone and wire, and rises at 5:30 a.m. to coincide with the working day back east. In other films, the New York–Los Angeles relationship is also antagonistic: in *The Damned Don't Cry*, the West Coast mobster, Nick Prenta, is a brash and cocky upstart who complains of his New York boss, 'I'm tired of sending the cream back east to a worn out guy who does nothing but sit back and watch a mousey bookkeeper add up what I made!' Moreover, where the films of the 1940s mostly present journeys cross-country by train, airplanes become the default thereafter.

The earliest of the film noirs to map the relationship between Los Angeles and New York is also the most spatially aware and perhaps the most emblematic of its moment. Speaking to the *Los Angeles Times* in 1946, Edgar G. Ulmer, the director of *Detour*, stated his interest in using cinema to understand 'life as it exists in this world'.[64] This was hardly surprising for a filmmaker who was a Czech expatriate trained in Vienna and Berlin and the co-director, with Robert Siodmak and Fred Zinnemann, of one of Weimar Germany's most important films, *Menschen am Sonntag* (*People on Sunday*, 1930), a realist portrait of ordinary Berliners on a summer weekend, filmed entirely on location. But Ulmer's interest in 'life as it exists in this world' *was* then a novelty for Hollywood and in *Detour* took shape in the story of Al (Tom Neal), a poorly paid piano player who is classically trained but works at the unimpressive 'Break O'Dawn' club in a New York shrouded in darkness and fog. In love with Sue (Claudia Drake), a singer who aspires to break into the movies, when Sue leaves town for Hollywood the transcontinental distance of their phone calls is underlined by Ulmer's intercutting of close-ups of their faces with shots of a telephone exchange and telephone lines running across the country. When Al follows Sue to Los Angeles to marry her, a map filmed in extreme close-up traces Al's journey hitch-hiking and on foot through Pittsburgh, Chicago and

Oklahoma. But bizarre twists of fate ensue in which Haskell, the driver of a car who offers Al a ride in Arizona, turns out to be a gangster and then dies during the night of mysterious causes, leaving Al in the frame for his murder. Taking Haskell's identity and his car, Al, in turn, gives a ride to a malevolent, dishevelled blonde who turns out to be Haskell's girlfriend, Vera, and threatens to report Al to the police. With Vera in tow, Al arrives in Los Angeles exhausted and under a cloud, his voice-over explaining, 'A few hours later we were in Hollywood. I recognized places Sue had written about. It struck me that far from being at the end of the trip there was a greater distance between Sue and me than when I started out.'[65] Not only has Sue not made it big in Hollywood and may be unemployed, but Al cannot go back to New York for fear of being arrested. His arrival in Los Angeles entails a spatial and a temporal rupture with a previous way of life and the shattering of his romantic and professional dreams.

As such, Ulmer's film echoes the rupture that he and many other film noir directors shared when they were exiled from Europe by fascism.[66] It also pessimistically recapitulates the route taken by thousands of impoverished migrant workers in the 1930s who became the subjects of Dorothea Lange and Paul Taylor's photo-journalistic study *American Exodus* (1939) and of John Steinbeck in *The Grapes of Wrath* (1939). And, in expressing profound disillusion with westward migration and a fatalistic sense of no going back, it sets a tone for later films about New York to Los Angeles journeys. In 1946 Siegfried Kracauer observed what he saw as a new postwar dispensation in American 'terror films', a term he used to describe many of what we now call film noirs, including *Shadow of a Doubt*, *Spellbound*, *Somewhere in the Night* and *The Lost Weekend*. The salient new feature of these films was that '[a]pprehension is accumulated; threatening allusions and dreadful possibilities evoke a world in which everybody is afraid of everybody else, and no one knows when or where the ultimate and inevitable horror will arrive'.[67] Ulmer's interview for the *Los Angeles Times* took place just after location shooting of his next film noir, *Strange Woman* (1946), and entailed a larger discussion of the continuing threat to Hollywood as the centre of American film production, and of its possible move back east. Ulmer explained that Hollywood was a better place to make movies in every respect because it offered a skilled workforce, favourable climate and technical facilities, but that its one weakness was a tendency towards 'strike conditions'.[68] This statement casts his narrative of professional musicians in Hollywood in *Detour* in a subversive light.[69] While film producers and studio executives in the late 1940s feared the possible collapse of the studio system, and film noirs inverted its classical conventions and positivity, its large numbers of exploited and unemployed workers lived out a real dystopia of Hollywood cinema in a climate of fear and insecurity that echoed what Kracauer described.

The Hollywood Strikes: A Geographical Interpretation

Al and Sue in *Detour* are typical of the protagonists of many film noirs who worked in Los Angeles' motion picture and entertainment industries but whose work was often temporary and insecure. In 1948 the labour relations commentator Anthony Dawson explained that behind 'the picture of opulence [of Hollywood cinema] . . . stretches a vast sea of men and women of all crafts and abilities striving and pressing for more constant employment in an industry which can use only a fraction of them even at capacity production'.[70] The industry's ever-present surplus of labour was at the root of the peculiar insecurity of its job market and was acutely felt by workers, especially given the recent memory of the Depression. In 1942, for example, the *New York Times* described 'Hollywood's worst sociological problem' as 'motion picture extra players . . . [who] cling desperately to their chance to starve to death'.[71] Of 7,000 extras in the business only 1,500 were thought to find more than ten days' work per year, and of 6,000 members of the Screen Actors Guild, no more than 350 were employed on any given day.[72] Dawson calculated average unemployment among skilled workers in the film unions at 31.95 per cent, while those who could find jobs were typically required to work between 54 and 60 hours per week.[73] As Donald Kraft has recently explained, the majority of musicians working in Los Angeles experienced 'painful social dislocation': a small elite employed at the studios made a comfortable living but most struggled to make ends meet by moonlighting or playing casually or part-time in clubs.[74]

In 1950 Dawson demonstrated that lack of tenure for workers was also seasonal in that the studios tended to concentrate the pre-production of films in the spring, shooting in the spring and summer, and post-production and distribution in the fall and winter – partly because of the climate but also because they could reduce their tax burden by striking sets and sending film negatives out of state by the end of the tax year every 31 March.[75] This heightened the instability of the labour market, a typical major studio having between seven and nine films in production in mid-summer but none in January. Security of employment was also relative to the size and output of each studio. A higher proportion of workers found year-round employment at the 'big five' studios (MGM, 20th Century-Fox, Warner Bros, Paramount, RKO), fewer at the 'little three' (Universal, United Artists, Columbia), and fewer still with the independents. For example, in 1947, 80 of 187 costumiers employed by MGM worked all year long, 25 of 78 employed at Columbia, 10 of 51 at Republic, and 5 of 115 at the smaller independents. Goldwyn and Roach studios employed 30 and 69 costumiers, respectively, but none of them worked all year.

Given these conditions, it is hardly surprising that the two major strikes that rocked the industry in 1945 and 1946–7 lasted ten months and thirteen months, respectively, shutting down most production and leading to extensive street fighting between picketers, strike breakers and police. These undercut the utopian content and form that characterized most Hollywood films of the studio era and presented a very different view of the industry than studio promotional films. They also interfered with the freedom to make movies that had been the essence of Hollywood for the moguls since the 1910s and which was expressed in 1946 by Eric Johnston, president of the Motion Picture Association of America (MPAA, successor to the MPPDA), with the words 'Utopia is production!'[76]

While film noirs gave Los Angeles new prominence and overturned its established iconography, the Hollywood strikes were defining events in the rise of the real Los Angeles after the Second World War. Their immediate causes lay in the distinctive labour politics of the studio system, but their unfolding and resolution played an important role in the formation of a new model of citizenship that was promoted as a broadening of the benefits of capitalism to embrace the working class, but which seemed to many the enforcement of a new political quiescence.[77] This formation took place across the United States and internationally during the Cold War, and over many decades. But it was led and shaped by developments more than 60 years ago in Los Angeles. These made it a geopolitical pressure point, connected to the rest of the world in new ways and providing a template for economic, social, political and cultural life in cities everywhere.

It is well known that Hollywood became one of the most visible crucibles of American anti-Communism, but less well known are the ways in which the public scandals, debates and political and policing practices of 'the McCarthy era' first surfaced many years earlier as a result of conflicts and considerations internal and local to the film industry in Los Angeles. The historical record reveals that a surprisingly straight line can be drawn between the determination of the Hollywood moguls to ensure the profitability of their industry, from its beginnings to the Depression, and the subsequent consolidation of a new rightist dispensation in American society and politics whose legacy remains today.

The austerities of the Depression forced a wave of concessions by trade unions at the studios in the face of management warnings of their imminent collapse and the actual receivership forced upon Fox, Paramount and RKO.[78] The era saw reductions of between 25 and 40 per cent in the average annual wage of technicians, painters, carpenters and plasterers,[79] while a proposal to cut all workers' pay by 50 per cent was only narrowly rejected.[80] Despite this, and the volatility of the labour market, studio management only begrudgingly recognized unions and sought to tamper with their organization to mitigate what management saw as their negative effects on profits. In 1933 the West Coast was connected to the rest of the nation in a new way when Nicholas Schenck, head of MGM, led an initiative by Hollywood moguls to contract the Chicago mafia to keep striking in the industry to a minimum by taking over its largest labour union, the International Alliance of Theatrical and Stage Employees (IATSE), and threatening radicals with blacklisting and physical intimidation. Following the end of Prohibition and the imprisonment of Al Capone, this development drew the mafia, now led by Frank 'The Enforcer' Nitti and his West Coast deputy Johnny Roselli, into the broad pattern of migration to California that characterized the 1930s for hundreds of thousands.[81] It also prefigured movies about mobsters in the movie business such as *Crashing Hollywood*, and in Southern California more generally, as in *The Damned Don't Cry*.

In 1934, at IATSE's national convention, Nitti successfully persuaded the union to elect one of his associates as its president and another its Hollywood representative, an achievement which Carey McWilliams attributed to the fact that in the convention hall 'there were more gunmen there than there were delegates'.[82] These associates, George Browne and Willie Bioff, supposed leaders of the film projectionists' union in Chicago who had organized a protection racket in its movie theatres in the 1920s, now extended their success west. Taking over IATSE, they guaranteed the producers there would be no more strikes in return for hefty payments of cash in brown paper bags, amounting to at least $1 million by 1939, plus a 2 per cent levy on all IATSE workers' pay. According to one studio executive who testified to the IRS years later, the deal saved the studios at least $14 million in improvements to pay and conditions that they would have had to grant to their workers otherwise.[83] Browne and Bioff were convicted of fraud and racketeering in 1941, as was Joseph Schenck for tax evasion, and Nitti on the same charge in 1943, but not before they had distorted labour relations in the studios in a lasting and destructive way.[84]

The Hollywood moguls' acceptance of Mafia assistance in the regulation of labour was not quite as remarkable at the time as it appears in retrospect. Mafia infiltration of labour unions was a feature of organized crime and an issue of concern to workers, civic leaders and law enforcement officials dating back to at least 1919, when the Chicago mafia established rackets among construction, bar, hotel and restaurant workers' unions, which regularly involved violence, including shootings, murders and bombings against genuine labour leaders and would-be striking workers, as well as business owners.[85] This situation intensified in the early 1930s when many entrepreneurs found themselves in exceptional economic difficulty and a significant proportion turned to racketeers as a means of suppressing the demands of labour. Indeed, the Hollywood film industry was in many respects typical of the kind of industry that lent itself to exploitation by racketeers. The legal historian Humbert Nelli has noted:

> Racketeering did not exist across the entire spectrum of the American business world, but was concentrated in specific industries and businesses that required modest amounts of capital or skill to enter and contained an over supply of labor. The tendency of racketeering to appear in small, unstable, and disorganized industries led Walter Lippman to observe in 1931 that it was essentially 'a perverse effort to overcome the insecurity of highly competitive capitalism'. Thus, rather than criminals forcing themselves on their victims, it was often the harried businessman faced with the constant threat of cut-throat competition, who turned to underworld elements and invited their help in dealing with excessive competition.[86]

Full public revelation of the extent of the corruption of IATSE was not made until the Kefauver Senate Committee on Organized Crime of 1950–51. However, it was widely recognized by film studio workers in the 1930s, understandably generating much resentment among them, and encouraging a good number to break away from IATSE in the hope of securing real bargaining power with producers.[87] The Conference of Studio Unions (CSU), which emerged as an umbrella group representing painters, set decorators, carpenters and machinists in the six-week strike of late spring 1937, was consolidated by a successful strike by animators at Walt Disney in 1941, and became the only viable challenge to the corruption of the dominant union. In his detailed published account, *Hollywood Labor Dispute: A Study in Immorality* (1950), Father George H. Dunne, a Jesuit priest involved in mediation between studio management and workers, presented the leader of the CSU, Herbert K. Sorrell, as 'a beacon of hope' to thousands of studio workers.[88] Sorrell was a former painter at Warner Bros whose pay as a union leader was capped at the average industrial wage of $250 and who voluntarily drew no pay when the workers in his union were out on strike.[89] And he became something of a folk hero in the Los Angeles labour movement for his dedication to the interests of workers and for defiance of both studio management and heavy-handed police tactics. Sorrell and a co-plaintiff made headlines when they were awarded damages for false arrest during strike action at Warner Bros in 1937.[90]

The increased radicalism of labour represented by Sorrell and the CSU was not unique to Hollywood at this time. Rather it reflected the long-standing tension in American labour history between the craft unionism of the American Federation of Labor (AFL), of which IATSE was a member union, and the then growing and more militant industrial unionism of the Congress of Industrial Organizations (CIO), which broke from the AFL in November 1935 as workers in mass production industries organized with greater discipline, and on a larger scale, than ever before because of the Depression. This tension between types of labour organization and their degrees of activism was exacerbated in Los Angeles by that city's relatively sudden rise as a city of industry, whose 4,500 factories were said in 1940 to employ 140,000 workers and produce goods worth $1 billion per year.[91] The tension was especially evident in the film industry in which 30,000 workers were responsible for an output of films worth $172 million annually, but whose business – the making of motion pictures – was partly industrial but also a craft, or even an art.[92] Los Angeles was now compared and competing as an industrial centre with New York, Chicago, Detroit and Philadelphia, but industries in those cities were blighted by strikes such as those by the United Auto Workers at General Motors in Flint, Michigan (the legendary 'Flint Sit Down Strike') in January and February 1937, and by the Steel Workers Organizing Committee at Republic Steel three months later. Such strikes were far bigger and more violent than anything known in Hollywood. In 1935 General Motors employed 135,000 workers, and the strike against Republic Steel culminated in the Memorial Day Massacre in Chicago on 30 May 1937, in which police shot and killed ten workers and wounded 30 more.[93] As noted in the previous chapter, censuses of the Los Angeles economy tended to distinguish between the Hollywood studio system and manufacturing industry in general, as did reports in the press. The CSU emerged in a space between IATSE and the CIO, but was linked with the latter in the press and received its moral and practical support, especially when labour unrest re-emerged with a vengeance after the Second World War.

Work stoppages affected the Hollywood studios in autumn 1944 and a one-day strike by film extras was led by the Screen Players Union in February 1945.[94] The following month, a dispute arose over the representation of unaffiliated set designers between the CSU, which claimed a membership of 12,000, and IATSE, said to represent about 16,000

Rioting outside Paramount Pictures studios, Tuesday, 23 October 1945.

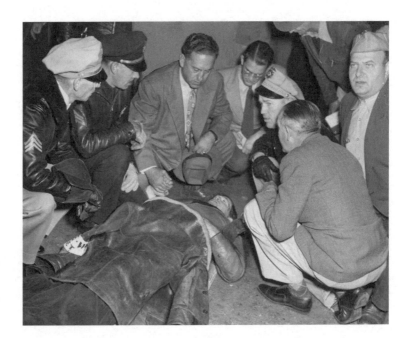

Herbert Sorrell, Conference of Studio Unions president, comforts a worker hit by a car at Warner Bros, Burbank, 29 October 1945.

workers.[95] CSU picketing shut down production at Warner Bros, MGM, Universal, Fox, RKO and Paramount, before spreading to Republic, PRC and other independent producers, as well as the Technicolor film processing labs.[96] This action continued for six months until October 1945, when it came to a head in several days of bitter street violence outside Warner Bros studios in Burbank. Seventy people were injured on the first day alone when IATSE members, management and film stars crossed the picket lines with the help of police and, according to credible reports by strikers, mafia thugs posing as disgruntled workers stirred up trouble.[97]

Reporting of these clashes was sometimes reasonably non-partisan, as in the *Los Angeles Times* of 6 October 1945:

> Inter-union enmities, kindled months ago by a strike over control of 77 set decorators, yesterday flared into a full-fledged riot at the gates of Warner Bros studio in which participants were knifed, clubbed, and gassed before police reserves from three cities and the county could restore order.[98]

As the violence continued, however, the *Times* made less effort to disguise its sympathies, reporting more colourfully on 24 October:

Motion picture
executives meet with
Los Angeles County
Sheriff Eugene
Biscailuz, Tuesday,
9 October 1945.

Featuring flailing nightsticks and fists and flying feet, Hollywood's grimmest mob scene yesterday was staged – without benefit of film cameras – at the gates of Paramount Studios as non-striking workers braved the gauntlet of massed 'peaceful' picketing which has hampered production for several days. Scores were injured, some seriously, including a policeman slugged and trampled as he attempted to give safe-conduct to workers battling their way to their jobs . . . Director of the mob scene was President Herbert K. Sorrell of the striking Conference of Studio Unions which has been locked for eight months in a jurisdictional contest with the non-striking International Alliance of Theatrical Stage Employees.[99]

Throughout the struggle, spokespeople for the MPAA played down the scale and impact of the strikes.[100] They characterized them as needless jurisdictional disputes not reflecting the generally good pay and conditions they argued were typical of the industry. And they reminded the public of the industry's recent patriotic service during the war when the studios had released morale-boosting films and raised funds for veterans' and other war-related charities.[101] In this, they no doubt had in mind not only how the strikes would appear to observers in Washington, DC, but also that some veterans in Los Angeles, more interested in their own right to work than in the right of workers to strike, were among the most vocal opponents of the CSU and organized counter-demonstrations against it.[102] However, the studios' stated position seemed disingenuous to many observers, especially as their response to the strike evolved: recruiting new workers from the industry's labour surplus rather than negotiating with those on strike; seeking to isolate the leadership and members of the CSU by breaking off union locals one at a time from its coalition;[103] offering closed shop union recognition to new workers wanting representation outside the CSU; and employing off-duty police as security guards.[104] Jack Warner, Samuel Goldwyn, Joseph and Nicholas Schenck, Louis B. Mayer and Harry Cohn petitioned the City and County of Los Angeles and the State of California to intervene and collaborated in seeking court injunctions against pickets and prosecutions of Sorrell and other CSU members for damages and contempt of court.[105] Warner Bros sued the Painters and Carpenters unions in the CSU for $3 million.[106]

Thirty-three weeks of strike, and three weeks of violence, massively restricted production at the studios and elicited the personal intervention of President Harry Truman, who encouraged mediation by the Department of Labor and the National Labor Relations Board (NLRB). On 24 October 1945 all sides agreed to 30 days of binding arbitration by an AFL-led board endorsed by William Green, AFL president, and Eric Johnston of the MPAA.[107] Claiming a victory, the CSU called off most pickets, although some continued at Warner Bros because Sorrell and 300 picketers were on trial for disturbing the peace there, and their case ran until February the following year.[108] The arbitration board, known as the Knight Committee after its chair, Felix H. Knight, visited Hollywood and held hearings before issuing a recommendation in December 1945. CSU workers were to return to work and be reassigned to their previous jobs, although studio management refused to comply with the latter request even when it was reiterated by the Committee eight months later.[109]

Throughout the first half of 1946, reports circulated that painters, carpenters and electricians with the CSU were returning to work only to find themselves forced by studio management to work on so-called 'hot' sets – that is, film sets dominated by IATSE workers who had been illegally hired by the studios during the strike of the previous October.[110] In mid-February the CSU threatened to strike for a reduction in the 48-hour working week that had been imposed during wartime and they demanded an improvement in hourly pay to account for their lack of tenure and seasonal employment.[111] MGM, Warner Bros, RKO, Paramount, Universal, Republic, Goldwyn Pictures, Columbia, 20th Century-Fox and Hal Roach Studios were threatened with pickets, in response to which studio management refused to negotiate for two months before agreeing to a wage increase of 10 per cent (18½ cents per hour) to 17,000 daily workers of all ranks.[112] While this was progress from the strikers' point of view, it did nothing to address job security nor their demand to have their union locals recognized outside of IATSE's closed shop. A new two-day strike ensued on 1 and 2 July 1946, which affected all studios and prompted a coordinated response by the police departments of Los Angeles, Culver City and Burbank. This, in turn, precipitated brief but violent clashes, hospitalizations and arrests, albeit on a smaller scale than before.[113] This time the strike was settled when studio management offered a 25 per cent wage increase, a 36-hour week for most workers, a recognition of Painters' Local 1421, the lynchpin of the CSU, and an agreement to abide by NLRB decisions. Shortly thereafter, in a ploy not likely to have alleviated tensions, Disney followed up an announcement that it would implement the pay rise with a further announcement that it was laying off 400 of its workforce of 1,000.[114]

On 26 September 1946 the dispute over 'hot' sets came to a head, leading to the most bitter phase of the strikes, which finally ended in October of the following year.[115] Amidst reports that movie stars including Mickey Rooney, Clark Gable and Greer Garson were crossing picket lines to work,[116] violent clashes took place on the streets outside Warner Bros and Paramount, and at MGM where Culver City police called in reinforcements from 'Inglewood, El Segundo, Santa Monica, Palos Verdes, Redondo, Hermosa, and Manhattan Beaches', as well as Los Angeles County sheriffs and the California Highway Patrol.[117] Pickets were established outside Republic in Studio City on 3 October and at Technicolor on 11 October. Outside Columbia on 15 November, the *Los Angeles Times* reported, 700 people were detained in 'what veteran police officers declared was the largest ever mass arrests made in California', many of the detainees immediately going on hunger strike in Lincoln Heights jail.[118] As lines hardened, the CSU demanded permanent local arbitration machinery for the Hollywood film industry, the issuing of signed contracts to all workers, and the return of all strikers to the jobs, pay and conditions they had held before the original strike the previous year.[119] Producers, meanwhile, publicly refused to meet with Sorrell unless the CSU first ended its strike and gave assurances no further strike action would be taken.[120] Throughout 1947, the stand-off received extensive coverage in the local and national press, which followed every twist of negotiations between the unions, employers and mediators, often daily and on the front page.

By late summer 1947, when chances of a breakthrough seemed slimmer than ever, Sorrell appealed on behalf of CSU members for mediation by the Los Angeles Interfaith Council, which comprised Catholic, Protestant and Jewish clergy and was chaired by Archbishop John J. Cantwell, who agreed to host a meeting at the Beverly Hills Hotel on 1 September.[121] All parties were invited but the producers' refusal to send representatives ensured the talks could have little effect.[122] In his final report, Stewart Meacham, director of the regional office of the NLRB, argued that '[i]t was the producers, and not the employees, who failed . . .'.[123] And in *Hollywood Labor Dispute*, Father Dunne argued that the moguls 'preferred to co-operate with gangsters rather than face the necessity of engaging in sincere collective bargaining with honest democratic trade unions'.[124]

Viewing the strikes as a 'lockout' calculated to make an example of the CSU's members, and ensure that no other challenge would ever emerge, Dunne pointed to what he called 'the historical continuity of partnership' between studio management and corrupt IATSE leaders, which persisted even after Browne and Bioff were prosecuted and re-placed by Richard Walsh and Roy Brewer.[125] Dunne's conclusion left no doubt as to the origins of the crisis, nor its exceptional social injustice:

> The record is clear. From 1934 to 1941 the producers worked hand in glove with the gangster elements who had seized control of the IATSE union to betray the interests of its rank and file members. In the years that followed they cooperated no less effectively to destroy the Conference of Studio Unions, which represented a kind of democratic and honest trade unionism which was a foreign, and therefore irritating, substance in the midst of the miasmic immorality which characterized the producers' conception of labor relations . . . The victims of this conspiracy have been thousands of honest American working men and women. Justice demands that those who victimized them be brought to heel and that restitution be made.[126]

At the end of October 1947, with no resolution in sight, and with the CSU rank and file struggling to cope with the hardship of extended unemployment, Sorrell allowed members of his own Painters union local a free vote on continuing or ending the strike. As they gradually returned to their jobs, Machinists and Carpenters remained on strike, and then Carpenters alone, their dispute continuing until June 1951.[127]

Although they were in generally good financial health in 1946, earning $316 million before tax out of a total income of $1.14 billion, in a record year at the box office, individual studios noted a reduction in net profits due to the industrial unrest. Columbia Pictures' annual report, for example, cited '[e]xtraordinary expenses resulting from jurisdictional strike at studios', which amounted to over $370,000, or 10 per cent of the studio's net profit for the year.[128] This was clearly a significant financial outgoing that no studio wanted to sustain, but other effects of the strikes were even more widespread and lasting. The defeat of the CSU was one of the more significant defeats of militant labour in United States history, given the visibility and symbolism of the film industry. But to fully appreciate its significance requires contextualizing the strikes within Los Angeles' longer hostility to labour unions, which distinguished it from older industrial cities back east and was one of the factors that drew film companies to the city in the first place.[129]

In the early days, anti-union sentiment was personified by Harrison Gray Otis, owner of the *Los Angeles Times*, which was so vocal in its support of police repression of the 1910 Los Angeles metalworkers' strike that its offices were bombed by radicals, resulting in twenty deaths. Together with the Los Angeles Chamber of Commerce, local business interests encouraged immigration to the region, in part to guarantee an over-supply of labour, which would keep wages low and hamper unionization efforts. The studio system came into being in an era that saw the most rapid growth in labour activism in United States history, the total number of unionized workers growing from two million in 1910 to five million ten years later, driven in part by the fervour of international socialism and communism before and after the October Revolution in 1917. Although the first serious effort by IATSE to organize Los Angeles film studio workers took place in 1914, producers quickly established their own representative body, the MPPDA, to promote an open shop. Years of difficulties led to the so-called Studio Basic Agreement of November 1926, which established a framework for determining wages and conditions and the arbitration of disputes by a committee composed equally of producers and union representatives. However, the studio moguls' natural inclination towards an individualistic system of credits and awards led them to establish the Academy of Motion Picture Arts and Sciences in 1927, a company union representing actors, directors, writers and cinematographers. Hence, studio management policy typified what labour historian Daniel Jacoby has called the 'corporate paternalism' of American big business at the time.[130]

In Los Angeles, more than in most other places, such paternalism was implicitly backed up by the threat of physical force. The Los Angeles Police Department developed a reputation for its proactive suppression of communists, demonstrations and visits by labour leaders.[131] In January 1924 the US Senate and State Department identified Los Angeles and San Pedro as two out of six key hotbeds of activity by the International Workers of the World (IWW) and as possible sites for a communist revolution supported by the Soviet Third International.[132] As Carey McWilliams put it in *California: The Great Exception* (1949), the state's labour struggles involved 'all of labor pitted against all of capital', without any half-measures.[133] Labour unions in California, while not revolutionary, tended to be more explicitly leftist than their counterparts in eastern states, partly because California's lack of a 'hereditary governing class' allowed a relatively active working class.[134] At the same time, the incumbent political machine was primarily Republican and labour struggles tended to be somewhat more turbulent than they were even in radical San Francisco where Democrats had historically held sway.

Labour unrest in the Hollywood film industry was further distinguished by a relatively high degree of specialization of work and an unusual hierarchy of grades, each encompassing a small number of workers, which ensured that class solidarity would always be complicated by competing interests. In the Hollywood strikes, the film industry became a key battleground in which the American working class publicly came to fight against itself. The strikes were characterized by a volatile mix of micro-conflicts and sympathetic actions, and took place in the context of other industrial actions across the Los Angeles region. In October 1945, for example, aircraft machinists downed tools at the Lockheed factory in Burbank to picket Warner Bros in support of the CSU, and thousands more from railroads, shipyards and the United Auto Workers were said to be ready to join the pickets.[135] Eighteen months later, individual locals shifted allegiances back and forth: the

Technicians employed at film laboratories defected from IATSE to the CSU;[136] and Electricians and Story Analysts left the CSU for IATSE.[137] But the CSU was always outnumbered by a larger alliance of up to 25,000 non-striking, mostly IATSE, workers. Among actors and extras there was an evolution from March 1945, when the Screen Actors Guild (SAG) allowed members to observe or ignore pickets according to their conscience, to February 1946, when SAG and the Screen Extras Guild (SEG) joined with IATSE, the Teamsters, Culinary Alliance, Plasterers and Musicians to publicly condemn the CSU.[138] Not only did these other groups not strike, they showed a complete disregard for CSU pickets and stood by while new, non-union workers were hired to fill the jobs of strikers.[139] On the one hand, Ronald Reagan, president of SAG, publicly alleged that 'the policy of the CSU is to win by force'.[140] On the other, a subcommittee of the US House Labor Committee (HLC) heard testimony that IATSE leaders intimidated members of the CSU's International Association of Machinists, pressuring them to switch sides, while IATSE members and Teamsters refused to work with CSU machinists when the latter did report for work.[141] Elsewhere in the city, major strikes occurred among Greyhound bus drivers, at telephone exchanges and oil refineries, with the US Navy being called in the latter case to keep the facilities running.[142]

Again and again, the Hollywood strikes were presented by studio management, IATSE and the press as superficial 'jurisdictional' disputes when, in fact, they represented a conflict between two ways of organizing labour: the CSU, focused on rank-and-file militancy, and IATSE, driven by a top-down model of industrial relations in which militancy was seen as a threat. In this, the strikes were not unique. As Mike Davis has explained in *Prisoners of the American Dream*, the immediate postwar years witnessed a nationwide wave of industrial unrest that was arguably the largest and most coordinated in American history, especially affecting heavy industries such as automobile and steel manufacturing.[143] In response, big business management led a concerted effort, with the endorsement of many union leaders, to break militant labour power. And the effort was particularly effective in the relatively conservative South and West where heavy industry and militancy were less well-established and the politics of much of the working class was gradually skewed to the right. In this spirit Eric Johnston, who had been director of the US Chamber of Commerce before he was made director of the MPAA in 1945, argued that, in responding to the Hollywood strikes, there was no point in studio executives 'trying to put a patch on an old wound'.[144] The de facto coalition of movie moguls, corrupt labour leaders and a newly ascendant Republican party in California became a driving force in what Davis calls the 'sudden riptide of anti-communism' that gripped government, big business, and unions across the United States.[145]

Most histories of Hollywood cinema after the Second World War have been more interested in the Hollywood blacklist than the Hollywood strikes. They have proposed that studio management responded to allegations of communism in the film industry reluctantly and under threat from television, falling audiences and the Paramount decrees.[146] Some accounts have emphasized that the threat the moguls faced from members of Congress who were intent on rooting out leftism was also a threat against themselves as Jews in so far as many prominent anti-communists were also anti-Semites.[147] Hence, the historically decisive Waldorf-Astoria declaration of 25 November 1947, in which Hollywood producers promised that the studios would no longer employ communists or former communists, is generally said to have been an unpalatable but necessary position taken to protect the movie business rather than because of any real anti-communist zeal on the moguls' part. In support, it is recorded that when Louis B. Mayer was tipped off in advance of the first film industry-related hearings of the House Un-American Activities Committee (HUAC) that he should dismiss any communists or ex-communists in MGM's employ, he did so, like other studios, to moderate the effects of anti-trust investigations by the government and calls by conservatives for greater censorship of films to guard against leftist political messages.[148]

To consider the history of Hollywood cinema and Los Angeles together, however, means to reflect on the blacklist and the strikes as related parts of a larger event, and reveals a different story. Firstly, the strikes preceded the blacklist, the second and longer strike coming to a close at the end of October 1947, just over two weeks before HUAC's film industry hearings, which began on November 17. Secondly, while the moguls had reason to be self-conscious about the positions they took in public, it is clear from their statements, press reports and the timing of events that anti-communism already provided a tool for the suppression of labour activism and helped to distract attention from the injustices of the studios' labour regime and the real infiltration of the movie business by the mafia. By circumscribing as unacceptable large swathes of labour union discourse and activity on the grounds that they were 'communist' or 'communistic', anti-communism served to ensure a more compliant workforce in the medium term. Of course, world-historical events fuelled anti-communism within and outside the United States. It had a long history since the 1910s when 'Red-baiting' emerged in response to Bolshevism and unionization in railroads and other industries. And after the Second World War it intensified, from the emergence of the 'Iron Curtain' to the Chinese Communist revolution of 1949, and the outbreak of the Korean War the following year. But Los Angeles and Hollywood exerted an unusual degree of influence upon its emergence and terms.

An early hint of the scandals surrounding Communism that would engulf Hollywood appeared in September 1930 when the US Congress Fish Committee investigated what the *New York Times* called 'Red activities', epitomized by the recent invitation to the Russian director Sergei Eisenstein to work at Paramount Pictures.[149] In March 1931 Charlie Chaplin was forced to deny rumours of his Communism that circulated in response to comments he made during a trip to Germany in the last days of the Weimar Republic to the effect that 'conditions in the United States were perhaps worse than here [in Germany]. Los Angeles has 100,000 unemployed film folk.'[150] In August 1934 James Cagney and other stars found it necessary to deny rumours they had given financial aid to Communists and Captain William F. Hynes, head of the intelligence squad of the LAPD, testified to a US Congressional Sub-Committee on un-American activities that stars such as Cagney were giving money out of a misguided philanthropy because they themselves 'were once poor persons'.[151] In October 1936, in a *Washington Post* article on attitudes in the Hollywood film community to the presidential election that would take place the following month, Louis B. Mayer admitted '[w]e've got Communists in Hollywood, yes; some of them drawing down $2,500 a week . . . They should pack their bags and start back to Moscow.'[152]

HUAC, which became the most prominent prosecutor of alleged communism in Hollywood after the Second World War, originated in the spring of 1938, when it was known as the Dies Committee for its chair, the Texan Democrat Martin R. Dies, and concentrated on investigating Nazi sympathizers in the United States. However, led by conservative Southern Democrats with Republican support, it soon came to focus on left-wing groups, beginning with an inquiry into claims that Communists had infiltrated another congressional committee, the La Follette Civil Liberties Committee, which was then hearing testimony on the use of organized violence and intimidation by employers against CIO workers.[153] The Dies Committee trained its sights on California. In August 1938, it heard evidence that 'Communistic activities' were noticeable among California longshoremen and agricultural workers and 'rampant among the studios of Hollywood'.[154] In the spring of 1939 it was asked to investigate the breaking away of a large union local from IATSE and sent agents to Hollywood who conferred with George Browne.[155] In February 1940, Mayor of Los Angeles Fletcher Bowron defensively declared 'Hollywood is not a hotbed of Communism, but a hotbed of patriotism', while attending the premiere at Grauman's Chinese Theater of *The Flag Speaks*, a documentary about the history of the US flag. This was accompanied by a parade down Hollywood Boulevard of 2,000 members of patriotic organizations and the California National Guard, and a ceremonial presentation made to Louis B. Mayer and producer Walter Wanger by the American Legion.[156]

On 14 August 1940 the first public naming of names of supposed Communists in Hollywood took place when testimony given to a Los Angeles County Grand Jury by one John R. Leech was leaked to the press. An editorial in the *New York Times* marvelled at the apparent lack of connection between the testimony and the five-year-old murder case that the grand jury was supposed to be investigating and contended that '[w]hat is sinister in the present episode is not the possible drop of communism in the vast sea of entertainment but the misuse of supposedly correct legal machinery to give irresponsible witnesses a chance to smear reputations'.[157] In their study of the Hollywood blacklist, Larry Ceplair and Steven Englund present evidence that Leech, who was described by the *Times* as 'a former Los Angeles County Communist Party organizer', was actually an agent for the LAPD and discredited as an unreliable witness at the time.[158] Setting in train a complex series of events that would have decisive effects for generations of Hollywood filmmakers, Senator Dies himself arrived in Los Angeles with uncannily good timing just three days later to give those individuals whose names had been leaked an opportunity to testify to clear their names in public (i.e. Herbert Biberman, Lester Cole and Samuel Ornitz, three of those named among the 'Hollywood Ten' ten years later).[159]

In July 1941 a bitter strike by Walt Disney's animators, who were affiliated to the CSU, caused Disney management to send a telegram to Washington, DC, demanding that Congress act in support of 'patriotic Americans' against '[a]gents of Communism'.[160] The following month, however, the strike ended successfully for the CSU with the strikers gaining union recognition, a 40-hour and five-day week, a 10 per cent wage increase, and the establishment of a board to review all layoffs proposed by management.[161] Given Disney's reputation as the strongest anti-union bastion of all the studios, this outcome boosted the CSU's credibility but also caused a redoubling of anti-Communist rhetoric. This was demonstrated again in 1941 when Joseph Schenck and IATSE leaders Browne and Bioff, in their trial for fraud and tax evasion, sought to defend themselves by deflecting blame onto what they described as the real threat to the Hollywood film industry and its workers – that is, Communism – to which they were among the first in Hollywood to make frequent reference.

While the war temporarily froze in place the ideological antagonisms gathering in the industry, anti-Communist investigations and rhetoric accelerated exponentially afterwards when, as Ingrid Scobie has put it, 'California led all other states in anti-subversive activity'.[162] In response to the strike of October 1945, Roy Brewer resurrected the anti-Communism that had been a staple of the Browne and Bioff era, alleging that 'the Communist Party openly entered this strike situation and made its boldest bid for power in the experience of Southern California labor'.[163] Making a distinction between the CSU and 'the legitimate labor movement in Los Angeles', he pressured the Los Angeles Central Labor Committee (CLC), local headquarters of the AFL, which had supported Browne and Bioff, to adopt a membership resolution banning Communists and to investigate Sorrell for Communist connections before voting for his removal from office.[164] This initiative took place, however, against a backdrop of declarations of support for the CSU by the United Auto Workers and other CIO unions, meetings between Sorrell and Los Angeles CIO representatives, and calls by the CIO for criminal charges against Sorrell to be dropped.[165]

The Brewer strategy, pursued by one workers' union against another, typified the internecine warfare between segments of the working class, which had long been a characteristic of American society but reached a crescendo in Los Angeles after the Second World War. As a sign of the perversion of class solidarity, Brewer's strategy entirely coincided with that of Senator Jack Tenney, chair of the California State Assembly Committee on Un-American Activities. Despite the fact that pickets at Warner Bros made a point of singing 'The Star-Spangled Banner' as police closed in with steel helmets, billy clubs and tear gas,

Tenney responded to the October 1945 strike by declaring himself 'amazed that a handful of revolutionary Communists can deny lawful owners the use of their property, inflict bodily injuries upon hundreds of citizens, defy orders of the courts of California, and openly and successfully defy all law enforcing agencies'.[166] Established in 1941, the Tenney Committee achieved a prominent role in California public life because of the state's strong anti-Communist tendency and the exposure of its long coastline to wartime threats from the Pacific.[167] A one-time professional piano player turned state assemblyman for the Democratic Party in 1933, Tenney had briefly been president of a Los Angeles musicians' union local but, ousted from that position in 1939, had gravitated toward the Republican Party, which he joined in 1944, disowning his many former associations with liberals and leftists.[168] For Tenney, investigation of the Hollywood film industry was but one (albeit prominent) political strategy aimed at protecting the state and its people from Communist subversion. Among his other initiatives in the California legislature were bills requiring the licensing by the state of all foreign-language schools, the filing with county authorities of an English-language translation of all foreign language newspapers, and the automatic abolition of any party whose registrations fell below 0.1 per cent of the total population of registered voters in the state.[169]

Additionally, Tenney led a concerted effort by conservative Republicans to thwart what they saw as dangerous liberal projects in California schools. He sponsored a bill to ensure that sex education was provided only by licensed physicians to children above eleventh grade, and to boys and girls in separate classes. Another bill called for the establishment of a State Assembly committee to approve all proposed public school curricula and textbooks, and another campaign aimed to have the state cancel the supposedly left-leaning history curriculum known as *Building America*. Although these efforts were not successful, they were so drawn out and high-profile as to have 'a stifling effect upon the Department of Education', generating fear among liberals and leftists in the community.[170] This was institutionalized by the establishment of anti-Communist loyalty oaths in Los Angeles County in 1947, the City of Los Angeles in 1948, and the State of California in 1950, the latter requiring an oath of all employees in public service, politicians, labour union members, lawyers and defence workers.[171]

The anti-Communist strategies that united Brewer and Tenney dovetailed in the hearings held to investigate Sorrell's supposed

Communism by the Los Angeles CLC in May 1946, which Brewer had initiated and at which Tenney testified. Here evidence gathered by Tenney Committee investigations was rehashed with a specific target in mind including, in a twist worthy of a low-grade B film noir, the first presentation in evidence of what was allegedly a Communist Party membership card from 1937 in the name of one 'Herbert Stewart', said to be an alias of, and signed by, the CSU leader Herbert Sorrell.[172] For two years after, the matter of Sorrell and the card was raised repeatedly by his critics, although attempts to make the charge stick proved difficult and the provenance and authenticity of the card were always in question.[173] Its next outing was on the other side of the country, in Washington, DC, as an item of evidence in the October 1947 HUAC hearings into the supposed Communism of Hollywood writers, directors and stars.

Although Gallup polls revealed that only 10 per cent of Americans seriously worried about Communist infiltration of Hollywood (and most of those who did were over 30, Republican, and not regular cinemagoers), the investigations of the Hollywood film industry by HUAC signalled a new kind and degree of federal government interest.[174] The infamous high-profile hearings that took place in Washington, DC, in 1947 and 1951 were preceded by investigations in person on the ground in Los Angeles by Democratic Congressman John S. Wood of Georgia, the chair of HUAC, who arrived to see for himself on 5 October 1946, just two weeks into the second of the Hollywood strikes.[175] Then, on 21 October 1947, when Hollywood luminaries travelled to the capital just one week before the second strike began to collapse, Adolphe Menjou, star of numerous comedy movies about the movies in the 1930s, presented to HUAC a photostat of Sorrell's supposed CP membership card, although he would not say who gave it to him.[176] Three days later, Walt Disney claimed of Sorrell that 'if he isn't a Communist he sure should be one',[177] and four days after that Roy Brewer testified that 'the Communist plan to control the motion picture industry as a whole . . . came dangerously close to success'.[178] Two weeks later again, in the shadow of the HUAC hearings but effectively endorsing the Committee's actions in retrospect, the moguls gathered for their highly publicized meeting at the Waldorf-Astoria Hotel in New York, at which they stated that they would no longer employ communists in the industry and would ban those known from their service. The location of the meeting was strategic, aiming to send a message of reassurance to conservative investors and government observers on the East Coast, but the message itself was a product of Los Angeles. If California set the pace in the implementation of loyalty oaths in public life, the moguls now did the same in the private sector. The *Stanford Law Review* dubbed their statement 'an outstanding example'[179] and the *New York Times* called it 'an unprecedented action in American industrial fields'.[180]

Sorrell publicly demanded to be allowed to testify to HUAC and appealed along with other members of the Painters union to Joseph Martin, Speaker of the House of Representatives, but was refused.[181] Instead, he and other workers were received by the House Labor Committee, chaired by Republican Congressman Fred A. Hartley of New Jersey, which had first held brief hearings on the Hollywood strikes in Washington, DC, on 8 March 1947 before following up with five weeks of hearings in Los Angeles that August and September.[182] A subcommittee sent to Los Angeles, chaired by Republican Congressman Carroll D. Kearns of Pennsylvania, heard testimony from Samuel Goldwyn and executives from Fox, Columbia and Warner Bros, as well as from Sorrell, Brewer and other labour leaders.[183] However, it was unable to achieve any breakthrough and returned to the capital where the Committee revisited the issue of the Hollywood strikes in February and March 1948, but now in a political environment that had been crucially changed by the HUAC hearings on Hollywood four months earlier. In Los Angeles and Washington, DC, Kearns showed little interest in hearing testimony from IATSE members that CSU members were communists and instead appears to have focused on the issue of possible continuing mafia connections with IATSE, and especially Willie Bioff, who was alleged by some to have regained influence behind the scenes in IATSE since his recent release from prison.[184] However, in a sign of the times, this line of inquiry was soon quashed by Kearns' own Republican colleagues on the HLC. In particular, Fred Hartley expanded the Committee's remit in February 1948 to look into the question of subversives and accepted testimony from Matthew Levy, attorney for IATSE, that the CSU had 'followed the Communist party line' by planning an industrial union in Hollywood, which would 'at the appropriate time join hands with the pro-Communist elements in the studio and especially in the Screen Writers Guild'.[185]

This was the same Fred Hartley who, just six months earlier, had successfully proposed legislation whose influence is still decisive in the American workplace today: the Taft-Hartley Act of 23 June 1947, which curtailed the right of workers to strike indefinitely, asserted a new executive power on behalf of the National Labor Relations Board to demand an end to strikes, and banned so-called jurisdictional strikes and secondary boycotts. The Act was conceived as a response to a national crisis of labour unrest but Southern California, and the Hollywood film industry in particular, played an important role in shaping it. On 2 September 1947, the day after the failed mediation efforts in the second strike by Archbishop Cantwell of Los Angeles, during Mass at St Vibiana's Cathedral, Fr Thomas F. Coogan declared from the pulpit that the Act 'denies basic rights of working men'.[186] Two weeks later, however, Senator Robert A. Taft, co-sponsor of the Act, and widely recognized as the leading Republican senator on domestic economic and social policy, made an address to the Republican Organizations of Los Angeles County in which he expressed his pleasure that the 1946 mid-term elections had made California 'a Republican State, which last year elected a Republican Governor [Earl Warren], a Republican Senator, and more than half of the Republican Congressmen'.[187]

The following month, the first ever case taken to the NLRB under the auspices of the Act was pursued by 42 Los Angeles film studio workers, both non-striking and striking, demanding that the Board order a return to work, determine jurisdictions for the different workers on each set, and fix penalties for unions continuing to strike.[188] In May 1948 Cecil B. De Mille travelled to Washington, DC, to give testimony to the HLC in which he pleaded for the instigation of federal right-to-work legislation and showed a twenty-minute film of picketing in the recent Hollywood strike as evidence that labour unions had pernicious effects.[189] Also that year, Hartley, in his book *Our New National Labor Policy*, singled out for praise the Republican Congressman Richard M. Nixon, who was a junior member of both the HLC and HUAC, not only for his important contribution to the successful prosecution of the Chambers-Hiss Soviet espionage case but for acting, in Hartley's words, as 'Hollywood's representative in Congress. An ex-service man, he reflected the resentment on the part of most veterans toward organized labor.'[190] And in 1950 the *Yale Law Journal*, in reviewing the first few years of the Act's operation, pointed to the case of *Schatte v. International Alliance* in which a member of the striking Carpenters' Union Local 946 of the CSU lost a claim for wrongful dismissal on the basis that, under the terms of the Taft-Hartley Act, his decision to strike had no justification in the first place.[191]

This unfortunate narrative illustrates that there was an inter-regional dynamic to the amplification of anti-communism in the United

States and that the most prominent prosecution of communists by agencies and individuals based in Washington, DC, was fuelled by agencies and individuals in Los Angeles.[192] Time and again, in the events of the day, a pattern revealed itself in which action was taken by the capital based upon initiatives and intelligence fed to it by reactionary elements on the West Coast who sought to bring the judgment of the federal government down upon their own community.

One of the notable features of the Hollywood strikes was their modest but publicly visible role in increasing routine urban-regional interaction between Los Angeles and other US cities of a kind that was an increasing fact of everyday life and narrativized in many film noirs. The people negotiating to resolve the strikes were among those who took advantage of the growth of air travel, flying back and forth between meetings held in Los Angeles, New York and Washington, DC, where many studio executives and government mediators were based, and in Chicago, San Francisco and Cincinnati, where the major unions were headquartered.[193] Certain flights from Los Angeles gained special attention, such as that made by Walter Pidgeon, Jane Wyman, Gene Kelly and Ronald Reagan as part of a Screen Actors Guild delegation that met with the AFL in Chicago in October 1946.[194] Indeed, it was standard practice for negotiations relating to Hollywood labour *not* to take place in Los Angeles in the 1930s and '40s and IATSE locals in Hollywood were forbidden from taking any industrial action without approval in advance from New York.[195] Because this restriction compounded the resentment felt by many Los Angeles studio workers at IATSE's closed shop and its mafia enforcement, it contributed to the increasingly militant determination of CSU members to achieve greater bargaining power through self-representation.[196] Carey McWilliams reflected years later that 'one of the things that was always wrong with labor relations in the industry was that the negotiations took place in New York instead of here [in Los Angeles]'.[197] Sorrell insisted that 'painters don't go for these contracts negotiated back in New York by men who have never seen the inside of a studio', and Congressman Carroll D. Kearns of the HLC, lamenting what he called the 'remote control' of labour issues, ventured that Hollywood studio workers 'could do things here pretty well if you didn't have to go away across the country to get approval'.[198] A hidden geographical dynamic shaped the strikes in so far as studio management seemed determined to ensure that control over film industry workers in Los Angeles remained vested in individuals and agencies on the other side of the country. The physical distance between the East and West Coasts, which contributed to the strikes, also made them more persistent and intense than they might otherwise have been.

If the focus by HUAC upon Hollywood may be said to have made the Cold War somehow cinematic, specific events in the history of the strikes uncannily resembled the film noirs then being made. At 8:30 p.m. on Monday, 30 October 1945, outside his home at 1153 North Norton Avenue, Glendale, three shots were fired at Herbert Sorrell's car as he reversed out of the driveway.[199] On 2 March 1946, Sorrell was abducted from 'a San Fernando Valley street . . . by three men in a black sedan', beaten, and later found in a critical condition, bound and gagged in the dirt near Inyokern, Kern County, about 100 miles northeast of Los Angeles.[200] Police at the picket lines outside Warner Bros in Burbank read the riot act to strikers using microphones and loudspeakers provided by the studio and mounted on studio trucks. In a bizarre inversion of the pilgrimages around Los Angeles made by movie fans, the jury in Sorrell's trial for contempt of court was taken on a tour of the Warner Bros studios and the streets outside. This, the *Los Angeles Times* explained, 'consumed a considerable part of the day looking over the scene of the rioting, the place where the official order was read against the mob, the spots where fighting took place and other points of connection with the case'.[201] And, finally, studio managers at Republic Pictures used the studios' own cameras to film pickets outside its walls, presumably for legal evidence, leading to a bizarre game of lights:

> The pickets used mirrors to slant sunlight into the lenses of cameras that were being used by the studios to make a record of how the pickets were behaving. On the other side, cameramen were reflecting some light of their own down on the picket lines and for a short time there was a battle of 'heliographs' but without greater casualties than smarting eyes.[202]

Long before the widespread establishment of the now standard practice whereby police and protesters often record each other's actions on digital video during major confrontations, this was an example of filming the real city on location but for very different purposes than the technique used in film noirs.

One response by the police, civic authorities and studio management to the Hollywood strikes was to condemn and prosecute the

A picketer outside Republic Pictures, Studio City, reflects sunlight in a mirror to dazzle surveillance cameramen, *Los Angeles Times*, 8 October 1946.

CSU, which they portrayed as a small minority of hard-line communist or communist-inspired agitators, despite the fact that its membership accounted for approximately two-fifths of the film industry's total workforce. Their other response, however, was to characterize picket lines as obstructions to freedom of movement in the streets and on sidewalks, and to try to use the law to define the kinds of movement that were and were not acceptable. This was especially evident around the imposing gates of the movie studios, which became the key sites of contestation. As explained in the previous chapter, these had been destinations for movie fans and markers of exclusivity through which ordinary folk could not pass. During the strikes, they became microcosms in a struggle for control of public space.

In March 1945, at the beginning of the first of the two major strikes, the *Los Angeles Times* reported, 'One of the largest crowds was at Warner Bros studios, where several thousand people milled around. Burbank police patrolled the highway, keeping the throng from blocking roads.'[203] That August, the Los Angeles Police Commission complained that, in contravention of laws, 'picket lines [in Hollywood] were so large that patrons could not get into theaters and that pedestrians were forced to step off the sidewalk'.[204] In October, Burbank City Council instituted by-laws to make a distinction between 'peaceful picketing' and 'mass picketing', where the latter phrase was used to describe any group of strikers blocking a thoroughfare, and especially the gates of a studio.[205] Thereafter, the strikes involved drawn-out stand-offs between strikers and non-strikers massed on opposite sides of the street and separated by traffic with occasional efforts by non-strikers to break through picket lines.

Violence at Warner Bros and other studios seems to have been frequently triggered by attempts to drive through pickets in automobiles, something that happened often, resulting in clashes of people and machines.[206] Press photographs of street-fighting between police, strikers and non-strikers present jarring compositions of bodies in action, mixed with overturned cars, the criss-crossing of streetcar lines and background clouds of tear gas and water spray as fire hoses are turned on pickets. These commotions of human limbs and demonstrative facial expressions have a density and lack of control that sets them apart from the relative absence of dynamic human pedestrian life then as now typical of large swathes of the real Los Angeles and mythicized in the empty streets of film noirs. They are also ironic given what we now know about Los Angeles' exceptionally dispersed growth and reliance on private automobiles, extensive suburban subdivisions and commercial strip development. These were already in evidence but accelerating significantly. By 1949 there was one car for every 3.9 persons in Los Angeles, compared to one for every 7.1 persons in Chicago, and one for every twelve in New York, while the population densities per square mile for the three cities in 1950 were 10,399 persons (Los Angeles), 17,409 (Chicago) and 26,046 (New York).[207]

Militant labour organization was made more difficult by these characteristics of the city, which were at odds with the conditions that had fostered mass demonstrations in other cities in history: as Christine Boyer has explained, from the late eighteenth century to the early twentieth, public spaces in large cities such as London, Paris, Berlin and New York, which had previously been designed as 'honorific place[s] celebrating the power of the king, queen, or aristocracy', were remade by political revolutions into a 'democratic public sphere' in which the 'repressed demands of the working and dangerous classes returned to haunt the streets'.[208] In the Hollywood strikes, however, the dispersal of the film studios in and around Los Angeles – some in Hollywood but others in Burbank, Studio City and Culver City – together with the significant distance between these and downtown Los Angeles, made the massing of strikers in large numbers a great challenge. The relative lack of a pedestrian culture, and the absence of large public spaces amenable to protesting crowds, made symbolic shows of strength by workers seem anachronistic and even impossible. Meanwhile, auto-mobility seems to have made it easier for police to congregate in large numbers: Burbank police, for example, regularly called in support from the nearby police departments of Glendale and Los Angeles, and from the Los Angeles County Sheriff's office.

Evidence that the authorities sought to restrict pedestrian move-ment in Los Angeles was provided in the *California Law Review* in 1951 by the legal historians Benjamin Aaron and William Levin, who argued that Los Angeles was at the forefront of a new national tendency for employers and police to use injunctions against strikers thanks to the Taft-Hartley Act.[209] Identifying the mass arrests of picketers outside

Columbia Pictures and other studios in 1946 as exemplary of the use of police to bust strikes, Aaron and Levin detailed the often strikingly prescriptive language used by city and county ordinances to circumscribe movement and assembly in public places:

> The injunctions are customarily rather lengthy and, in some respects, quite detailed in their use of language. Restraints against picketing also usually forbid 'standing', 'sitting', 'loitering', 'gathering', 'assembling', 'marching', 'parading', 'walking', 'stopping', or 'stationing, placing, or maintaining any pickets at the place of'. Those against violence prohibit 'intimidating', 'coercing', 'threatening', 'molesting', 'pushing', 'elbowing', 'shouldering', and the catch-all 'otherwise physically contacting the person or clothing of'. Other restrictions upon picket-line conduct include prohibitions against 'lewd or boisterous talk or shouting or yelling'.[210]

One of the typical strategies pursued by Los Angeles courts in granting injunctions was to place restrictions on the number of people allowed on any one picket line, usually stipulating a maximum of three, each ten to twenty feet apart, regardless of the size of the industry being picketed, the number of workers on strike, the location of the picket line or the other kinds of activity going on nearby. For Aaron and Levin, the courts' tendency to 'regulate picket-line activities with extreme particularity' suggested 'somewhat unrealistic' expectations.[211]

While Sorrell was detained by police on numerous occasions, the most serious charges he faced, in a law suit against him and 400 other strikers, were rioting, failure to disperse, and contempt of court for failing to abide by the court's stipulation that no more than eighteen pickets (that is, eighteen people in total) could be placed at any one time outside the main gate of Warner Bros and the seven other entrances to its site of more than 60 acres.[212] Prior to their arrest, the strikers, whose numbers were much larger than allowed, circumvented the court order by placing pickets on the gates in accordance with the law and having the rest of those in attendance parade up and down on the street in front – initially, it was not an offence to parade without a permit in Burbank although the City Council soon changed the law.[213]

In this respect, the Hollywood strikes exemplified the rise of the 'corporate city' identified by the political economist David M. Gordon as the key development in American urbanization after the Second

World War and one in which suburbanization and political quiescence went hand in hand.[214] Examining the relationship between class, industrial organization and the internal geography of American cities, Gordon observes that, until the 1870s, factories and working-class residential areas were typically concentrated in city centres, with residential districts internally differentiated by ethnic group and the middle classes congregating in emerging suburbs, facilitated by the growth of public transport. Subsequently, however, labour unrest migrated from small towns and the countryside into cities where downtowns became hotspots of social conflict. In the early twentieth century, aided by the automobile, industrial development was increasingly led by corporations whose 'search for stability, predictability, and security' led them to move their operations from urban to suburban areas, thus contributing to the city's further dispersal.[215] Citing as an example the relationship between Chicago and Gary, Indiana, in the 1900s, and the book-length study by Graham Taylor, *Satellite Cities: A Study of Industrial Suburbs* (1915), Gordon explains that in suburbs industrialists found to their satisfaction that union organization was less successful and unruly. This was especially the case in so-called 'Sunbelt' cities in the Southwest after the Second World War, which saw the culmination of this long pattern of development because they 'meet the tests of *qualitative efficiency* better than old cities. They have developed a form which lends itself to control of workers better than the older form.'[216]

Conference of Studio Unions march and picket flanked by police and bystanders, Warner Bros, Burbank, October 1945.

In leading the decentralization of industry in Los Angeles in the 1910s and '20s, the film studios helped to drive the decentralization of residential and commercial land use while articulating those processes in a mostly positive way in slapstick comedies. The events of the Hollywood strikes, however, foregrounded some of the negative effects that decentralization had for later generations in real life and cinematic representation. Los Angeles' suburbanization did not lead merely to a new urban form but extended and reinforced a particularly strong manifestation of the individualism generally characteristic of United States society, based upon notions of a right to private property and a right to work. The links between those and the city's distinctive spatiality had been officially expressed by Arthur W. Kinney, Industrial Commissioner of the Los Angeles Chamber of Commerce, back in 1918:

> In this region a favorable climate makes for contented and efficient labor. Here the home life of the worker is almost ideal. They live in modest modern bungalows surrounded by flowers and plots of green grass . . . The nights are cool, the days are pleasant, and the factory worker goes to his employment refreshed and invigorated. This means that there exists here a remarkable efficiency of labor . . .[217]

After the Second World War Los Angeles' further growth as an objectively existing city and as a collection of filmed images was informed by similar thinking. But the two aspects were often defined by their opposition: in film noirs, critiques of the city's dominant mythology and iconography proliferated even as the city became a key site in the formation of a new vision of the worker as a stakeholder in capitalism. This new vision, in turn, became a pillar of the postwar *pax Americana* and was global in its reach.

Moreover, urban planning and construction in Los Angeles were as profoundly torn apart by the ideological conflicts of the day as the motion picture industry. Continuing the liberal and leftist traditions of the New Deal, progressive urban reformers in the late 1940s sought to implement large-scale public housing projects, such as Elysian Park Heights in the Chavez Ravine, to accommodate returning veterans, the working poor and displaced migrants from Los Angeles' slums.[218] But efforts at collectivist, high-density and socially mixed development were overcome by the privatizing and decentralizing forces of commercial real estate developers, conservative citizens groups, industrial corporations, the police and the courts. And a similarly decisive role was played by anti-communist allegations and prosecutions, led by Republican public representatives – for example, in the purge of progressive reformers in the Los Angeles Housing Authority, which came to a head in 1952–3.

Meanwhile, Los Angeles' boosterist tradition continued apace: a special feature in the *New York Times* in 1949, for example, eulogizing the city's lifestyles and constant growth, explained 'Why people go to Los Angeles – and stay there' with a long list of no-brainers each accompanied by an upbeat photo:

> Because of job opportunities; Because they dress as they please; Because the food is good – and cheaper; Because the movies lend enchantment; Because the suburbs offer pleasant living; Because drive-ins include even a church; Because it is a fine place to raise children; Because of the city's screwball streak; Because the sun shines bright.[219]

Such accounts generally hid Los Angeles' social divisions and the turbulence of its physical growth. In 1954 work began on clearing Chavez Ravine for Dodger Stadium instead of public housing, and on Bunker Hill downtown for a new central business district. Also in 1954, the newly opened Hollywood Freeway cut like a knife through the eastern half of Hollywood and between it, Edendale and Los Feliz, in which filmmaking had once been key.[220] But by that time neither film noir nor the Hollywood studio system was in its heyday any more.

Epilogue

In the late 1950s and the '60s, a series of significant transformations took place in Los Angeles, its film industry and its cinematic representation. The city was spatially and experientially reorganized around its freeway network while its global economic, political and demographic importance was confirmed. The decline of the studio system accelerated, as independent production, art cinema and underground film took off. And the proliferation of types of cinema made Los Angeles' cinematic image even more ubiquitous, though also more fragmented than before. Taken together, these transformations constitute an important punctuation mark in the history of the real and imaginary subjects of this book, and a point at which to bring my study to a close while making connections between that history and more recent times.[1]

As the middle-aged and middle-class audiences to whom film noir had been primarily addressed deserted cinema-going for television and other pastimes, the city's image was increasingly shaped by the attitudes of teenagers and young adults. Alienated from the region's boosterist mythology and the formulae of the silver screen, this newly significant demographic responded with deliberately subcultural behaviour of a kind that had existed in the past, but had been largely ignored by Hollywood cinema.[2] For example, *Rebel Without a Cause* (Nicholas Ray, 1955) drew public attention to the issues of teenage rebellion and juvenile delinquency, which manifested themselves acutely in Los Angeles because of its good weather and high rates of automobile ownership. Revolving around the dysfunctional family life of Jim Stark (James Dean), his romance with the maladjusted Judy (Natalie Wood) and his friendship with the loner Plato (Sal Mineo), the film was produced by Warner Bros in rich colour and CinemaScope, endowing the image

273

of the city with a new degree of spectacle. But, at this time, films with youth subculture themes and settings were more often produced on low budgets by independent companies in the exploitation film industry and with a less moralistic tone. This was evident in the American International Pictures release *A Bucket of Blood* (Roger Corman, 1959), a parody of the Beatnik artists' scene in Venice Beach, in which a young layabout with no talent becomes a celebrated sculptor by killing his subjects, covering them in plaster and displaying them for the appreciation of existentialist art connoisseurs. In its choice of setting, the film recognized that district of Los Angeles as one of the leading centres of dissent from the Cold War consensus, but its mockery of the Beatnik artist accused artisanal rather than industrial culture of dissimulation. By contrast, authentic deconstructions *were* achieved by real artists and filmmakers in Los Angeles' burgeoning underground scene as the work of Kenneth Anger, Curtis Harrington and others expanded the earlier, but more sporadic, avant-garde filmmaking of Robert Florey and Maya Deren.[3]

Glamour and sex appeal of the kind promoted by the studios were among the primary targets of avant-garde film, but those values were extended in a fully commercial way by films such as *Beach Party* (William Asher, 1963) and *Beach Blanket Bingo* (William Asher, 1965). These appealed to teenage audiences with an appetite for high school girls in bikinis, muscular college men in shorts, seaside romance, rock 'n' roll, surfing and the Southern California sun. Hence Los Angeles film culture was deeply split during its 'Endless Summer', at least until the late 1960s when an increasingly large and visible youth counterculture was announced in the drinking, brawling and sacrilege of bikers in *The Wild Angels* (Roger Corman, 1966) and political demonstrations in *Wild in the Streets* (Barry Shears, 1968).[4] These films ambivalently celebrated and condemned their subjects, but they were consistent in promoting young people as an especially creative force in Los Angeles, whose postwar population growth was the most rapid of any city in the United States, and which was now the centre not only of American feature film production but of television and the music business too. Films with very low budgets, such as *A Bucket of Blood*, continued to use sets for interiors, but filmmakers and audiences increasingly valued location filming for navigation of places that were apart from the mainstream: the beatnik cafés of Venice, the surfing beaches of Malibu and the back roads of the Hollywood Hills. This was another cinema of automobility but, unlike slapstick comedy, one that had little patience for the regimentation of suburban bungalows and streets. Instead, its new geography implied the end of the studio era: the Sunset Strip had once been home to big bands and the high life of the stars at Ciro's and the Trocadero but, by the late 1960s, when that role had been usurped by Las Vegas and Palm Springs, The Fifth Estate and the Whisky A Go-Go made the Strip a hub of counterculture and revolt.

The geographical specificity of the films spoke to a need to counter the sprawling homogeneous consumer capitalism of much of the Los Angeles landscape. Boosterist sources continued to speak in glowing terms of the city's expansion: for example, the Citizens National Bank of Los Angeles declared in its book *Los Angeles: Industrial Focal Point of the West* (1963): 'OPPORTUNITY . . . Los Angeles is on the move . . . moving up and . . . moving from within . . . Los Angeles is the focal point of the Air age and now the even newer Space age. It is in the path of progress.'[5] In such accounts Los Angeles' exceptionally large size was presented as a guarantor of profits, its economic opportunity underpinned by its horizontal expanse and its then still-new freeway system, which was celebrated for making possible a productive new mobility for citizens and businesses. The freeways had been under construction since the late 1940s but were attended by growing public ambivalence. Early reports recognized the scale of the city as a problem to be solved by engineering. The *Los Angeles Times* predicted a 'city of freeways' hinging upon a growing transport nexus around, but bypassing, downtown.[6] Sociologists evaluated the 'ecological considerations' of the 'superhighway' when applied to 'the greatest land area of any city in the world, specifically 453 square miles'.[7] A particularly frank exploration in the *New York Times* marvelled that Los Angeles' 60 miles of freeways, more than any other US city, were expected to grow to 900 miles by 1980, but with dubious net benefit to society: 'Here, nestled under its blanket of smog, girdled by bands of freeways, its core eviscerated by concrete strips and asphalt fields, its circulatory arteries pumping away without focus, lies the prototype of Gasopolis, the rubber-wheeled living region of the future.'[8] One of the first scholarly studies to elaborate on a growing crisis of decentralization, Arthur Grey's 'Los Angeles: Urban Prototype' (1959), pointed to an alarming decline of downtown, the weakening of social interaction by a retail-dominated cityscape, 'political fractionalization', the failure 'to evolve an integrated pattern' of housing and the destruction of open space.[9]

During much of the 1960s, youth subculture films rejecting the instrumental city sat awkwardly side-by-side with films produced and released by the majors that updated the city's sun-drenched iconography in less controversial ways. *Sex and the Single Girl* (Richard Quine, 1964), *The Swinger* (George Sidney, 1966) and *Don't Make Waves* (Alexander Mackendrick, 1967) were romantic comedies with all-star casts that characterized Los Angeles as a place of sex-obsessed, but good-natured, suburban mayhem. However, cinematic critiques of Los Angeles emerged in films that incorporated the modernist influences of European art cinema. Many of the most innovative films were made by foreigners who, like Blaise Cendrars and other foreign visitors 30 years before, saw a telling landscape of the future. *Point Blank* (John Boorman, 1967), *Model Shop* (Jacques Demy, 1969), *Zabriskie Point* (Michelangelo Antonioni, 1970) and *The Outside Man* (Jacques Deray, 1972) portrayed a place of armed aggression, hard-edged modern architecture, commercial kitsch and constant automobility. In *Point Blank* and *The Outside Man*, these features were presented within an updated film noir (or 'neo-noir') format, while *Model Shop* and *Zabriskie Point* concentrated on the anomie caused by Los Angeles' effacement of nature and the war in Vietnam.

By that time it had become commonplace to think of Los Angeles as a city whose development said something about the future of human civilization. A sense of its widespread significance was conveyed by the aerial views of the urban landscape from helicopters or planes that many films deployed, extending the camera's perceptive field while implying a greater sense of emptiness than ever before. In the 1950s Los Angeles was described as a 'natural experimental laboratory' and 'the progenitor of urban change throughout the United States'.[10] In the following decade it was an 'endless spread', 'a new non-society by the sea', 'instant architecture in an instant townscape' or, in the words of Jean-Luc Godard, simply 'a big garage'.[11] Critical voices increasingly recognized what boosterist accounts did not admit – that an over-reliance on automobiles, runaway freeway building and urban sprawl had destructive potential and effects.

The fate of some districts seemed likely to compound the layered traces of lost pasts in Los Angeles' history and visual culture. Downtown was in seemingly terminal decline as a commercial and social hub: the buildings in its beaux arts and art deco business district, often used for locations in silent comedies, had fallen derelict or been taken over by low-rent activities, and its last Victorian enclave, Bunker Hill, a frequent stomping ground for film noir, had been razed to the ground for a new financial centre. Hollywood was no longer the business and symbolic anchor of the film industry it had been in movies about the movies, but a dilapidated environment of poverty and crime, populated by fast-food outlets, porno theatres and souvenir stores for tourists.[12] Other districts, whose neglect was even greater, and which had never much featured in movies, experienced even more troubling upheaval. The largely African American neighbourhood of Watts was torn apart by riots in 1965 that caused 34 deaths and tens of millions of dollars worth of damage, while the largely Latino East Los Angeles exploded in a wave of mass protest culminating in the Chicano Moratorium five years later, in which the journalist Ruben Salazar and three others were killed. In common with many other cities across the United States, official agencies increasingly pointed to a crisis and called for urban reform, for example in the *Concept for the Los Angeles General Plan* produced by the Los Angeles Department of City Planning (1970), and the Los Angeles County Board of Supervisors' *General Plan of Los Angeles County* (1973).[13]

Many films implied that Los Angeles was the nation's limit case of rampant urban growth, suburban conformity and televisual superficiality, leading to crises of identity and mental breakdown.[14] This was true of perhaps the most famous film of the era set in Los Angeles, *The Graduate* (Mike Nichols, 1967), which focused on the frustration of college graduate Benjamin Craddock (Dustin Hoffman) in the face of the staid middle-class marriage and career in the plastics industry that his parents have planned for him. In *The Graduate*, as in many other films of the era, the activity of driving at speed through Los Angeles becomes a prominent subject for representation in its own right as Benjamin rejects the mansions and swimming pools of Beverly Hills by driving off in his red Alfa Romeo Spider. Inverting such images of mobility, Peter Bogdanovich's *Targets* (1968) recounted, in a deliberately cold way, the obsession with guns of an outwardly typical San Fernando Valley teenager, much less well-off than Craddock, whose disgust with his parents leads him to kill them in their bungalow before going on a shooting spree, sniping at cars on the Ventura Freeway and the audience at a drive-in movie theatre in Van Nuys, which is showing horror movies from the studio era.

John Cassavetes's *Faces* (1968), Robert Altman's *The Long Goodbye* (1973) and Hal Ashby's *Shampoo* (1975) also generally insisted on filming the real city on location, rendering Los Angeles as a patchwork of horizontal, high-speed and depthless landscapes with hand-held and vehicle-mounted cameras, and rapid zooming and panning, to a degree unprecedented in American narrative film. With these techniques,

277

filmmakers grappled with the challenges of representing what the geographer Kevin Lynch called the lack of 'imageability' and the accentuated 'kinesthetic sensations' that typified life in Los Angeles.[15] Mostly made in colour and widescreen, they also often echoed what Peter Plagens has called the 'Los Angeles Look' of Billy Al Bengston and Ed Ruscha, whose 'cool, semi-technological, industrially pretty art' often drew on movie iconography.[16] Indeed, like other visual arts, cinema showed Los Angeles as 'pre-emptively Pop'.[17]

That many of these films involved no shooting in studios at all testified to the collapse of the studio system. From 1946 to 1969 cinema-going in the United States fell from 100 million to 15 million tickets sold per week; the studios' annual revenues dropped from $1.8 billion to $350 million; and the number of feature films produced dwindled from an average of 500 to 100 per year.[18] In response, the Hollywood majors concentrated on film financing and distribution while film production by independent companies on location became the norm. So-called 'run-away' productions diminished the importance of Los Angeles' movie lots and sound stages, and were matched by a rise in 'offshore' production, driven by the increasing importance of foreign markets to the industry's revenue.[19] As I explained in chapter One, these developments combined with the gradual absorption of the majors into diversified multinational corporations to prompt the widespread disposal of buildings and land by MGM, Fox and other studios. Hence the 1960s and '70s witnessed a reversal of much of the construction undertaken at such expense and with such fanfare between 40 and 60 years before. The studios' simulacral qualities persisted in *Singin' in the Rain* (Stanley Donen, 1952) and *A Star is Born* (George Cukor, 1954) but were disillusioned beyond repair in *Hollywood Boulevard* (Joe Dante, 1976) and *California Suite* (Herbert Ross, 1978).

Despite the progressive deconstruction of Los Angeles' inherited cinematic image as a place of opportunity, beauty and wealth, many films continued to be set in relatively comfortable locales such as Hollywood, Beverly Hills, Santa Monica and Malibu, and most paid no attention to social and economic inequality between the white middle class and minority groups. As we have seen, even when deliberately shooting beyond the studios' walls, most Hollywood films of Los Angeles from the 1910s to the 1950s marginalized, suppressed or distorted non-Anglo experiences and iconographies. This situation showed signs of improvement, for example, in the very late film noir *The Crimson Kimono*

(Samuel Fuller, 1959), which was shot in Little Tokyo and sympathet-
ically portrayed the friendship of two police detectives and Korean War
veterans, one Anglo, one Japanese American. But a fuller exploration
of race and urban space took place in 'blaxploitation' thrillers such as
Sweet Sweetback's Baadaaasss Song (Melvin Van Peebles, 1971), filmed on
a low budget in Watts. Centred upon a black male hustler sympathetic
to the Black Panthers, the film used *cinéma vérité*, jump-cutting and
psychedelic effects to document impoverished sections of Los Angeles
previously absent from the screen. Subsequent examples such as *Foxy
Brown* (Jack Hill, 1974) were more formulaic, but the Hollywood
studio system was further rebuked for marginalizing racial minorities
in social studies such as *Killer of Sheep* (Charles Burnett, 1977) and other
films by the so-called 'LA Rebellion' directors of UCLA.[20] Diversity was
also added to Los Angeles' cinematic image by popular comedies about
Latinos such as *Cheech & Chong: Up in Smoke* (Lou Adler, 1977) and
realist portraits of migrant workers such as *El Norte* (Gregory Nava, 1983).

Subsequently, Los Angeles became important for the 'New Black
Realism' of *Boyz N the Hood* (John Singleton, 1991) and *Menace II
Society* (Albert and Allen Hughes, 1993), which were shot on modest
budgets in a relatively flat, televisual style. These became controversial
because of their focus on the deprivation, endemic drug use and street
violence that blighted South Central Los Angeles before and after the Los
Angeles riots of 1992, while racial conflict was addressed by white filmmakers concentrating on white protagonists in *Colors* (Dennis Hopper,
1988) and *Falling Down* (Joel Schumacher, 1993). However, some of
the most telling films on race were historical. For example, *Come See the
Paradise* (Alan Parker, 1990), *American Me* (Edward James Olmos,
1992) and *Devil in a Blue Dress* (Carl Franklin, 1995) delved into Los
Angeles' social history of the mid-twentieth century, reinserting the
racial diversity that Anglo culture and the studio system preferred not
to see at the time.

Whichever community has been their focus, many films since the
early 1970s have explored the value and sustainability of ethnic minority
communities in a polyglot city shaped by transnational capitalism,
globalization and the strong arm of the Los Angeles Police Department.
The latter themes have received expression of a different kind in disaster
films set in Los Angeles, from *Earthquake* (Mark Robson, 1974) to
Volcano (Mick Jackson, 1997), which have undercut Los Angeles' status
as the second largest American city with a sense of its propensity for

catastrophe. They have also been at the forefront of the cinema's increasing reliance on blockbusters and special effects, foregrounding the spectacular collapse of skyscrapers, homes and freeways, and the sights and sounds of shattering glass, concrete and steel. Such spectacle had begun to be important in the 1950s: *Them!* (Gordon Douglas, 1954), for example, revolved around a threat to Los Angeles by giant mutant ants, playing upon the city's proximity to the Nevada and New Mexico deserts, where the military-industrial complex worked in secret at Los Alamos and Area 51. The science fiction apocalypse of Los Angeles came into its own in *Blade Runner* (Ridley Scott, 1982) during the renewed Cold War of the Reagan era. Its futuristic vision emphasized the city's Asian and Latino populations and location shooting in downtown's landmark Bradbury Building (1893) and the Ennis House (1924) by Frank Lloyd Wright in Los Feliz. However, being entirely high-rise, with no suburbs or beaches, and filmed entirely at night, its Los Angeles was much less recognizable than others. *Terminator 2: Judgment Day* (James Cameron, 1991) was also filmed on location, but mostly by day, the entire film being one long chase in which an evil android disguised as an LAPD patrolman pursues a good android (Arnold Schwarzenegger) and a boy he has orders to protect. While the film was pioneering for its computer-generated imagery and $100 million budget, it arguably derives more meaning from the extensive real city it maps, through a shopping mall and suburban streets in Sherman Oaks, along storm drains and freeways, out into the desert, and back for a showdown in a steel mill in the industrial district of Fontana.[21]

Such films shared with film noir a dystopian inversion of urban history and myths, echoing sociological critiques of late twentieth-century Los Angeles as a 'fortified city' full of 'interdictory space'.[22] As such, they drew attention to some of the outcomes of the privatization of urban space to which Los Angeles' film industry had contributed in the construction of its studios, its representation of transport and suburbia, and its labour economy. Now science fiction films intensified Los Angeles' status as a geopolitical pressure point by facilitating collaborations between the film industry and the military-industrial complex.[23] They also intersected with art cinema's version of Los Angeles by emphasizing a synthetic and monotonous built environment dominated by data and signs, a landscape described by Baudrillard as 'a sort of luminous, geometric, incandescent immensity' and by Christine Boyer as the leading edge of 'CyberCities'.[24] However, the reliance of science fiction films on relentless spectacle arguably constrained the effect of any critique they meant to propose.

A certain 'etherealization' of the real city can also be seen in the numerous big budget crime thrillers, from *Die Hard* (John McTiernan, 1988) to *Collateral* (Michael Mann, 2004), which have stylized Los Angeles as a city of sleek corporate architecture disturbed only by automatic weapons fire and explosions.[25] Movies about the movies, such as *The Player* (Robert Altman, 1992) and *Mulholland Drive* (David Lynch, 2001), have explored thwarted artistry, ruthless ambition and murder to standardize an image of the Hollywood film industry as dystopia, but without the moral judgement of movies about the movies of the 1920s or the positive sense of mass culture of the 1930s. European insights have been extended by the German director Wim Wenders, whose meditative thriller *The End of Violence* (1997) posited a network of surveillance cameras monitoring the city for deviant behaviour. And recent representations of race by women directors, such as *What's Cooking?* (Gurinder Chadha, 2000) and *Real Women Have Curves* (Patricia Cardoso, 2002), have interwoven explorations of gender with narratives of diaspora at a time when Los Angeles has been overtaken in size by Mexico City, São Paulo, Mumbai, Lagos and Shanghai.[26]

In all of these, Los Angeles and its parts are repeatedly named, although 'Hollywood' and the film industry lack the physical presence and organization they once had. This is also true of what is surely the most prominent recent tendency, the numerous off-beat Los Angeles dramas emanating from the 'indie' film industry, from *Pulp Fiction* (Quentin Tarantino, 1994), to *Magnolia* (Paul Thomas Anderson, 1999) and *Crash* (Paul Haggis, 2004). In these, features of Los Angeles that were remarkable in earlier films – palm trees, sunshine, the ocean, freeways, gas stations, mini-malls, motels, parking lots and the automobile – have become ubiquitous and banal. Multiple narrative strands have brought together disparate quirky characters from various parts of the urban region, and extended driving sequences, in which little happens but mundane conversation or presentation of the passing landscape, have served to underline the endlessness of Los Angeles' low-rise, low-density and commercialized urban environment.[27]

These films have not generally sought to critique this environment, nor have they shown much consciousness of the racial and socio-economic exclusivity of the West Los Angeles and San Fernando Valley settings that dominate them. Rather they have proceeded on the basis of an ironic knowing of the city's history and dysfunction, and within these terms they have arguably served to acclimatize audiences to the present-day landscapes, lifestyles and rhythms of Los Angeles, by acknowledging its commodification of everyday life, its tendency to sudden and random violence, and its apparently limitless size. Notably, the aerial shot of the city at night, appearing as a flickering matrix of lights as far as the eye can see, has become a regular visual metaphor, while the most striking narrative device has been the use of chance as a determining factor. An earthquake occurs at a strategic moment in *Short Cuts* (Robert Altman, 1993), relieving the building tension that permeates the relationships of the underpaid waitress, uptight cop, drunk hippies, world-weary nightclub singer and children's party clown whose several trajectories the film loosely describes, while in *Magnolia* a similar function is performed by a heavy shower of frogs falling from the sky. What ultimately unites these films, and marks them out as an important new stage in Los Angeles' cinematic history, is an effort to demonstrate that the myriad individuals who populate the city can achieve meaningful interpersonal connections despite the postmodern tendency of human contact to seem like a series of transactions and despite the apparent separation of individuals in the city's endless physical terrain.

Today it has become a commonplace to describe Los Angeles in hyperbole. Claimed by Edward Soja and other commentators as the place where 'it all comes together', the Los Angeles Metropolitan Area, comprising Los Angeles and Orange Counties, has a population of 12.6 million and total land area of 5,700 square miles, while the larger five-county region has a total population of approximately 18 million and covers 35,000 square miles.[28] If the five-county region were to become a state in the United States, it would automatically become the fourth in terms of total personal income after New York, California and Texas, and if it were to declare independence as a nation state it would be the eleventh most powerful in the world in gross national product, slightly behind South Korea but ahead of the Netherlands.[29] Perhaps the most striking aspect of the recent relationship between cinema and the city in Los Angeles has been a disjuncture between its objective status as one of 'the most propulsive and superprofitable industrial growth poles in the world economy' and the small scale of very recent films such as *In Search of a Midnight Kiss* (Alex Holdridge, 2007), *Yes Man* (Peyton Reed, 2008), *(500) Days of Summer* (Marc Webb, 2009) and *The Kids Are All Right* (Lisa Cholodenko, 2010).[30] As interest increases in redeveloping

Los Angeles in sustainable ways, these films rely on what might be called 'low carbon' narratives in which the most significant movement around the city is by van, motorcycle, scooter, subway or walking, and the freeway is shunned in favour of more humane green spaces and downtown's increasingly appreciated historic core. These films provide glimpses of a possible positive future while suggesting a city now better at dealing with its past.[31] And their representations may be mirrored in real world plans for a 44-acre 'Hollywood Central Park' to cover the Hollywood Freeway from Santa Monica Boulevard to Hollywood Boulevard in a district, no longer so shaped by motion pictures, that has the least green space per capita of any district in Los Angeles.[32] While Los Angeles has been especially notable for nearly 100 years for the interaction and disjuncture between cinema and the city, these developments may portend a new urban ecology of the movies.

Appendix

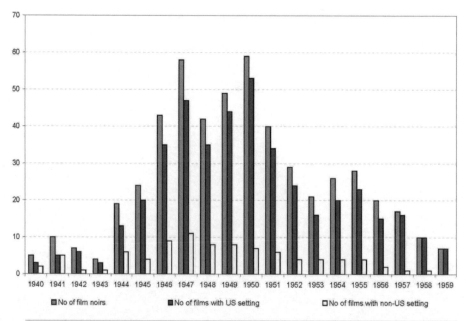

Table 5. Number of American film noirs, 1940–59, and number with US and non-US settings.

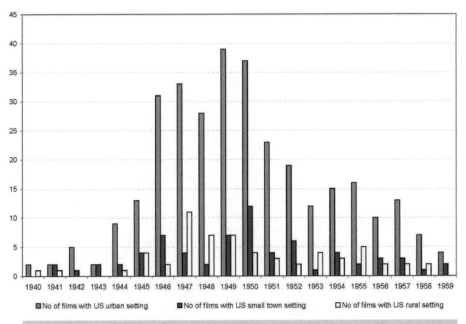

Table 6. Number of film noirs with US urban, small town and rural settings.

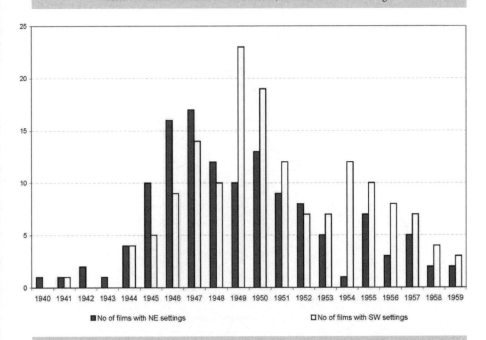

Table 7. Number of film noirs with Northeast and Southwest settings.

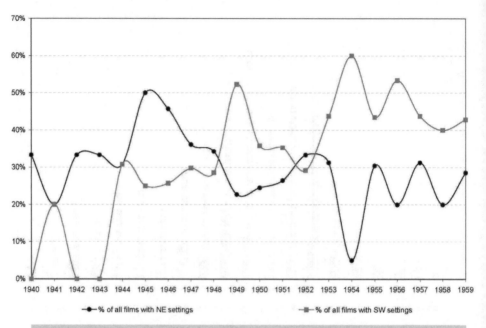

Table 8. Percentage of film noirs with Northeast and Southwest settings.

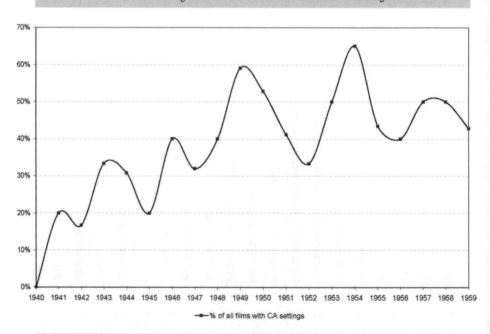

Table 9. Percentage of film noirs with California settings.

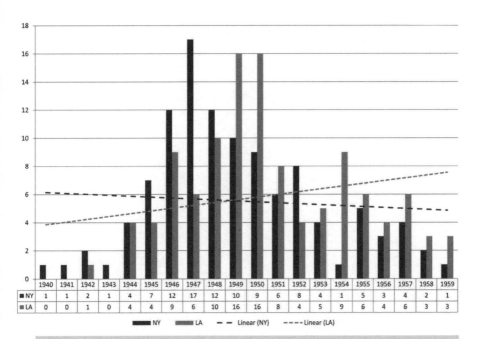

	1940	1941	1942	1943	1944	1945	1946	1947	1948	1949	1950	1951	1952	1953	1954	1955	1956	1957	1958	1959
■ NY	1	1	2	1	4	7	12	17	12	10	9	6	8	4	1	5	3	4	2	1
■ LA	0	0	1	0	4	4	9	6	10	16	16	8	4	5	9	6	4	6	3	3

■ NY ■ LA   – – Linear (NY)   - - - - Linear (LA)

Table 10. Number of film noirs with New York and Los Angeles settings.

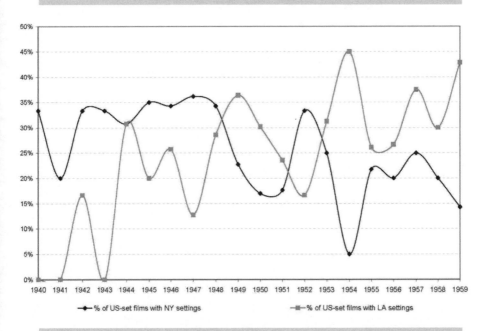

—◆— % of US-set films with NY settings   —■— % of US-set films with LA settings

Table 11. Percentage of film noirs with settings in New York and Los Angeles.

287

References

Introduction

1 Ralph Hancock, *Fabulous Boulevard* (New York, 1949), p. 6.
2 See, for example, Aida Hozic, *Hollyworld: Space, Power, and Fantasy in the American Economy* (Ithaca, NY, and London, 2001); Edward Dimendberg, *Film Noir and the Spaces of Modernity* (Cambridge, MA, 2004); Allen J. Scott, *On Hollywood: The Place, the Industry* (Princeton, NJ, 2005); David James, *The Most Typical Avant-Garde: History and Geography of Minor Cinemas in Los Angeles* (Berkeley, CA, 2005).
3 See, for example, Alain Silver and James Ursini, *Los Angeles Noir: The City as Character* (Santa Monica, CA, 2005); John Bengtson, *Silent Traces: Discovering Early Hollywood through the Films of Charlie Chaplin* (Santa Monica, CA, 2006); Rosemary Lloyd, *Los Angeles: Then and Now* (San Diego, CA, 2007); Marc Wanamaker and Robert W. Nudelman, *Early Hollywood* (Charleston, SC, 2007).
4 See 'LA as Subject', University of Southern California, www.usc.edu; 'Los Angeles Mapped', Library of Congress, www.loc.gov; Philip J. Ethington, 'Los Angeles and the Problem of Urban Historical Knowledge', University of Southern California, www.usc.edu; and the blogs 'historylosangeles', http:// historylosangeles.blogspot.com, and 'The 1947 Project', www.1947project.com.
5 In 2010 the museum was projected for completion in 2012 on a site near the intersection of Sunset Boulevard and Vine Street in Hollywood; in April 2011, the Academy website indicated that 'current economic realities' had put the project on hold. As of January 2012, the project has restarted but is planned to be housed in the former May Company department store building, now part of the LA County Museum of Art on the Miracle Mile section of Wilshire Boulevard. See www.oscars.org.

1 The Trace

1 Walter Benjamin, 'On Some Motifs in Baudelaire', in *Walter Benjamin: Selected Writings, IV: 1938–1940*, ed. Howard Eiland and Michael W. Jennings (Cambridge, MA, 2006), pp. 313–55 (315).
2 Marcel Proust, *À la recherche du temps perdu*, vol. I (Paris, 1962), p. 44, quoted in ibid., p. 315.
3 Here I am paraphrasing the definition of 'utopia' in the *Oxford English Dictionary*, 2nd edn (Oxford, 1989). See also Dora Beale Polk, *The Island of California: A History of the Myth* (Spokane, WA, 1991).
4 Quoted in Michael J. Gonzalez, *This Small City Will Be a Mexican Paradise: Exploring the Origins of Mexican Culture in Los Angeles,*

1821–1846 (Albuquerque, NM, 2004), p. 65.

5 Quoted ibid., p. 67.

6 See Robert M. Fogelson, *The Fragmented Metropolis: Los Angeles, 1850–1930* (Cambridge, MA, 1967, revd Berkeley, CA, 1993), p. 15.

7 These are statistics for the County of Los Angeles. See 'Counting California' website, 'Historical Census Populations of Places, Towns, and Cities in California, 1850–1990', data extraction result, 3 March 2007, University of California Libraries, http://countingcalifornia.cdlib.org.

8 See Carey McWilliams, *Southern California: An Island on the Land* (New York, 1946, repr. Layton, UT, 1973), p. 102; and Kevin Starr, *Americans and the California Dream, 1850–1915* (New York and Oxford, 1973), p. 60.

9 James Miller Guinn, 'Some Early California Industries that Failed' [1906] in *A Southern California Historical Anthology: Selections from the Annual and Quarterly Publications of the Historical Society of Southern California, 1883–1983*, ed. Doyce B. Nunis (Los Angeles, CA, 1984), pp. 203–14 (203).

10 Quoted in Fogelson, *The Fragmented Metropolis*, pp. 124–5.

11 Harris Newmark, *Sixty Years in Southern California, 1853–1913* [1916] (Los Angeles, CA, 1970).

12 Ibid., p. 650.

13 Ibid., p. 651. Upper case in original.

14 Joel Snyder, 'Territorial Photography', in *Landscape and Power*, ed. W.J.T. Mitchell (Chicago, IL, 2002), pp. 175–201 (182–3).

15 William Alexander McClung, *Landscapes of Desire: Anglo Mythologies of Los Angeles* (Berkeley, CA, 2000), esp. pp. 149–53; Jennifer Watts, 'Picture Taking in Paradise: Los Angeles and the Creation of Regional Identity, 1880–1920', in *The Nineteenth-Century Visual Culture Reader*, ed. Vanessa R. Schwartz and Jeannene M. Przyblyski (New York, 2004), pp. 218–32.

16 See Michael Dawson, 'Photography South of Point Lobos', in *LA's Early Moderns*, ed. William Deverell, Michael Dawson, Victoria Dailey and Natalie Shivers (Glendale, CA, 2003),

pp. 217–315.

17 *Los Angeles Today*, Los Angeles Chamber of Commerce and the Neuner Company (Los Angeles, CA, 1915), n.p.

18 See Fogelson, *The Fragmented Metropolis*, pp. 43–84, and Mansel Griffiths Blackford, 'Businessmen and the Regulation of Railroads and Public Utilities in California during the Progressive Era', *The Business History Review*, XLIV/3 (1970), pp. 307–19.

19 *Los Angeles Today*, n.p.

20 Charles G. Clarke, *Early Filmmaking in Los Angeles* (Los Angeles, CA, 1976), p. 13.

21 *Edison Films Catalog*, March 1900, p. 23, cited in Library of Congress, American Memory Collection, Early Motion Pictures 1897–1920, online exhibit, http://hdl.loc.gov/loc.mbrsmi/edmp.0024.

22 Ibid., July 1901, p. 43, http://hdl.loc.gov/loc.mbrsmi/edmp.1881.

23 Ibid., July 1901, p. 43, http://hdl.loc.gov/loc.mbrsmi/edmp.1627.

24 Paula Scott, *Santa Monica: A History on the Edge* (San Francisco, CA, 2004), p. 45.

25 Edna Monch Parker, 'The Southern Pacific Railroad and Settlement in Southern California', *Pacific Historical Review*, VI/2 (1937), pp. 103–19 (103).

26 Ibid., p. 105.

27 Ibid., p. 111.

28 Quoted in William A. Spalding, *History and Reminiscences: Los Angeles City and County*, vol. 1 (Los Angeles, CA, 1931), p. 327.

29 The boat used by the cameraman was 'a launch furnished by Mr. Eager, President of the California Construction Co.', which was responsible for the works. See *Edison Films Catalog*, Sept. 1902, pp. 54–5, http://hdl.loc.gov/loc.mbrsmi/edmp.1968.

30 Eileen Bowser, *The Transformation of Cinema, 1907–1915* (Berkeley, CA, 1994), p. 152.

31 Clarke, *Early Filmmaking in Los Angeles*, p. 29.

32 Dates provided from ibid., p. 21; Bowser, *The Transformation of Cinema*, p. 151; Anthony Slide, *Early American Cinema* (Metuchen, NJ, and London, 1994), p. 27; and *Motion Picture*

Herald, 11 March 1944, p. 35.

33 See Clarke, *Early Filmmaking in Los Angeles*, p. 25, and Marc Wanamaker and Bob Birchard, 'The Historic Film Studios: All-Star Feature Corporation (1913–1915)', part 1, *Classic Images*, no. 151 (January 1988), pp. 40–44 (40).

34 Clarke, *Early Filmmaking in Los Angeles*, p. 21.

35 These accounts are in Slide, *Early American Cinema*, p. 27; Spalding, *History and Reminiscences*, p. 356; Wanamaker and Birchard, 'The Historic Film Studios', part 1, p. 40; and 'How the Movies Began in LA', *Los Angeles Evening Herald and Express*, 8 October 1938, Margaret Herrick Library, Academy of Motion Picture Arts and Sciences (hereafter AMPAS), clippings file.

36 See 'Col. Selig's 50 Years: Anniversary Notes on the Longest Career in the Industry', *Motion Picture Herald*, 11 March 1944, pp. 35–6; Slide, *Early American Cinema*, p. 27; Wanamaker and Birchard, 'The Historic Film Studios', part 1, p. 40.

37 Clarke, *Early Filmmaking in Los Angeles*, p. 22; Bowser, *The Transformation of Cinema*, p. 152; Wanamaker and Birchard, 'The Historic Film Studios', part 1, p. 41.

38 Clarke, *Early Filmmaking in Los Angeles*, pp. 32–3.

39 Slide, *Early American Cinema*, p. 23.

40 See *Los Angeles Times*, 1 January 1915, p. VI46.

41 *Los Angeles Times*, 12 March 1911, p. II.1.

42 Ibid.

43 See Wanamaker and Birchard, 'The Historic Film Studios', part 1, p. 42; Slide, *Early American Cinema*, 200; Clarke, *Early Filmmaking in Los Angeles*, p. 30; Kevin Brownlow, *Hollywood: The Pioneers* (London, 1979), p. 90; *Motion Picture World*, 10 March 1917, *Los Angeles Examiner*, 4 October 1958 and *Variety*, 8 October 1958, Margaret Herrick Library, AMPAS, clippings file; and *Los Angeles Times*, 25 September 1940, pp. A1, A2.

44 Clarke, *Early Filmmaking in Los Angeles* pp. 30, 34; and Richard Koszarski, *An Evening's Entertainment: The Age of the Silent Feature Picture, 1915–1928* (Berkeley, CA, 1994), p. 4.

45 Clarke, *Early Filmmaking in Los Angeles*, p. 45;

Wanamaker and Birchard, 'The Historic Film Studios', part 1, p. 42.

46 Exteriors for *The Birth of a Nation* were filmed in the San Fernando Valley.

47 Ralph Hancock, *Fabulous Boulevard* (New York, 1949), p. 10.

48 Remi Nadeau, *Los Angeles: From Mission to Modern City* (New York, 1960), p. 214.

49 *Los Angeles Times*, 12 March 1911, p. III.

50 Allen J. Scott, *On Hollywood: The Place, the Industry* (Princeton, NJ, 2005), p. 1.

51 Ibid., p. 24.

52 Wanamaker and Birchard, 'The Historic Film Studios', part 1, p. 41.

53 Clarke, *Early Filmmaking in Los Angeles*, p. 19.

54 William C. De Mille, *Hollywood Saga* (New York, 1939), p. 45.

55 *Los Angeles Evening Herald and Express*, 8 October 1938, Margaret Herrick Library, AMPAS, clippings file. Edison's suits against Selig preceded the foundation of the MPPC as such, which Selig eventually joined after a settlement. See *Hollywood Reporter*, 19 July 1948, Margaret Herrick Library, AMPAS, clippings file.

56 William A. Johnston (editor of *Motion Picture News*), 'The Structure of the Motion Picture Industry', *Annals of the American Academy of Political and Social Science*, no. 128 (November 1926), pp. 20–29.

57 Nadeau, *Los Angeles*, p. 205.

58 Slide, *Early American Cinema*, p. 63.

59 Bowser, *The Transformation of Cinema*, pp. 149–50.

60 In 1926 R. W. Pridham, president of the Los Angeles Chamber of Commerce, described Los Angeles as 'The Citadel of the Open Shop'. See Fogelson, *The Fragmented Metropolis*, p. 130.

61 The few scholarly accounts of the early Hollywood film industry that make reference to real estate or labour do so fairly briefly: e.g. Koszarski, *An Evening's Entertainment*, p. 100, and Robert Sklar, *Moviemade America: A Cultural History of American Movies* (New York, 1994), pp. 75, 170.

62 *Motion Picture World*, 8 April 1911, p. 768.

63 *Motion Picture World*, 2 December 1911,

p. 1677.

64 *Los Angeles Times*, 14 January 1912, p. VI9.

65 *Los Angeles Times*, 27 January 1918, p. 116.

66 *Los Angeles Evening Herald and Express*, 8 October 1938, Margaret Herrick Library, AMPAS, clippings file.

67 De Mille, *Hollywood Saga*, pp. 62–3. Emphasis in original.

68 Jesse Lasky Jr, *Whatever Happened to Hollywood?* (New York, 1973), p. 8.

69 Clifford M. Zierer, 'Hollywood – World Center of Motion Picture Production', *Annals of the American Academy of Political and Social Science*, no. 254 (November 1947), pp. 12–17 (17).

70 *Los Angeles Times*, 14 January 1912, p. VI9.

71 Zierer, 'Hollywood – World Center of Motion Picture Production', p. 13.

72 Gregory Paul Williams, *The Story of Hollywood: An Illustrated History* (Los Angeles, CA, 2006), p. 3.

73 James Miller Guinn, *A History of California, and an Extended History of Los Angeles and Environs* (Los Angeles, 1915).

74 Harry Carr, *Los Angeles – City of Dreams* (New York, 1935), p. 272.

75 De Mille, *Hollywood Saga*, p. 82.

76 Ibid., p. 97.

77 Anita Loos, *A Girl Like I* (New York, 1966), p. 77.

78 Catherine Parsons Smith, 'Founding the Hollywood Bowl', *American Music*, XI/2 (1993), pp. 206–42.

79 *Motion Picture World*, 8 April 1911, p. 768.

80 Clarke, *Early Filmmaking in Los Angeles*, p. 34.

81 The location used for the race track scenes may have been Los Angeles' Ascot Park race track.

82 *Los Angeles Times*, 2 January 1929, p. D12.

83 Ibid..

84 Quoted in Kevin Starr, *Inventing the Dream: California through the Progressive Era* (New York and Oxford, 1986), p. 89.

85 There is a brief glimpse of an African American man driving a horse and carriage on South Spring Street in the film of that name by the Edison Company. On the other hand, Edison films emphasized the relatively large non-Anglo

population of San Francisco, for example, in *Arrest in Chinatown, San Francisco* (1897), *Parade of Chinese* (1898) and *San Francisco Chinese Funeral* (1903).

86 Bowser, *The Transformation of Cinema*, p. 165. Conversely, Jacques Aumont has argued that later Biograph films by Griffith, such as *An Unseen Enemy* (1912), which were made in studios in New York, were typified by a notable 'figurative closure'. See Jacques Aumont, 'Griffith: the Frame, the Figure', in *Early Cinema: Space, Frame, Narrative*, ed. Thomas Elsaesser (London, 1990), pp. 349–50.

87 Chon A. Noriega, 'Birth of the Southwest: Social Protest, Tourism, and D. W. Griffith's Ramona', in *The Birth of Whiteness: Race and the Emergence of US Cinema*, ed. Daniel Bernardi (New Brunswick, NJ, 1996), pp. 203–26.

88 Ibid., p. 211.

89 See Fogelson, *The Fragmented Metropolis*, pp. 85–117.

90 *Los Angeles Times*, 12 March 1911, p. III.

91 Clarke, *Early Filmmaking in Los Angeles*, p. 19.

92 *Los Angeles Times*, 12 March 1911, p. III.

93 Ibid., 14 January 1912, p. VI9.

94 Fogelson, *The Fragmented Metropolis*, p. 78, and Andrew Lees, *Cities Perceived: Urban Society in European and American Thought, 1820–1940* (Manchester, 1985), p. 5.

95 Data from Fogelson, *The Fragmented Metropolis*, p. 79.

96 Ibid., p. 84.

97 *Motion Picture World*, 8 April 1911, p. 768; Bowser, *The Transformation of Cinema*, p. 159.

98 See, for example, *Motion Picture World*, 2 December 1911, p. 1677; 9 October 1915, p. 272.

99 Ibid., 8 April 1911, p. 768.

100 Ibid., 9 October 1915, p. 272.

101 *Los Angeles Times*, 15 September 1915, p. III0.

102 *Photoplay Art* (February 1916), p. 4; Slide, *Early American Cinema*, pp. 63–4; *Motion Picture World*, 15 January 1916, p. 409.

103 *Los Angeles Times*, 27 January 1918, p. 116; 1 January 1915, p. VI46.

104 Sharon Zukin, *Landscapes of Power: From Detroit*

to *Disney World* (Berkeley, CA, 1991), p. 5.

105 Norman M. Klein, *The History of Forgetting: Los Angeles and the Erasure of Memory* (London and New York, 1997).

106 Date from Slide, *Early American Cinema*, pp. 54–6.

107 See Marc Wanamaker and Bob Birchard, 'The Historic Film Studios', part 2, *Classic Images*, no. 152 February 1988), pp. 51–5 (52).

108 Koszarski, *An Evening's Entertainment*, pp. 1–4.

109 Quoted in ibid., p. 6.

110 Spalding, *History and Reminiscences*, p. 327, and Janet L. Abu-Lughod, *New York, Chicago, Los Angeles: America's Global Cities* (Minneapolis, MN, 1999), p. 149.

111 Quoted in Paula Scott, *Santa Monica*, p. 39.

112 Josh Stenger, 'Lights, Camera, Faction: (Re)Producing "Los Angeles" at Universal's CityWalk', in *Hollywood Goes Shopping*, ed. David Desser and Garth S. Jowett (Minneapolis, MN, 2000), pp. 277–308.

113 *Motion Picture World*, 9 October 1915, p. 272.

114 Ibid.

115 Robert C. Duncan, 'The Ince Studios', *Picture Play*, 1 March 1916, pp. 25–6; quoted in Slide, *Early American Cinema*, pp. 84–5.

116 Clarke, *Early Filmmaking in Los Angeles*, p. 53. Clarke became an assistant cameraman for Universal Pictures around 1915, later working as director of photography on *Stand-In* (Tay Garnett, Walter Wanger Prods, 1937) and *Miracle on 34th Street* (George Seaton, 20th Century-Fox, 1947). See Charles G. Clarke and Anthony Slide, *Highlights and Shadows: The Memoirs of a Hollywood Cameraman* (Metuchen, NJ, 1989).

117 Wanamaker and Birchard, 'The Historic Film Studios', part 1, p. 43.

118 At this time, silent film libraries such as the Eastin-Phelan Company, released compilations of candid footage of the stars, directors and producers of the early industry on 16mm film and videotape. See *Memories of the Silent Stars*, Blackhawk Films, Eastin-Phelan Company, Davenport, IA, 1974.

119 Wanamaker and Birchard, 'The Historic Film Studios', part 2, p. 51.

120 Gene Fernett, *American Film Studios: An Historical Encyclopedia* (Jefferson, NC, 1988), pp. 119–20. The Ince Studio subsequently became, and remains, the independent rental facility known as Culver City Studios, restored in the 1980s.

121 *Los Angeles Times magazine*, 16 December 1979, p. 1.

122 *Box Office*, 31 July 1967, p. w-2.

123 Bill Murphy, *The Dolphin Guide to Los Angeles and Southern California* (New York, 1962), p. 84.

124 *Hollywood Citizen News*, 3 October 1958; *Los Angeles Examiner*, 4 October 1958; and *Variety*, 8 October 1958, Margaret Herrick Library, AMPAS, clippings file.

125 *Los Angeles Times*, 25 September 1940, pp. A1–A2.

126 See *Motion Picture Herald*, 11 March 1944, pp. 35–6; *Los Angeles Examiner*, 17 July 1948, *Hollywood Reporter*, 19 July 1948, and *Los Angeles Evening Herald and Express*, 8 October 1938, Margaret Herrick Library, AMPAS, clippings file.

127 *Los Angeles Examiner*, 17 July 1948, Margaret Herrick Library, AMPAS, clippings file.

128 *Los Angeles magazine*, January 1963, p. 18; and *Los Angeles Times*, 4 April 2000, Margaret Herrick Library, AMPAS, clippings file; and *Wilshire Independent*, 13 September 2000, pp. 1–2.

129 *Life and Death in Hollywood: The Sensational Picture Document of Hollywood's Most Turbulent Years* (Cincinnati, OH, 1950), pp. 60–66.

130 Ibid., p. 81.

131 Ibid., p. 4.

132 *Los Angeles Times*, 22 March 1925, p. B10.

133 *Los Angeles Times*, 24 June 1928, p. B7.

2 Navigation

1 On Hollywood cinema's cultural imperialism, see, for example, Ruth Vasey, *The World According to Hollywood, 1918–1939* (Madison, WI, 1997).

2 Dennis Cosgrove, *Apollo's Eye: A Cartographic Genealogy of the Earth in the Western Imagination* (Baltimore, MD, 2001), p. 46.

3 Ibid., p. xi.

4 Ibid., p. 85.

5 Ibid., p. 86.

6 Richard Koszarski, *An Evening's Entertainment: The Age of the Silent Feature Picture, 1915–1928* (Berkeley, CA, 1994), p. 102; Richard Koszarski, *Hollywood on the Hudson: Film and Television in New York from Griffith to Sarnoff* (New Brunswick, NJ, and London, 2008), pp. 179–227.

7 On Biograph, see Eileen Bowser, *The Transformation of Cinema, 1907–1915* (Berkeley, CA, 1994), p. 159; on Selig, see Charles G. Clarke, *Early Filmmaking in Los Angeles* (Los Angeles, CA, 1976), p. 21; on Nestor, see *Los Angeles Times*, 25 September 1940, pp. A1, A2.

8 *Motion Picture Studio Directory, 1918*, published by *Motion Picture News* (New York, 1918), p. 300.

9 Ibid., pp. 117, 119, 123, 137.

10 Ibid., pp. 65, 161.

11 Ibid., p. 199.

12 Ibid., pp. 30–31.

13 Zukor Collection, File #4, AMPAS.

14 Ibid.

15 Ibid.

16 Zukor Collection, File #11, letter from Jesse Lasky to Adolph Zukor, 18 July 1928.

17 *Motion Picture Studio Directory, 1923–24*, published by *Motion Picture News* (New York, 1924), p. 270.

18 Ibid. pp. 242–3.

19 William A. Johnston, 'The Structure of the Motion Picture Industry', *Annals of the American Academy of Political and Social Science*, no. 128 (November 1926), p. 21.

20 *Journal of the Society of Motion Picture Engineers*, XI, no. 29 (April 1927), pp. 34–44 (34).

21 Ibid., pp. 39–40.

22 Ibid., p. 38.

23 Ibid., XII, no. 33 (April 1928), pp. 13–15, pp. 18–20 (18).

24 Ibid., p. 20.

25 Society of Motion Picture Engineers, *Transactions of the Society of Motion Picture Engineers, 1916–1929*, p. 4.

26 Neal Gabler, *An Empire of their Own: How the Jews Invented Hollywood* (New York, 1988).

27 Charlie Chaplin, *My Autobiography* (London, 1964), p. 319.

28 Zukor Collection, File #4.

29 *Bankers' Magazine* (September 1925), p. 326; see also *Bankers' Magazine* (July 1921), p. 313.

30 Janet Wasko, *Movies and Money: Financing the American Film Industry* (Norwood, NJ, 1982), p. 120.

31 *Film Year Book 1927*, published by *Film Daily* (New York, 1927), p. 739.

32 Ibid., p. 740.

33 Zukor Collection, File #11.

34 Robert McLaughlin, *Broadway and Hollywood: A History of Economic Interaction* (New York, 1974), p. 2.

35 Ibid., p. 35.

36 *Pantomime*, 3 June 1922, p. 20.

37 *Los Angeles Times*, 19 March 1923, p. 118.

38 See Anthony Slide, *Early American Cinema* (Metuchen, NJ, and London, 1994), pp. 108–9.

39 Charlie Chaplin, *Charlie Chaplin's Own Story*, ed. Harry M Geduld [1916] (Bloomington, IN, 1985), pp. 105, 112.

40 Ibid., p. 115.

41 Ibid., p. 138.

42 *New York Times*, 8 May 1927, p. SM8.

43 Carey McWilliams, 'Los Angeles', *Overland Monthly and Out West Magazine*, LXXXV/5 (May 1927), p. 135.

44 *Los Angeles Times*, 17 June 1928, p. B4.

45 Rockwell D. Hunt, 'Cultural Progress in Los Angeles and Environs', *Overland Monthly and Out West Magazine*, 1 July 1931, p. 18.

46 McWilliams, 'Los Angeles', p. 135.

47 The Historical Census Populations of California, 1850–1990, Counting California, University of California Libraries, http://countingcalifornia.cdlib.org, accessed 3 March 2007; and 'Rank by Population of the 100 Largest Urban Places', United States Census Bureau, www.census.gov, accessed 3 March 2007.

48 Richard Longstreth, *City Center to Regional Mall: Architecture, the Automobile, and Retailing in Los Angeles, 1920–1950* (Cambridge, MA, 1998), p. 21.

49 Ibid., p. 6.

50 See Leo Marx, 'Pastoralism in America', in *Ideology and Classic American Literature*, ed. Sacvan Bercovitch and Myra Jehlen (New York, 1986), pp. 36–69; Leo Marx, *The Machine in the Garden: Technology and the Pastoral Ideal in America* (New York, 1967).

51 Reyner Banham, *Los Angeles: The Architecture of the Four Ecologies* (New York, 1971), p. 238.

52 Ibid., p. 143.

53 Richard S. Weinstein, 'The First American City' in *The City: Los Angeles and Urban Theory at the End of the Twentieth Century*, ed. Allen J. Scott and Edward W. Soja (Berkeley, CA, 1998), pp. 22–46 (22).

54 See Robert M. Fogelson, *The Fragmented Metropolis: Los Angeles, 1850-1930* (Cambridge, MA, 1967, revd Berkeley, CA, 1993), pp. 145–7.

55 Critical studies of slapstick comedy have provided valuable insights but have tended to focus on narrative, performance, class, gender and modernity, without extended consideration of place. For example, Kristine Karnick and Henry Jenkins, *Classical Hollywood Comedy* (London and New York, 1995); and Rob King, *The Fun Factory: The Keystone Film Company and the Emergence of Mass Culture* (Berkeley, CA, 2009). Recently place *is* a concern in Charles Wolfe, 'California Slapstick Revisited', in *Slapstick Comedy*, ed. Tom Paulus and Rob King (New York and London, 2010), pp. 169–89.

56 Fredric Jameson, 'Notes on Globalization as a Philosophical Issue', in *The Cultures of Globalization*, ed. Fredric Jameson and Masao Miyashi (Durham, NC, 1998), p. 63.

57 Tom Gunning, 'Crazy Machines in the Garden of Forking Paths: Mischief Gags and the Origins of American Film Comedy', in Karnick and Jenkins, pp. 87–105, pp. 87–93.

58 Tom Gunning, 'The Cinema of Attractions: Early Film, its Spectator, and the Avant-Garde', in *Early Cinema: Space, Frame, Narrative*, ed. Thomas Elsaesser (London, 1990), pp. 56–62 (59); Tom Gunning, *D. W. Griffith and the Origins of American Narrative Film: The Early Years at Biograph* (Urbana, IL, 1994), pp. 41–4.

59 Gunning, 'The Cinema of Attractions', ibid., p. 60; Kristin Thompson, 'The Stability of the Classical Approach after 1917', in David Bordwell, Janet Staiger and Kristin Thompson, *The Classical Hollywood Cinema: Film Style and Mode of Production to 1960* (London, 1985), p. 231.

60 See William K. Everson, *American Silent Film* (New York, 1978), p. 262.

61 Siegfried Kracauer, *Theory of Film* (Oxford, 1960, repr. Princeton, NJ, 1997), pp. 42, xlix.

62 Walter Benjamin, 'On Some Motifs in Baudelaire', in *Walter Benjamin: Selected Writings, IV: 1938–1940*, ed. Howard Eiland and Michael W. Jennings (Cambridge, MA, 2006), p. 328.

63 Ibid.

64 Giuliana Bruno, *Atlas of Emotion: Journeys in Art, Architecture, and Film* (London and New York, 2007), p. 166.

65 Lynn Kirby, *Parallel Tracks: The Railroad and Silent Cinema* (Exeter, 1997), pp. 6–7. See also Stephen Kern, *The Culture of Time and Space* (Cambridge, MA, 1983).

66 Stanley Corkin, *Realism and the Birth of the Modern United States* (Athens, GA, 1996), pp. 51, 109.

67 Ibid., p. 75.

68 Alan Dale, *Comedy is a Man in Trouble: Slapstick in American Movies* (Minneapolis, MN, 2000), p. 37.

69 John Bengtson, *Silent Traces: Discovering Early Hollywood through the Films of Charlie Chaplin* (Santa Monica, CA, 2006), p. 131, makes the connection with Chaplin's childhood in Lambeth in the East End of London. Multi-storey tenements were rare in Los Angeles: low-grade bungalows, courtyard housing or shacks were more common. See Dana Cuff, *The Provisional City: Los Angeles Stories of Architecture and Urbanism* (Cambridge, MA, 2000), p. 25.

70 According to Bengtson, the set was built on the Lone Star lot on the corner of Cahuenga Boulevard and Romaine Street in Hollywood but the chase was shot on location at the real intersection of Marchessault Street and Alameda Street near the Plaza in downtown Los Angeles.

71 Noel Burch, 'A Primitive Mode of Representation?', in *Early Cinema*, ed. Elsaesser, pp. 220–27 (220).

72 *Safety Last* was successful, being described by *Variety* magazine as 'a money maker for its exhibitor as well as its producer'. See review in *Variety*, 5 April 1923, Margaret Herrick Library, AMPAS, clippings file.

73 Harold Lloyd and W. W. Stout, *An American Comedy* (New York, 1928), pp. 145–6. The vertical climb features in other Harold Lloyd films, including *Ask Father* (1919), *High and Dizzy* (1920) and *Feet First* (1930). Chaplin made an earlier department store film, *The Floorwalker* (1916), shot entirely indoors.

74 I know only two silent slapstick comedies whose titles named parts of Los Angeles: Chaplin's *Kid Auto Races at Venice* (1914) and Laurel and Hardy's *45 Minutes from Hollywood* (1926). As in *Safety Last*, however, there were textual clues that indicated the films' locations: for example, a shot of the 'Sunset Pharmacy' on Sunset Boulevard in Chaplin's *Laughing Gas* (1914); signs for 'California Oranges' and the 'Venice Racing Derby' on the boardwalk in Lloyd's *Number, Please?* (1920), a window of the 'Palms Branch of Citizen State Bank' in his *Get Out and Get Under* (1920), and the letters 'LA GAS' emblazoned on a gas depot in his *Girl Shy* (1924); also the brass door plate of the 'Harry H. Culver and Company' offices in Culver City in Laurel and Hardy's *Putting Pants on Philip* (1927), and a sign on a streetcar in *County Hospital* (1932) indicating its route from 'Vernon Ave to Slauson & Santa Fe'.

75 Lloyd and Stout, *An American Comedy*, p. 117.

76 Longstreth, *City Center to Regional Mall*, pp. 24–43. Hamburger's, with floor space of over 500,000 sq. ft, was the largest department store west of Chicago.

77 Ibid., p. 23; see also Carl Wilbur Condit and Sarah Bradford Landau, *Rise of the New York Skyscraper, 1865–1913* (New Haven, CT, 1996), p. x.

78 See Leon Smith, *Famous Hollywood Locations* (Jefferson, NC, 1993), pp. 63–7.

79 Longstreth, *City Center to Regional Mall*, p. 33.

80 Benjamin, 'Some Motifs', pp. 326–7. See also Janet Ward, *Weimar Surfaces: Urban Visual Culture in 1920s Germany* (Berkeley, CA, 2001).

81 Walter Benjamin, 'The Paris of the Second Empire in Baudelaire', *Walter Benjamin: Selected Writings, iv: 1938–1940*, ed. Howard Eiland and Michael W. Jennings (Cambridge, MA, 2006), pp. 43–5.

82 Benjamin, 'Some Motifs', p. 331.

83 Benjamin, 'Paris of the Second Empire', p. 31.

84 See Richard Longstreth, *The Drive-In, the Supermarket, and the Transformation of Commercial Space in Los Angeles, 1914–1941* (Cambridge, MA, 2000), p. xv.

85 Venice also appeared in Chaplin's *Tillie's Punctured Romance* (1914), *By the Sea* (1915), *His New Profession* (1914), *The Adventurer* (1917), *Shoulder Arms* (1918) and *The Circus* (1928), as well as Lloyd's *Number, Please?* (1920) and Keaton's *The High Sign* (1920). The pier and amusements at Wilmington appeared in Chaplin's *A Busy Day* (1914), while Santa Monica was in Harold Lloyd's *A Sailor Made Man* (1921) and Keaton's *The Love Nest* (1923).

86 These included Chaplin's *Mabel's Dramatic Career* (1913), *Twenty Minutes of Love* (1914) and *Recreation* (1914), Mack Sennett's *A Muddy Romance* (1913) and Roscoe Arbuckle's *A Flirt's Mistake* (1914), all made at Echo Park in Edendale. Westlake Park (now MacArthur Park) was used in Chaplin's *Twenty Minutes of Love* (1914) and *Between Showers* (1914); Lincoln Park in Chaplin's *Work* (1915) and *A Woman* (1915) and Lloyd's *Haunted Spooks* (1920); Hollenbeck Park in Chaplin's *His Trysting Place* (1914), Roscoe Arbuckle's *Fatty's Chance Acquaintance* (1915) and *Fatty's Tintype Tangle* (1915), Lloyd's *Girl Shy* (1924), and Laurel and Hardy's *Men O'War* (1929).

87 In this film, made just a few days before *Kid Auto Races at Venice*, Chaplin has not yet developed the character of the Tramp but portrays a similar character who is dressed in a morning coat with a top hat and a cane.

88 Other relevant films include *The Star Boarder* (aka *The Landlady's Pet*, 1914), *His Favorite Pastime* (1914), *The Knockout* (1914), *Cruel Cruel Love* (1914), and *Police* (1916).

89 Walter Benjamin, 'Naples', in *Walter Benjamin: Selected Writings*, I: *1913–1926*, ed. Marcus Bullock and Michael Jennings (Cambridge, MA, 1996), p. 416.

90 Quoted in Greg Hise, *Magnetic Los Angeles: Planning the Twentieth Century Metropolis* (Baltimore, MD, 1997), p. 10. See also Greg Hise, 'Industry and the Landscapes of Social Reform', in *From Chicago to LA: Making Sense of Urban Theory*, ed. Michael J. Dear (Thousand Oaks, CA, 2002), pp. 100–102.

91 *Los Angeles Today*, Los Angeles Chamber of Commerce and the Neuner Company (Los Angeles, CA, 1915), n.p.

92 See Nikolaus Pevsner, *Pioneers of Modern Design: From William Morris to Walter Gropius* [1936] (New Haven, CT, 2004), pp. 36–57, 124–45.

93 Weinstein, 'The First American City', p. 26.

94 Herbert Hoover, 'The Home As An Investment', in W. B. Meloney, *Better Homes for America* (New York, 1922). Text available online at Project Gutenberg, at www.gutenberg.org.

95 Longstreth, *City Center to Regional Mall*, p. 10.

96 Fogelson, *The Fragmented Metropolis*, p. 146.

97 Benjamin, 'Paris of the Second Empire', p. 30.

98 See Sabine Hake, 'Chaplin's Reception in Weimar Germany', *New German Critique*, no. 51 (Autumn 1990), pp. 87–111.

99 Benjamin, 'Some Motifs', p. 328.

100 A sign advertising the prominent Hollywood real estate developer C. E. Toberman is visible on Hollywood Boulevard in the later Lloyd feature film *Movie Crazy* (Clyde Bruckman, 1932).

101 Marx, *The Machine in the Garden*.

102 Longstreth, *City Center to Regional Mall*, pp. 11–12.

103 *A Selected Traffic Program compiled by the Los Angeles Traffic Commission*, usually known as *The Los Angeles Plan*, Los Angeles Traffic Commission, December 1922, p. 6.

104 Ibid., p. 3.

105 Ibid., p. 14.

106 Longstreth, *City Center to Regional Mall*, p. 13.

107 Ibid., p. 13.

108 See Mark S. Foster, 'The Model-T, the Hard Sell, and Los Angeles's Urban Growth: The Decentralization of Los Angeles during the 1920s', *Pacific Historical Review*, XLIV/4 (1975), pp. 459–84 (464).

109 Quoted in *Los Angeles Plan*, p. 7. On Burnham, see Peter Hall, *Cities of Tomorrow: An Intellectual History of Urban Planning and Design in the Twentieth Century* (Oxford and Malden, MA, 2002), pp. 191–7.

110 *Los Angeles Plan*, p. 7; *A Major Traffic Street Plan for Los Angeles*, Frederick Law Olmsted, Harland Bartholomew and Charles Henry Cheney, for the Traffic Commission of the City and County of Los Angeles, Los Angeles, 1924.

111 Ibid., pp. 11–12.

112 Fogelson, *The Fragmented Metropolis*, p. 143.

113 Ibid., p. 142.

114 *Los Angeles Plan*, p. 22.

115 Data from Longstreth, *City Center to Regional Mall*, p. 16; quotation from *Los Angeles Times*, 29 February 1920, II, p. 1.

116 For contemporary accounts, see *Los Angeles Times*, 20 July 1924, p. 4; 25 January 1925, p. 7; 19 November 1925, p. A5.

117 Jean Baudrillard, *America* (London and New York, 1988), pp. 52–5.

118 *Parks, Playgrounds, and Beaches for the Los Angeles Region: A Report Submitted to the Citizens' Committee on Parks, Playgrounds, and Beaches*, by Olmsted Brothers and Bartholomew and Associates (1930), reprinted in Greg Hise and William Deverell, *Eden by Design: The 1930 Olmsted-Bartholomew Plan for the Los Angeles Region* (Berkeley, CA, 2000), p. 85.

119 Quoted in Longstreth, *City Center to Regional Mall*, p. 15.

120 According to Bengston, *Silent Traces*, pp. 31–7, the exteriors were filmed on Apablasa St in

Chinatown, an area also used for locations in
Griffith's *Broken Blossoms* (1919), Chaplin's *The
Kid* (1921) and Keaton's *The Goat* (1921).

121 Jack Richmond, *Hollywood: The City of a
Thousand Dreams, The Graveyard of a Thousand
Hopes* (Los Angeles, CA, 1928), pp. 12.

122 Jacqueline Stewart, *Migrating to the Movies:
Cinema and Black Urban Modernity* (Berkeley,
CA, 2005), p. 93. Stewart explains that one of the
most significant independent African American
film companies, the Lincoln Motion Picture
Company, was founded in Los Angeles in the
late 1910s to make films for primarily African
American audiences. Stewart, pp. 202–10.

123 Merrill Schleier, *Skyscraper Cinema: Architecture
and Gender in American Film* (Minneapolis, MN,
2009), p. 20.

124 *Los Angeles Times*, 11 July 1915, p. VI2.

125 *Wall Street Journal*, 9 July 1919, p. 13.

126 Ibid.

127 *Los Angeles Times*, 17 February 1924, p. F4.

128 Longstreth, *Drive-In*, p. 23.

129 Olmsted-Bartholomew Report, pp. 77–8.

130 Ibid., p. 111.

131 Ibid., p. 109.

132 Ibid., pp. 78 and 85.

133 Ibid., p. 151.

134 Ibid., p. 111.

135 *Los Angeles Times*, 2 January 1929, p. D12.

136 The banning of Keystone took place in 1918.
See Bengtson, *Silent Traces*, pp. 42–3.

137 *Motion Picture World*, 9 October 1915, p. 272.

138 To confirm the dimensions of early film studios
in Los Angeles, I have relied on the block-by-
block maps of Los Angeles produced by the
Sanborn Fire Insurance Company of New
York in 1913, 1919, 1924 and 1929. A
comprehensive collection of these is held at
the Map Library, Special Collections, Young
Research Library, UCLA. Additionally, on the
Robertson-Cole studio, see *Los Angeles Times*,
5 September 1920, p. VI; on Paramount, see
Los Angeles Times, 29 March 1926, p. AI; on
United Artists, see Tommy Dangcil, *Hollywood
Studios* (Charleston, SC, 2007), p. 75; on the
Jesse D. Hampton Studios, see *Los Angeles*

Times, 7 September 1919, p. VI; on Columbia
Pictures, see *Los Angeles Times*, 11 April 1926,
p. EII.

139 Clarke, *Early Filmmaking in Los Angeles*, p. 41;
Los Angeles Times, 4 November 1923, p. 16.

140 *Film Year Book 1927*, p. 742. An alternative
figure of 78 acres is given in *Los Angeles Times*,
19 October 1930, p. DI.

141 Dangcil, *Hollywood Studios*, p. 86.

142 *Los Angeles Times*, 20 June 1927, p. AI. See
also Sennett Collection, File #1166, AMPAS,
two-page untitled inventory of Mack Sennett
properties for 1931.

143 *Los Angeles Times*, 1 January 1915, p. VI46 and
21 June 1929, p. D4. Other significant land
holdings in the region included the campus of
UCLA (430 acres), Loyola University (200 acres),
Westwood Golf Club (180 acres) and Griffith
Park Airport (157 acres). See Olmsted Report,
Appendix II, pp. 143–8, 247–52.

144 In this respect the early film industry appears
to have resembled the oil industry. See Nancy
Quam-Wickham, '"Another World": Work,
Home, and Autonomy in Blue-Collar Suburbs',
in *Metropolis in the Making: Los Angeles in the
1920s*, ed. Tom Sitton and William Deverell
(Berkeley, CA, 2001), pp. 123–42 (130).

145 Hise, 'Industry and the Landscapes of Social
Reform', p. 113.

146 *Los Angeles Times*, 27 September 1931, p. D2.

147 Mel Scott, with Alvin Lustig and Bob
Holdeman, *Cities Are for People: The Los Angeles
Region Plans for Living* (Los Angeles, 1942),
p. 22.

148 In 1922, Los Angeles County became the first
in the United States to institute county-level
planning. Ibid., p. 22. In 1929 the Los Angeles
City Planning Commission specified height
limits for each type of building, ratios of lot size
to floor space, and minimum requirements for
off-street parking. Los Angeles Board of City
Planning, *City Planning Impressions*, 1929, n.p.,
first page. However, as late as 1930, only 48 per
cent of the City of Los Angeles was actually
zoned, according to David Gebhard and
Harriette Von Breton, *Los Angeles in the Thirties:*

1931–1941, 2nd edn (Santa Monica, CA, 1989), p. 19.

149 Fogelson, *The Fragmented Metropolis*, p. 154.

150 Johnston, 'The Structure of the Motion Picture Industry', p. 21.

151 On the national trend, see *Los Angeles Times*, 1 July 1923, p. VII.

152 Federico Bucci, *Albert Kahn: Architect of Ford* (New York, 2002). Ford factories were decisive in this innovative reconfiguration. At the Mack Avenue and Picquette Avenue plants near downtown Detroit, the first Ford manufacturing had taken place in old, adapted buildings in which components and finished goods were moved up and down between floors by elevator, and even Highland Park was dominated by structures with several storeys. The River Rouge plant, by contrast, horizontalized production and moved it away from the city.

153 On these scandals, see Gary Alan Fine, 'Scandal, Social Conditions, and the Creation of Public Atttention: Fatty Arbuckle and the "Problem of Hollywood"', *Social Problems*, XLIV/3 (1997), pp. 297–323; Lary May, *Screening Out the Past: The Birth of Mass Culture and the Motion Picture Industry* (Chicago, IL, and London, 1983), pp. 200–236; and Kenneth Anger, *Hollywood Babylon* (New York, 1975), pp. 27–87.

154 See Heidi Kenaga, 'Making the "Studio Girl": The Hollywood Studio Club and Industry Regulation of Female Labour', *Film History*, XVIII/2 (2006), pp. 129–39 (133).

155 *Wall Street Journal*, 16 December 1922, Margaret Herrick Library, AMPAS, clippings file; see also *Los Angeles Times*, 14 December 1922, p. I28.

156 Quoted in Bucci, *Albert Kahn*, pp. 58–9.

157 See Hise and Deverell, *Eden by Design*, p. 10.

158 Quoted ibid., p. 33.

159 Ibid.

160 Ibid.

161 Richmond, *Hollywood: The City of a Thousand Dreams*, pp. 14–15.

162 *Los Angeles Times*, 4 November 1923, p. V3. This development was announced but never took place. See Marc Wanamaker, *Westwood*

(Charleston, SC, 2010), pp. 116.

163 *Los Angeles Times*, 19 March 1923, p. II8.

164 Zukor Collection, File #6.

165 Longstreth, *City Center to Regional Mall*, pp. 5, 81, 82.

166 Zierer, 'Hollywood – World Center of Motion Picture Production', p. 14; Hise, *Magnetic Los Angeles*, p. 43.

167 *Los Angeles Times*, 25 July 1926, p. EI.

168 Approximately half of the film processing of the Los Angeles film industry was carried out in the East until the establishment of the Standard Film Laboratories in Hollywood. *Los Angeles Times*, 11 July 1920, p. VI.

169 For example, Carl Laemmle sought to attract the construction of a department store on the northwest corner of Hollywood and Vine in 1929–30; see Longstreth, *City Center to Regional Mall*, p. 89; movie stars such as John Barrymore and Wallace Beery invested in the Los Angeles Guaranty Building and Loan Association, run by local financier Gilbert Beesemyer; see *Los Angeles Times*, 3 September 1932, p. 12 and 27 September 1939, p. 1.

170 *New York Times*, 21 September 1937, p. 29.

171 *Motion Picture World*, 9 October 1915, p. 272; Hise, *Magnetic Los Angeles*, p. 40.

172 *Los Angeles Times*, 27 June 1926, p. K10.

173 Richard Lewis Ward, *A History of the Hal Roach Studios* (Carbondale, IL, 2006), p. 39.

174 'Culver City: The City of Opportunities', Harry H Culver & Co., Los Angeles to Venice Properties, Culver City, California, promotional brochure, 21 August 1923.

175 *Los Angeles Times*, 26 December 1926, p. B8; 22 August 1926, p. 14.

176 *Los Angeles Times*, 5 December 1926, p. E3.

177 Burbank had previously been dominated by china manufacturing, canning and trucking. *Los Angeles Times*, 5 April 1926, p. E14. Subsequently, nearby Toluca Wood was developed to house workers in Burbank's aircraft and motion picture industries. See James Thomas Keane, *Fritz B. Burns and the Development of Los Angeles* (Los Angeles, CA, 2001), p. 76.

178 *Los Angeles Times*, 20 June 1927, p. A2.

179 Ibid., 8 April 1928, p. EI.

180 Ibid., 13 November 1927, p. E3; 20 November 1927, p. E5.

181 Ibid., 17 July 1927, p. E8; 21 August 1927, p. E7; 2 October 1927, p. E4; 8 April 1928, p. EI.

182 Ibid., 20 June 1927, p. AI; 18 September 1927, p. E8; 21 July 1929, p. D4.

183 Ibid., 22 July 1928, p. E5.

184 Ibid., 2 October 1927, p. E4; 23 October 1927, p. GIO. A new bus route was also intended to connect film studios from Culver City through Hollywood, Burbank and Studio City. Ibid., 27 June 1926, p. EI.

185 Ibid., 25 December 1927, p. F4; 26 February 1928, p. E8; 22 April 1928, p. E4. The total population of San Fernando Valley increased from 19,592 in 1920 to 54,217 in 1930 to 112,001 in 1940. See Gebhard and Von Breton, *Los Angeles in the Thirties*, p. 22.

186 *Los Angeles Times*, 2 October 1927, p. E4.

187 Ibid., 2 June 1929, p. E4.

188 Ibid., 4 September 1927, p. F5.

189 Ibid., 20 October 1929, p. D8.

190 Ibid., 27 May 1928, p. EIO.

191 Laurel and Hardy films not set in Los Angeles include *Sailors Beware* (1927), set on a cruise ship; *With Love and Hisses* (1927), on basic training for the US Army; *Flying Elephants* (1928), which takes place in the Stone Age; and *Double Whoopee* (1929), set in a plush Manhattan hotel.

192 The Dutch artist Piet Schreuders has forensically counterpointed film stills from Laurel and Hardy films shot on location in Culver City with the history of its buildings and businesses. See 'The Shortest Main Street in the World', *Furore* (Amsterdam), no. 19 (March 1999).

193 Other films of this type included *That's My Wife* (1929), *Blotto* (1930), *Their First Mistake* (1931) and *Helpmates* (1932).

194 In *Busy Bodies* (1933), Laurel and Hardy begin driving happily through Beverly Hills to work in a lumber yard where, after many comic turns, they accidentally cut their car in half by driving it through a band saw.

195 *Los Angeles Times*, 24 August 1930, p. DI.

196 Hise and Deverell, *Eden by Design*, p. 6.

197 Re-zoning in Hollywood is discussed in *Los Angeles Times*, 27 September 1931, p. D2.

198 Sennett's business difficulties partly stemmed from the fact that he had been caught off guard by technology, initially equipping his new studios at Studio City for silent film and then having to quickly retool them for sound; his studios were inherited by Republic Pictures. *Los Angeles Times*, 22 July 1928, p. E8; 16 September 1928, p. E5; 14 October 1928, p. D5. See also Ward, *A History of the Hal Roach Studios*, pp. 84–98.

199 Gilbert Beesemyer, general manager of the Los Angeles Guaranty Building and Loan Association, and one of the directors of the CMPD, was convicted in 1931 of defrauding 24,000 investors in the building and loan company of nearly $8 million. See *New York Times*, 13 December 1930, p. 15; *Los Angeles Times*, 3 January 1931, p. A2.

3 The Simulacrum

1 Undated quote in Scott Eyman, *Ernst Lubitsch: Laughter in Paradise* (Baltimore, MD, 2000), p. 197. Presumably the quote dates from the release of Lubitsch's comedy *So This is Paris* (1926).

2 Jean Baudrillard, *Simulacra and Simulation* (Ann Arbor, MI, 1994), p. 1.

3 Ibid., p. 12.

4 Histories of Hollywood cinema such as David Bordwell, Janet Staiger and Kristin Thompson, *The Classical Hollywood Cinema: Film Style and Mode of Production to 1960* (London, 1985), pp. 271–2, and Richard Koszarski, *An Evening's Entertainment: The Age of the Silent Feature Picture, 1915–1928* (Berkeley, CA, 1994), pp. 102–9, refer briefly to the construction of film studio buildings.

5 Richard Longstreth, *City Center to Regional Mall: Architecture, the Automobile, and Retailing in Los Angeles, 1920–1950* (Cambridge, MA, 1998) and *The Drive-In, the Supermarket, and*

the Transformation of Commercial Space in Los Angeles, 1914–1941 (Cambridge, MA, 2000).

6 See Dana Cuff, The Provisional City: Los Angeles Stories of Architecture and Urbanism (Cambridge, MA, 2000), p. 5.

7 Ibid., p. 4. See also OMA, Rem Koolhaas and Bruce Mau, S, M, L, XL (New York, 1997).

8 Cuff, The Provisional City, p. 43. For example, Cuff points to Vincent Scully, American Architecture and Urbanism (New York, 1969).

9 Cuff, The Provisional City, p. 18.

10 Halsey, Stuart & Company, 'The Motion Picture as a Basis for Bond Financing' (1927), in The American Film Industry, ed. Tino Balio (Madison, WI, 1985), pp. 195–217 (197).

11 Mae Huettig, 'Economic Control of the Motion Picture Industry' (1944), excerpted in American Film Industry, ed. Balio, pp. 285–310 (287–8).

12 Los Angeles Times, 27 January 1918, p. 116.

13 William A. Spalding, History and Reminiscences: Los Angeles City and County, vol. 1 (Los Angeles, CA, 1931), p. 414.

14 Ibid., p. 444.

15 Ibid. Estimates of the industry's total employment vary: for example, the Los Angeles Times gave the figure of 25,000 people employed. See Los Angeles Times, 6 May 1928, p. E2. Allen J. Scott cites conservative statistics from the United States Department of Commerce, indicating the total grew from 12,852 in 1927, to 16,417 in 1933, and 30,408 in 1937. Allen J. Scott, On Hollywood: The Place, the Industry (Princeton, NJ, 2005), p. 26.

16 Koszarski, An Evening's Entertainment, pp. 102–4.

17 Los Angeles Times, 1 April 1935, p. A1; 2 January 1940, p. C7; 8 April 1940, p. A4.

18 Spalding, History and Reminiscences, p. 467.

19 Janet L. Abu-Lughod, New York, Chicago, Los Angeles: America's Global Cities (Minneapolis, MN, 1999), p. 237.

20 Greg Hise, 'Industry and the Landscapes of Social Reform', in From Chicago to LA: Making Sense of Urban Theory, ed. Michael J. Dear (Thousand Oaks, CA, 2002), p. 111.

21 Spalding, History and Reminiscences, pp. 419–20; Mel Scott, with Alvin Lustig and Bob Holdeman,

Cities Are for People: The Los Angeles Region Plans for Living (Los Angeles, 1942), p. 39; Nancy Quam-Wickham, '"Cities Sacrificed on the Altar of Oil": Popular Opposition to Oil Development in 1920s Los Angeles', Environmental History, III/2 (1998), pp. 189–209.

22 Spalding, History and Reminiscences, pp. 465–7.

23 Allen J. Scott and Edward W. Soja, eds, The City: Los Angeles and Urban Theory at the End of the Twentieth Century (Berkeley, CA, 1998), p. 8; and Mel Scott, Metropolitan Los Angeles: One Community (Los Angeles, 1949), p. 41.

24 H. S. McKee, 'Business Conditions and the Outlook', Los Angeles, Gillis Papers, July 1915, quoted in Robert M. Fogelson, The Fragmented Metropolis: Los Angeles, 1850–1930 (Cambridge, MA, 1967, revd Berkeley, CA, 1993), p. 123.

25 See Fogelson, The Fragmented Metropolis, pp. 125–6, and Mike Davis, 'Sunshine and the Open Shop: Ford and Darwin in 1920s Los Angeles', in Metropolis in the Making: Los Angeles in the 1920s, ed. Tom Sitton and William Deverell (Berkeley, CA, 2001), pp. 103–4.

26 Los Angeles Times, 11 July 1920, p. VI.

27 Ibid., 21 October 1921, p. 113.

28 Bankers' Magazine, 4 October 1921, pp. 31–2.

29 Spalding, History and Reminiscences, pp. 414–44.

30 Los Angeles Times, 23 April 1928, p. A9.

31 New York Times, 16 October 1932, p. X5; 29 March 1936, p. SM10. See ibid., 19 April 1939, p. 18, on the US tour of Crown Prince Olav and Crown Princess Martha of Norway, who visited the World's Fair in New York, an automobile factory in Detroit, Abraham Lincoln's tomb in Springfield, Illinois, Yellowstone National Park, the Grand Canyon, Boulder Dam and a film studio in Los Angeles.

32 David James, Allegories of Cinema: American Film in the Sixties (Princeton, NJ, 1989), pp. 5–12.

33 Los Angeles Times, 11 April 1926, p. B2.

34 Ibid., 21 December 1908, p. 17.

35 Ibid., 23 April 1916, p. VI2.

36 Ibid., 26 January 1919, p. III1; 19 March 1923, p. 118.

37 William A. Johnston, 'The Structure of the Motion Picture Industry', Annals of the

American Academy of Political and Social Science, no. 128 (November 1926), p. 20.

38 For the argument that the Hollywood film industry could not become fully Fordist due to its particular 'technological, organizational, and employment structures', see Michael J. Dear, ed., *From Chicago to LA: Making Sense of Urban Theory* (Thousand Oaks, CA, 2002), p. 169. Clifford Zierer argued in 1947 that '[t]he motion picture industry is not a manufacturing industry in the usual sense'. Clifford M. Zierer, 'Hollywood – World Center of Motion Picture Production', *Annals of the American Academy of Political and Social Science*, no. 254 (November 1947), p. 17. Allen J. Scott takes a similar position in *On Hollywood*, pp. 4–6.

39 *Los Angeles Times*, 1 September 1915, p. III.

40 Ibid., 11 April 1926, p. B2, and 1 October 1928, p. A3.

41 Johnston, 'The Structure of the Motion Picture Industry', p. 22.

42 *Journal of the Society of Motion Picture Engineers*, XII, no. 33 (April 1928), pp. 13–14.

43 Federico Bucci, *Albert Kahn: Architect of Ford* (New York, 2002), p. 48. As Bucci notes, p. 62, the Ford Motor Company built a large Assembly Building at Long Beach, California, in 1926.

44 W. E. Garity and J. L. Ledeen, 'The New Walt Disney Studio', *Journal of the Society of Motion Picture Engineers*, vol. XXXVI (1941), pp. 3–29 (29).

45 Ibid., p. 8.

46 Ibid., p. 15.

47 In addition to Baudrillard's *Simulacra and Simulation*, quoted above, see, for example, Louis Marin, 'Utopic Degeneration: Disneyland', in *Utopics: The Semiological Play of Textual Spaces*, trans. Robert A. Vollrath (New York, 1984), pp. 239–58; and Michael Sorkin, 'See You in Disneyland', in *Variations on a Theme Park: The New American City and the End of Public Space*, ed. Michael Sorkin (New York, 1992), pp. 205–32.

48 These three films are held in the Film and Television Archive at UCLA: *Universal Studios and Stars* (1912–27), UCLA catalog #VA11747M;

William Fox Studios and Stars (1915–27), UCLA video item catalog #VA19592M; *A Trip to Paramountown* (1922), UCLA catalog #VA4707M.

49 UCLA catalog #VA11747.

50 UCLA catalog #VA19365M.

51 Statistics rounded up to the nearest whole number from Jack Alicoate, ed., *Film Daily Year Book of Motion Pictures 1927* (New York, 1927), pp. 737–66.

52 MGM was one of those studios in Los Angeles at this time that did its own processing and printing of films on-site.

53 Statistics rounded up to the nearest whole number from Jack Alicoate, ed., *Film Daily Year Book of Motion Pictures 1935* (New York, 1935), pp. 900–921.

54 At first Fox Realty was responsible for the studios at Hollywood and Westwood, valued between $4.5 million and $4.8 million in total, buildings on them valued at about $2.5–3 million, and the Fox building in Oakland, California, probably valued around $400,000. *Film Daily Year Book 1927*, p. 741; *New York Times*, 7 April 1927, p 34; *Los Angeles Times*, 8 April 1927, p. 18.

55 *New York Times*, 7 November 1920, magazine section, p. 50; Richard Koszarski, *Hollywood on the Hudson: Film and Television in New York from Griffith to Sarnoff* (New Brunswick, NJ, and London, 2008), p. 101.

56 *Hartford Courant*, 24 July 1928, p. 1; Janet Wasko, *Movies and Money: Financing the American Film Industry* (Norwood, NJ, 1982), pp. 70–72.

57 John Parke Young, 'Industrial Background', in *Los Angeles: Preface to a Master Plan*, ed. George W. Robbins and L. Deming Tilton (Los Angeles, 1941), p. 69.

58 *Southwest Builder and Contractor*, 21 October 1921, p. 1.

59 Spalding, *History and Reminiscence*, pp. 403, 411, 422, 431, 450, 461.

60 Ibid.

61 *Los Angeles Times*, 5 December 1926, pp. E1, 3 (E1).

62 *Los Angeles Times*, 22 July 1928, p. E5.

63 *Los Angeles Times*, 13 November 1916, p. III, pp. 1–2. I have rounded these figures to two decimal places.

64 Spalding, *History and Reminiscences*, pp. 401, 419–20.

65 *Southwest Builder and Contractor*, 27 February 1920, p. 15; 29 October 1920, p. 13; 14 October 1921, p. 19; 29 August 1924, p. 58.

66 For example, *The American Architect*, 23 April 1919, p. 12.

67 *Pacific Coast Architect* (October 1927), p. 65.

68 *Pacific Coast Architect* (May 1927), p. 74; (July 1927), p. 58.

69 Charlie Chaplin, *My Autobiography* (London, 1964), pp. 150–51.

70 *Los Angeles Times*, 1 September 1915, p. III.

71 'Facts About the Mack Sennett Studios', undated two-page inventory (probably *c.* 1923 because it contains a reference to the 'recently completed' Sennett film *Suzanna*, which was made that year); also 'Mack Sennett Studio', one-page inventory dated 20 January 1925 and revised 15 January 1927, Sennett Collection, File #1166, AMPAS.

72 Janet Staiger, 'Dividing Labor for Production Control: Thomas Ince and the Rise of the Studio System', *Cinema Journal*, XVIII/2 (Spring 1979), pp. 16–25 (16).

73 *Motion Picture World*, 9 October 1915, p. 272. This total included: one stage 175 × 220 ft, two stages each 50 × 80 ft, and a fourth stage, last to be built, 360 × 160 ft.

74 *Los Angeles Times*, 9 January 1916, p. VI.

75 Anthony Slide, *Early American Cinema* (Metuchen, NJ, and London, 1994), p. 90, reports that four stages opened in February 1916, and Staiger, 'Dividing Labor for Production Control', p. 22, reports that eight stages were completed. Press reports of the day indicate that eight were definitely planned but they, and subsequent photographs and maps, suggest that only five were actually built. *Los Angeles Times*, 9 January 1916, p. VI.

76 Ibid., 9 January 1916, p. VI. According to Koszarski, *An Evening's Entertainment*, p. 83, the Triangle façade was built by Harry Aitken.

77 *Los Angeles Times*, 16 June 1918, p. VI.

78 Ibid., 11 September 1927, p. G14. See also 23 March 1926, p. A10.

79 Ibid., 22 December 1918, p. IIII, and 26 January 1919, p. IIII.

80 Ibid., 15 June 1919, p. VI. Hollywood Studios, Inc. had previously been Hollywood General Studios.

81 Ibid., 7 September 1919, p. VI.

82 Ibid., 5 September 1920, p. VI, and 21 November 1920, p. IIII5.

83 Ibid., 26 September 1920, p. III28.

84 Ibid., 2 October 1920, p. III.

85 Ibid., 19 March 1923, p. II8.

86 Ibid.

87 Ibid., 21 November 1920, p. IIII5.

88 Ibid., 5 May 1926, p. A9; 24 August 1926, p. A2; *Berkeley Daily Gazette*, 18 March 1926, p. 9.

89 *Los Angeles Times*, 14 November 1925, p. A7; 19 September 1926, p. E9; 15 March 1927, p. A10.

90 See Douglas Gomery, 'The Coming of Sound: Technological Change in the American Film Industry', in *American Film Industry*, ed. Balio, pp. 242–5; Donald Crafton, *The Talkies: American Cinema's Transition to Sound, 1926–1931* (Berkeley, CA, 1999), pp. 89–100.

91 *Los Angeles Times*, 3 June 1928, p. F3.

92 Ibid., 1 October 1928, p. A3.

93 Ibid., 19 October 1930, pp. D1, D3.

94 Ibid.

95 *Los Angeles Times*, 21 February 1926, p. B7; 28 January 1926, p. A1; 22 August 1926, p. 14; 21 October 1928, p. D3.

96 *Film Daily Year Book 1927*, p. 742; *Los Angeles Times*, 21 July 1929, p. D4.

97 Ibid., 19 October 1930, p. D1, D3, and 10 August 1929, p. A3.

98 *Chicago Daily Tribune*, 1 January 1926, p. 21; *Los Angeles Times*, 11 April 1926, p. B2.

99 Ibid., 22 January 1927, p. A8; 29 March 1926, p. A1.

100 Ibid., 11 April 1926, p. E11.

101 Ibid., 19 October 1930, p. D1, D3; 8 April 1928, pp. E1, 3, p. 3.

102 Ibid., 25 May 1930, p. D5.

103 Ibid., 19 October 1930, p. D1, D3.

104 Ibid., 24 March 1934, p. A1; 1 September 1935, p. 10; 30 September 1935, p. A1.

105 Ibid., 30 June 1935, p. 3.

106 In addition to Sanborn Fire Insurance Maps, commercial maps of Los Angeles generally indicated the location and extent of the largest film studios. See, for example: Security First-National Bank of Los Angeles, *Map of Los Angeles, Hollywood, and Adjacent Cities*, 1938; Shell Corporation, *Street Map of Los Angeles*, 1941; US Geological Survey, *Los Angeles: Hollywood Quadrangle*, 1953; all held at the UCLA Map Library. Also very useful are the Benjamin and Gladys Thomas and the Spence and Fairchild Air Photo Archives at the UCLA Department of Geography.

107 *Los Angeles Times*, 27 January 1918, p. II6.

108 Ibid., 12 March 1911, p. III.

109 Ibid., 9 January 1916, p. VI.

110 *Motion Picture World*, 9 October 1915, p. 272.

111 *Los Angeles Times*, 15 June 1919, p. VI; Zukor Collection, File #4, 'Authority for Expenditure', 28 May 1921. The Christie Comedy Company also improved its open stages to cope with the rainy season, as did B. P. Schulberg and Louis B. Mayer when they overhauled the abandoned former Selig studio in Edendale. See *Los Angeles Times*, 26 January 1919, p. III1, and 28 August 1923, p. 18.

112 *Southwest Builder and Contractor*, 27 February 1920, p. 15; 29 October 1920, p. 13; 14 October 1921, p. 19; 29 August 1924, p. 58.

113 See Nikolaus Pevsner, *Pioneers of Modern Design: From William Morris to Walter Gropius* [1936] (New Haven, CT, 2004), p. 113.

114 Paul Scheerbart, 'Glass Architecture' (1914), in Ulrich Conrads, *Programs and Manifestoes of Twentieth Century Architecture* (Cambridge, MA, 1971), p. 32.

115 On what he called 'the beginning of iron construction' and its role in the rise of the modern cosmopolitan environment, see Walter Benjamin, 'Paris, Capital of the Nineteenth Century', in *Walter Benjamin: Selected Writings*, III: *1935–1938*, ed. Howard Eiland and Michael W. Jennings (Cambridge, MA, 2002), pp. 32–49 (33).

116 Pevsner, *Pioneers of Modern Design*, pp. 109–13.

117 Anne S. Cunningham, *Crystal Palaces, American Garden Conservatories* (Princeton, NJ, 2000), pp. 5, 41; Scott Rutherford and Kevin J. Holland, *Classic American Railroad Terminals* (Minneapolis, MN, 2001), p. 24.

118 Robert Hugh Kargon and Arthur P. Molella, *Invented Edens: Techno-cities of the Twentieth Century* (Cambridge, MA, 2008), pp. 16–17.

119 Brent Richards and Dennis Gilbert, *New Glass Architecture* (New Haven, CT, 2006), p. 14.

120 Alan Blanc, *Architecture and Construction in Steel* (Oxford, 1993), pp. 455, 463. See also Kristin Thompson, 'Mercury Vapor Lamps and Diffused Sunlight', in Bordwell, Staiger and Thompson, *The Classical Hollywood Cinema*, pp. 271–3.

121 Reyner Banham, *Theory and Design in the First Machine Age* (Cambridge, MA, 1980), p. 69.

122 Herman Muthesius in the Deutscher Werkbund *Jahrbuch*, 1913, quoted in Banham, *Theory and Design*, p. 80.

123 Quoted in Pevsner, *Pioneers of Modern Design*, p. 161.

124 Giancarlo Consonni, 'Preface', in Bucci, *Albert Kahn*, p. 17.

125 Greene and Greene used a timber frame in the archetypal Gamble House (1908). See Neil Jackson, 'Metal Frame Houses of the Modern Movement in Los Angeles: Part I: Developing a Regional Tradition', *Architectural History*, XXXII (1989), pp. 152–72 (152).

126 The average floor space of supermarkets in Los Angeles increased from 4,000 sq. ft to 8,000 sq. ft in the 1920s, to 10,000 sq. ft in 1935 and 20,000 sq. ft by the end of the 1930s. It continued to increase in the 1940s and '50s. See Longstreth, *The Drive-In*, pp. 91–110, 178.

127 On Neutra, see Thomas S. Hines, *Richard Neutra and the Search for Modern Architecture* (Berkeley and Los Angeles, CA, 1994). For an authoritative account of modernist architecture in Los Angeles, see Hines, *Architecture of the Sun: Los Angeles Modernism, 1900–1970* (New York, 2010).

128 Chaplin, *My Autobiography*, pp. 412, 413.

129 *Los Angeles Times*, 28 June 1929, p. A10.

130 Ibid.

131 *Los Angeles Times*, 5 August 1928, p. E1.

132 Ibid.

133 Ibid. See also *Los Angeles Times*, 21 October 1928, p. D6.

134 Ibid. For a discussion of the challenges, and the artificiality, of recording sound in these new studio buildings, see Emily Thompson, *The Soundscape of Modernity: Architectural Acoustics and the Culture of Listening in America, 1900–1933* (Cambridge, MA, 2002), pp. 267–81.

135 *Los Angeles Times*, 3 March 1929, p. E7.

136 Pevsner, *Pioneers of Modern Design*, p. 20.

137 Bucci, *Albert Kahn*, pp. 79–84.

138 *Los Angeles Times*, 4 August 1935, p. 16.

139 Ibid., 9 January 1916, p. VI.

140 Ibid., 4 November 1923, p. 16.

141 Ibid., 13 November 1927, p. E3; 20 November 1927, p. E5; 18 December 1927, p. E7.

142 Ibid., 10 November 1929, p. D1.

143 Ibid.

144 Ibid., 29 March 1926, p. A1.

145 Bucci, *Albert Kahn*, p. 31.

146 See Natalie Shivers, 'A New Creative Medium', in *LA's Early Moderns*, ed. William Deverell, Michael Dawson, Victoria Dailey and Natalie Shivers (Glendale, CA, 2003), pp. 135–9.

147 James A. Larsen, Academy Films, 'Design and Construction of a Motion Picture Production Sound Stage', *Journal of the Society of Motion Picture and Television Engineers*, LXVII/4 (1958), pp. 260–63 (260). See also Catherine Croft, *Concrete Architecture* (London, 2004), pp. 62–5.

148 *Los Angeles Times*, 8 April 1928, pp. E1, 3, p. 3.

149 Ibid., 10 November 1929, p. D1.

150 MGM Art Department Collection, File #76, AMPAS.

151 Ibid.

152 Ibid.

153 Ibid.

154 Ibid.

155 Ibid.

156 Internal memorandum, 'Destruction of Stock Sets', dated 18 November 1936, from J. J. Cohn to Cedric Gibbons, MGM Art Department Collection, File #76, AMPAS; see also internal memorandum dated 27 November 1936, from E. J. Mannix to Cedric Gibbons and J. J. Cohn.

157 Similar big-budget, studio-bound tendencies were visible too at other studios, especially RKO, Paramount and Fox.

158 Postcard, copyright Glen G. Stone, California Postcard Company, Los Angeles, California, c. 1920, Charles G. Clarke Collection, Folder #42, AMPAS.

159 *Los Angeles Times*, 4 November 1923, p. 16.

160 Ibid., 16 August 1925, p. F2. See also Zierer, 'Hollywood – World Center of Motion Picture Production', p. 16.

161 For recent architectural histories, see, for example, Charles Jencks, *Heteropolis: Los Angeles: The Riots and the Strange Beauty of Hetero-architecture* (London, 1993); Jim Heimann, *California Crazy and Beyond: Roadside Vernacular Architecture* (San Francisco, CA, 2001); James Steele, *Los Angeles Architecture: The Contemporary Condition* (London, 1998).

162 Dr E. Debries, *Hollywood As It Really Is* (London, 1930), pp. vi–vii, viii–ix.

163 Young, 'Industrial Background', pp. 196, 197.

164 *Los Angeles Times*, 23 April 1916, p. VI2.

165 Thomas S. Hines, 'The Blessing and the Curse: The Achievement of Lloyd Wright', in Alan Weintraub, Thomas S. Hines, Eric Lloyd Wright and Dana Hutt, *Lloyd Wright: The Architecture of Frank Lloyd Wright Jr* (London, 1998), pp. 12–37 (17).

166 Quoted in J. A. Jackson, 'Photoplay Architecture', *Los Angeles Times*, 19 February 1922, p. VIII5.

167 *Los Angeles Times*, 21 February 1926, p. B7.

168 Anthony Dawson, 'Patterns of Production and Employment in Hollywood', *Hollywood Quarterly*, IV/4 (1950), pp. 338–53.

169 David Frisby, *Cityscapes of Modernity* (Cambridge, 2001), p. 107.

170 George Simmel, 'The Ruin' (1907), in *George Simmel, 1858–1918*, ed. Kurt H. Wolff (Columbus, OH, 1958), p. 259.

171 Ibid., p. 265.

172 For examples of such critiques, see Sharon

Zukin, *Landscapes of Power: From Detroit to Disney World* (Berkeley, CA, 1991); and Edward W. Soja, 'Inside Exopolis: Scenes from Orange County', in *Variations on a Theme Park*, ed. Sorkin, pp. 94–122; and Mike Davis, *City of Quartz: Excavating the Future in Los Angeles* (New York, 1992), pp. 246–8.

173 *Motion Picture World*, 9 October 1915, p. 272.

174 Bucci, *Albert Kahn*, p. 127.

175 *Los Angeles Times*, 9 January 1916, p. VI.

176 Ibid., 16 June 1918, p. VI.

177 *Warner Bros Studios and Stars (1923–1927)*, produced by William Horsley, UCLA catalog #VA22187M.

178 James E. Shelton, Vice-President, Security Trust and Savings Bank, Los Angeles, 'Los Angeles Bids for Next ABA Convention', *Bankers' Magazine* (September 1925), p. 326.

179 Charles Fletcher Scott, 'Welcome Intelligentsia', *Overland Monthly and Out West Magazine*, 1 July 1931, pp. 11–12 (12).

180 *Los Angeles Times*, 4 February 1940, p. 19.

181 Mike Davis, *Ecology of Fear: Los Angeles and the Imagination of Disaster* (New York, 1999).

182 On the history of flooding in Los Angeles, see Jared Orsi, *Hazardous Metropolis: Flooding and Urban Ecology in Los Angeles* (Berkeley, CA, 2004).

183 *New York Times*, 13 March 1938, p. 169.

184 I have rounded these figures to the nearest million from *Film Daily Year Book 1927*, pp. 750, 754, 763.

185 *Los Angeles Times*, 9 January 1916, p. VI.

186 Ibid., 24 May 1923, p. III0.

187 Ibid., 10 November 1929, p. D1.

188 Ibid., 19 October 1930, p. D1, D3.

189 Ibid., 22 November 1916, p. 112.

190 Ibid., 27 February 1921, p. 17.

191 Ibid., 18 March 1926, p. A3.

192 Ibid., 16 August 1926, p. A1.

193 Ibid., 11 September 1927, p. G14.

194 Ibid., 12 December 1927, p. A2.

195 Zukor Collection, File #12, telegram from S. R. Kent to Adolph Zukor, 17 January 1929.

196 Display ad #46, *Los Angeles Times*, 8 July 1917, p. 110.

197 Ibid.

198 *Los Angeles Times*, 7 November 1920, p. 110, and 6 November 1920, p. 14.

199 Ibid., 5 November 1923, p. 14.

200 Ibid.

201 Flann O'Brien, *The Third Policeman* (1940) (Normal, IL, 1999), p. 87.

202 *Los Angeles Times*, 20 May 1925, p. C7.

203 Ibid.

204 Ibid.

205 Ibid.

206 Charlie Chaplin, *Charlie Chaplin's Own Story*, ed. Harry M Geduld (1916) (Bloomington, IN, 1985), p. 140.

207 *Forum*, January 1920, p. I6; *Life*, 26 February 1925, p. 6; *Los Angeles Times*, 2 January 1929, p. H6.

208 According to the AFI Catalog, 29 feature films about the Hollywood film industry were released between 1921 and 1928. These were: *A Small Town Idol* (Erle Kenton, 1921), *Her Face Value* (Thomas N. Heffron, 1921), *The Speed Girl* (Maurice Campbell, 1921), *Doubling for Romeo* (Clarence Badger, 1922), *Night Life in Hollywood* (Fred Caldwell, 1922), *Dangerous Hour* (William Hughes Curran, 1923), *The Extra Girl* (F. Richard Jones, 1923), *Hollywood* (James Cruze, 1923), *Mary of the Movies* (John McDermott, 1923), *Souls for Sale* (Rupert Hughes, 1923), *Inez from Hollywood* (Alfred Green, 1924), *In Hollywood with Potash and Perlmutter* (Alfred Green, 1924), *The Legend of Hollywood* (Renaud Hoffman, 1924), *Married Flirts* (Robert G. Vignola, 1924), *Merton of the Movies* (James Cruze, 1924), *Goat Getter* (Albert Rogell, 1925), *Go Straight* (Frank O'Connor, 1925), *My Neighbor's Wife* (Clarence Geldert, 1925), *Bluebeard's Seven Wives* (Alfred Santell, 1926), *Broken Hearts of Hollywood* (Lloyd Bacon, 1926), *Ella Cinders* (Alfred Green, 1926), *The Hollywood Reporter* (Bruce Mitchell, 1926), *Miss Brewster's Millions* (Clarence Badger, 1926), *The Skyrocket* (Marshall Neilan, 1926), *Naughty Nanette* (James Leo Meehan, 1927), *Stranded* (Phil Rosen, 1927), *The Last Command* (Josef von Sternberg, 1928) and *Show People* (King Vidor, 1928). Most of these were

melodramas, some comedies.

209 The two tallest buildings we see were, in fact, the Guaranty Building (John C. Austin and Frederick M. Ashley, 1923–4) and the Security Trust Savings Bank (John and Donald B. Parkinson, 1920–22), both on Hollywood Boulevard. See Longstreth, *City Center to Regional Mall*, p. 92.

210 *45 Minutes from Hollywood* was the first film in which both Stan Laurel and Oliver Hardy appeared, although they appeared in two separate supporting roles and not yet as a comic duo.

211 Chaplin made two other films set in movie studios, *The Masquerader* (1914) and *Behind the Screen* (1916).

212 Jack Richmond, *Hollywood: The City of a Thousand Dreams, The Graveyard of a Thousand Hopes* (Los Angeles, CA, 1928), p. 6.

213 Ibid.

214 Ibid.

215 Walter Benjamin, *The Arcades Project*, ed. Rolf Tiedemann (Cambridge, MA, 1999), pp. 463–4.

216 Walter Benjamin, 'Naples', in *Walter Benjamin: Selected Writings*, I: *1913–1926*, ed. Marcus Bullock and Michael Jennings (Cambridge, MA, 1996), p. 416.

217 *Film Year Book 1927*, p. 13.

218 David Karnes, 'The Glamorous Crowd: Hollywood Movie Premieres between the Wars', *American Quarterly*, XXXVIII/4 (1986), pp. 553–72 (554 and 556).

219 See Maggie Valentine, *The Shows Starts on the Sidewalk: An Architectural History of the Movie Theater, Starring Charles S. Lee* (New Haven, CT, 1994), p. 194.

220 Harris Allen, AIA, 'Recent California Theatres', *Pacific Coast Architect* (July 1927), pp. 10–29 (10).

221 S. Charles Lee, 'Influence of West Coast Designers on the Modern Theater', *Journal of the Society of Motion Picture Engineers*, L/4 (1948), pp. 329–36 (329).

222 See also James Y. Dunbar, 'Space Acoustics', *Journal of the Society of Motion Picture Engineers*, XLIX/4 (1947), pp. 372–88.

223 Longstreth, *The Drive-In*, p. 93.

224 Valentine, *The Shows Starts on the Sidewalk*, p. 97.

225 *Los Angeles Times*, 4 August 1935, p. 16.

226 Thomas S. Hines, 'Richard Neutra's Hollywood: A Modernist Ethos in the Land of Excess', *Architectural Digest*, LIII (April 1996), p. 64.

227 Simon Dixon, 'Ambiguous Ecologies: Stardom's Domestic Mise en Scène', *Cinema Journal*, XLII/2 (2003), pp. 81–100 (86).

228 Jeffrey Charles and Jill Watts, 'Un(Real) Estate: Marketing Hollywood in the 1910s and 1920s', in *Hollywood Goes Shopping*, ed. David Desser and Garth S. Jowett (Minneapolis, MN, 2000), pp. 253–76 (265).

229 Kevin Brownlow, 'Harold Lloyd: A Renaissance Palace for One of the Silent Era's Greatest Comic Pioneers', *Architectural Digest*, Academy Awards Edition (April 1990), pp. 160–65.

230 Dixon, 'Ambiguous Ecologies', p. 81.

231 *Pacific Coast Architect*, December 1927, p. 9.

232 Ibid.

233 *Photoplay*, May 1929, p. 35.

234 *Pacific Coast Architect*, December 1927, p. 9.

235 Ibid.

236 Ibid., p. 63.

237 Ibid.

238 Harry Carr, *Los Angeles – City of Dreams* (New York, 1935), p. 264.

239 Ibid., p. 272.

240 *Los Angeles Times*, 30 May 1937, p. 15.

241 Ibid.

242 The other films are: *Married in Hollywood* (Marcel Silver, 1929), *The Talk of Hollywood* (Mark Sandrich, 1929), *Showgirl in Hollywood* (Mervyn LeRoy, 1930), *Playthings of Hollywood* (William A. O'Connor, 1930), *The Cohens and Kellys in Hollywood* (John Francis Dillon, 1932), *Hollywood Speaks* (Eddie Buzzell, 1932), *Make Me a Star* (aka *Gates of Hollywood*, William Beaudine, 1932), *Broadway to Hollywood* (Willard Mack, 1933), *Going Hollywood* (Raoul Walsh, 1933), *Secrets of Hollywood* (George M. Merrick, 1933), *Hollywood Hoodlum* (B. Reeves Eason, 1934), *Hollywood Party* (Roy Rowland, 1934), *365 Nights in Hollywood* (George Marshall, 1934), *Another Face* (aka *It Happened*

in *Hollywood*, Christy Cabane, 1935), *Hollywood Boulevard* (Robert Florey, 1936), *Hollywood Round-Up* (Ewing Scott, 1937), *Hollywood Cowboy* (Ewing Scott, 1937), *It Happened in Hollywood* (Harry Lachman, 1937), *Sophie Lang Goes West* (aka *Sophie Lang in Hollywood*, Charles Riesner, 1937), *Crashing Hollywood* (Lew Landers, 1938), *Keep Smiling* (aka *Hello Hollywood*, 1938), *Hollywood Cavalcade* (Irving Cummings, 1939) and *The Jones Family in Hollywood* (Malcolm St Clair, 1939).

243 Other examples include *Let's Go Places* (Frank R. Strayer, 1930), *Movie Crazy* (Clyde Bruckman, 1932), *Bombshell* (Victor Fleming, 1933), *Hard to Handle* (Mervyn LeRoy, 1933), *Here Comes Carter* (William Clemens, 1936), *Talent Scout* (William B. Clemens, 1937), *Something to Sing About* (Victor Schertzinger, 1937), *The Stand-In* (Tay Garnett, 1937), *The Affairs of Annabel* (Ben Stoloff, 1938), *Boy Meets Girl* (Lloyd Bacon, 1938).

244 *Los Angeles Times*, 4 January 1935, p. 19; 6 February 1938, p. C1.

245 *Studio Murder Mystery*, released in June 1929, was made with sound in the earliest days of the technology, and concerns a studio in which we can see both silent and sound films being made side by side.

246 See David James, *The Most Typical Avant-Garde*, pp. 39–47 and Brian Taves, *Robert Florey: The French Expressionist* (Metuchen, NJ, 1987).

247 Critical reviews suggest that audiences appreciated the portrait of Hollywood in *Hollywood Boulevard* but were disappointed that it was complicated by the story's tragic elements and critique. See *Motion Picture Herald*, 22 August 1936; *Hollywood Reporter*, 31 July 1936; *Variety* 31 July 1936 and 23 September 1936, Margaret Herrick Library, AMPAS, clippings file.

248 See, for example, Giuliana Muscio, *Hollywood's New Deal: Culture and the Moving Image* (Philadelphia, PA, 1996).

249 An earlier but less self-conscious instance occurs in *What Price Hollywood*, from which *A Star is Born* heavily borrowed; subsequent examples may be found in the 1960s art film *Model Shop*

(Jacques Demy, 1968) and the 1990s thriller *Heat* (Michael Mann, 1995), to name just two. Its content and form have also become iconic in Julius Shulman's celebrated photograph of Case Study House #22 (Pierre Koenig, 1959–60), 1960. See Elizabeth Armstrong, ed., *Birth of the Cool: California Art, Design, and Culture at Midcentury* (New York and Newport Beach, CA, 2007), p. 35.

250 David Gebhard and Harriette Von Breton, *Los Angeles in the Thirties: 1931–1941*, 2nd edn (Santa Monica, CA, 1989), p. 6.

251 Donald Albrecht, *Designing Dreams: Modern Architecture in the Movies* (London, 1987), p. xii.

252 James Sanders, *Celluloid Skyline: New York and the Movies* (London, 2002), pp. 243–67, 296–312.

253 Albrecht, *Designing Dreams*, p. xii, acknowledges both New York and Los Angeles as centres of modernist architecture but indicates that most films with modernist settings were set in New York.

254 Robert Florey, *Hollywood d'hier et d'aujourd'hui*, with a preface by René Clair (Paris, 1947), especially pp. 85–90. For other international perspectives, see Umberto Colombini, *Hollywood Visione che incanta* (Turin, 1929); César Miró, *Hollywood: La ciudad imaginaria* (Hollywood, CA, 1939); and Anton Wagner, *Los Angeles: the development, life and form of the Southern Californian metropolis*, trans. Gavriel D. Rosenfeld, not published, Getty Research Institute for the History of Art and the Humanities, Los Angeles, 1997.

255 Yvan Noé also wrote a study of Hollywood in which he described it as 'the greatest factory of lies *in the world*', but he must be differentiated from his compatriots in that he worried about its Jewish backing and has been identified by historians of French cinema with the right rather than the left wing of French interwar politics. See Yvan Noé, *L'Épicerie des rêves* (Paris, 1933), pp. 8–9; and Richard Abel, *French Film Theory and Criticism, 1907–1939* (Princeton, NJ, 1993), pp. 8, 12. All translations in this section are my own.

256 Ehrhard Bahr, *Weimar on the Pacific: German*

Exile Culture in Los Angeles and the Crisis of Modernism (Berkeley, CA, 2008).

257 J. Kessel, *Hollywood: Ville Mirage* (Paris, 1936), pp. 12–14. Of course, associations of Hollywood with appearance rather than substance were also evident in celebrated novels such as Nathanael West's *The Day of the Locust* (1939), F. Scott Fitzgerald's *The Last Tycoon* (1941) and Evelyn Waugh's *The Loved One* (1948). See John Parris Springer, *Hollywood Fictions: The Dream Factory in American Popular Literature* (Norman, OK, 2000) and Chip Rhodes, *Politics, Desire, and the Hollywood Novel* (Iowa City, IA, 2008).

258 Kessel, *Hollywood: Ville Mirage*, p. 7.

259 Ibid., p. 10.

260 Blaise Cendrars, *Hollywood: La Mecque du Cinéma* (Paris, 1936), p. 23.

261 Ibid., p. 39.

262 Ibid., pp. 21–2.

263 Ibid., p. 54.

264 Jean Baudrillard, *America* (London and New York, 1988), p. 51. See also Jean-François Lyotard, *Pacific Wall* [1979] (Venice, CA, 1989).

265 Kessel, *Hollywood: Ville Mirage*, pp. 169–70.

4 Geopolitical Pressure Point

1 *Los Angeles Times*, 13 November 1953, p. A4.

2 Tino Balio, ed., *The American Film Industry* (Madison, WI, 1985), pp. 401–2.

3 *New York Times*, 9 April 1950, pp. 14, 40–41 (14).

4 Ibid.

5 See United States Census Bureau, *Population of the 100 Largest Cities and Other Urban Places in the United States, 1790–1990*, by Campbell Gibson, 1998, at www.census.gov.

6 Mike Davis, *City of Quartz: Excavating the Future in Los Angeles* (New York, 1992), p. 67.

7 Allen J. Scott and Edward W. Soja, eds, *The City: Los Angeles and Urban Theory at the End of the Twentieth Century* (Berkeley, CA, 1998), p. 9.

8 See United Nations, Department of Economic and Social Affairs, Population Division, *World Urbanization Prospects: The 2005 Revision,*

File 14: The 30 Largest Urban Agglomerations Ranked by Population Size, 1950–2015, at www.un.org.

9 For Jameson, *Klute* (Alan J. Pakula, 1971), *The Parallax View* (Pakula, 1974), *Three Days of the Condor* (Sydney Pollack, 1975) and *All the President's Men* (Pakula, 1976) concern 'the figuration of conspiracy as an attempt . . . to think a system [multinational capitalism] so vast that it cannot be encompassed by the natural and historically developed categories of perception with which human beings normally orient themselves'. Fredric Jameson, *The Geopolitical Aesthetic: Cinema and Space in the World System* (Bloomington, IN, and London, 1995), pp. 1–2. Los Angeles became an important setting for similar films in *The Long Goodbye* (Robert Altman, 1973) and *Chinatown* (Roman Polanski, 1974). See also my own 'A Nostalgia for Modernity: New York, Los Angeles, and American Cinema in the 1970s', in *Screening the City*, ed. Mark Shiel and Tony Fitzmaurice (London and New York, 2003), pp. 160–79.

10 Jameson briefly alludes to film noir as a forerunner of this kind. Jameson, *The Geopolitical Aesthetic*, p. 150.

11 Paul Schrader, 'Notes on Film noir', in *Film Genre Reader*, ed. Barry Keith Grant (Austin, TX, 1986), pp. 167–82 (174).

12 I note Steve Neale's explanation that in the United States in the 1940s and '50s what are now called 'film noirs' were typically referred to as 'crime melodramas' or 'thrillers'. See Steve Neale, *Genre and Hollywood* (London and New York, 1999), pp. 142–67. Though aware of Neale's important differentiation of the terms, I use 'film noir' as a flag of convenience to manage a large body of films that have more similarities than differences, and around which an exceptionally large volume of literature has grown in which the term 'film noir' has been effectively standardized. At the same time, my argument is not reliant on the term 'film noir' – indeed, I hope to maintain critical distance from it by highlighting its geographical limitations.

13 Mary Ann Doane, *The Desire to Desire: The Woman's Film of the 1940s* (Bloomington, IN, 1987), and *Femmes fatales: Feminism, Film Theory, and Psychoanalysis* (New York, 1991); J. P. Telotte, *Voices in the Dark: The Narrative Patterns of Film noir* (Urbana, IL, 1989); Frank Krutnik, *In a Lonely Street: Film noir, Genre, Masculinity* (London, 1991); James Naremore, *More than Night: Film noir in its Contexts* (Berkeley, CA, 1998).

14 In addition to Telotte, Krutnik and Naremore, these are Nicholas Christopher, *Somewhere in the Night: Film noir and the American City* (New York, 1997); Spencer Selby, *Dark City: The Film noir* (Jefferson, NC, 1997); Joan Copjec, ed., *Shades of Noir* (London and New York, 1993); Andrew Dickos, *Street with No Name: A History of the Classic American Film noir* (Lexington, KY, 2002); Paula Rabinowitz, *Black and White and Noir* (New York, 2002); Kelly Oliver and Benigno Trigo, *Noir Anxiety* (Minneapolis, MN, 2002).

15 Raymond Borde and Etienne Chaumeton's now canonical *Panorama du film noir* (1955), for example, available in English translation as *Panorama of Film noir, 1941–1953* (San Francisco, 2002), makes a small number of specific references to New York, Los Angeles, Chicago and San Francisco, but homogenizes them in terms of what they see as a distinctively American modernity and toughness, and without differentiating between their districts or moments in their historical evolution. See also Nino Frank, 'Un nouveau genre "policier": l'aventure criminelle', *L'Écran français*, no. 61 (August 1946), pp. 8–9.

16 Edward Dimendberg, *Film Noir and the Spaces of Modernity* (Cambridge, MA, 2004), pp. 6, 19.

17 Eric Avila, *Popular Culture in the Age of White Flight: Fear and Fantasy in Suburban Los Angeles* (Berkeley, CA, 2004), pp. 65–105.

18 I have compiled the filmography from Michael L. Stephens, *Film noir: A Comprehensive, Illustrated Reference to Movies, Terms, and Persons* (Jefferson, NC, 1995); Selby, *Dark City*; Michael F. Keaney, *Film noir: 745 Films of the Classic Era, 1940–1959* (Jefferson, NC, 2003); Arthur Lyons, *Death on the Cheap: The Lost B Movies of Film noir* (Cambridge, MA, 2000); Alain Silver and Elizabeth Ward, *Film noir: An Encyclopedic Reference to the American Style* (Woodstock, NY, 1979); and the American Film Institute Catalog of Feature Films, 1893–1971, at www.afi.com. The body of films I call 'film noir' is deliberately broad, including many historically important smaller groups of films such as gothic noir, boxing films, prison films, semi-documentary crime films and *film gris*. See Peter Stanfield, 'A Monarch for the Millions: Jewish Filmmakers, Social Commentary, and the Postwar Cycle of Boxing Films', and Thom Andersen, 'Red Hollywood', in *'Un-American' Hollywood: Politics and Film in the Blacklist Era*, ed. Frank Krutnik, Steve Neale, Brian Neve and Peter Stanfield (New Brunswick, NJ, 2008), pp. 79–98 and 225–63, respectively; also Thomas Schatz, *Boom and Bust: American Cinema in the 1940s* (Berkeley, CA, 1999), pp. 232–9 and 378–92. Unlike the widest definitions, such as Keaney's, I do not include *noir* westerns such as *Yellow Sky* (William Wellman, 1948), *noir* serials such as *The Shadow* (James W. Horne, 1940), or films of non-US origin. In the filmography, I have identified the most important settings on a film-by-film basis by reference to the films, production reports, contemporary film reviews and the AFI Catalog. I have tabulated these settings chronologically, by date of the film's first US release, and geographically, by differentiating between US and non-US settings, urban, small-town and rural settings, specific cities by name, and major US regions from the Eastern seaboard to California.

19 Naturally, there are some methodological limits to the geographical specificity of the analysis. It allows me to identify the key settings in each film but, where a film is set in more than one place, it does not allow me to identify the amount or proportion of time spent in each place, nor the dramatic significance of the place relative to others in any given film; it does not allow me to specify whether a setting is recreated

in the studio or shot on location (nor, if shot on location, *where* on location); and it does not allow me to indicate the degree to which such and such a setting is specifically identified in a film through visual cues, captions, dialogue or other intra- or extra-diegetic information, although in my tabulation I have specifically included a category for those films which are set in cities that are not named at all, for example John Huston's *The Asphalt Jungle* (1950). However, these limits do not hamper the interpretation I provide in this essay.

20 Table Aa22-35, *Historical Statistics of the United States,* ed. Susan B. Carter et al. (Cambridge, 2006); http://hsus.cambridge.org.

21 1950 saw a spike in representations of the American northwest because in that year seven films were set, in whole or in part, in San Francisco. These were *Born to be Bad*, *D.O.A.*, *The Man Who Cheated Himself*, *No Man of Her Own*, *Once a Thief*, *Shakedown* and *Woman on the Run*.

22 Kirkpatrick Sale, *Power Shift: The Rise of the Southern Rim and its Challenge to the Eastern Establishment* (New York, 1976), pp. 207–71.

23 United States Census Bureau, *Demographic Trends in the Twentieth Century, Census 2000 Special Reports*, November 2002, p. 19.

24 Ibid.

25 Avila, *Popular Culture in the Age of White Flight*, pp. 73–80; Mike Davis, 'Bunker Hill: Hollywood's Dark Shadow', in *Cinema and the City: Film and Urban Societies in a Global Context*, ed. Mark Shiel and Tony Fitzmaurice (Oxford and Malden, MA, 2001), pp. 33–45; Dimendberg, *Film Noir and the Spaces of Modernity*, pp. 151–65.

26 Ibid., pp. 36–46.

27 Other examples of the film noir about the Los Angeles movie business include *Hollywood Story* (William Castle, 1951) and *The Bad and the Beautiful* (Vincente Minnelli, 1952).

28 *Wall Street Journal*, 8 August 1947, pp. 1, 4. See also *Los Angeles Times*, 29 June 1947, pp. C1, and *New York Times*, 12 May 1946, p. 47.

29 *Los Angeles Times*, 23 May 1948, p. C2.

30 Ibid.

31 *New York Times*, 7 February 1949, p. 15.

32 *Los Angeles Times*, 20 January 1949, p. 21.

33 *Daily News*, 20 January 1949, Margaret Herrick Library, AMPAS, clippings file.

34 Ibid.

35 *Lady in the Lake* (Robert Montgomery, 1947) and *The Brasher Doubloon* (John Brahm, 1947) were the final two of seven screen adaptations of Chandler's writings in the 1940s until a second wave of them occurred in the late 1960s and '70s.

36 On this evolution, see Krutnik, *In a Lonely Street*, pp. 92–164.

37 Paul Kerr, 'Out of What Past? Notes on the B film noir', in *The Hollywood Film Industry: A Reader*, ed. Paul Kerr (London, 1986), pp. 220–44.

38 On the lack of representations of the working class in earlier Hollywood cinema, see Steven J. Ross, *Working-Class Hollywood: Silent Film and the Shaping of Class in America* (Princeton, NJ, 1998).

39 On this authoritarian implication of the police procedural film, see Christopher P. Wilson, *Cop Knowledge: Police Power and Cultural Narrative in Twentieth-Century America* (Chicago, IL, 2000), pp. 57–93. Wilson emphasizes the cumulative and normative effects of the repetition and humanization of police routines over time in literature, cinema and television. Some of the writers and directors of police procedurals in the late 1940s were politically liberal or leftist, but their efforts at critique were neutered by the producers and studios for whom they worked, and suppressed altogether by the full implementation of the blacklist in 1951. See Rebecca Prime, 'Cloaked in Compromise: Jules Dassin's "Naked" City', in *'Un-American' Hollywood*, ed. Krutnik, Neale, Neve and Stanfield, pp. 142–51.

40 On these films, see James Sanders, *Celluloid Skyline: New York and the Movies* (London, 2002), pp. 327–36 and 390–92; and Eddie Muller, *Dark City: The Lost World of Film Noir* (New York, 1998).

41 David C. Perry and Alfred J. Watkins, 'Regional Change and the Impact of Uneven Urban Development', in *The Rise of the Sunbelt Cities*, ed. David C. Perry and Alfred J. Watkins (Beverly Hills, CA, 1977), pp. 23, 49.

42 *Los Angeles Times*, 2 January 1940, p. C7.

43 Janet L. Abu-Lughod, *New York, Chicago, Los Angeles: America's Global Cities* (Minneapolis, MN, 1999), pp. 192, 233, 245.

44 *Los Angeles Times*, 3 March 1940, p. H4.

45 Ibid.

46 Ibid.

47 Ibid.

48 Ibid.

49 Donald L. Singer, 'Upton Sinclair and the California Gubernatorial Campaign of 1934', in *A Southern California Historical Anthology: Selections from the Annual and Quarterly Publications of the Historical Society of Southern California, 1883–1983*, ed. Doyce B. Nunis (Los Angeles, CA, 1984), pp. 351–78. For a contemporary report, see *New York Times*, 29 August 1934, pp. 1–2.

50 *Los Angeles Times*, 14 October 1934, p. 18.

51 On labour activism in other California industries, see Anne Loftis, *Witnesses to the Struggle: Imaging the 1930s California Labor Movement* (Reno, NV, 1998).

52 *New York Times*, 2 October 1947, p. 2. See also *New York Times*, 10 July 1947, p. 23; 3 August 1947, pp. 10, 17–18; and Edward C. Maguire, Coordinator of the Motion Picture Industry of the City of New York, 'New York Motion Picture Production', *Journal of the Society of Motion Picture Engineers*, L (January 1948), pp. 4–5.

53 *Los Angeles Times*, 25 February 1950, p. 2.

54 Quoted in Janet Wasko, *Movies and Money: Financing the American Film Industry* (Norwood, NJ, 1982), p. 110.

55 Flora Rheta Schreiber, 'New York: A Cinema Capital', *Quarterly of Film, Radio, and Television*, VII/3 (1953), pp. 264–73.

56 James P. Kraft, 'Musicians in Hollywood: Work and Technological Change in Entertainment Industries, 1926–1940', *Technology and Culture*, XXXV/2 (1994), pp. 289–314.

57 For an early indication of the studios' nervousness about the advent of television, see *Los Angeles Times*, 2 January 1940, p. E3. On the relationship between New York, Los Angeles and television, see *New York Times*, 13 June 1948, p. XX20; *Los Angeles Times*, 23 February 1955, p. 24; 14 October 1959, p. A10.

58 *New York Times*, 14 December 1947, p. X4.

59 Ibid., 17 October 1949, p. 39.

60 *Los Angeles Times*, 15 February 1946, p. 14; see also *New York Times*, 15 July 1946, p. 47.

61 *New York Times*, 16 August 1947, p. 26.

62 Carey McWilliams, 'Culture and Society in Southern California', *Annals of the American Academy of Political and Social Science*, CCXLVIII (November 1946), pp. 209–13 (209).

63 Ibid.

64 *Los Angeles Times*, 15 December 1946, p. B1. See also Noah Isenberg, 'Perennial Detour: The Cinema of Edgar G. Ulmer and the Experience of Exile', *Cinema Journal*, XLIII/2 (2004), pp. 3–25.

65 *Detour* was produced on a budget of $30,000 and was shot over one week in June 1945. While much of its action took place in New York and Los Angeles interiors and was filmed in the studio, it used location filming for its Arizona sequences and rear projections of second unit photography of actual street scenes for its Los Angeles exteriors. Working for the independent producers of Poverty Row, location filming had the added attraction for Ulmer that it was relatively affordable. In relation to his film *Strange Woman* (1946), Ulmer explained that 'we can figure on New York primarily as a location, and not as a studio setup' but that New York will continue to be used because 'it costs more to duplicate nature on a sound stage than to shoot it in the raw!' *Los Angeles Times*, 15 December 1946, p. B3.

66 On German and other Central European writers and filmmakers in Hollywood in the 1930s and '40s, see Ehrhard Bahr, *Weimar on the Pacific: German Exile Culture in Los Angeles and the Crisis of Modernism* (Berkeley, CA, 2008), and Anton Kaes, 'A Stranger in the House: Fritz Lang's "Fury" and the Cinema of Exile', *New German*

Critique, no. 89 (Spring–Summer 2003), pp. 33–58.

67 Siegfried Kracauer, 'Hollywood's Terror Films: Do They Reflect an American State of Mind?' (1946), *New German Critique*, no. 89 (Spring–Summer 2003), pp. 105–11 (106).

68 *Los Angeles Times*, 15 December 1946, p. B3.

69 The veiled articulation of critique in film noirs by leftist and left-liberal filmmakers is explored in Paul Buhle, 'The Hollywood Left: Aesthetics and Politics', *New Left Review*, I/212 (July–August 1995), pp. 101–19; Paul Buhle and Dave Wagner, *Radical Hollywood: The Untold Story Behind America's Movies* (New York, 2002); and Krutnik, Neale, Neve and Stanfield, ed., *'Un-American' Hollywood*.

70 Anthony A. P. Dawson, 'Hollywood's Labor Troubles', *Industrial and Labor Relations Review*, I/4 (1948), pp. 638–47 (640).

71 *New York Times*, 1 March 1942, p. X3.

72 Ibid., and Dawson, 'Hollywood's Labor Troubles', p. 641.

73 Dawson, 'Hollywood's Labor Troubles', p. 643, and Mike Nielsen and Gene Mailes, *Hollywood's Other Blacklist: Union Struggles in the Studio System* (London, 1995), p. 51.

74 Kraft, 'Musicians in Hollywood', p. 314.

75 Anthony Dawson, 'Patterns of Production and Employment in Hollywood', *Hollywood Quarterly*, IV/4 (1950), pp. 345–6.

76 Quoted in Nielsen and Mailes, *Hollywood's Other Blacklist*, p. 143. Johnston made this statement in an address to the 1946 IATSE annual convention.

77 Perry and Watkins, 'Regional Change and the Impact of Uneven Urban Development', pp. 39–40; also Perry and Watkins, 'People, Profit, and the Rise of the Sunbelt Cities', in *The Rise of the Sunbelt Cities*, ed. David C. Perry and Alfred J. Watkins (Beverly Hills, CA, 1977), pp. 277–306.

78 See Colin Shindler, *Hollywood in Crisis: Cinema and American Society,1929–1939* (New York and London, 1996), p. 7.

79 See *Los Angeles: A Guide to the City and its Environs*, Writers' Program of the Work Projects Administration in Southern California (1941) (New York, 1951), p. 78.

80 Murray Ross, 'Labor Relations in Hollywood', *Annals of the American Academy of Political and Social Science*, CCLIV (November 1947), pp. 58–64 (61).

81 See Thomas Repetto, *American Mafia: A History of Its Rise to Power* (New York, 2004); and Gerald Horne, *Class Struggle in Hollywood, 1930–1950: Moguls, Mobsters, Stars, Reds, and Trade Unionists* (Austin, TX, 2001).

82 Carey McWilliams, 'Honorable in All Things: The Memoirs of Carey McWilliams', interviewed by Joel R. Gardner, Oral History Program, Department of Special Collections, Charles E. Young Research Library, University of California, Los Angeles, transcript of Tape 5, 14 July 1978, p. 214.

83 John Cogley, *Report on Blacklisting*, I: *The Movies* (New York, 1956), cited in Nielsen and Mailes, *Hollywood's Other Blacklist*, fn. 44, p. 70.

84 Efforts to expose the existence of an alliance of film producers, IATSE leaders and the mafia were led by radical labour unions in 1937 and 1938, but only came to fruition when the attention of the FBI and other agencies in Washington, DC, was gained in 1939. See Tim Adler, *Hollywood and the Mob* (London, 2007), pp. 100–1.

85 See Virgil W. Peterson, 'Rackets in America', *Journal of Criminal Law, Criminology, and Police Science*, XLIX/6 (1959), pp. 583–9.

86 Humbert Nelli, *The Business of Crime* (New York, 1976), p. 243, cited in Barbara Alexander, 'The Rational Racketeer: Pasta Protection in Depression Era Chicago', *Journal of Law and Economics*, XL/1 (1997), pp. 175–202 (193–4).

87 Nielsen and Mailes, *Hollywood's Other Blacklist*, pp. 73, 78.

88 Fr George H. Dunne, *Hollywood Labor Dispute: A Study in Immorality* (Los Angeles, 1950), p. 23.

89 *Los Angeles Times,* 27 March 1947, p. 1; 1 September 1947, pp. 1, 2; and 27 October 1947, p. 1.

90 Ibid., 21 April 1938, p. A2; 7 July 1938, p. A3; 22 December 1939, p. A10.

91 Ibid., 2 January 1940, p. C7.

92 Ibid. Similar but slightly different figures are ibid., 8 April 1940, p. A4.

93 Daniel Jacoby, *Laboring for Freedom: A New Look at the History of Labor in America* (Armonk, NJ, and London, 1998), pp. 85, 125.

94 *Los Angeles Times,* 3 February 1945, p. A1.

95 CSU membership was estimated by the *Los Angeles Times* at a somewhat lower figure, between 6,000 and 10,000 members. *Los Angeles Times,* 12 March 1945, p. 1; 12 February 1946, p. 1; and 16 February 1946, pp. 1, 4; also *Variety,* 6 February 1946, pp. 3, 12, and 13 February 1946, p. 3.

96 *Los Angeles Times,* 13 March 1945, p. 1.

97 Ibid., 9 October 1945, pp. 1–3; 24 October 1945, pp. 1, 12; 19 December 1945, p. A2.

98 Ibid., 6 October 1945, p. 1.

99 Ibid., 24 October 1945, pp. 1, 12.

100 Ibid., 3 February 1945, p. A1.

101 Ibid., 12 March 1945, p. 1; 19 March 1945, p. 1.

102 Opponents of the CSU regularly claimed that the strikes were an insult to recently returned veterans who deserved the right to work unhindered. The Cecil B. De Mille Foundation for Political Freedom provided assistance to unemployed veterans who were unable to cross the pickets, and a small number of veterans maintained a picket of CSU headquarters in the autumn of 1945. Herbert Sorrell and other CSU spokespeople alleged that veterans' 'protests' were actually paid for by the studios and that most of those veterans protesting were IATSE members. Some members of the CSU were also veterans. See *Los Angeles Times,* 11 November 1945, pp. A1–A2; 13 November 1945, p. A1; and 14 November 1945, p. 2.

103 Ibid., 16 April 1945, p. 11.

104 Ibid., 14 October 1945, pp. 1–2, and 20 March 1946, p. 12.

105 See ibid., 11 October 1945, p. 1; 12 October 1945, p. 1; 13 October 1945, p. 1; 16 October 1945, pp. 1, 8; 22 October 1945, p. 1; and 23 October 1945, pp. 1, 2.

106 Ibid., 5 October, 1946, p. 8.

107 Ibid., 25 October 1945, pp. 1, 4, and 26 October 1945, pp. 1, 4.

108 Ibid., 26 October 1945, p. 4; 31 October 1945,

pp. 1, 6; 19 December 1945, p. A1; 15 February 1946, pp. A1, A3; *New York Times,* 21 February 1946, p. 13; 21 February 1946, p. 7; and *Los Angeles Times,* 22 February 1946, p. 8.

109 Dunne, *Hollywood Labor Dispute,* pp. 27–31; Ross, 'Labor Relations', p. 64; *Los Angeles Times,* 26 August 1947, pp. A1–A2.

110 *Los Angeles Times,* 25 September 1946, pp. A1, A3. The Painters Union, one of the key elements of the CSU, had additional power because it also represented Screen Story Analysts.

111 See *New York Times,* 14 February 1946, p. 4, 15 February 1946, p. 15, and 16 February 1946, p. 3; *Los Angeles Times,* 27 November 1945, p. 8, 14 December 1945, p. A3, and 12 February 1946, p. 1.

112 *Los Angeles Times,* 13 February 1946, pp. 1–2; *New York Times,* 17 April 1946, p. 1; *Los Angeles Times,* 17 April 1946, p. 1.

113 Ibid., 1 July 1946, pp. A1, 3, and 3 July 1946, pp. 1–2.

114 Ibid., 27 July 1946, p. 2; 1 August 1946, p. 2; and 30 July 1946, p. A1.

115 Ibid., 11 November 1946, p. A1; 26 September 1946, pp. 1–2; and 8 October 1946, p. 1.

116 Ibid., 27 September 1946, pp. 1, 2.

117 Ibid., 27 September 1946, pp. 1, 2; 4 October 1946, p. 1; and 12 October 1946, pp. 1–2.

118 Ibid., 16 November 1946, pp. 1, 3; 19 November 1946, pp. 1–2. The vast majority of detainees were ultimately charged only with misdemeanours such as blocking an entrance. Ibid., 7 March 1947, p. 9.

119 Ibid., 25 November 1946, pp. 1–2.

120 Ibid., 29 November 1946, p. 1.

121 Ibid., 31 December 1946, p. 7.

122 Ibid., 1 September 1947, pp. 1–2; *New York Times,* 1 September 1947, p. 30; *Los Angeles Times,* 2 September 1947, p. A1.

123 Meacham quoted in Dunne, *Hollywood Labor Dispute,* p. 26. See also *New York Times,* 23 August 1947, p. 2.

124 Dunne, *Hollywood Labor Dispute,* p. 19. Dunne's account relies on his own experiences together with a number of authoritative sources, including testimony and the judge's findings in the

resolution of the estate of Frank Nitti, September 1948 through November 1949, in Chicago tax court; the report of Stewart Meacham to the NLRB; and testimony to the (Kearns) House Committee on Education and Labor. Dunne testified to that committee that a Paramount official had lobbied his superiors to suppress his outspoken interventions, and that he had been directly approached by a Twentieth Century-Fox official for the same purpose.

125 Ibid., 24; *New York Times*, 29 August 1947, p. 18.
126 Dunne, *Hollywood Labor Dispute*, pp. 42, 44. Dunne's view was anticipated by Dawson, 'Hollywood's Labor Troubles', pp. 638–47.
127 *Los Angeles Times*, 27 October 1947, p. 1; 28 October 1947, p. A1; and 21 June 1951, p. A3.
128 Dawson, 'Hollywood's Labor Troubles', pp. 638–9.
129 Richard Koszarski, *Hollywood on the Hudson: Film and Television in New York from Griffith to Sarnoff* (New Brunswick, NJ, and London, 2008), p. 100.
130 Daniel Jacoby, *Laboring for Freedom: A New Look at the History of Labor in America* (Armonk, NJ, and London, 1998), p. 93.
131 *New York Times*, 9 August 1927, p. 2; 6 October 1927, p. 9; 29 June 1932, p. 3; and 27 February 1930, p. 19.
132 Ibid., 23 January 1924, p. 6.
133 Carey McWilliams, *California: The Great Exception* (New York, 1949, repr. Berkeley, CA, 1998), p. 127.
134 Michael Kazin, 'The Great Exception Revisited: Organized Labor and Politics in San Francisco and Los Angeles, 1870–1940', *Pacific Historical Review*, LV/3 (1986), pp. 371–402 (381).
135 *Los Angeles Times*, 11 October 1945, p. 1; 12 October 1945, p. 1.
136 Ibid., 18 October 1946, p. 2.
137 Ibid., 3 February 1947, p. 2; *New York Times*, 22 March 1947, p. 2.
138 See *Los Angeles Times*, 13 March 1945, p. 2, and 16 October 1945, pp. 1, 8; *New York Times*, 17 February 1946, p. 4; *Los Angeles Times*, 16 February 1946, p. 1, and 1 July 1946, pp. A1, 3.
139 Ibid., 6 April 1945, p. 1, and 16 April 1945, p. 11.
140 Ibid., 19 November 1946, p. 7.
141 Ibid., 29 August 1947, pp. A1–A2.
142 Ibid., 6 October 1945, p. 2, and 6 October 1945, pp. 1–2, 4.
143 Mike Davis, *Prisoners of the American Dream: Politics and Economy in the History of the US Working Class* (London and New York, 1986), pp. 82–93, 117–21.
144 *Los Angeles Times*, 18 October 1945, p. 1.
145 Davis, *Prisoners of the American Dream*, p. 88.
146 See, for example, Thomas Schatz and Gorham Kindem, 'The Postwar Motion Picture Industry', in Schatz, *Boom and Bust*, pp. 285–328; John Cogley, 'HUAC: The Mass Hearings', excerpted from *Report on Blacklisting*, I: *The Movies* (1956), in Balio, *American Film Industry*, pp. 487–509; Otto Friedrich, *City of Nets: A Portrait of Hollywood in the 1940s* (Berkeley, CA, 1997), pp. 291–338.
147 See, for example, Neal Gabler, *An Empire of their Own: How the Jews Invented Hollywood* (New York, 1988), pp. 311–86. Jon Lewis has added an important interpretation of the blacklist as the result of 'a larger transformation of the film industry from its roots in entrepreneurial capital to a more corporatist, conglomerate mode'. Jon Lewis, '"We Do Not Ask You to Condone This": How the Blacklist Saved Hollywood', *Cinema Journal*, XXXIX/2 (2000), pp. 3–30 (5).
148 It was Mayer himself who first put forward this explanation in testimony he gave in court in response to a suit against MGM for wrongful dismissal taken by Lester Cole, who would later be named as one of the Hollywood Ten. See *New York Times*, 9 December 1948, p. 3, and 10 December 1948, p. 5.
149 Ibid., 27 September 1930, p. 9.
150 Chaplin quoted in ibid., 15 March 1931, p. 12.
151 *New York Times*, 18 August 1934, p. 5, and 9 August 1934, pp. 1, 6. In his testimony, Hynes estimated that there were perhaps 4,000–5,000 Communist Party members in California, of whom 2,000 were in Los Angeles, along with about 20–25,000 sympathizers.
152 *Washington Post*, 14 October 1936, p. X16.
153 Patricia Cayo Sexton, *The War on Labor and the*

315

Left: Understanding America's Unique Conservatism
(Boulder, CO, 1991), pp. 144–5.

154 *Los Angeles Times*, 15 August 1938, pp. 1, 3.

155 Ibid., 29 March 1939, p. 4. Nielsen and Mailes,
Hollywood's Other Blacklist, p. 65, argue that it was
George Browne who requested that the Dies
Committee investigate Communist infiltration
of Hollywood labor unions.

156 *Los Angeles Times*, 19 February 1940, p. 6.

157 *New York Times*, 16 August 1940, p. 14.

158 Ibid.; Larry Ceplair and Steven Englund, *The
Inquisition in Hollywood: Politics in the Film
Community, 1930–60* (Garden City, NY, 1979,
repr. Urbana, IL, 2003), p. 157.

159 *New York Times*, 17 August 1940, p. 13. Others
among the Hollywood Ten were active supporters
of the CSU: Dalton Trumbo was one of the
signatories to a statement against police tactics,
and Edward Dmytryk and Ring Lardner Jr
attended picket lines at Warner Bros. See *Los
Angeles Times*, 10 October 1945, pp. 1, 2, and 12
October 1945, pp. 1, 3, p. 3.

160 *Los Angeles Times*, 15 July 1941, p. A2.

161 *New York Times*, 10 August 1941, p. X3.

162 Ingrid Winther Scobie, 'Jack B. Tenney and the
"Parasitic Menace": Anti-Communist Legislation
in California, 1940–1949', *Pacific Historical
Review*, XLIII/2 (1974), pp. 188–211 (189).

163 *Los Angeles Times*, 26 October 1945, p. 4.

164 Ibid., 14 February 1946, p. 2.

165 Ibid., 8 March 1947, p. A3; 11 September 1947,
p. 1; and 20 September 1947, p. 4.

166 Ibid., 9 October 1945, p. 2, and 20 February
1946, p. 2.

167 Ibid., 25 May 1941, p. 14.

168 Scobie, 'Jack B. Tenney and the "Parasitic
Menace"', pp. 191–3.

169 Ibid., pp. 194–200.

170 Ibid., p. 206.

171 Harold W. Horowitz, 'Report on the Los Angeles
City and County Loyalty Programs', *Stanford Law
Review*, V/2 (1953), pp. 233–46; John W. Caughey,
'Farewell to California's "Loyalty" Oath', *Pacific
Historical Review*, XXXVIII/ 2 (1969),
pp. 123–8.

172 *Los Angeles Times*, 7 May 1946, p. 2; 13 August

1946, p. 6.

173 *Los Angeles Times*, 25 February 1948, p. 2;
4 March 1948, p. 2; 13 March 1948, p. 2. See
also ibid., 26 February 1948, p. 1, and *New York
Times*, 30 August 1947, p. 28. By all accounts,
testimony that Sorrell gave directly to the Tenney
Committee and the House Labor Committee
was witty in ridiculing spurious allegations of
communism and the motivations of those
pursuing them, as well as pugnacious in
defending the bona fides of the CSU. It was
reported that Sorrell had forced a Russian-born,
admitted Communist out of the Painters Local
644. See *Los Angeles Times*, 26 February 1948,
p. 1, and 30 September 1948, p. A2.

174 Lewis, p. 8.

175 *Los Angeles Times*, 5 October 1946, p. 1.

176 *New York Times*, 22 October 1947, pp. 1, 3.

177 *Los Angeles Times*, 25 October 1947, pp. 1, 3.

178 *Washington Post*, 29 October 1947, pp. 1, 2.

179 Harold W. Horowitz, 'Loyalty Tests for
Employment in the Motion Picture Industry',
Stanford Law Review, VI/3 (1954), pp. 438–72
(439).

180 *New York Times*, 26 November 1947, p. 1.

181 *Los Angeles Times*, 29 October 1947, p. 2, and
13 November 1947, p. 11.

182 *Los Angeles Times*, 9 March 1947, pp. 1–2.

183 *Los Angeles Times*, 25 July 1947, p. 4. In Los
Angeles, Kearns briefly attended the Cantwell
talks but the meeting failed to reach resolution.
See ibid., 2 September 1947, p. A1.

184 Ibid., 4 March 1948, p. 2, and 9 March 1947,
pp. 1, 2; McWilliams, 'Honorable in All Things',
p. 221; Horne, *Class Struggle in Hollywood*, p. 25.

185 *Los Angeles Times*, 26 February 1948, p. 2.

186 Ibid., 2 September 1947, pp. A1, A12.

187 Clarence E. Wunderlin, Jr, ed., *The Papers of
Robert A Taft*, III: *1945–1948* (Kent, OH, 2003),
p. 311.

188 *Los Angeles Times*, 31 October 1947, pp. 1, 5.

189 Ibid., 12 May 1948, pp. 1, 4. The Taft-Hartley
Act emboldened calls from businesses across the
United States for so-called 'right-to-work' laws,
which would allow any worker to be employed
without having to join a union or pay union dues.

Such laws became particularly prevalent in southern and western states, although not in California.

190 Fred A. Hartley, *Our New National Labor Policy: The Taft-Hartley Act and the Next Steps* (New York, 1948), p. 30; see also Clarence E. Wunderlin, *Robert A Taft: Ideas, Tradition, and Party in US Foreign Policy* (Lanham, MD, 2005), p. 146.

191 'Diversity Jurisdiction under Section 303 (b) of the Taft-Hartley Act', *Yale Law Journal*, LIX/3 (1950), pp. 575–80.

192 Earlier film industry scandals also had an inter-regional dynamic. The 1921 case in which the film comedian Roscoe 'Fatty' Arbuckle was arrested for the alleged rape of Virginia Rappe in a San Francisco hotel was fuelled partly by anti-Los Angeles sentiment among influential San Franciscans. See Gary Alan Fine, 'Scandal, Social Conditions, and the Creation of Public Atttention: Fatty Arbuckle and the "Problem of Hollywood"', *Social Problems*, XLIV/3 (1997), p. 310. There was also a geographical dimension to condemnations of Hollywood by conservative Christians in the Midwest. See 'Moving Picture Morals Attacked and Defended', *Current Opinion* (April 1922), p. 505.

193 *Los Angeles Times*, 8 July 1945, p. 1; 22 October 1945, pp. 1–2; 31 December 1946, p. 7.

194 Ibid., 6 October 1946, p. 1. In October 1947, stars opposed to HUAC, including Humphrey Bogart, Lauren Bacall, John Huston, Paul Henreid and Gene Kelly flew to Washington, DC. See *Los Angeles Times*, 29 October 1947, p. 2.

195 Ibid., 6 April 1945, p. 6.

196 Nielsen and Mailes, *Hollywood's Other Blacklist*, pp. 73, 78.

197 McWilliams, 'Honorable in All Things', p. 214.

198 Sorrell quoted in Laurie Pintar, 'Herbert K. Sorrell as the Grade-B Hero: Labor Militancy and Masculinity in the Studios', *Labor History*, XXXVII/3, pp. 392–416 (405); Kearns quoted in *Los Angeles Times*, 15 August 1947, p. A1, 14.

199 Ibid., 31 October 1945, pp. 1, 6.

200 Ibid., 3 March 1947, p. 1; *New York Times*, 4 March 1947, p. 22.

201 *Los Angeles Times*, 27 February 1946, p. 7.

202 Ibid., 8 October 1946, pp. 1–3.

203 Ibid., 13 March 1945, p. 2.

204 Ibid., 29 August 1945, p. A2.

205 Ibid., 23 October 1945, pp. 1–2.

206 Ibid., 6 October 1945, p. 1.

207 *New York Times magazine*, 4 September 1949, p. 37.

208 M. Christine Boyer, *The City of Collective Memory: Its Historical Imagery and Architectural Entertainments* (Cambridge, MA, 1998), pp. 7–8.

209 Benjamin Aaron and William Levin, 'Labor Injunctions in Action: A Five-Year Survey in Los Angeles County', *California Law Review*, XXXIX/1 (1951), pp. 42–67.

210 Ibid., p. 55.

211 Ibid., p. 65.

212 Sorrell was arrested with approximately 400 other strikers outside Warner Bros on 10 October 1945, but their thirteen-week trial, which concluded in April 1946, was a public relations disaster for Burbank City Council. Charges of failure to disperse, disturbing the peace and riot were dropped against all but nine defendants. The remaining nine, including Sorrell, were convicted of the lesser charge of failure to disperse and fined $500 each, later reduced to $50 each. One of the nine was convicted of disturbing the peace. See *Los Angeles Times*, 7 October 1945, p. 1; 11 October 1945, pp. 1–2; 5 March 1946, p. A2; 24 April 1946, p. 2; 25 April 1946, p. A2; 28 April 1946, p. 2; 10 May 1946, p. A1; 15 May 1946, p. 4.

213 *Los Angeles Times*, 12 October 1945, pp. 1–2 and 23 October 1945, pp. 1–2.

214 See David M. Gordon, 'Class Struggle and the Stages of Urban Development', in *The Rise of the Sunbelt Cities*, ed. Perry and Watkins, pp. 55–82 (79).

215 Ibid., pp. 72–7

216 Ibid., p. 80.

217 *Los Angeles Times*, 27 January 1918, p. 116.

218 Dana Cuff, *The Provisional City: Los Angeles Stories of Architecture and Urbanism* (Cambridge, MA, 2000), pp. 272–309; Thomas S. Hines, 'Housing, Baseball, and Creeping Socialism: The Battle of Chavez Ravine, Los Angeles, 1949–1959', *Journal*

of *Urban History*, VIII/2 (1982), pp. 123–43. James Thomas Keane, *Fritz B. Burns and the Development of Los Angeles* (Los Angeles, CA, 2001), p. 180, explains the influential opposition to public housing of Fritz B. Burns, one of the giants of Los Angeles real estate and a prominent Republican. For parallel developments in the visual arts, see what Plagens calls 'the painting witch-hunt of 1947–52', in Peter Plagens, *Sunshine Muse: Art on the West Coast, 1945–1970* (Berkeley, CA, 1974, repr. 1999), p. 23.

219 *New York Times*, 4 September 1949, p. 94.

220 For contemporary accounts of the explosion of freeway building in the 1950s, and its physical and social effects, see *Los Angeles Times*, 3 November 1952, p. 3; 13 September 1954, p. 3; and *New York Times*, 3 March 1959, p. 1.

Epilogue

1 This periodization is supported by Dear's description of the period of 'high modernism' in Los Angeles' planning history; Allen J. Scott's tracing of a new wave of 'industrial-urban development' after 1955; and Edward Soja's analysis of its cultural history after HUAC, Disneyland and 'mass suburbanization'. See Michael Dear, *The Postmodern Urban Condition* (Malden, MA, and Oxford, 2000), p. 108; Allen J. Scott, *Metropolis: From the Division of Labor to Urban Form* (Berkeley, CA, 1988), p. 160; and Edward Soja, *Postmetropolis: Critical Studies of Cities and Urban Regions* (Malden, MA, and Oxford, 2000), p. 137. On the shift in Hollywood cinema history at this time, see David Bordwell, Janet Staiger and Kristin Thompson, *The Classical Hollywood Cinema: Film Style and Mode of Production to 1960* (London, 1985), pp. 9–10; and Peter Lev, *T he Fifties: Transforming the Screen, 1950–1959* (Berkeley, CA, 2003), pp. 216–18.

2 See, for example, Daniel Hurewitz, *Bohemian Los Angeles and the Making of Modern Politics* (Berkeley, CA, 2007); John Arthur Maynard, *Venice West: The Beat Generation in Southern California* (New Brunswick, NJ, 1991).

3 David James, *The Most Typical Avant-Garde: History and Geography of Minor Cinemas in Los Angeles* (Berkeley, CA, 2005), pp. 187–227.

4 Mike Davis, *City of Quartz: Excavating the Future in Los Angeles* (New York, 1992), p. 65.

5 Citizens National Bank of Los Angeles, *Los Angeles: Industrial Focal Point of the West* (Los Angeles, 1963), p. 1.

6 *Los Angeles Times*, 3 November 1952, p. 3.

7 E. Gordon Ericksen, 'The Superhighway and City Planning: Some Ecological Considerations with Reference to Los Angeles', *Social Forces*, XXVIII/4 (1950), pp. 429–30.

8 *New York Times*, 3 March 1959, p. 1.

9 Arthur L. Grey, Jr, 'Los Angeles: Urban Prototype', *Land Economics*, XXXV/3 (1959), pp. 235–7.

10 Ericksen, 'The Superhighway and City Planning', p. 430; Grey, 'Los Angeles: Urban Prototype', p. 242.

11 Kevin Lynch, *The Image of the City* (Cambridge, MA, 1960), p. 40; *Chicago Tribune*, 20 November 1966, p. H32; Reyner Banham, *Los Angeles: The Architecture of the Four Ecologies* (New York, 1971), p. 3; Jean-Luc Godard, roundtable discussion with Agnès Varda and others, University of Southern California, 27 February 1968, published in the *Los Angeles Free Press*, 15 March 1968, p. 25.

12 For contemporary discussion, see Charles Higham, 'Hollywood Boulevard 1965', *Sight & Sound*, XXXIV/4 (1965), p. 177–9; LA Department of City Planning, *Hollywood Community Plan: Implementation Report*, City Case Plan 18473, September 1970; Michael Wood, 'Hollywood's Last Picture Show', *Harper's Magazine* (January 1976), pp. 79–82.

13 Los Angeles Department of City Planning, *T he Concept for the Los Angeles General Plan*, Los Angeles, January 1970; Los Angeles County Board of Supervisors and Regional Planning Commission, *General Plan of Los Angeles County*, Los Angeles, June 1973.

14 Michael B. Katz and Mark J. Stern, *One Nation Divisible: What America Wants and What it is Becoming* (New York, 2008), p. 164.

15 Lynch, *The Image of the City*, pp. 41–2.

16 Peter Plagens, *Sunshine Muse: Art on the West Coast, 1945–1970* (Berkeley, CA, 1974, repr. 1999), p. 120.

17 Ibid., p. 139.

18 Tino Balio, ed., *The American Film Industry* (Madison, WI, 1985), pp. 401–2; Douglas Ayer, Roy E. Bates and Peter J. Herman, 'Self-Censorship in the Movie Industry: A Historical Perspective on Law and Social Change', in Gorham Kindem, ed., *The American Movie Industry: The Business of Motion Pictures* (Carbondale, IL, 1982), pp. 220–21.

19 See Mel Gussow, 'Movies Leaving Hollywood Behind', *New York Times*, 27 May 1970, p. 36.

20 See Paula Massood, 'An Aesthetic Appropriate to Conditions: *Killer of Sheep*, (Neo)Realism, and the Documentary Impulse', *Wide Angle*, XXI/4 (1999), pp. 20–41.

21 On the production history of *Terminator 2*, see Tino Balio, '"A Major Presence in all of the World's Important Markets": the Globalization of Hollywood in the 1990s', in *Contemporary Hollywood Cinema*, ed. Stephen Neale and Murray Smith (New York and London, 1998), p. 59. For wider discussion of contemporary Hollywood cinema, including many of the films referred to here, see Mike Hammond and Linda Ruth Williams, eds, *Contemporary American Cinema* (New York and London, 2006).

22 On Los Angeles as a 'fortified city', see Mike Davis, 'Fortress Los Angeles: The Militarization of Urban Space,' in *Variations on a Theme Park: The New American City and the End of Public Space*, ed. Michael Sorkin (New York, 1992), pp. 154–80; on 'interdictory space', see Steven Flusty, *Building Paranoia: The Proliferation of Interdictory Space and the Erosion of Spatial Justice* (West Hollywood, CA, 1994), pp. 16–17.

23 Aida Hozic, *Hollyworld: Space, Power, and Fantasy in the American Economy* (Ithaca, NY, and London, 2001), pp. 135–68; and 'Uncle Sam Goes to Siliwood: Of Landscapes, Spielberg and Hegemony', *Review of International Political Economy*, VI/3 (1999), pp. 289–312.

24 Jean Baudrillard, *America* (London and New York, 1988), p. 51; M. Christine Boyer, 'The Imaginary Real World of Cyber Cities', *Assemblage*, no. 18 (August 1992), pp. 114–27.

25 Ibid., p. 116. I borrow the term 'etherealization' from Boyer, who uses it to point to what she sees as a tendency in some postmodernist descriptions of Los Angeles to favour hyperbole over historical and political analysis and understanding.

26 See Deepak Narang Sawhney, *Unmasking LA: Third Worlds and the City* (New York, 2002); David Rieff, *Los Angeles: Capital of the Third World* (London, 1992); and Eric J. Heikkila and Rafael Pizarro, eds, *Southern California and the World* (Westport, CT, 2002). Having spent the 1960s and '70s as sixth largest city in the world by population, according to the UN, Los Angeles slipped to tenth place in 2000. It is projected to be fifteenth in the world in 2015. See United Nations, Department of Economic and Social Affairs, Population Division, *World Urbanization Prospects: The 2005 Revision, File 14: The 30 Largest Urban Agglomerations Ranked by Population Size, 1950–2015*, at www.un.org.

27 See Hsuan L. Hsu, 'Racial Privacy, the LA Ensemble Film, and Paul Haggis's *Crash*', *Film Criticism*, XXXI/1–2 (2006), pp. 132–56.

28 Edward W. Soja, *Postmodern Geographies: The Reassertion of Space in Critical Social Theory* (London and New York, 1989), p. 190; Los Angeles Economic Development Corporation, *LA Stats*, May 2000, pp. 4–5; Los Angeles Economic Development Corporation, *Essential Southern California: An Economic Atlas of Southern California*, 1998, pp. 10.

29 Ibid., pp. 10, 14.

30 Soja, *Postmodern Geographies*, p. 191.

31 For example, on recent efforts at ecological improvement in Los Angeles, such as the restoration of the Los Angeles river, see Robert Gottlieb, *Reinventing Los Angeles: Nature and Community in the Global City* (Cambridge, MA, 2007), pp. 135–72.

32 Alexa Hyland, '101 Freeway Park Proposal Ramping Up', *Los Angeles Business Journal*, 5 April 2010, at www.labusinessjournal.com.

Select Bibliography

Anger, Kenneth, *Hollywood Babylon* (New York, 1975)

Armstrong, Elizabeth, ed., *Birth of the Cool: California Art, Design, and Culture at Midcentury* (New York and Newport Beach, CA, 2007)

Avila, Eric, *Popular Culture in the Age of White Flight: Fear and Fantasy in Suburban Los Angeles* (Berkeley, CA, 2004)

Bahr, Ehrhard, *Weimar on the Pacific: German Exile Culture in Los Angeles and the Crisis of Modernism* (Berkeley, CA, 2008)

Banham, Reyner, *Los Angeles: The Architecture of the Four Ecologies* (New York, 1971)

Baudrillard, Jean, trans. Chris Turner, *Simulacra and Simulation* [1981] (Ann Arbor, MI, 1994)

Bengtson, John, *Silent Traces: Discovering Early Hollywood through the Films of Charlie Chaplin* (Santa Monica, CA, 2006)

Benjamin, Walter, *Selected Writings*, ed. Marcus Bullock, Howard Eiland, Michael W. Jennings and Gary Smith, 5 vols (Cambridge, MA, 2006)

Borde, Raymond, and Etienne Chaumeton, *Panorama of Film noir, 1941–1953* [1955] (San Francisco, CA, 2002)

Bordwell, David, Janet Staiger and Kristin Thompson, *The Classical Hollywood Cinema: Film Style and Mode of Production to 1960* (London, 1985)

Bowser, Eileen, *The Transformation of Cinema, 1907–1915* (Berkeley, CA, 1994)

Boyer, M. Christine, *The City of Collective Memory: Its Historical Imagery and Architectural Entertainments* (Cambridge, MA, 1998)

Bruno, Giuliana, *Atlas of Emotion: Journeys in Art, Architecture, and Film* (London and New York, 2007)

Bucci, Federico, *Albert Kahn: Architect of Ford* (New York, 2002)

Carr, Harry, *Los Angeles – City of Dreams* (New York, 1935)

Clarke, Charles G., *Early Filmmaking in Los Angeles* (Los Angeles, CA, 1976)

Corkin, Stanley, *Realism and the Birth of the Modern United States* (Athens, GA, 1996)

Cosgrove, Dennis, *Apollo's Eye: A Cartographic Genealogy of the Earth in the Western Imagination* (Baltimore, MD, 2001)

Crafton, Donald, *The Talkies: American Cinema's Transition to Sound, 1926–1931* (Berkeley, CA, 1999)

Cuff, Dana, *The Provisional City: Los Angeles Stories of Architecture and Urbanism* (Cambridge, MA, 2000)

Davis, Mike, *City of Quartz: Excavating the Future in Los Angeles* (New York, 1992)

De Mille, William C., *Hollywood Saga* (New York, 1939)

Dear, Michael J., ed., *From Chicago to LA: Making Sense of Urban Theory* (Thousand Oaks, CA, 2002)

Desser, David, and Garth S. Jowett, eds, *Hollywood Goes Shopping* (Minneapolis, MN, 2000)

Deverell, William, Michael Dawson, Victoria Dailey and Natalie Shivers, eds, *LA's Early Moderns*

(Glendale, CA, 2003)

Dimendberg, Edward, *Film Noir and the Spaces of Modernity* (Cambridge, MA, 2004)

Dunne, Fr George H., *Hollywood Labor Dispute: A Study in Immorality* (Los Angeles, CA, 1950)

Florey, Robert, *Hollywood d'hier et d'aujourd'hui* (Paris, 1947)

Fogelson, Robert M., *The Fragmented Metropolis: Los Angeles, 1850–1930* (Cambridge, MA, 1967, revd Berkeley, CA, 1993)

Gabler, Neal, *An Empire of Their Own: How the Jews Invented Hollywood* (New York, 1988)

Gottlieb, Robert, *Reinventing Los Angeles: Nature and Community in the Global City* (Cambridge, MA, 2007)

Hines, Thomas S., *Architecture of the Sun: Los Angeles Modernism, 1900–1970* (New York, 2010)

Hise, Greg, *Magnetic Los Angeles: Planning the Twentieth Century Metropolis* (Baltimore, MD, 1997)

Horne, Gerald, *Class Struggle in Hollywood, 1930–1950: Moguls, Mobsters, Stars, Reds, and Trade Unionists* (Austin, TX, 2001)

Hozic, Aida, *Hollyworld: Space, Power, and Fantasy in the American Economy* (Ithaca, NY, and London, 2001)

Hurewitz, Daniel, *Bohemian Los Angeles and the Making of Modern Politics* (Berkeley, CA, 2007)

James, David, *The Most Typical Avant-Garde: History and Geography of Minor Cinemas in Los Angeles* (Berkeley, CA, 2005)

Jameson, Fredric, *The Geopolitical Aesthetic: Cinema and Space in the World System* (Bloomington, IN, and London, 1995)

Jencks, Charles, *Heteropolis: Los Angeles: The Riots and the Strange Beauty of Hetero-architecture* (London, 1993)

King, Rob, *The Fun Factory: The Keystone Film Company and the Emergence of Mass Culture* (Berkeley, CA, 2009)

Klein, Norman M., *The History of Forgetting: Los Angeles and the Erasure of Memory* (London and New York, 1997)

Koszarski, Richard, *An Evening's Entertainment: The Age of the Silent Feature Picture, 1915–1928* (Berkeley, CA, 1994)

Krutnik, Frank, Steve Neale, Brian Neve and Peter

Stanfield, eds, *'Un-American' Hollywood: Politics and Film in the Blacklist Era* (New Brunswick, NJ, 2008)

Lasky Jr, Jesse, *Whatever Happened to Hollywood?* (New York, 1973)

Longstreth, Richard, *City Center to Regional Mall: Architecture, the Automobile, and Retailing in Los Angeles, 1920–1950* (Cambridge, MA, 1998)

Loos, Anita, *A Girl Like I* (New York, 1966)

Lynch, Kevin, *The Image of the City* (Cambridge, MA, 1960)

McClung, William Alexander, *Landscapes of Desire: Anglo Mythologies of Los Angeles* (Berkeley, CA, 2000)

McWilliams, Carey, *Southern California: An Island on the Land* (New York, 1946, repr. Layton, UT, 1973)

Nadeau, Remi, *Los Angeles: From Mission to Modern City* (New York, 1960)

Neale, Steve, *Genre and Hollywood* (London and New York, 1999)

Newmark, Harris, *Sixty Years in Southern California, 1853–1913* [1916] (Los Angeles, CA, 1970)

Perry, David C., and Alfred J. Watkins, eds, *The Rise of the Sunbelt Cities* (Beverly Hills, CA, 1977)

Pevsner, Nikolaus, *Pioneers of Modern Design: From William Morris to Walter Gropius* [1936] (New Haven, CT, 2004)

Sale, Kirkpatrick, *Power Shift: The Rise of the Southern Rim and its Challenge to the Eastern Establishment* (New York, 1976)

Schatz, Thomas, *Boom and Bust: American Cinema in the 1940s* (Berkeley, CA, 1999)

Schleier, Merrill, *Skyscraper Cinema: Architecture and Gender in American Film* (Minneapolis, MN, 2009)

Scott, Allen J., *On Hollywood: The Place, the Industry* (Princeton, NJ, 2005)

Scott, Mel, *Metropolitan Los Angeles: One Community* (Los Angeles, CA, 1949)

Shiel, Mark, and Tony Fitzmaurice, eds, *Cinema and the City: Film and Urban Societies in a Global Context* (Oxford and Malden, MA, 2001)

—, *Screening the City* (London and New York, 2003)

Sitton, Tom, and William Deverell, eds, *Metropolis in the Making: Los Angeles in the 1920s* (Berkeley,

CA, 2001)

Soja, Edward W., *Postmetropolis: Critical Studies of Cities and Urban Regions* (Malden, MA, and Oxford, 2000)

Spalding, William A., *History and Reminiscences: Los Angeles City and County*, vol. 1 (Los Angeles, CA, 1931)

Starr, Kevin, *Inventing the Dream: California through the Progressive Era* (New York and Oxford, 1986)

Stewart, Jacqueline, *Migrating to the Movies: Cinema and Black Urban Modernity* (Berkeley, CA, 2005)

Valentine, Maggie, *The Show Starts on the Sidewalk: An Architectural History of the Movie Theater, Starring Charles S. Lee* (New Haven, CT, 1994)

Williams, Gregory Paul, *The Story of Hollywood: An Illustrated History* (Los Angeles, CA, 2006)

Zukin, Sharon, *Landscapes of Power: From Detroit to Disney World* (Berkeley, CA, 1991)

Acknowledgements

The germination, research, and writing of this book has encompassed six years and spanned Los Angeles and several other cities. In LA, I am grateful to the staff in general and to individual staff members at a number of institutions who were especially helpful to me in my work: Barbara Hall, Kristine Krueger and Faye Thompson at the Margaret Herrick Library of the Academy of Motion Picture Arts and Sciences; Christina Rice and Terri Garst at the Los Angeles Public Library; Octavio Olvera and Brandon Barton at the Charles E. Young Research Library at UCLA; David Deckelbaum at UCLA's Henry J. Bruman Map Library; Jennifer Watts, Suzanne Oatey and Erin Chase at the Huntington Library; and William J. Burke at the John Randolph Haynes and Dora Haynes Foundation. Additionally, I am grateful for the assistance of staff in the Benjamin and Gladys Thomas Air Photo Archives of the UCLA Department of Geography and at the Getty Research Institute. Also at UCLA, in the Film and Television Archive, Mark Quigley frequently gave me his expert advice in identifying and tracking down rare films; Nick Browne kindly welcomed me to the Department of Film, Television, and Digital Media where I gained from his immense knowledge of the city and its film history; Tom Hines was an excellent interlocutor on those subjects, and on LA architecture and design – as well as a good friend, whose hospitality I enjoyed. Mike Davis provided sponsoring advice and some challenging questions, while he and Alessandra Moctezuma generously hosted me for dinner at their home. Nessa O'Shaughnessy graciously provided accommodation in La Jolla.

The single most intensive phase of writing this book took place at Princeton University where the resources and staff of the Firestone Library proved of vital importance. During the academic year 2006–7, I had the privilege of being a fellow of the Shelby Cullom Davis Center for Historical Studies, as a result of which I owe a debt of gratitude to many people. Gyan Prakash, who was then Director of the Center, went out of his way to generate an atmosphere of intellectual innovation and rigour, and a full schedule of enlightening lectures and other events on the theme of utopia and dystopia, a theme in which Los Angeles has always been deeply enmeshed. I am also grateful to Michael Gordin, Dan Rodgers, Sheldon Garon, Bill Jordan and the other members of the Center's Executive Committee who helped to make the Davis Center a truly inspiring place in which to work. Much of the inspiration also came from the other people who were Davis Center fellows during my time: Anne Maria Makhulu, David Pindar, John Kriege, Shira Robinson, Ravi Vasudevan and Luise White. Their research was fascinating, urgent and authoritative, and they were great fun to hang out with as well. The Center's Manager, Jennifer Houle, did a thoroughly professional job and also has my thanks. In the Department of History, of which the Davis Center forms a part, I enjoyed opportunities to discuss my work with Jeremy Adelman and Philip Nord, and I was grateful for the administrative support of its Manager, Judith Hanson. In History and in other departments I also benefited from discussions with (and the friendship of) Maria Di Battista, Angela Gleason, Gaetana Marrone-Puglia, Paul Miles, Sarah Whiting and Michael Wood.

Finally, I learned a lot of value to my own research from lectures by, and conversations with, visiting speakers to the Davis Center, including James Donald, Ruben Gallo, Fredric Jameson, Anton Kaes, Ranjani Mazumdar and Ravi Sundaram.

I am pleased to acknowledge that the research and writing of this book has been generously supported by funding from a variety of sources. The Shelby Cullom Davis Center for Historical Studies, Princeton University, provided a substantial fellowship and research expenses; the School of Arts & Humanities, King's College London, and the Central Research Fund of the University of London, both funded research trips from London to LA; and the British Academy has kindly supported the costs of copyright and reproductions for many of the illustrations in this book.

At King's College London, where it is a pleasure to teach, I have been supported by my colleagues in the Department of Film Studies, and especially by two successive Heads of Department – Ginette Vincendeau and Sarah Cooper – who have helped me arrange sabbatical and research leave and to make related applications for funding. I have also enjoyed learning from, as well as teaching, many of my graduate students while doing my own work on LA. Those who have taken my MA class on 'Cinema and the City' are too numerous to name, but I reserve a special thanks for the innovative ideas and research of my own PhD students, Maurizio Cinquegrani, Martha Shearer and Lawrence Webb, and those of other PhD students – Louis Bayman, Sofia Bull and Ryan Powell – who participated in the 'Spatiality and Representation' reading group in 2007–8. Outside Film Studies at King's, my own thinking on cinema and cities has been expanded by exchanges with David Green, Loretta Lees and other colleagues in the Cities Group of the Department of Geography.

I have been fortunate enough to be invited to deliver parts of this book in the form of several lectures and conference papers, which have provided important testing grounds for my theories and findings. I am grateful to these colleagues and institutions who invited me to speak and responded to what I said (in chronological order from 2006 to 2011): Vincent Guigueno and Stéphane Füzessery, at the École des hautes études en sciences sociales, Paris, and the École nationale des ponts et chaussées, Marne-la-Vallée; Alan Marcus and Rajin-der Dudrah at the University of Manchester; Andrew Hussey and Christoph Lindner at the University of London Institute in Paris; Karen Beckman and Timothy Corrigan at the University of Pennsylvania; Alastair Philips at Warwick University; Sarah Durcan and Declan Long at the National College of Art and Design, Dublin; David Craggs and Katherine Jones, the graduate student convenors of the Cities Group seminar series at King's; at the University of Cambridge, the graduate students Micah Trippe, who convened the City Seminar, and Matilda Mroz, who convened the Screen Media Research Seminar, both held at the Centre for Research in the Arts, Social Sciences and Humanities, and to members of the faculty, Zygmunt Baranski, François Penz, David Trotter and Andrew Webber. In addition, at these and similar events, I have gained ideas and perspective from discussions of cinema and the city in Los Angeles, and related contexts, with Dudley Andrew, Stan Corkin, Stephanie Donald, Matthew Gandy, Sue Harris, Jon Lewis, Paula Massood, Laura Mulvey, Geoffrey Nowell-Smith and Nezar Al Sayyad. I am fortunate to have had the benefit of their insights and their company.

I am especially conscious of the fact that a number of scholars who are also friends have devoted exceptional amounts of time and effort to support my project: Stephen Barber, who first encouraged me to write this book and to publish it with Reaktion; Steve Neale, Tom Hines (again) and Merrill Schleier, who generously agreed to read and comment in detail on substantial portions of the manuscript; and the two anonymous readers for Reaktion who read the entire manuscript with tremendous care and attention. Vivian Constantinopoulos, editorial director at Reaktion, has been encouraging, patient and thorough. It's been a pleasure to work with her and her team.

Finally, it's hard to know what words to use to thank my family for their love and support. Diarmuid, Deirdre, Sonia, Hebe, Eva, Joseph, Evelyn, James, Amy and Dan have shown interest and sponsoring concern in countless large and small ways. But, most of all, I thank my wife and hero, Alyce, and our prima ballerina, Anouk, who, after all, first learned to crawl in LA.

Photo Acknowledgements

The author and publishers wish to express their thanks to the below sources of illustrative material and/or permission to reproduce it.

Reproduced courtesy of the Academy of Motion Picture Arts and Sciences, Beverley Hills, California: pp. 37, 58, 60, 78, 87, 130, 131, 135, 146, 151, 155, 156, 161, 164, 174, 180, 196, 199; reproduction courtesy of the John Randolph Haynes and Dora Haynes Foundation: p. 9, 34; Huntington Library, San Marino, California: pp. 175, 193; from the *Journal of the Society of Motion Picture Engineers*, vol. XXXVI, January 1941: p. 138; Library of Congress, Washington, DC (Motion Picture, Broadcasting, and Recorded Sound Division): pp. 26, 27, 28, 29, 30; photos courtesy of Los Angeles Public Library: pp. 48, 169, 176, 248, 249, 250, 270; from the *Los Angeles Times*: 9 January 1916 (p. 148), 16 August 1926 (p.179), 4 September 1927 (p. 122), 25 September 1940 (p. 64), 8 October 1946 (p. 267) and 8 January 1958 (p. 63); from *Pacific Coast Architect*, October 1927: p. 145; from George Rosenthal, *Life and Death in Hollywood* (Cincinnati, 1950): p. 67; from Mel Scott, *Metropolitan Los Angeles: One Community* (Haynes Foundation, Los Angeles, 1949): pp. 9, 34; © M. Shiel: p. 284, 285, 286, 287; from William A. Spalding, *History and Reminiscences: Los Angeles City and County* (Los Angeles, 1931): pp. 45, 119; courtesy of UCLA Film and Television Archive, Los Angeles, Archive Research and Study Center: p. 140.

Index

A Star is Born 201–2, *203*, 205, 206, 278
Academy of Motion Picture Arts and Sciences 17, 75, 255
actuality films, early short 18, 23, 25–31, 40, 86
air travel, rise in 237–8
American Exodus 242
anti-Communism 244–5, 255, 257–65, 272
    socialism, perceived threat of 235–6
apartment blocks, use of, film noir 229–30, 231
Arbuckle, Roscoe 'Fatty' 71, 115
architecture
    criticism of artificiality 169–70
    film stylization of 281
    modernist *see* modernist architecture
    Spanish Revival 122, 148, 170–71, 173–4, 192, 194, 202, 218, 223–4
    studio architecture *see* studio architecture
    suburban 96–7, *96*
Art Work on Southern California (Chapin) 23
automobile orientation 104, 106–7, 111–12, 276
    traffic and methods of transport, slapstick comedies 100–105, 107
avant-garde films 274

Balboa Studios 36, 66–7, 144
Balshofer, Fred J. 36, 149
Baudrillard, Jean 128, 129, 139, 209, 280
beach and ocean settings, film noir 222–3
Berkeley, Busby, *Hollywood Hotel* 200, *201*, 202, 203, 204, 205–6, 237
Beverly Hills 8, 57, 67, 113, 192, 236
    homes in 192, 194, 202

portrayed in films 220, 223, 224, 277
The Big Bluff 238, 240
The Big Sleep 220, 226, 227, 230
Biograph 32, 33, 40, 47, 70, 74, 84, 148
The Birth of a Nation 38, 79
Bison film company 36, 47
The Black Angel 217, 218, *218*, 228, 230–32
Blade Runner 280
'blaxploitation' thrillers 279
    see also racial diversity
Boggs, Francis 33, 36
boosterism 20–21, 22, 24–5, 50, 69, 73, 82, 272, 275
Border Incident 224–5, 233
Borderline 224, 225
Bosworth, Hobart 33
Brewer, Roy 253, 260, 261–2, 263
Bronx studios 136, 154
Brunton, Robert 59, 73, 154
Building a Harbor at San Pedro 30–31, *30*
Burbank
    air travel to New York from 237–8
    land zoning 114
    manufacturing industry in 133, 144
    picketing by-laws 267, 268, 269
    rise in importance of 121
    see also First National; Universal Pictures; Walt Disney; Warner Bros.

Cagney, James 192, 258
Caught in a Cabaret 108–9, *109*
CBS 61, 64, 204

Cendrars, Blaise, *Hollywood: La Mecque du cinéma* 208–9
Century Film Corporation fire 178–9, *179*
Chapin, Lou V., *Art Work on Southern California* 23
Chaplin, Charlie 66, 69, 85
    Caught in a Cabaret 108–9, *109*
    Communist links, alleged 258
    Easy Street 86–7, *87*
    fanciful sets 167
    Film Johnnie 185, 190
    films made, but not set, in Los Angeles 86–7
    gendering of narrative space 108
    Kid Auto Races at Venice 93–4, *94*
    Los Angeles, move to 79
    Mabel's Married Life 94–5, *95*
    Making a Living 95–8, *96*, *99*
    Show People, cameo in 186
    on sound, coming of 159
    suburbs, filming in 93–4
    success, dealing with 182
    transportation in films 100–101
    Wall Street, dislike of 76
    see also Keystone Company; Lone Star Film Company
Chaplin Studio 61, 135
    building investment 153
    as cultural-historic monument 62
    English cottage-style architecture 173–4
chase sequences, movement and narrative, slapstick comedies 84–6, 87, 88, 91, 93–4, 97–8, 101–4, 111, 126
Christie Studios 117, 122, 144, 167, 173
cinemas *see* movie theatres
cities, descriptions of film studios as 136–7
Cinemascope 236
Clarke, Charles, *Early Filmmaking in Los Angeles* 32, 39, 47, 54, 61
climate 40–41, 44–5, 46–50, 83–4, 98–9, 116
Cohn, Harry 76, *250*, 251
Columbia Pictures 32, 35, 45
    construction investment 153
    sound and soundproofing 160
    value of assets 113, 142, 254
    workers' security of employment 244
    workers' strike action 252, 254, 269

commerce
    commercial architecture 159, 226–7
    and decentralization 118, 271–2, 281–2
    and industrial growth 212–13
    and industrial output 132–4, 135–6
construction industry, growth of 143–5, 146–55, 168
The Corner of Madison and State Streets, Chicago 26, *27*
corruption *see* scandals, public
The Count of Monte Cristo 33
County Hospital 125–6, *125*
Crashing Hollywood 201, 202–3, 205, 206
The Crimson Kimono 278–9
Criss Cross 221–2, *221*, 228, 233
crowds, mobilizing for marketing purposes 58–9
Culver City 32, 74
    and Better Homes in America 120
    City Hall *125*, 126
    as City of Opportunities 120–21
    land zoning 114
    rise in importance of 119–21
    significant buildings, lack of 126
    slapstick comedies 83, 85, 88, 123–6
    studio architecture, construction and scale 131
    studio building conservation 62
    suburban landscape, portrayal of 124–6
    see also Goldwyn Studios; MGM; New York Motion Picture Company (NYMPC); Roach, Hal
The Damned Don't Cry 238, *238*, 240, 241
De Mille, Cecil B. 41–2, 55, 65, 66, 77
    and Academy of Motion Picture Arts and Sciences 75–6
    construction investment 148
    and Olmsted-Bartholomew report 116
    right-to-work legislation, request for 264
    The Squaw Man 18, 36–7, 47–9, *48*, 51
    and Studio City 122
De Mille, William C. 60, 61, 139
    Hollywood Saga memoir 39, 41–2, 46
    Ince studio takeover 60, 61
    studio fire damage 179
decentralization, effects of 90–1, 113–19, 127, 269–72
    see also individual districts
Depression, effects of 127, 154, 243, 244–5
Desilu studio 61
Detour 226, 238, *240*, 241–3

disaster movies 279–80
Disney *see* Walt Disney
D.O.A. 217, 226, 227, 232, 233
Double Indemnity 214, 217–18, 219, 220, 224, 226, 228, 230, 232, 233
downtown Los Angeles
    congestion in 107, 113
    decline of 116, 214, 221–2, 275, 276
    department stores in 90–91, 92–3
    film noirs 219–20, 227, 234
    slapstick comedies 83, 85, 88, 91–8
    see also Biograph; Griffith, D.W.; Roach, Hal; Selig Company

Early Filmmaking in Los Angeles (Clarke) 32, 39, 47, 54, 61
Easy Street 86–7, *87*
Echo Park 94–5, *95*
Edendale 32, 37, 56, 59
    economic investment in 54
    open stages 154
    slapstick comedies 83, 85, 93
    studio architecture, construction and scale 131
    studio growth, lack of 114, 173, 272
    see also Fox Studios; Keystone Company; New York Motion Picture Company (NYMPC); Roach, Hal; Selig Company
Edison Company 21, 50, 51, 74
    actuality films, early short 18, 23, 25–31, 40, 86
    Building a Harbor at San Pedro 30–31, *30*
    The Corner of Madison and State Streets, Chicago 26, *27*
    Going through the Tunnel 28, *29*
    Herald Square (New York) 26, *27*
    South Spring Street, Los Angeles 26, *26*
    Sunset Limited, Southern Pacific Railway 27–8, *28*
editing, effect on understanding of space 85–6, 90
The End of Violence 281
Essanay 33, 40, 71
ethnic minorities, marginalization of 82, 109–10
    see also racial diversity
European art cinema, influence of 276, 281
The Extra Girl 183, 186, *187*, 203

Fairbanks, Douglas 6, 49, 75, 116, 154, 194
Famous Players-Lasky 37, 59, 70, 71, 72–4
    construction investment 144

financial success 77
fire damage 179
glass shooting stage 156
In-Vis-O advertisement 145, *145*
relocation 117–18, 122, 135, 136, 162
shooting stages *155*
The Squaw Man 36–7, 47–9, *48*
staff automobile ownership 111
value of assets 141, 178
see also Lasky, Jesse
film industry
    actuality films, early short 18, 23, 25–31, 40, 86
    base for creative personnel 71–2, 75–6
    contracting of Broadway stars 78–9
    decline of studio system 11, 63, 127, 211, 236, 273, 278
    early growth of 18, 53–6
    early studios 56–68
    editing, effect on understanding of space 85–6, 90
    employment levels 132–3, 168, 243–4
    film city, origins of term 136–7
    film stars' homes 192–4
    film studio redistribution and creation of space 113–18
    film studios' map *34*
    films made, but not set, in Los Angeles 86–7, 88–9
    financial success 76–8, 132–3
    first feature film 36–7
    first film screening in Los Angeles 25
    first film serial in Los Angeles 65
    first film studios in Los Angeles 32–3, 36, 132–3
    geographical split in 70–71
    Hollywood referenced in films 195–202
    and House Un-American Activities Committee investigation 65, 257
    as industrial machine 136
    Los Angeles as film capital 71–2
    modern urban subject, and role of film 85–90
    mortality of stars, fascination with 65–6
    movies about movies *see* movies about movies
    personnel, private property of 192–4
    real and studio architecture and artefacts, blurring between 168, 170–71, 179–82
    'real life' filming, move away from 128–9
    reality and illusion, contrast between 203, 206, 207, 208

relocation fears 235–6
rental studios 59, 61, 149
salary levels 78
small scale of recent films 282–3
studio architecture *see* studio architecture
studio production, growing preference for 163–6
studio system, collapse of 278
studios as cities 129–72
studios, origins of 31–56
suburbs, filming in 93–4, 95–8, 100–103
urbanization, problems associated with 112–13
see also individual film companies and films
Film Johnnie 185, 190
film noir 166, 195, 223–4
  apartment blocks, use of 229–30, 231
  beach and ocean settings 222–3
  The Big Bluff 238, 240
  The Big Sleep 220, 226, 227, 230
  The Black Angel 217, 218, *218*, 228, 230–32
  Border Incident 224–5, 233
  Borderline 224, 225
  Bunker Hill in 221–2
  class stratification and architectural styles 230–31
  commercial architecture and public buildings 226–7
  The Crimson Kimono 278–9
  Criss Cross 221–2, *221*, 228, 233
  critical literature on 214–15
  The Damned Don't Cry 238, *238*, 240, 241
  darkness and light, use of contrast between 232–3
  and decline of the studio system 214, 223–4
  Detour 226, 238, *240*, 241–3
  D.O.A. 217, 226, 227, 232, 233
  Double Indemnity 214, 217–18, 219, *220*, 224, 226, 228, 230, 232, 233
  films produced, number of 215
  flashbacks and ellipses, use of 231–2
  geographic dispersal, emphasis on 219–20, 271
  The Harder They Fall 238, *239*, 240–41
  He Walked by Night 219, 220–21, *220*, 226, 227, 228, 230, 232, 233
  In a Lonely Place 222, 223–4, *223*, 226, 227, 230, 233
  Kiss Me Deadly 218–19, 220, 221–3, *222*, 226, 227, 230
  law enforcement, moral prominence to 232–3

  Los Angeles, rise of, and decline of New York 233–43
  The Man I Love 238, 239–40
  and Mexican border, close proximity of 224–5
  Murder My Sweet 218, 219–20, *219*, 222, 226, 228, 230, 231
  New York settings 216, 287
  New York to Los Angeles journeys, depiction of 238–42
  Nobody Lives Forever 237, 238, 239
  Pitfall 218, 222, 227–8, 230, *230*, 231, 233
  Plunder Road 214, 233
  settings 201, 202, 213, 215–33, 284–7
  street names, use of precise 218–20
  strike history resemblance 266, 268
  The Strip 228–9, *229*, 232
  studio shooting 226
  Sunset Boulevard 223
  and Sunset Strip 228–9, *229*, 239
  They Won't Believe Me 238, 240, 241
  This Gun for Hire 217, 225, 226, 230, 233
  and understanding of real world 241–3, 271
  urban history and myths 280
  working class, lack of portrayal of 233
fine art, Los Angeles as centre of 22–4
Fine Arts Studio 37
First National
  construction investment 137, 162, 171, 235
  relocation 113, 121, 153
  studio sets and offices 171, 183
  see also Vitagraph; Warner Bros
Florey, Robert
  Hollywood Boulevard 198–9, *199*, 203, 205–6, 278
  Hollywood d'hier et d'aujourd'hui memoir 206
Ford, Francis Ford 113, 154, 179–80
Fordism 115–16, 136, 137–8, 158
  45 Minutes from Hollywood 184–5, *185*
Fox Studios 32, 36, 127, *130–31*
  construction investment 148, 150–52, 154, 162, 168
  contracting of Broadway stars 78–9
  El Dorado set 150
  exterior standing sets 168
  fire damage 178
  Fox Hills 35, 136, 150–51, *151*, 162, 168, 173

Fox-Case Corporation 150
  glass shooting stages 173
  Gothic-style architecture 173
  increase in value of 117
  Kid Auto Races at Venice 93–4, *94*
  promotional film 139
  receivership 245
  redevelopment of 67–8, 150–51
  relocation 38, 40, 113
  sound, investment in 150–53
  studio space 163, 164
  value of assets 141, 142, 178

Get Out and Get Under 102–3, *103*, 104, 110
Gibbons, Cedric 163–5, *166–7*, 170–71
Gill, Irving 96, 163, 266
Girl Shy 104, 110–11, *110*
Glendale 32, 66, 74, 114
  Kalem 32, 33, 35, 36, 40
  portrayal in film 219, *220*, 228
Going through the Tunnel 28, *29*
Goldwyn, Samuel 65, 66, 77, 116
Goldwyn Studios 60, 134, 183
  workers' security of employment 244
  workers' strike action *250*, 251, 252
  see also MGM (Metro-Goldwyn-Mayer)
The Graduate 277
Greene, Charles and Henry 96
Griffith, D.W. 39, 56, 66, *67*, 70, 79, 147, 170
  The Birth of a Nation 38, 79
  as guardian of middle-class culture 86
  long shots and panning as innovative techniques
  52
  Native and Spanish Americans, representation of
  50–53
  Ramona 18, 33, 37, 50–53, *53*
  The Unchanging Sea 18, 33, 42–4, *43*, 48, 50, 51

Hampton, Jesse B. 113, 149
Hancock, Ralph 7, 38
The Harder They Fall 238, *239*, 240–41
He Walked by Night 219, 220–21, *220*, 226, 227, 228,
  230, 232, 233
Herald Square (New York) 26, *27*
Hollywood: La Mecque du cinéma (Cendrars) 208–9
Hollywood: Ville mirage (Kessel) 207–8, 209–10

Hollywood
  anti-Communism in 244–5, 255, 257–65, 272
  as arts focal point, reasons for 47
  Blondeau's Tavern 46
  Business Center *119*
  cinema capital, promoted as 134
  Cinemascope 236
  corruption scandals 127, 246
  decline and dereliction of 276–7
  Depression, effects of 127, 154, 243, 244–5
  early history of land 45–7
  emergence of 32
  exaggerated sense of place 128–9
  exploitation of young women, accusations of 186–8
  first studio 36, *64*
  French filmmakers migration to 206–7
  Hollywood Boulevard *45*, 63, 118, 184, 190
  Hollywood Central Park plans 283
  Hollywoodland sign 192
  investment in 119
  location filming 91, 198–9
  Los Angeles before 19–31
  Los Angeles decentralization, effects of 119
  Mafia and unions 245–7, 249, 253
  modernist architecture 204
  movie premieres, home of 119
  name, origin of 46
  NBC Radio City 154, 204
  overshadows Los Angeles 182–5, 195, 198, 207–8
  and political change 244–5
  post-war insecurity and criticism of 211–12
  property values, increase in 117
  published critiques of 206–10
  and racial diversity 279
  racial unrest 277
  'real life' filming, move away from 128–9
  real and studio architecture, confusion between
  168
  reality and illusion, contrast between 203, 206,
  207, 208
  referenced in films 195–202
  rental studios 149
  settings, ability to create 48–50, 188
  sex scandals 206
  slapstick comedy *see* slapstick comedy
  social and economic inequalities in 208–9

sound, and rise of studio system 128–9, 134–5, 196
Standard Film Laboratories 134
strikes *see* strikes
studio architecture, construction and scale 131
studio construction investment 148–54
Sunset Strip 228–9, *229*, 239
technical companies, base for 127
teenagers and young adults, effect on industry 273–4
union recognition 245–56
Valentino statue 66
westerns, early 44–5
workers' wage levels 245
see also Columbia Pictures; First National; Nestor Studio; Paramount; Robertson-Cole Company; United Artists
Hollywood Boulevard 198–9, *199*, 203, 205–6, 278
Hollywood d'hier et d'aujourd'hui memoir (Florey) 206
Hollywood Hotel 200, *201*, 202, 203, 204, 205–6, 237
Hollywood Saga memoir (De Mille) 39, 41–2, 46
Hollywood Studios Inc. 59, 148, 149, 156
Hollywood Walk of Fame 63
Horsley, David and William 36, 37, 41, 56, 63–5
construction investment 144
liquidation sale 179
shooting stages 154
Hot Water 104, *105*, 108

I Do 100, *101*
immigration 13, 50–53, 55, 71, 76, 235, 242, 254
In a Lonely Place 222, 223–4, *223*, 226, 227, 230, 233
Ince, Thomas 36, 60, 62, 120, 148
see also New York Motion Picture Company (NYMPC); Triangle studios
'indie' film industry 281–2
infrastructure improvements, Los Angeles 105–6, 112–13, 118
freeway system 122, 170, 191, 272, 275, 276
Iverson Movie Ranch 48

Kalem 32, 33, 35, 36, 40
Kessel, Joseph, *Hollywood: Ville mirage* 207–8, 209–10
Keystone Company 35, 36, *37*
construction investment 136, 144, 146–7, *146*, 162

fanciful sets 167
relocation 113
relocation to Studio City 121–2
shooting stages 154
staff automobile ownership 111
see also Chaplin, Charlie; Sennett, Mack
Kid Auto Races at Venice 93–4, *94*
Kiss Me Deadly 218–19, 220, 221–3, *222*, 226, 227, 230

Laemmle, Carl 40, 76, 116
The Land of Sunshine (magazine) 23, 50
land zoning and city planning 82, 114
landscape 40–41, 44–5, 46–50, 83–4, 98–9, 116
Lasky, Jesse 39, 41, 56, 76, 117–18
Lasky Feature Play Company 35, *48*
see also Famous Players-Lasky
Laurel and Hardy 69, 83, 85, 123–4
County Hospital 125–6, *125*
Putting Pants on Philip 123–4, *123*
Should Married Men Go Home? 124–5
Sons of the Desert 127
Lee, S. Charles 190–91, 205
Lloyd, Harold 69, 83, 85–6
films made, but not set, in Los Angeles 88–9
gendering of narrative space 108
Get Out and Get Under 102–3, *103*, 104, 110
Girl Shy 104, 110–11, *110*
Greenacres estate 192, 193, *193*
Hot Water 104, *105*, 108
I Do 100, *101*
Movie Crazy 197–8, *198*, 202, 205, 206
New York and Middle America settings 87–8
Number, Please? 101–2, *102*, 110
racialization in films 109–11
Safety Last 83, 88–90, *89*, 91–3, 98, 107, 109
transportation in films 100–101
Loew's studio 77, 141
see also MGM (Metro-Goldwyn-Mayer)
Lone Star Film Company 37, 59, 83
see also Chaplin, Charlie
Los Angeles
aerial views of urban landscape 276, 282
anti-Communism in 244–5, 255, 257–65, 272
Arts and Crafts and Garden City movements, influence of 99

Atheneum 80
before Hollywood 19–31
boosterism 20–21, 22, 24–5, 50, 69, 73, 82, 272, 275
Broadway's changing status 90–91
Bunker Hill 90, 91, 221–2, 272, 276
Burbank *see* Burbank
Cahuenga Public Market 104
Chinatown 109, *109*
City Beautiful design 106, 116, 127, 158
City Hall 134, 220–21, *220*
climate and landscape 40–41, 44–5, 46–50, 83–4, 98–9, 116
contemporary interest in history of 16–17
Culver City *see* Culver City
department stores, expansion of 90–91, 92–3
downtown *see* downtown
early history 20–21
Echo Park 94–5, *95*
economic and physical growth 8–12, 53–6, 212–13, 234
Edendale *see* Edendale
as film capital 71–2
film industry *see* film industry
film representation of 7–8
freeway system 122, 170, 191, 272, 275, 276
Glendale *see* Glendale
highway recreation 107–8
Hollyhock House 170
Hollywood *see* Hollywood
house building design 158
house building and ownership 99, 130
immigration 13, 51, 55, 71, 76, 235, 242, 254
infrastructure improvements 105–6, 112–13, 118, 122, 170, 191, 272, 275, 276
Land of Sunshine identity 21
The Los Angeles Plan (1922) 105–6
Lovell House 159, 204
map of communities *9*
mass entertainment industry 237
middle class majority 50–51, 82, 86, 92, 278–9
movie theatres *see* movie theatres
multi-centred development and porosity of landscape 98, 103, 189
natural disasters 177
New Deal, effects of 212, 271

and New York, cultural distance between 71–6, 78–80
and New York, journeys between, cinematic representation of 237–8
Pershing Square, criticism of 117
population growth 54–5, 81, 107, 114, 118, 212, 215, 216, 282
property values, increase in 117
referenced in films 201–2, *203*
Robinson's department store 91
Santa Monica *see* Santa Monica
skyscrapers, lack of 90
streetcar system 105–6, 118
suburban development *see* suburban development
Sunset Route Railroad 21, 27–8, *28*
television and theatre production 237
The Tower theatre, Broadway 190
Thomas Tally's Kinetoscope Parlor 25
traffic congestion and accidents 105–6, 107
universities 80–81
urban development patterns 98–9
urban space organization, success of 81
urban sprawl, effects of 276, 277–8, 280–82
Venice *see* Venice
Los Angeles Today (brochure) 24–5
Lubin, Sigmund 32, 40, 55

Mabel's Married Life 94–5, *95*
Mafia and unions 245–7, 249, 253
Making a Living 95–8, *96*, 99
The Man I Love 238, 239–40
maps and mapping 9, 16–17, 20, 34–5, 69–70, 86, 90, 183, 220, 241, 280
Mayer, Louis B. 65, 75, 76, 134, 140, 259
    on Communism 257, 258
    political involvement 235
    retake policy 165
    Spanish Revival style home 170–71
    workers' strike action *250*, *251*
    see also MGM (Metro-Goldwyn-Mayer)
Metro Pictures 59, 148, 153, 178, 179
MGM (Metro-Goldwyn-Mayer) 32, 60, 62, 120, 134, *135*
    communist workers, dismissal of 257
    construction investment 122, 160
    dismantling and moving of stages 162

French filmmakers 206
glass shooting stage *156*, 189
MGM *Studio Tour* 174, 182
modernist architecture, portrayal of 205
promotional film 139–41, *140*, 148
property room *180*
retake policy 164–5, 167
shooting in studio, preference for 163–6
sound studios 160, *161*
The Strip 228–9, *229*
studio space 163–7, 189
Thalberg Building 204
Triangle studios, acquisition of 153
value of assets 142
workers' security of employment 244
workers' strike action 252
see also Goldwyn Studios; Loew's studio; Mayer,
Louis B.; New York Motion Picture Company
(NYMPC); Triangle studios
middle class majority 50–51, 82, 86, 92, 278–9
modernist architecture
and coming of sound 205–6
Hollywood 204
International Style 191, 205, 206
and New York settings 205
popularizing 11–12, 159, 170, 171–2, 194–5,
204–5
see also architecture
Motion Picture Association of America (MPAA) 244,
250–51, 256–7
Motion Picture News 71–2, 74–5
Motion Picture Patents Company (MPPC) 39, 40
Motion Picture Producers and Distributors of America
(MPPDA) 67, 76, 115–16, 134, 254
Motion Picture Studio Directory 71–2, 74
Movie Crazy 197–8, *198*, 202, 205, 206
movie theatres 189–92, 205
box office decline 211, 236, 278
sell-off and Paramount decrees 211, 236
movies about movies, and line between reality and
fantasy 182–9, 196–206, 281
cameo roles 203–4
character doubling 202–3
sound and modernist *mise en scène*, combination
of 205–6
see also film industry

Murder My Sweet 218, 219–20, *219*, 222, 226, 228,
230, 231
music recording 237

NBC Radio City 154, 204
Nestor Studio 36, 44–5, 46, 63–4, 70, 113
bronze memorial 64–5, *64*
Neutra, Richard 159, 204
New York
corporate management and distribution 70–71
film noir settings 216, 287
film studios, attempts to attract 235, 236
Herald Square (New York) 26, *27*
Los Angeles, cultural distance between 71–6,
78–80
Los Angeles, journeys between, cinematic representation of 237–8
Los Angeles, reaction to success of 233–5
New York to Los Angeles journeys, depiction of
238–42
unions' headquarters in 265–6
see also Edison; Vitagraph
New York Motion Picture Company (NYMPC) 32
construction investment 144, 145, 147–8, 162
glass shooting stage 155
Inceville 35, 36, 59–60, *60*, 61, 62, 112, 136,
147–8
staff automobile ownership 111
Triangle studios *see* Triangle studios
see also Ince, Thomas; MGM (Metro-Goldwyn-
Mayer)
Newmark, Harris, *Sixty Years in Southern California*
21–2
Nixon, Richard M. 264
Nobody Lives Forever 237, 238, *239*
Number, Please? 101–2, *102*, 110

Olmsted-Bartholomew report 107–8, 112, 116, 127

Paramount Pictures 32, 37, 50
Communist links, alleged 258
construction investment 153, 154
Double Indemnity 214, 217–18, *219*, *220*, 224,
226, 228, 230, 232, 233
fire risks 178
In-Vis-O advertisement 145, *145*

modernist architecture, portrayal of 205
promotional film 139
receivership 245
Spanish Revival-style architecture 173
The Studio Murder Mystery 196–7, *196*, 206
studio space 163, 164, 165
value of assets 113, 142
workers' strike action *248*, 250, 252
photography, Los Angeles as centre of 22–4
Pickford, Mary 52, 55, 76, 78, 116, 194
Pitfall 218, 222, 227–8, 230, *230*, 231, 233
Plunder Road 214, 233
political change, and Hollywood 244–5
Putting Pants on Philip 123–4, *123*

racial diversity 279–80
    'blaxploitation' thrillers 279
    ethnic minorities, marginalization of 82, 109–10
    and Hollywood 279
    Native and Spanish Americans, representation of 50–53
    racialization in films 108–10
Ramona 18, 33, 37, 50–53, *53*
Reagan, Ronald 256, 265
Rebel Without a Cause 273–4
Republic 244, 252, 266, *267*
Revier, Harry 36, 37, 39, 47
RKO (Radio-Keith-Orpheum) 32, 58, 59, 61
    construction investment 153, 162, 204
    fire risks 178
    French filmmakers 206
    largest stage in the world claim 163
    modernist architecture 174, 205
    monorail system 163
    Murder My Sweet 218, 219–20, *219*, 222, 226, 228, 230, 231
    receivership 245
    value of assets 142
    workers' strike action 252
Roach, Hal 33, 35, 55, 83
    American Colonial style home 170
    and automobile industry 112
    construction investment 113, 144
    Get Out and Get Under 102–3, *103*, 104, 110
    I Do 100, *101*
    Number, Please? 101–2, *102*, 110
    studio decline 127
    workers' security of employment 244
    workers' strike action 252
Robertson-Cole Company 35, 59, 113, 145, 150
Rolin Film Company *see* Roach, Hal
rural space 25, 27, 32, 41, 46, 103, 187, 201, 215, 224

Safety Last 83, 88–90, *89*, 91–3, 98, 107, 109
San Fernando Valley 32, 41, 47–8, 82, 114, 118–19, 131, 153
    see also Studio City
Santa Monica 32, 33, 42–3, 44, 50, 58–9, 222
    construction investment 122, 130, 131, 204
    rise of 28–9
    slapstick comedies 83, 93
scandals, public 115–16
    corruption scandals 127, 246
    sex scandals *see* sex scandals
Schenck, Joseph M. and Nicholas 77, 116, 235, 245, 246, *250*, 251, 260
science fiction films 280–81
Screen Actors Guild 243, 256, 265
Sea Hawk 164
Selig Company 32, 35, 40, 41, 44, 47, 55, 70
    construction investment 144
    glass shooting stage 155
    relocation 33, 36, 40
Selig, William
    law suits against 39–40
    Special Academy Award 65
Sennett, Mack 66, 127, 148
    see also Keystone Company
sex scandals 10
    exploitation of young women, accusations of 186–8
    see also scandals, public
Should Married Men Go Home? 124–5
Show People 156, 183, *183*, 185–6, 188–9, 190
Sixty Years in Southern California (Newmark) 21–2
slapstick comedies 69–70
    building interiors and exteriors, contrast between 95, 102
    chase sequences, movement and narrative 84–6, 87, 88, 91, 93–4, 97–8, 101–4, 111, 126
    gendering of narrative space 108

ideological biases 70
location filming 83–4, 86–97, 184–5, 188–9
public parks, filming in 94–5
racialization in 108–10
sound, coming of, and use of studios 127
suburbs, filming in 93–4, 95–8, 100–103
traffic and methods of transport 100–105, 107
see also Chaplin, Charlie; Laurel and Hardy;
Lloyd, Harold
socialism, perceived threat of 235–6
see also anti-Communism
Society of Motion Picture Engineers (SMPE) 75–6
Sons of the Desert 127
Sorrell, Herbert K. 247, 248, 250, 251, 253, 254, 260,
261–2, 263, 265, 266, 269
see also strikes
sound, and rise of studio system 127, 128–9, 134–5,
196
South Spring Street, Los Angeles 26, 26
Southern Pacific Railroad 21, 25, 27–8, 28, 29–30
The Squaw Man 18, 36–7, 47–9, 48, 51
Standard Film Laboratories 134
strikes 213, 235–6, 244–7, 248–57, 260–61, 263–7
automobiles driving through picket lines 248,
267–8
Conference of Studio Unions (CSU) 247–9, 251–4,
255–6, 259–60, 262, 263, 264, 265, 267, 270
'hot' sets and labour disputes 251, 252
industrialization and labour activism 247–8, 254–6
and inter-union conflict 256–7
Mafia and unions 245–7, 249, 253
mass demonstrations, logistical problems 268
media coverage of 249–50, 252, 253, 266, 267
pedestrian movement restrictions 268–9
and rise of corporate city 269–70
studio gates, focus of 267
and Taft-Hartley Act 263–4, 268–9
trade union recognition, Hollywood 245–56
trade unions and corporate city rise 269–70
and urban-regional interaction and travel, increase
in 265–6
worker specialization conflicts 255–6
see also Sorrell, Herbert K.; Tenney, Senator Jack
The Strip 228–9, 229, 232
studio architecture 129–31
building conservation 62, 64–5

building permits, lack of 171
buildings, redevelopment of 61–3, 66–8
concrete and prefabrication 162–3
concrete sound stages 159–62
construction industry, growth of 143–5, 146–55
construction and scale 131–2
dismantling and moving of stages 162–3
early studios 146–50
exterior standing sets 167–8
film city, use and origins of term 136–9
fire risks 177–8
glass construction 161–2
glass shooting stages 155–9, 173
historicism in 173–5
internal 137–8
permanent and temporary sets, use of 165–6
promotional films 139–41, 173–4, 175, 182
props owned by studios 179–82
sets, striking of, to relieve tax burden 171
sets and studio offices, similarities between 171
shooting stages 131, 138, 140, 141, 148–9,
154–62, 167
shooting stages, and prefabrication 162–3
sound, investment in 150–53
sound, and soundproofing 159–60
studio buildings and artefacts, auctioning of
179–81
studio gates, security of 175–7
temporary nature of 172
'tilt-up' construction 162–3
and use of space 162–4
value of assets 141–2
Studio City 13, 113, 121–3, 122, 162
The Studio Murder Mystery 196–7, 196, 206
suburban development 81–2, 83–4, 189, 269–71
and moral reform 115–16
and slapstick comedies, filming 93–4, 95–8,
100–103
and threat to public spaces 112–13
see also individual districts
suburbanization 70, 84, 111, 137, 236, 270–71
Sunset Boulevard 223
Sunset Limited, Southern Pacific Railway 27–8, 28

Targets 277
Technicolor, workers' strike action 249, 252

Tenney, Senator Jack 260–62
    see also strikes
Terminator: Judgment Day 280
That's Right, You're Wrong 201, 203–4, 205, 206, 237
Them! 280
They Won't Believe Me 238, 240, 241
This Gun for Hire 217, *225*, 226, 230, 233
trade union recognition, Hollywood 245–56
    see also strikes
Triangle studios 35, 56, 60, 113, 147–8, *149*
    construction investment 145, 150, 162
    fire risks 178
    glass shooting stage 155–6, 159, 189
    neoclassical-style architecture 174, 175, *175*
    see also Ince, Thomas; MGM (Metro-Goldwyn-Mayer)
Twentieth Century Fox 62, *63*, 252

The Unchanging Sea 18, 33, 42–4, *43*, 48, 50, 51
United Artists 32, 59, 76, 113, 244
    construction investment 113, 149, 153, 154
    fanciful sets 167
    financial crisis 236
    United Artists Theater Building 204
Universal Pictures 32, 35, 36, 40, 208
    Behind the Screen studio tour 173
    The Black Angel 217, 218, *218*, 228, 230–32
    construction investment 57, 144, 153
    Universal International Pictures Building 204
    logo 69
    promotional films 139
    shooting stages 154
    sound, coming of 159
    staff automobile ownership 111
    Universal City 57–9, *58*, 63, 121, 136, 154, *174*
    value of assets 141, 142, 178
    workers' strike action 252
urbanization 29, 82, 84, 112, 121–2, 177, 194, 215, 234, 269
urban planning 10, 12–13, 16, 82, 170, 271

Valentino, Rudolph 66
Venice
    slapstick comedies 83, 85, 93, 93–4, 101–2, *102*
    Venice Beach 33, 274
Vitagraph 33, 35, 37, 40, 153

construction investment 144, 148
fanciful sets 167
    see also First National

Walt Disney Studios 138–9, *138*, 204–5
    worker layoffs 252
    workers' strike 247, 259–60
Warner Bros 32, 35, 76, 127
    The Big Sleep 220, 226
    construction investment 153, 192
    French filmmakers 206
    neoclassical-style architecture 175, 192
    Rebel Without a Cause 273–4
    relocation 113, 121
    Sea Hawk 164
    Spanish Revival-style architecture 173
    studio building 161–2, 235–6
    studio space 163, 164, *164*
    value of assets 141, 142
    Warner Bros Studios and Stars 175
    workers' strike action 247, *248*, *250*, 251, 252, 255, 266, 267, 269
    see also First National
westerns, early, Hollywood 44–5
Westwood 113, 114, 190, 191–2
    see also Christie Studios; Fox Studios
working class, lack of portrayal of, film noir 233
The World's a Stage 182–3, 187
Wright, Frank Lloyd 170, 204

youth subculture themes 273–5

Zukor, Adolph 72–4, 77–8, *78*, 117–18